SECURITIES MARKET IN JAPAN

2022

JAPAN SECURITIES RESEARCH INSTITUTE

Published by
Japan Securities Research Institute
Taiyo Life Insurance Nihombashi Building
2-11-2, Nihombashi, Chuo-ku,
Tokyo 103-0027, Japan
Telephone (+81) 3-6225-2326
Facsimile (+81) 3-6265-1552

ISBN 978−4−89032−823−9

The book is a translation of "Illustrated Guide: 2022 Securities Markets in Japan"
(prepared by the Japan Securities Research Institute), which was published in Japanese,
into English. It includes quotations from or references to descriptions of laws and
regulations such as the Financial Instruments and Exchange Act; however, it is the laws and
regulations in Japanese themselves that have legal effect and the translations given herein
are only for your reference. For legal matters, see the laws and regulations
in Japanese described in the official journal.

PREFACE

"The Securities Market in Japan: An Illustrated Guide 2022" explains the structures, functions, history and current status of Japan's securities markets in a simple and user-friendly manner. We have been publishing this guide every two years since 2008, with the content revised as appropriate for those with an interest in the securities market.

At the time of publication of the previous edition in 2020, it was difficult to anticipate the global spread of coronavirus (COVID-19) and the enormous impact it would have on the economy and society. However, it can be said that the securities market has successfully managed to withstand the various effects of the pandemic without excessive disruption during this period. On the other hand, the medium- and long-term challenges facing Japan's securities markets, such as financial digitalization, cross-sectoral regulation by function, reform of exchange market structures, stable asset formation for the general public, corporate governance reform and sustainability issues, are becoming more and more urgent. The basic structure of the 2022 edition is unchanged from the previous edition. However, to accurately reflect changes in circumstances, we have added sections on The Development of Digital Finance, The Revision of TSE Market Segments, and The Stewardship Code (Part 2), as well as a description of new regulations on solicitation of investment in OTC securities. In addition, we have updated the commentary and data in this book where necessary in light of recent developments.

In addition to "The Securities Market in Japan," Japan Securities Research Institute also publishes "The Securities Market in the U.S.," "The Securities Markets in Europe," and "The Securities Markets in Asia" every few years. These contain concise descriptions of the current status and history of securities markets in various countries, and provide a general overview of securities markets across the world.

As with our previous publications, this book was compiled by a group of specialists, including researchers and research fellows at Japan Securities Research Institute and experts at the Japan Securities Dealers Association (JSDA), the Japan Exchange Group (JPX), Japan Securities Finance (JSF) and Japan Investment Advisers Association, who took part in writing the sections respectively assigned to them (see page iii for the assignment of writing tasks). Chiaki Wakazono (Senior Researcher) and Nakako Zushi (Researcher) at Japan Securities Research Institute were responsible for the overall compilation.

It is difficult to predict exactly how securities markets will change post-COVID, but understanding the current status and history of securities and capital markets is now more important than ever. We sincerely hope that this book will be useful for all those who have an interest in this topic.

March 2022

KIICHIROU MASUI
President
Japan Securities Research Institute

CONTENTS

CHAPTER XI   Financial Instruments Exchange, etc. (2)

CHAPTER XII   Financial Instruments Business (Securities Business)

CHAPTER I

The Securities Market and the National Economy

1. What Is a Security?

The financial markets provide a marketplace through which funds are channeled from sectors with idle cash (lenders) to cash-short sectors (borrowers), and the types of financing arranged on these markets are divided in terms of intermediaries into indirect and direct financing. Indirect financing means a form of transaction in which a financial institution acquires a primary security (due bills and notes, etc.) from a borrower with a fund raised by issuing an indirect security (certificates of deposit and insurance policies, etc.). In direct financing, a borrower raises funds by issuing a primary security (equity and debt securities, etc.) to lenders through a market intermediary. The marketplace on which direct financing is arranged is the securities market, and it is divided into a primary market (where securities are issued and distributed) and a secondary market (where securities are bought and sold).

Generally, the term "security" refers to instruments that give their legal holders the rights to money or other property. They are designed to facilitate the assignment of such rights and have the characteristic of combining rights and certificates. More specifically, securities are issued in various forms, such as stocks and bonds issued by business corporations; notes, checks, and bills of lading; government securities issued by national governments; and municipal bonds issued by local public bodies. Of these, securities traded in the securities markets are called "securities under the Financial Instruments and Exchange Act (FIEA)," as defined in Paragraphs 1 and 2, Article 2 of that law. Paragraph 1 defines securities whose interests are represented by securities or certificates that are physically issued as listed in the table on the right.

Paragraph 2 of Article 2 sets forth the definition of deemed securities. In the former part of the paragraph rights presented by securities that are listed in the preceding paragraph are deemed to be securities by themselves in cases where no physical certificates are issued. The latter part of the paragraph then goes on to define deemed securities as rights other than those represented by securities or certificates. The scope of the definition has been substantially

Table I-1.   The Definition of Securities under the Provisions of Paragraphs
2-1 and 2-2 of FIEA

Paragraph 2-1 Securities
1. Government securities
2. Municipal bond securities
3. Bonds issued by special public corporations
4. Specified corporate bonds as provided for in the Act on the Liquidation of Assets
5. Corporate bonds
6. Subscription certificates issued by special public corporations
7. Preferred shares as provided for in the Law Concerning Preferred Shares in Cooperative Financial Institutions
8. Preferred subscription certificates or new preferred subscription rights certificates as provided for in the Act on the Liquidation of Assets
9. Stock certificates or subscription right/warrant certificates
10. Beneficiary certificates of investment trusts or foreign investment trusts
11. Investment certificates or bonds issued by investment corporations, investment equity subscription rights certificates or investment certificates issued by foreign investment corporations
12. Beneficiary certificates of loan trusts
13. Beneficiary certificates of special-purpose trusts as provided for in the Act on the Liquidation of Assets
14. Beneficiary certificates of certificate-issuing trusts as provided for in the Trust Law
15. Commercial paper
16. Mortgage securities
17. Foreign securities: foreign certificates that have the attributes of any type of securities as defined in Items 1 through 9 and Items 12 through 16 hereof
18. Beneficiary certificates of foreign loan claims trusts
19. (Financial) options securities or certificates
20. Foreign depository securities or receipts
21. Securities or certificates designated by government ordinance

Paragraph 2-2 Deemed Securities
(General description of the former clause)
Interests represented by securities that are listed in the preceding paragraph in cases where no physical certificates are issued
(Latter clause)
1. Beneficiary interests in trusts
2. Beneficiary interests in foreign trusts
3. Partnership interests in general or limited partnership companies (*gomei gaisha or goshi gaisha*), as designated by government ordinance, or interests in limited liabilities companies (*godo gaisha*)
4. Partnership interests in foreign corporations, with the attributes of interests defined in any of the preceding items
5. Interests in collective investment schemes as comprehensively defined
6. Interests in foreign collective investment schemes
7. Other interests as designated by government ordinance

Source: Based on Toshiro Ueyanagi, Yutaka Ishitoya, and Takeo Sakurai, *Shin Kin'yu Shohin Torihiki-ho Handobukku*, Nippon Hyoronsha, 2006, and Etsuro Kuronuma, *Kin'yu Shohin Torihiki-ho Nyu-mon*, Nihon Keizai Shimbun, 2006, and the Financial Instruments and Exchange Act as listed in e-Gov's legal data service.

widened compared with that of the former law, and, specifically, there are comprehensive provisions in Item (v) of the paragraph for the FIEA to be applicable to various types of collective investment vehicles, or funds. In addition to securities, the FIEA applies to derivatives trading in domestic financial instruments exchanges, over-the-counter markets and foreign markets.

The electronically recorded transferable rights added to Article 2, paragraph 3 of the Act are the rights of each paragraph of Article 2 represented in property value that can be transferred using an electronic platform under Article 2, and are included in the category of Paragraph (1) Securities. In addition, by a Cabinet Office Ordinance, property values including deemed securities, etc. that are transferred by means of an electronic platform are defined as Electronically Recorded Transferable Rights to Be Indicated on Securities, etc.

2. Corporate Financing

The term "business corporation" (excluding financial service institutions) means economic entities whose objective is to make a profit from such activities as the production and sale of goods or services. Business corporations invest funds in real assets (such as facilities and products in inventories) to carry out production and marketing activities on a continuing basis. Business corporations raise the necessary funds by various means.

Funds raised by business corporations are divided into internal funds (those generated in the ordinary course of the production and sale of goods or services) and external funds (those raised from external sources), according to the method employed to raise them. Technically, internal reserves and depreciation charges are included in internal funds. They are considered the most stable means of corporate financing as corporations are not required to repay the principal of, or pay interest or dividends on, such funds. In actuality, however, business corporations cannot meet their funding requirements with internal funds alone, and most of the requirements have to rely on external funds. External funds are divided into three categories of loans, equity and corporate bond, according to the method employed to raise them. Loans are obtained primarily from banking institutions. This method of raising funds is termed "indirect financing." Business corporations issue equity share at the time of their incorporation, and issue additional equity shares (an increase of capital) to finance the expansion of their production capacity or for other purposes. As business corporations are not required to repay the principal thus raised, or pay interest thereon, the proceeds from the issuance of equity shares constitute the most stable form of funds among external funds. As is the case with equity shares, corporate bonds are also an instrument for rais-

Chart I-1.   Corporate Financing

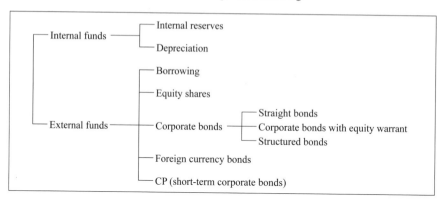

Note: Internal reserves refer to a company's after-tax income less any dividends and officers' bonuses. Depreciation charges are recognized as the economic benefits of tangible fixed assets, such as buildings and machinery, that are consumed each year and recorded as expenses. In other words, they are reserves for facility replacement.

ing funds from the capital markets, and issuers have to redeem them on or by a predetermined date of redemption and pay a definite rate of interest on them. Corporate bonds are largely divided into straight bonds (SB), corporate bonds with subscription rights/warrants, and structured bonds (see Chapter V regarding corporate bonds with subscription rights/warrants and structured bonds). The issuance of equity shares or corporate bonds is recognized as a means of raising funds by the "direct financing" method.

A survey of changes that have occurred in the amount of funds raised by companies from external sources as a percentage of the outstanding balance of financial debts shows that bank borrowings have tended to decrease. This tendency was triggered by the fact that following the liberalization and inter-nationalization of the financial markets, businesses have actively sought to raise funds by selling new shares and corporate bonds on the market. Since the 2000s, funds raised through the issue of securities have outpaced those obtained through bank borrowings, and direct finance has become the main-stay of corporate financing structure in Japan. The total amount of funds raised has increased substantially, with the exception of a sharp drop in 2008 as a result of the Global Financial Crisis, and securities have accounted for about 60% of total funds raised. In particular, the proportion of funds raised by equities has been over 50% in recent years. On the other hand, the amount raised through corporate bonds has been increasing, due to monetary easing in response to the pandemic.

With the enhancement of stock market for startups and the deregulation of the corporate bond market creating a fund-raising route through the capital

Table I-2.   Percentage of Funds Raised and Invested by the Corporate Sector

(balances at fiscal year-end)

	1980	1985	1990	1995	2000	2005	2010	2014	2016	2018	2019	2020
Management												
Cash and demand deposits	10.0	7.6	6.6	9.1	13.3	15.5	18.4	15.4	14.8	15.9	17.8	19.2
Time deposits	14.5	14.8	12.8	10.8	7.7	4.1	6.3	5.0	6.0	4.3	5.5	5.4
CDs	0.1	1.2	1.1	2.6	3.3	1.5	1.8	1.3	1.5	1.2	1.2	1.3
Trusts	1.3	1.4	0.7	1.3	0.3	0.3	0.3	0.3	0.4	0.5	0.5	0.6
Investment trusts	0.1	0.6	0.2	0.4	1.0	0.7	1.8	0.5	1.2	0.1	0.1	0.2
Securities	15.7	25.9	30.9	24.2	22.9	36.4	19.4	32.1	32.3	34.3	30.5	31.9
(equity shares)	13.5	23.5	28.1	22.6	19.6	33.4	16.3	30.2	30.3	32.4	28.3	29.5
(debt securities)	2.2	2.3	2.8	1.6	3.3	3.0	3.1	1.9	2.0	1.9	2.2	2.3
Inter-business credits	45.5	35.2	30.5	35.3	33.5	24.4	27.1	20.2	19.4	20.1	19.3	17.1
Others	12.7	13.2	17.2	16.3	18.2	17.1	24.9	25.2	24.4	23.5	25.1	24.4
Total	312.4	483.5	835.7	783.2	738.9	950.3	792.6	1,110.9	1,146.1	1,192.0	1,139.6	1,229.6
Financing												
Borrowing	42.2	39.5	36.5	40.2	36.2	22.4	31.3	22.7	24.4	23.6	26.4	24.5
Securities	27.1	38.1	43.1	38.6	42.0	58.2	42.5	58.1	54.8	58.2	54.8	60.0
(equity shares)	23.1	33.9	37.3	32.7	35.2	52.9	35.2	52.9	50.0	53.3	49.2	54.7
(corporate bonds)	2.2	2.6	2.3	3.8	5.3	4.1	5.8	3.8	3.6	3.9	4.4	4.4
(foreign currency bonds)	1.8	1.6	2.6	1.5	0.6	0.8	0.8	1.0	1.1	0.7	0.7	0.6
(CPs)	–	–	0.8	0.6	0.9	0.4	0.7	0.4	0.1	0.2	0.5	0.3
Inter-business credits	24.3	17.0	14.6	15.4	16.2	12.8	15.4	11.1	11.9	12.2	12.1	9.8
Others	6.4	5.5	5.8	5.8	5.6	6.6	10.8	8.1	8.9	6.0	6.7	5.7
Total	477.4	760.6	1,358.7	1,351.7	1,198.0	1,421.8	1,056.7	1,521.3	1,658.8	1,748.5	1,598.8	1,871.5

Notes: 1. In percentages and trillions of yen.
2. Time and savings deposits include foreign currency deposits.
3. Figures in parentheses are a breakdown of securities, and equity shares include equity subscriptions.
4. Investment of equity shares is based on market prices and that of new shares issued in the years up to fiscal 1990, inclusive, is based on the capital plus capital reserve and that is based on the market prices since fiscal 1995.
Source: Compiled from the Flow of Funds Account data published on the web site of the Bank of Japan.

markets for large and small-to-medium enterprises, the prevalence of securities-based financing is expected to remain stable in the coming years.

3.   The Securities Market and Public Finance

Public finance is a type of economic activity carried out by the government (national and local). More specifically, the government conducts administrative services (law enforcement and education, etc.) and public investment

Chart I-2.   Changes in the Balance of Outstanding Public Securities and the Degree of Dependence on Public Securities

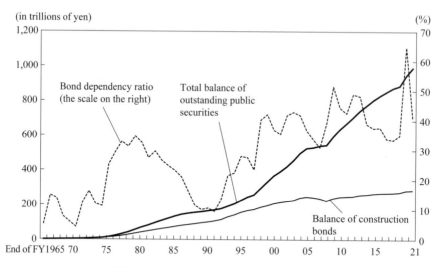

Notes: 1. Figures for fiscal 2021 are estimates.
2. Based on straight government bonds.
Source: Compiled from the data issued by the Ministry of Finance.

based on the revenue largely from taxes. In practice, the government adjusts its fiscal policies in response to economic trends. When government expenditures exceed revenues, the deficit is met mainly by issuing public bonds (government and municipal government bonds).

A survey of changes that have occurred in the balance of outstanding public bonds and the government's dependency on debt financing shows that the government had issued special government bonds (deficit-financing) in fiscal 1965, the first time since the end of World War II, under a supplementary budget and also that the government has issued a series of construction bonds on a continuing basis since fiscal 1966. However, both the bond dependency ratio and the balance of outstanding government debt securities had remained at a low level until the first half of the 1970s. As tax revenues had leveled off due to an economic slowdown that began in the second half of the 1970s, the government had no choice but to issue a large amount of government bonds, and their outstanding balance had increased sharply to ¥71 trillion at the end of fiscal 1980. As a result, government bonds came to carry an increasing weight in the securities market, and the influence of government fiscal policies on the securities market had taken on a growing importance. In order to improve the fiscal situation, a fiscal restructuring policy was adopted from

Table I-3.   Changes in JGB and Short-Term Government Bill Ownership by Investor Type

(in percentages)

Types of investors	FY2009	FY2011	FY2013	FY2014	FY2015	FY2016	FY2017	FY2018	FY2019	End of Dec. 2020
General government	1.9	1.9	2.3	2.1	0.4	0.4	0.3	0.3	0.3	0.2
Public pension funds	9.2	7.9	7.1	5.5	4.9	4.4	4.0	3.8	3.3	3.0
Fiscal loan funds	0.2	0.1	0.1	0.3	0.0	0.0	0.0	0.0	0.0	0.0
Bank of Japan	8.8	9.6	20.0	26.3	33.8	39.4	41.8	43.2	44.2	44.7
Banks	47.2	45.4	35.6	30.8	24.8	20.3	18.4	15.6	15.0	16.3
Life, nonlife, and other insurance companies	18.0	19.1	19.6	19.6	20.4	19.7	19.5	19.5	19.5	18.0
Pension funds	3.4	3.2	3.5	3.4	3.3	3.0	2.9	2.8	2.8	2.6
Overseas	5.6	8.3	8.2	9.4	10.2	10.7	10.9	12.7	12.9	13.3
Households	4.0	2.9	2.0	1.5	1.1	1.2	1.1	1.2	1.2	1.1
Others	1.9	1.6	1.6	1.1	1.0	0.9	0.9	0.9	0.8	0.7

Notes: 1. Figures for the end of fiscal 2020 are preliminary figures.
2. "Government bonds" includes "FILP bonds."
3. Banks include Japan Post Bank, securities investment trusts and securities companies.
4. Life, nonlife, and other insurance companies include Japan Post Insurance.
5. Others are composed of nonfinancial corporations and private nonprofit institutions serving households.
Source: Compiled from Saimu kanri ripoto 2021 (Debt Management Report 2021) published by the Ministry of Finance and the Flow of Funds Account data published by the Bank of Japan.

fiscal 1981. Once public bond dependency was reduced and increases in the balance of outstanding public bonds had been curbed, economic stimulus measures implemented in response to the prolonged recession since the 1990s and the financial crisis in 2008 have led to an increase in the issuance of public bonds. The public bond dependency ratio has been on a declining trend since 2009, when it was 51.5%, but jumped again to 64.8% in 2020 due to the COVID-19 pandemic. The balance of outstanding public bonds also continues to increase and is expected to reach approximately ¥990 trillion by the end of fiscal 2021.

Looking at the ownership structure of Japanese government bonds (JGB) as shown in the table below right, the ownership of banks (including Japan Post Bank) who were previously major holders, has declined up to 2019. This has been particularly evident after the introduction of quantitative and qualitative monetary easing by the Bank of Japan in April 2013. Meanwhile, the Bank of Japan has considerably increased its percentage of ownership and as of the end of 2020, its ownership ratio was a remarkable 44.7%.

Public pension funds, who used to be stable investors premising their investments on long-term ownership, have reduced their investment percentage to 3.0% as of the end of 2020, following a review in October 2014 by the Government Pension Investment Fund (GPIF) of its distribution of investment assets and a reduction in its domestic bond investment ratio. On the other hand, ownership by overseas investors has increased significantly. With the sovereign debt crisis in Europe in 2010 amongst other factors, ownership by overseas investors has been on the rise, reaching 13.3% at the end of 2020. When considering the problem of Japan's budget deficit, trends in overseas investors' ownership of JGBs should be closely monitored.

4. Financial Assets Held by the Household Sector

Looking at the financial assets held by the household sector of Japan (excess savings) in terms of the flow of funds, the ratio of household surpluses to nominal gross domestic product (GDP) peaked in the mid-1990s and then declined and stabilized. However, it subsequently increased sharply to approximately 7.7% in fiscal 2020 (from approximately 3.1% in fiscal 2019). Households' financial assets had piled up to stand at approximately ¥1,946 trillion as of the end of fiscal 2020, with a higher amount held in cash and deposits compared to the previous year. This potentially reflects households' desire to secure liquidity in response to the COVID-19 pandemic.

A survey of changes in the management of financial assets of the household sector found the following three characteristics. First, while the component ratio of cash and demand deposits has been rising, time deposits, which used to carry the largest weight within financial assets, has tended to decrease since the 1980s. This tendency of the component ratio is mainly due to the low interest rate policy and the quantitative and qualitative monetary easing measures adopted by the Bank of Japan. Second, the ratios of insurance and annuities rose consistently through to the end of fiscal 2000 and have since remained stable. This trend likely reflects that Japan has already become an aging society. Third, the weight of securities in household financial assets, especially stocks, declined considerably due to the sluggish stock market following the collapse of the economic bubble and the sharp sell-off in stock prices caused by the financial crisis in 2008. However, despite the turbulence in the stock market in the first half of 2020 due to the pandemic, the ratio recovered to 12.4% by end of fiscal 2020 with the market recovery trend after the end of 2012.

A comparison of household investment in financial assets between Japan and other countries (in the case of Japan, those of nonprofit-making institu-

Table I-4.   Percentage Composition of Financial Assets of Individuals

(at fiscal year-end)

	1980	1985	1990	1995	2000	2005	2010	2015	2020
Cash and demand deposits	9.8	7.7	7.2	8.2	11.6	21.0	23.6	26.1	37.0
Time deposits	48.7	44.9	40.2	41.9	42.5	29.7	31.6	26.5	23.4
Trusts	4.5	4.0	3.7	3.4	1.5	0.4	0.2	0.2	0.3
Insurance funds	13.4	16.3	20.8	25.4	27.2	25.8	28.4	29.7	30.5
Investment trusts	1.2	2.3	3.4	2.3	2.4	3.4	3.6	4.2	4.8
Securities	16.1	19.7	19.6	13.9	9.7	15.3	8.6	11.0	12.4
(equity shares)	13.2	16.0	16.9	11.5	7.7	13.0	6.2	9.8	11.1
(debt securities)	2.8	3.7	2.6	2.5	2.0	2.3	2.4	1.2	1.2
Others	6.3	5.2	5.2	4.9	5.1	4.4	4.1	2.7	3.0
Total amount	372.0	626.8	1,017.5	1,256.5	1,388.8	1,516.6	1,480.6	1,754.4	1,945.8

Notes: 1. Composition in percentages and totals in trillions of yen.
2. Time and savings deposits include negotiable and foreign-currency deposits.
3. Figures in parentheses are a breakdown of securities, and equity shares include equity subscriptions.
4. Equity shares are based on market prices.
Source: Compiled from the Flow of Funds Accounts data published on the web site of the Bank of Japan.

Table I-5.   Comparison of Japanese and U.S. Household Assets Composition (as of March 31, 2019)

	Japan	United States	Euro area
Cash and demand deposits	54.3%	13.3%	34.3%
Bonds	1.4%	4.2%	1.8%
Investment Trusts	4.3%	13.2%	9.6%
Stocks, etc.	10.0%	37.8%	18.2%
Insurance and annuity	27.4%	29.0%	33.8%
Others	2.7%	2.5%	2.3%

Source: Compiled from the Bank of Japan's "Comparison of the flow of funds between Japan, the United States and the Euro area" (August 20, 2021).

tions providing services to households are not included) as of the end of March 2021 still shows a large difference in the preference for types of assets. While Japanese households hold 54.3% of their funds in cash deposits and 14.3% of their funds in securities (including investment trusts), their American counterparts holds 13.3% of their funds in the former and 51.0% in the latter. In Europe, the figures are 34.3% and 27.8%, respectively. In choosing appropriate investment assets, while it is necessary to take into a consideration a wide range of differences, including social security systems, among the regions, these figures suggest that Japanese households prefer assets that guarantee principal, the Americans choose those with higher performance potential and Europeans sit somewhere between the two.

In Japan, however, the direct link between households and the securities markets is becoming stronger with the spread of defined contribution pension plans and the Nippon Individual Saving Account (NISA), a small-amount investment tax exemption scheme, the expansion of membership in individual-type defined contribution pension plans (iDeCo), and the introduction of installment-type NISA plans. In addition to an enhancement of investment trusts and exchange traded funds (ETFs), there is a demand for the dissemination of practical financial knowledge, as well as the provision of high-quality financial services.

5. Investment Behavior of Foreigners (Inbound Securities Investment)

Over a period of years after the war, international financial and capital transactions were banned, in principle. However, since the Foreign Exchange and Foreign Trade Act was amended in December 1980 (the new Foreign Exchange and Foreign Trade Act), the system of licensing international financial and capital transactions was changed from the prior permission system to the filing system, making them free in principle. Furthermore, by virtue of an amendment to the new Foreign Exchange and Foreign Trade Act in April 1998 (one of the main reforms under what was locally called "the Japanese version of the Big Bang"), the filing system of currency transactions was abolished, completely liberalizing direct financial transactions with overseas customers.

Looking at inbound securities investment in recent years, foreign investors were net buyers of Japanese stocks following the stock market crash in 2002, net sellers after the financial crisis in 2008, and net buyers again during the sharp rally in stock prices from the end of 2012. Since 2014 they have been either modest net buyers or net sellers of Japanese stocks. However, the volume of stocks bought and sold by foreign investors has increased sharply since 1999, and as a result the difference between the two has fluctuated widely. In 2020, when the market was particularly volatile due to coronavirus, the volume of stocks bought and sold was close to the record levels of 2018.

On the other hand, the sales of medium/long-term bonds by foreign investors exceeded their purchase in 1999 after the abolition of securities transaction taxes, during the depreciation of the yen in 2002 and 2003 and during

Table I-6. Inbound Securities Investment

(¥100 million)

Calendar year	Equity and investment fund shares			Debt Securities (excluding bills)			Net balance
	Bought	Sold	Net	Bought	Sold	Net	
2000	835,593	837,932	−2,339	571,013	470,246	100,767	98,429
2001	779,015	741,061	37,954	522,905	504,878	18,027	55,981
2002	644,372	657,039	−12,667	582,775	618,928	−36,153	−48,819
2003	790,641	692,870	97,771	619,163	641,269	−22,106	75,666
2004	1,161,630	1,056,357	105,273	727,773	683,161	44,612	149,885
2005	1,675,176	1,548,934	126,241	873,775	811,451	62,324	188,565
2006	2,671,452	2,590,472	80,981	1,035,501	970,532	64,969	145,950
2007	3,371,648	3,330,228	41,419	1,123,120	1,023,179	99,941	141,360
2008	2,640,366	2,714,152	−73,786	895,747	933,021	−37,274	−111,060
2009	1,453,977	1,453,694	283	504,203	574,104	−69,900	−69,617
2010	1,736,099	1,717,710	18,389	695,100	688,976	6,125	24,513
2011	1,974,084	1,971,556	2,528	884,363	838,985	45,379	47,906
2012	1,867,789	1,846,517	21,272	811,683	790,007	21,676	42,948
2013	3,942,020	3,783,603	158,416	838,677	873,965	−35,288	123,128
2014	4,115,951	4,089,468	26,483	762,694	676,154	86,540	113,022
2015	5,231,108	5,228,502	2,606	802,426	727,168	75,258	77,865
2016	4,955,097	5,011,755	−56,658	965,053	921,289	43,764	−12,894
2017	5,167,744	5,162,228	5,515	803,430	761,290	42,140	47,655
2018	5,817,386	5,877,281	−59,896	841,269	817,331	23,938	−35,958
2019	4,776,114	4,779,757	−3,643	1,081,377	981,491	99,886	96,243
2020	5,712,328	5,805,004	−92,676	1,043,869	1,069,475	−25,607	−118,283

Note: Up to 2004, figures were compiled based on "Changes in In-and Out-Bound Securities Investment (on a settlement basis)." Since 2005 and thereon, figures have been compiled based on "International Transactions in Securities (based on reports from designated major investors)."
Source: Compiled from materials listed on the web site of the Ministry of Finance.

the financial turmoil in 2008 and 2009 to cover arbitrage positions, and in 2013 when the Bank of Japan introduced quantitative and qualitative easing. However, recent trends show more purchase of bonds over sales, and trading levels remain high. As was the case with stocks, the bond transaction level has stepped up since 1999, with the result that the difference between purchases and sales has fluctuated substantially. This trend may be explained by active arbitrage trading by foreign hedge funds in addition to the expanded market for medium-term government notes (with a maturity of two to five

Table I-7.   Balance of Inbound Securities Investment and Related Indicators

Year-end	Stocks (¥b)		Bonds (¥b)		TOPIX	Interest rate (%)	¥/$ (¥)
2000	63,222	(30.4)	32,981	(15.8)	1,283.67	1.640	114.90
2001	49,563	(24.7)	33,546	(16.7)	1,032.14	1.365	131.47
2002	40,757	(21.4)	27,799	(14.6)	843.29	0.900	119.37
2003	60,085	(28.2)	27,108	(12.7)	1,043.69	1.360	106.97
2004	77,393	(31.2)	33,846	(13.6)	1,149.63	1.435	103.78
2005	132,842	(40.8)	41,428	(12.7)	1,649.76	1.470	117.48
2006	149,277	(43.5)	49,579	(14.5)	1,681.07	1.675	118.92
2007	142,031	(39.4)	60,203	(16.7)	1,475.68	1.500	113.12
2008	68,625	(23.4)	50,650	(17.3)	859.24	1.165	90.28
2009	76,372	(26.6)	42,236	(14.7)	907.59	1.285	92.13
2010	80,537	(26.4)	42,877	(14.0)	898.80	1.110	81.51
2011	65,841	(20.7)	45,730	(14.4)	728.61	0.980	77.57
2012	83,556	(23.2)	49,504	(13.8)	859.80	0.795	86.32
2013	152,323	(32.3)	50,168	(10.6)	1,302.29	0.740	105.37
2014	169,144	(29.2)	64,434	(11.1)	1,407.51	0.320	119.80
2015	186,919	(30.7)	72,623	(11.9)	1,547.30	0.265	120.42
2016	181,530	(28.0)	83,001	(12.8)	1,518.61	0.040	117.11
2017	219,841	(32.1)	95,167	(13.9)	1,817.56	0.045	112.65
2018	176,300	(26.1)	102,615	(15.2)	1,494.09	− 0.005	110.40
2019	209,923	(28.6)	118,340	(16.1)	1,721.36	− 0.025	109.15
2020	219,657	(27.8)	117,051	(14.8)	1,804.68	0.020	103.33

Notes: 1. Bonds include only long-term debt securities.
2. Figures given in parentheses are component ratios (%) to the total debts to overseas lenders.
3. Interest rate signifies the yield on 10-year government bonds newly issued and distributed on the secondary market.
4. ¥/$ represents the closing spot rates on the Tokyo market.
Source: Compiled based on the data released by the Ministry of Finance and the Bank of Japan.

years) and other infrastructural factors.

Looking at the trend in the balance, it turned upward again in 2003 due to a recovery in stock prices, increasing to approximately ¥149 trillion at the end of 2006, but remained stagnant from 2010 to 2012 due to the impact of the global financial crisis. Subsequently, with the recovery of the stock market, the balance increased to approximately ¥220 trillion at the end of 2020. The balance of domestic debt securities held by overseas investors, long- and medium-term bonds and notes combined, also increased steadily to a total of

Table I-8. Percentages of Japanese Stocks and Bonds Held by Investors
of Different Regions

(in percentages)

Year-end	United States	Europe	Asia	Cayman Islands	Others
Equity securities					
2014	47.4	36.9	5.4	0.6	9.8
2015	49.1	36.0	5.7	0.7	8.4
2016	49.9	34.9	6.2	1.0	8.1
2017	50.2	34.0	7.3	0.9	7.5
2018	52.6	32.5	6.4	0.9	7.6
2019	54.2	30.9	6.7	0.9	7.3
2020	51.7	33.1	7.1	0.7	7.5
Debt securities (bonds and notes)					
2014	21.9	33.7	21.6	6.1	16.6
2015	22.6	40.0	19.3	6.2	11.9
2016	20.4	40.7	22.0	5.8	11.2
2017	22.9	42.9	22.3	4.1	7.8
2018	23.1	47.9	17.8	4.3	7.0
2019	21.3	50.1	16.9	4.2	7.5
2020	23.7	54.0	12.7	3.2	6.3

Note: Stocks refer to equity and investment fund interests; bonds refer to medium- and long-term bonds.
Source: Compiled on the basis of data from the Ministry of Finance.

approximately ¥117 trillion at the end of 2020. Looking at the breakdown of ownership by region, Japanese stock ownership by European investors is on a slightly declining trend, while American ownership remains high, accounting for a share of 51.7% at the end of 2020. For debt securities on the other hand, contrary to stocks, American investors' share was 23.7% at the end of 2020, while European investors increased their share to nearly 54%. Asian bond holdings were 22.3% in 2017, close to the share of American investors, but gradually declined to only 12.7% at the end of 2020.

6. Development of digital finance

Digital finance is a general term to describe blockchain-based financial services developed with distributed ledger technology (DLT). It can be applied to transactions of securities and commodities as well as to payments and re-

Chart I-3. Digitalization of Finance Industry

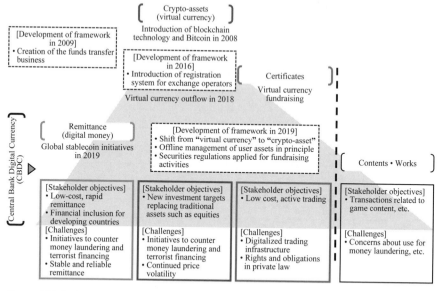

Source: FSA Study Group on Digital and Decentralized Finance.

Chart I-4. Regulatory System for Security Tokens

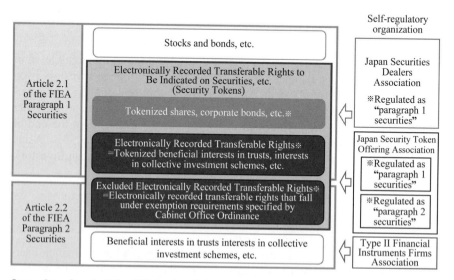

Source: Japan Security Token Offering Association, JSTOA overview and future initiatives.

mittances using crypto-assets (virtual currencies).

DLT is a system for the decentralized management of records related to the transfer and ownership of assets and rights whereby the transaction details are recorded by the relevant parties via a shared ledger over the internet. In the securities market, DLT can be applied as a decentralized infrastructure in various fields such as issuance, distribution, and settlement. Atypical example of its application is fundraising through the issuance of digital tokens. In the United States, large amounts of funds were raised through initial coin offerings (ICOs) in 2017−18.

Regarding digital tokens with such securities characteristics, the revised Financial Instruments and Exchange Act (FIEA), which came into effect in Japan in May 2020, defines paragraph (2) securities, whose rights can be transferred via an electronic information processing system, as "electronically recorded transferable rights." By adding these to paragraph (1) securities, they are subject to the same disclosure regulations as stocks and other securities. In addition, those who buy, sell, or solicit these instruments are required to register as a Type I Financial Instruments Business Operator (see Chapter XII). However, for liquidity considerations, securities separately specified by the Financial Services Agency in accordance with Cabinet Office Ordinance are treated as paragraph (2) securities.

In response to the revised FIEA, the FSA has determined that, since electronically recorded transferable rights and paragraph (1) securities where no certificate has been issued are defined by the Cabinet Office Ordinance as "Electronically Recorded Transferable Rights to Be Indicated on Securities, etc.," a wider range of instruments can be treated as Security Tokens (digital tokens for securities). The "Study Group on Digital and Decentralized Finance" set up at the FSA in July 2021 is also considering further measures.

As described above, the establishment of laws and regulations in Japan has made it easier to issue and distribute securities utilizing DLTs within the framework of the securities market. As described in Chapter V, Daiwa Securities and Daiwa Food & Agriculture issued Japan's first digital corporate bonds in February 2021 through a so-called private placement, while SBI Securities issued ¥100 million in digital corporate bonds in April 2021 through a public offering. Mitsubishi UFJ Trust and Banking Corporation managed a digital securitization and sale of real estate in August 2021. This shows that the issuance of security tokens backed by corporate bonds and financial assets is now increasingly commonplace in Japan.

CHAPTER II

The History of the Japanese Securities Market

1. The Securities Market in the Prewar Period

If we take the point of origin of Japan's securities market to be the first issuance of securities, it occurred in 1870 with the issue of a foreign currency denominated government bond bearing 9% interest in London, England. If we consider the birth of a secondary market based on a legal ordinance, it happened in 1878 with the establishment of stock exchanges in Tokyo and Osaka. Whichever definition is used, Japan's securities market has been in existence for about 140 years. The stock exchanges started off as markets for trading in public debt, such as old and new public bonds and *Chitsuroku* bonds. Although the stocks of the exchanges and of banks were later listed, public debt accounted for most of the trading for some time. Around 1886, there was a period of rapidly emerging mainly railway and textile companies that ushered in more active trading in stocks.

The formation of corporations (*kabushiki kaisha*) in Japan was not related to the huge capital investments that are required to develop the heavy chemical industry. Instead, the corporation was introduced to deal with the low level of capital accumulation in the economy. In conjunction with that action, schemes were established to facilitate the paying in of capital, such as the stock installment payment system and stock collateral loans. As a result, the corporations set up in the Meiji era were mostly small companies primarily involved in light industry and they really could be considered corporations in name only in terms of their generally intended function of raising capital. The turning point for that function in Japan came with the shift in the composition of industry toward the heavy industry prompted by World War I. Only then did the country see a sharp increase in large albeit mainly financial combine (*zaibatsu*)-related companies with paid-in capital exceeding ¥5 million.

There were practically no shares of major companies listed on stock exchanges in the secondary market because the *zaibatsu* held exclusive ownership of their group companies. And as a result of the lack of investment capital and inadequate credit provision by banks before World War II, the secondary market developed mainly around future trading called settlement

Chart II-1.   Changes in Stock Prices (Long-term margin transactions) (1878−1920)

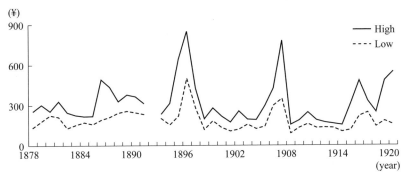

Source: Complied from *Tokyo shoken torihikisho no nijyunen shi-kisoku to tokei* (A 20-year History of the Tokyo Stock Exchange-Regulations and Statistics).

Chart II-2.   Stock Price Movement (Major Stock Price Index) (1921−1944)

Source: Complied from *Tokyo shoken torihikisho tokei nenpo* (Tokyo Stock Exchange Annual Statistics Reports) and *nisho tokei geppo* (Japan Securities Exchange Monthly Statistics Reports).

dealings and forward transactions. Even the main trading issues of exchanges' stocks were subject to speculative investment. For that reason, the prewar stock market can be characterized as being speculative. Another characteristic that can be pointed out in retrospect is the imposition of wartime regulations. Following the Showa depression, the government sought to achieve economic recovery by devaluing the currency to promote exports and by creating inflation through expansive government spending, principally on the military. After the outbreak of the Sino-Japanese War, the government implemented a wartime regime and imposed regulations on the securities market. The government restricted the issuance of securities for nonessential indus-

Table II-1.   Issues Listed on the Tokyo Stock Exchange

(as of end of 1878)

Bonds: New and old public bonds, *Chitsuroku* public bonds, *Kinroku* public, bonds, *Kigyo* public bonds Stocks: Tokyo Stock Exchange, Daiichi National Bank, Tokyo Kabutocho Rice Merchant Association, and Tokyo Kakigara-cho Rice Merchant Association

Source: Complied from *Tokyo shoken torihikisho no gojyunen shi* (A 50-year History of the Tokyo Stock Exchange).

Table II-2.   Number of Issues Listed on the Japan Securities Exchange, by Industry

(as of May 31, 1945)

Subscription certificates, 2; banks, trust companies, and insurance companies, 64; investment companies, colonization companies, and securities companies, 28; stock exchanges, 2; railroad and electric railroad companies, 62; transportation and communication companies, 28; gas and electric utilities, 43; mining companies, 86; shipbuilding and machinery companies, 232; steel companies, metal companies, and smelting companies, 81; textile industrial companies, 58; sugar manufacturing and milling companies, 18; food processing companies and fisheries companies, 29; chemical companies, 65; ceramics companies, 25; paper and pulp, printing, and tanning companies, 26; other industrial companies, 31, rubber and tobacco companies, 23; land, building, and warehousing companies, 17; commercial companies, 46

Source: Japan Securities Exchange.

tries, instituted planned corporate bond issuance, put controls on stock prices, and introduced a licensing system for securities companies. Japan's 11 stock exchanges, furthermore, were merged into the Japan Securities Exchange in 1943.

2. The Period of Postwar Economic Rehabilitation (1945–54)

After the war, Japan was placed under the control of the general headquarters (GHQ) of the supreme commander for the Allied powers. There was immediate movement within Japan's securities industry to reopen the market. At one point, in fact, the Ministry of Finance decided to restart the stock exchanges on October 1, 1945. However, the GHQ did not approve this, and the market was not reopened. The securities industry continued to enthusiastically lobby for a restart of market operations, but the GHQ rejected the idea as premature

Chart II-3.   Stock Price Movements (1949−1954)

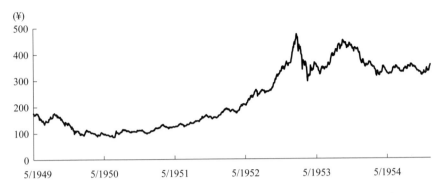

Source: Compiled from Nomura Securities' *Shoken tokei yoran* (Manual of Securities Statistics).

Table II-3.   Number of Members and Listed Companies of Each Exchange at Establishment

	Establishment	No. of members (at the time the fund was established)	Listings
Tokyo Stock Exchange	May 16, 1949	116 official members, 12 specialists	681
Osaka Securities Exchange	May 16, 1949	76 official members, 11 specialists	523
Nagoya Stock Exchange	May 16, 1949	50 official members, 8 specialists	268
Kyoto Stock Exchange	July 4, 1949	41 members	217
Kobe Stock Exchange	July 4, 1949	34 members	189
Hiroshima Stock Exchange	July 4, 1949	28 members	119
Fukuoka Stock Exchange	July 4, 1949	29 members	181
Niigata Stock Exchange	July 4, 1949	24 members	176
Sapporo Securities Exchange	April 1, 1950	17 members	103

Source: Complied from *shoken torihiki iinkai hokokusho* (a Securities and Exchange Commission Report).

and instead gave priority to economic reforms (land reform, dismantling of the *zaibatsu*, and labor reform) and political and social reforms. Consequently, it took nearly four years to reopen the stock exchanges, during which time the Japan Securities Exchange remained closed. This has been the only blank period in the operation of exchanges in the history of the securities market in

Table II-4.   Member Securities Companies at the Establishment of Tokyo Stock Exchange
(April 1, 1949)

Nikko Securities, Tamazuka Securities, Yamaichi Securities, Yachiyo Securities, Taguchi Securities,
Maruhiro Securities, Nitto Securities, Yamazaki Securities, Kaneju Securities, Irimaru Securities,
Yamayoshi Securities, Aizawa Securities, Kokusai Heiwa Securities, Marusui Securities,
Toyama Securities, Meiwa Securities, Sekitani Securities, Daiwa Securities, Sekito Securities,
Shinko Securities, Nomura Securities, Matsuya Securities, Tokuda Securities, Sanko Securities,
Yamaka Securities, Kanaman Securities, Bokutoku Securities, Naruse Securities, Daifuku Securities,
Rokushika Securities, Daito Securities, Oda Securities, Tokyo Daiichi Securities, Ninomiya Securities,
Yamakanou Securities, Osawa Securities, Obuse Securities, Marusan Securities, Tabayashi Securities,
Kakumaru Securities, Koyanagi Securities, Tsukuba Securities, Chiyoda Securities,
Nippon Kangyo Securities, Tachibana Securities, Marusugi Securities, Mie Securities,
Haratada Securities, Maruya Securities, Fukuyama Securities, Irinaka Securities, Ikko Securities,
Rokko Securities, Nippon Sangyo Securities, Toyo Securities, Totan Securities, Toko Securities,
Tokyo Showa Securities, Tokyo Shinei Securities, Tokyo Jiyu Securities, Chugai Securities,
Marukuni Securities, Ikanagashira Securities, Kaga Securities, Kadoman Securities,
Yoshikawa Securities, Yoshimura Securities, Taihei Securities, Taiyo Securities, Tanaka Securities,
Takai Securities, Taishichi Securities, Taisei Securities, Naigai Securities, Nakahara Securities,
Nakajima Securities, Hachisu Securities, Ueno Securities, Ono Securities, Osaka Shoji, Oda Securities,
Yamani Securities, Yamawa Securities, Fukuri Securities, Yamamaru Securities, Yamafumi Securities,
Yamasachi Securities, Yamasan Securities, Marutoyo Securities, Maruwa Securities,
Marusan Securities, Maruju Securities, Matsui Securities, Fuso Securities, Koiei Securities,
Ebisu Securities, Ando Securities, Yamata Securities, Sanshin Securities, Sansei Securities,
Sakai Securities, Kyowa Securities, Kyodo Securities, Misawaya Securities, Miki Securities,
Shimizu Securities, Shinei Securities, Jujiya Securities, Juzen Securities, Joichi Securities,
Jonan Securities, Hinode Securities, Hiyama Securities, Hirahara Securities, Central Securities,
Marugo Securities
Specialists: Daiichi to Daijuni Jitsuei Securities

Source: Compiled from *Tokyo shoken torihikisho no jyunen shi* (A 10-year History of the Tokyo Stock
Exchange).

Japan.

Despite trading being halted on the floors of the stock exchanges and official secondary market, the demand for securities trading persisted even in the
confusion of postwar Japan. Securities trading naturally emerged at the offices of securities companies in the form of over-the-counter (OTC) trading.
When it became clear, moreover, that the stock exchanges were not going to
restart anytime soon, "group transactions," which involved institutionalized
OTC trading at fixed places and times in parallel with the OTC trading at individual securities companies, also got under way. By the end of 1945, group
transactions, which first emerged in Tokyo and Osaka, had spread to exchanges in Nagoya, Niigata, Kyoto, Kobe, Hiroshima, and Fukuoka, among
others.

It would, of course, have been difficult to reopen the stock exchanges
merely by continuing the prewar exchange organization and securities legislation. To democratize the securities industry, the Japanese government com-

menced the formulation of a new legal framework. In 1947, it promulgated the Securities and Exchange Law, which drew on the Securities and Exchange Act of the United States. Initially, only those articles of the law dealing with the Securities and Exchange Commission, which was patterned after the U.S. Securities and Exchange Commission (SEC), were enforced. Then a full-scale revision of the law was promulgated in 1948. This amended law formed the legal framework for the new postwar securities market, replacing the licensing system for securities companies with a system of registration with the regulatory authority and putting in place such regulations as the separation of banking and securities businesses.

Stock exchanges were established in Tokyo, Osaka, Nagoya, and other cities from May 1949. The GHQ, however, instructed Japan's Securities and Exchange Commission to ensure the strict observance of its Three Principles of Market Operation: (1) recognize transactions in order of the occurrence, (2) concentrate trading on exchanges, and (3) prohibit futures trading. All exchanges pledged to strictly follow these principles, enabling the long-awaited reopening of stock exchanges (participants in group transactions and the issues they had traded moved en masse to these stock exchanges and restarted trading on a cash transaction basis only). Because, however, it was difficult to match buys and sells based only on actual demand, a movement got under way in the industry to push for the revival of prewar forward transactions for the purpose of introducing temporary demand. Since the management of the exchanges and the GHQ were against this proposal, a margin trading system modeled on the U.S. margin trading system was introduced in 1951.

3. The Securities Market during the First Period of Rapid Economic Growth (1955‒64)

As made clear in the title of an economic white paper issued in 1956, The Post-War Period Is Over, in the first half of the 1950s Japan had finished with its postwar recovery and was heading into its first period of rapid economic growth. Japan's *Jinmu* and *Iwato* booms in the mid-1950s and from 1958 to 1961, respectively, were representative of the change. Against a backdrop of favorable growth in corporate performances, stock prices rose almost universally during the period from the latter half of 1955 to July 1961. An investment trust boom at the time also contributed to the rising securities market.

Japan had introduced a postwar securities investment trust system in 1951, but the market for these investment trusts struggled until 1955. From 1956 on, however, stock prices surged, and the outstanding principal of investment trusts expanded sharply. Investment trusts became such a force in the securities market that they were referred to as "the whale in the pond." Another

Chart II-4.   Stock Price Movements (TSE's Modified Stock Price Average) (1955–1964)

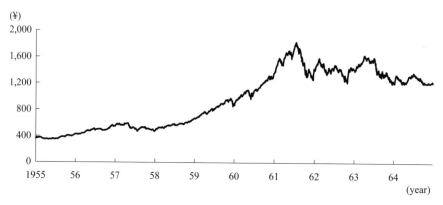

Source: Compiled from Nomura Securities' *Shoken tokei yoran* (Manual of Securities Statistics) and the Tosho tokei nenpo (TSE Annual Report).

Table II-5.   Changes in Assets of Stock Investment Trusts and Bond Investment Trusts (Principal basis)

(millions of yen)

	Stock Investment Trusts					Bond Investment Trusts				
	Sales (A)	Cancellation (B)	Redemption (C)	Year-end Principal	Net asset change (D=A−(B+C))	Sales (A)	Cancellation (B)	Redemption (C)	Year-end Principal	Net asset change (D=A−(B+C))
1955	26,381	31,792	13,640	59,519	−19,051					
1956	51,431	27,163	16,039	67,748	8,229					
1957	92,544	16,178	7,199	136,915	69,166					
1958	106,412	25,741	7,890	209,695	72,780					
1959	182,480	58,876	3,219	330,081	120,385					
1960	362,066	87,945	−	604,202	274,120					
1961	588,205	155,751	9,810	1,026,845	422,643	244,490	88,470	−	156,020	156,020
1962	347,116	229,174	14,161	1,130,627	103,781	83,819	107,160	−	132,679	−23,341
1963	331,873	274,226	17,884	1,170,388	39,761	109,857	71,021	−	171,515	38,836
1964	330,158	293,573	45,415	1,161,558	−8,829	122,332	84,811	−	209,036	37,521
1965	196,829	349,502	42,556	966,328	−195,229	120,665	110,132	−	219,569	10,533

Source: Compiled from *Shokenshintaku sanjyugonen shi* (35-year History of Securities Investment Trusts).

Table II-6.   Categories of Investible Custody Securities and Investment Uses

(millions of yen)

	Total Assets Under Management	Category			Investment Area	
		Special debt	Of above, bank debentures	Corporate bonds	Deposited collateral	Others
Sept. 1958	62,701	61,984	61,384	568	53,812	5,283
Sept. 1959	108,347	107,602	105,381	673	88,793	19,420
Sept. 1960	146,076	144,875	141,666	969	116,061	30,015
Sept. 1961	139,833	138,552	134,794	1,239	116,988	22,845
Sept. 1962	154,284	152,127	143,946	2,005	129,030	25,254
Sept. 1963	209,197	205,337	196,967	3,386	156,319	52,877
Sept. 1964	249,079	244,685	235,557	3,714	195,891	53,189

Source: Compiled from the Securities Bureau of the Ministry of Finance, *Nenpo* (Annual Report).

factor in the bull market was the system of "investable custody." Under that system, securities companies borrowed bank debentures (primarily discount bank debentures) that they had sold in the market on a commission basis from unspecified multiple customers for a predetermined fee through a custody system. The securities companies then raised capital from small and medium-sized financial institutions or in the call money market by using the bank debentures as collateral and invested it in stocks or bonds through their own proprietary trading accounts. In this manner, against the backdrop of an expanding economy and bullish securities market, OTC trading value rose sharply, and the number of companies approved to sell their securities OTC grew rapidly, concentrated mainly on start-up and growth companies. To deal with the rapid expansion in the OTC market, the Tokyo, Osaka, and Nagoya stock exchanges each established Second Sections.

Japan, though, was striving to balance its current account, and when the balance of payments fell into the red it tightened the money supply. When the interest rate was raised in July 1961 to improve the balance of international payments, Japanese companies began liquidating their stockholdings. In combination with corporations' focus on increasing capital, this trend caused a worsening in the demand-supply balance for stocks. The resultant drop in stock prices forced an end to the investment trust boom, as the mechanism that had been driving up stock prices reversed and caused further declines in stock prices. The increase in the official discount rate also produced a rise in the number of redemptions of bond investment trusts, especially by companies. This action placed a great financial burden on the securities companies, which were forced to buy bonds that were being removed from the pool of investment trust assets. These factors became a cause of panic in the securities market.

For that reason, the market took such steps as urging business corporations to rearrange their financing plans (cutting back or postponing their planned increase of capital) and persuading commercial banks to make loans secured by bonds to four bond investment trusts. Despite these efforts, stock prices kept declining, partially because of the market reaction to the assassination of U.S. President Kennedy. To deal with the issues, the industry formed stock purchasing organizations. In January 1964, banks and securities companies contributed capital to create the Japan Joint Securities Co., Ltd., while in January 1965 a group of securities companies jointly established the Japan Securities Holding Association. Both of these organizations carried out share purchasing operations in the market and assumed ownership of shares held by investment trusts with the aim of improving the demand and supply balance in the stock market. In the latter part of May 1965, however, the news that Yamaichi Securities Co., Ltd., was on the verge of bankruptcy hit the market, plunging it into a state of panic.

4. The Securities Market during the Second Period of Rapid Economic Growth (1965−74)

The curtain opened on the 10-year period from 1965 onward with a securities panic. At the end of the first half of fiscal 1964 (September 30, 1964), the cumulative earnings of securities companies in Japan amounted to a loss of ¥26.4 billion. And Yamaichi Securities' performance had deteriorated particularly badly; by March 31, 1965, the company had racked up a loss of ¥28.2 billion, compared with total capital of only ¥8 billion. On May 21, 1965, it finally was revealed that Yamaichi Securities was on the brink of failure. To avoid a loss of confidence in the market, a move was made to bail the company out. In the late night on May 28, the government invoked Article 25 of the Bank of Japan Act and announced that Yamaichi Securities would receive a special loan from the Bank of Japan without any required collateral and for an unlimited amount (in actual fact some collateral was secured). Stock prices continued to fall for some time following the announcement but staged a rally when the government made clear that it intended to issue deficit-covering bonds for the first time since the war. Meanwhile, the panic in the securities market also served as the basis for a reorganization of the securities industry. The government amended the Securities and Exchange Act, introducing a licensing system for securities companies. This forced many

Chart II-5. Stock Price Movement (TSE's Modified Average, TOPIX) (1965-1974)

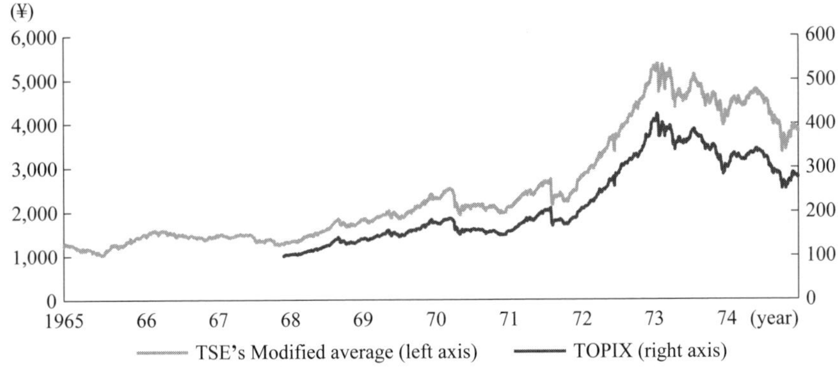

Source: Compiled from data the *Shoken tokei yoran* (Manual of Securities Statistics), the *Nihon Keizai Shimbun*, and the *Tosho tokei nenpo* (TSE Annual Report).

securities companies to combine their operations, or merge, to prepare for the new system. In combination with the securities companies that had their registration revoked around the time of the securities panic and those that dissolved their operations, the number of securities companies at the time of the conversion to the new licensing system declined to 277 companies, compared with 593 companies at the end of 1963.

During the decade from 1965 to 1974, progress was made in internationalizing Japan's securities market. In 1964, Japan became an Article 8 country member of the International Monetary Fund (IMF), joined the Organization for Economic Cooperation and Development (OECD), and publicly promised to liberalize capital transactions. Consequently the government implemented measures to liberalize the capital market in five stages beginning in July 1967. This process steadily eased the restrictions on ownership of Japanese stock by foreigners, and they were finally fully lifted with the exception of certain stock categories. The liberalization of capital transactions was not limited to foreign investors; foreign issuers and intermediates were also able to operate in Japan's securities market. In 1970, the Asian Development Bank started issuing yen-denominated foreign bonds in Japan. Foreign shares were made available to buy in Japan in 1972. The Tokyo Stock Exchange established a Foreign Section in 1973. Around the same time, foreign securities companies commenced setting up operations in Japan. Merrill Lynch opened a Tokyo branch in 1972, becoming the first foreign securities company to receive a securities business license in Japan.

The liberalization of capital transactions also meant that it was then possible for foreign companies to acquire Japanese companies. Japanese compa-

Table II-7.   Changes in Number of Securities Companies

	Changes in the number of companies		Companies at financial year-end	Number of Business Offices	Total Capital (in ¥ mil.)	Per-Company Capital (¥ mil.)
	Increase	Decrease				
FY1948	959	11	948			
1949	292	113	1,127	1,889	3,014	2.7
1950	18	209	936	1,601	3,454	3.7
1951	11	109	838	1,642	3,767	4.5
1952	71	73	836	1,794	6,683	8.0
1953	52	52	836	2,105	10,115	12.1
1954	11	83	764	1,997	10,713	14.0
1955	2	66	700	1,901	10,826	15.5
1956	7	55	652	1,848	12,022	18.4
1957	7	77	582	1,904	18,062	31.0
1958	7	32	557	1,984	19,569	35.1
1959	15	26	546	2,233	29,221	53.5
1960	36	30	552	2,565	39,094	70.8
1961	48	10	590	2,841	74,991	127.1
1962	23	12	601	2,934	78,114	130.0
1963	8	16	593	2,893	100,573	169.6
1964	0	82	511	2,424	126,118	246.8
1965	0	86	425	2,109	125,599	295.5
1966	2	30	397	2,009	118,632	298.8
1967	0	113	284	1,869	119,955	422.4
1968	0	7	277	1,572	119,904	432.9

Note: Figures for "Number of Business Offices" and "Capital" for the years preceding 1959 are as of the end of the calendar year concerned.
Source: Compiled from the Securities Bureau of the Ministry of Finance, Nenpo (Annnual Report).

Table II-8.   Changes in Stock Ownership Among Investor Categories

By Owner FY	1965	1966	1967	1968	1969	1970	1971	1972	1973	1974	1975
National and local government organizations	0.3%	0.2%	0.3%	0.3%	0.3%	0.3%	0.2%	0.2%	0.2%	0.2%	0.2%
Corporations — Financial institutions	26.8%	29.8%	30.6%	32.0%	31.9%	32.3%	33.9%	35.1%	35.1%	35.5%	36.0%
Corporations — Securities companies	5.4%	5.4%	4.4%	2.1%	1.4%	1.2%	1.5%	1.8%	1.5%	1.3%	1.4%
Corporations — Business corporation, etc.	21.0%	18.6%	20.5%	21.4%	22.0%	23.1%	23.6%	26.6%	27.5%	27.1%	26.3%
Corporations — Foreign corporations	1.9%	1.7%	1.7%	2.1%	3.1%	3.0%	3.4%	3.4%	2.8%	2.4%	2.5%
Corporate investor total	55.1%	55.5%	57.2%	57.6%	58.4%	59.6%	62.4%	66.9%	66.9%	66.3%	66.2%
Individual — Individuals and others	44.4%	44.1%	42.3%	41.9%	41.1%	39.9%	37.2%	32.7%	32.7%	33.4%	33.5%
Individual — Foreign investors	0.2%	0.2%	0.2%	0.2%	0.2%	0.2%	0.2%	0.1%	0.1%	0.1%	0.1%
Individual investor total	44.6%	44.3%	42.5%	42.1%	41.3%	40.1%	37.4%	32.8%	32.8%	33.5%	33.6%

Note: Investment trust portion is included in financial institutions.
Source: Compiled from Kabushiki bunpu jokyo chosa (Survey of Stock Distribution Status).

nies countered this new possibility by focusing on building stable shareholder bases. If companies held shares with each other, this reduced the number of shares available in the market, making it easier to defend against takeover attempts. Share crossholdings were viewed from the perspective of takeover prevention. Later, after Japanese companies switched the form of their capital increases from making rights issues to existing shareholders at par value to making public offerings of stock at market prices, issuers pursued share crossholdings from the point of view of the desirability of high share prices in case of public offering. As a result, there was a change in the shareholding composition of the market, with the proportion of corporate shareholdings increasing and the proportion of individual investor shareholdings declining.

5.   Measures Taken to Cope with the Oil Crisis (1975‾84)

At the end of the previous 10-year period, there had been a succession of major events that shook the Japanese economy, including the Nixon Shock (1971), the introduction of a floating exchange rate system (1973), and the first oil shock (1973.) The second oil shock occurred later, in 1979. With Japanese companies practicing energy conservation management in the face of back-to-back oil crises, the government seemed intent on getting through the crises using a fiscal expansion strategy. Underpinning that strategy was the massive issuance of deficit-covering Japanese government bonds (JGBs).

As previously mentioned, government bond issuance after the war got started in fiscal 1965. The main feature of those bonds was that they were issued at low interest rates without regard to market conditions and were forcibly allocated among financial institutions belonging to the underwriting syndicate according to their capital strength. Maintaining this artificially fixed, low interest rate market meant that financial institutions could not be permitted to sell the JGBs in the market freely. Since at the time the government was trying to keep JGB issuance within the scope of the growth in the money supply, the Bank of Japan purchased almost all JGBs that had been held by the financial institutions for one year (liquidity policy). The reason, in fact, that JGB issuance after the oil shocks was said to be massive was that JGB issuance after fiscal 1975 exceeded the growth in the money supply.

With the massive issuance of JGBs, the liquidity policy reached its limits, making it impossible to avoid issuing JGBs in the public market. Accordingly, the government approved, with some restrictions, JGB sales on the bond market in 1977. Following this change, the restrictions on sales were liberalized in stages, resulting in the deregulation of the JGB secondary market. The interest rate yields for JGB subscribers, on the other hand, were the base rates given by the regulated interest rate structure in Japan. To deregulate

Chart II-6. Stock Price Movement (TSE's Modified Average, Nikkei Dow Average and TOPIX) (1975−1984)

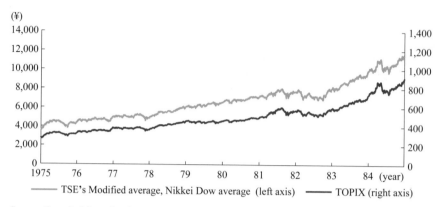

Source: Compiled from data from the *Nihon Keizai Shimbun*, the *Tosho tokei nenpo* (TSE Annual Report), and the *Shoken tokei nenpo* (Annual Securities Statistics).

Chart II-7. Change in JGB Issuance and Outstanding Balance (until the end of FY2020)

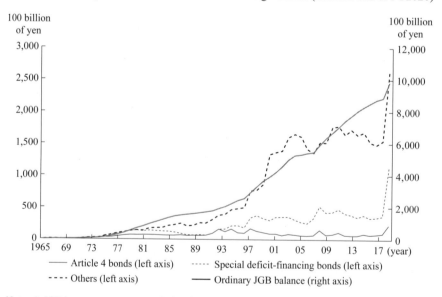

Notes: 1. JGB issuance amounts are calculated on a proceeds basis.
2. Special deficit-financing bonds include temporary-bridging, tax-reduction offset, and disaster-recovery special public bonds.
3. Others represents the total of pension plan funding special deficit-financing bonds, reconstruction bonds, FILP bonds, and refunding bonds.
Source: Compiled from the web site of the Ministry of Finance.

these rates would have forced the government to change its artificially regulated interest rate policy. For that reason, there was a great deal of resistance to the deregulation of the JGB primary market within the government, and deregulation proceeded at a snail's pace. When, however, the designated underwriting syndicate refused to underwrite the planned issuance of JGBs in June 1981, the issuance conditions for JGBs were deregulated, setting the stage for the deregulation of the different types of long-term interest rates.

Internationalization proceeded at this time. During the period from 1975 to 1984, Japan's trade surplus with the United States ballooned, causing trade and economic friction between the two countries. Perceiving the reason for the problem to be the closed nature of Japan's financial, capital, and service markets, the United States demanded the overall reform of Japan's economic structure. As part of that process, the two countries formed the Japan-U.S. Yen/Dollar Committee. The United States argued that deregulated financial and capital markets driven by a market mechanism would enable the optimum allocation of capital in Japan. It therefore pushed strongly for the removal of various restrictions placed on those markets by the Japanese government that it considered obstructive to open markets. In this manner, internationalization formed the basis for financial deregulation in Japan.

6. Developments before and after the Economic Bubble (1985–89)

In a Japan-U.S. Yen/Dollar Committee Report released in 1984, the United States brought pressure on Japan to liberalize its financial and capital markets and to internationalize the yen. The Japanese government responded by liberalizing the domestic financial market through such actions as deregulating interest rates on bank deposits. It also moved to improve foreign financial institutions' access to the Japanese market through such measures as opening up membership on the Tokyo Stock Exchange (TSE). As the first step toward internationalizing the yen, the government liberalized the Euroyen market. The TSE, meanwhile, heeded the request of the government to open its membership by revising the fixed number of membership seats in its Articles of Incorporation in 1985 and accepting its first round of new members. A total of three rounds were eventually conducted, resulting in seats on the TSE for 25 foreign securities companies.

The deregulation of interest rates began in 1985 with the deregulation of interest rates on large deposits. After that, the deregulation of interest rates on deposits progressed rapidly. As a result, the Bank of Japan's open interest rate for fund raising jumped to 53% in 1989, from 7.5% at the end of 1984, greatly increasing fund procurement costs for banks. Major corporations concurrently shifted their financing from bank loans to security issuance, resulting

Chart II-8.   Stock Price Movement (Nikkei Dow and TOPIX) (1985–1989)

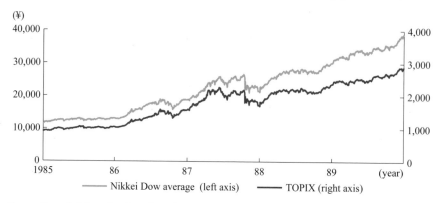

Nikkei Dow average (left axis)   TOPIX (right axis)

Source: Compiled from data from the *Nihon Keizai Shimbun* and the *Shoken tokei nenpo* (Annual Securities Statistics).

Chart II-9.   Yen to US$ Exchange Rate and Japan's Official Discount Rate

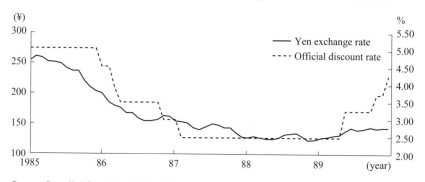

Source: Compiled from the web site of the Bank of Japan.

in a decline in the balance of loans being extended by major banks to their core customer base (heavy industry). To cope with the loss of business, the leading Japanese banks expanded the scope of their loan operations to include real estate, construction, and other industries and launched international operations. They also began planning to enter the securities business, creating friction between the banking and securities industries.

In 1985, the Plaza Accord was signed, after which the yen appreciated sharply against the U.S. dollar. The rate movement raised concerns about a strong yen-related economic recession in highly export-dependent Japan. The Bank of Japan's reaction was to implement successive reductions in the offi-

Table II-9.   Stock Trading Composition by Investor Category

(100 million shares)

	Total Brokerage Trading	Individuals	Foreigners	Life and Non-Life Insurance Companies	Banks	Investment Trusts	Corpora-tions	Others
1983	1,250.7	59.5%	15.9%	1.3%	3.5%	4.4%	9.3%	6.1%
1984	1,344.5	54.6%	17.3%	1.2%	5.3%	4.4%	11.5%	5.7%
1985	1,615.6	49.5%	15.4%	1.2%	10.6%	5.0%	11.6%	6.6%
1986	2,772.0	41.7%	13.8%	1.1%	16.1%	5.4%	15.4%	6.5%
1987	3,683.4	36.8%	12.4%	1.0%	21.5%	5.6%	17.0%	5.8%
1988	3,979.2	34.8%	9.1%	1.2%	24.7%	6.8%	17.7%	5.7%
1989	3,395.1	32.3%	10.8%	1.2%	25.4%	10.0%	14.6%	5.7%

Note: Total brokerage trading equals the buying and selling of all securities companies on the first and second sections of the TSE, Osaka, and Nagoya exchanges.
Source: Compiled from the *Tosho yoran* (TSE Fact book).

cial discount rate from January 1986 onward, and the economy responded by entering a recovery phase. Amid this low interest rate climate, Black Monday rocked the U.S. market on October 19, 1987, causing nations around the world to initiate monetary easing to avert recessions. Japan, meanwhile, was still in an economic recovery phase, and its official discount rate remained at a low level. Consequently, the price of land and stocks continued to rise. Against this backdrop of asset inflation, corporations began taking advantage of their ability to raise capital through bank loans and securities, using finan-cial engineering, or *zaitech*, to boost their financial income. Financial institu-tions, hurt by the decline in loan balances, also aggressively invested capital in securities. Heated investment in securities pushed the Nikkei Dow index up from ¥12,716.52 (September 30, 1985) before the Plaza Accord to a re-cord high of ¥38,915.87 at the end of 1989.

New trading methods were also introduced during this period, commenc-ing with bond futures trading in 1985. Stock index futures trading was intro-duced in 1987, and stock index options in 1989. Japan's securities market thus gained a full complement of cash, future, and options trading.

Chart II-10.   Stock Price Movement (Nikkei Dow and TOPIX) (1990−1995)

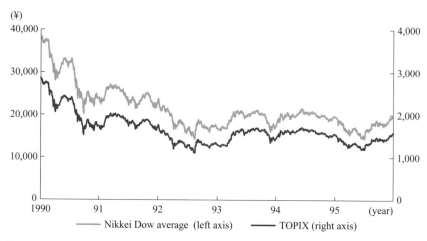

Nikkei Dow average (left axis) ────── TOPIX (right axis)

Source: Compiled from data from the *Nihon Keizai Shimbun* and the *Shoken tokei nenpo* (Annual Securities Statistics).

7. The Reform of the Financial System after the Stock Market Scandals (1990−95)

The debate on financial system reform began in Japan in the mid-1980s. It arose in response to the global trend toward financial deregulation and to the change in the financing methods of Japanese corporations. The Financial System Research Council took the lead in the debate of revising in the specialized financial institution systems including the separation of long-term interest rates from short-term interest rates, commercial banks from trust banks, and the banking industry from the securities industry. These systems were the pillars of the postwar financial system in Japan. The Financial System Research Council, however, was positive about banks being allowed to enter the securities business and decided that the best approach would be to allow mutual entry into the banking, trust and securities businesses based on wholly owned subsidiaries. It requested the Securities and Exchange Council to revise the system separating the banking and securities industries. But the Securities and Exchange Council was wary of allowing banks into the securities business, recognizing that the securities industry overall was far less enthusiastic about this idea than the banking industry. The Securities and Exchange Council nevertheless decided to approve mutual entry through subsidiaries on the condition that firewalls were established between subsidiaries and parent companies. And for the time being bank subsidiaries, in-

Table II-10.   Establishment of Securities Subsidiaries of Banking Institutions

Month/Year	Companies Starting New Securities Business
Jul. 1993	IBJ Securities (currently Mizuho Securities), LTCB Securities (currently UBS Securities), and Nochu Securities (currently Mizuho Securities)
Nov. 1993	Sumitomo Trust Securities (liquidated in 2000) and Mitsubishi Trust Securities (currently Mitsubishi UFJ Morgan Stanley Securities)
Jul. 1994	Asahi Securities (dissolved in 1999)
Aug. 1994	Yasuda Trust Securities (currently Mizuho Securities)
Nov. 1994	Sakura Securities (currently Daiwa Securities), Sanwa Securities (currently Mitsubishi UFJ Morgan Stanley Securities), Daiichi-Kangyo Securities (currently Mizuho Securities), Fuji Securities (currently Mizuho Securities), Mitsubishi Diamond Securities (currently Mitsubishi UFJ Morgan Stanley Securities), and Sumitomo Capital Securities (currently Daiwa Securities)
Mar. 1995	Tokai International Securities (currently Mitsubishi UFJ Morgan Stanley Securities)
Apr. 1995	Hokkaido Takushoku Securities (dissolved in 1998)
May 1995	Mitsui Trust Securities (terminated business in 1999)
Oct. 1995	Toyo Trust Securities (liquidated in 1999)
Nov. 1996	Shinkin Securities and Yokohama City Securities (both liquidated in 1999)
Aug. 1997	Tokyo Forex Securities (currently ICAP Totan Securities), and Nittan Brokers Securities (currently Central Totan Securities)
Nov. 1997	Ueda Tanshi Securities (dissolved in 2001)
Oct. 1998	Hitachi Credit Securities (currently DBJ Securities)

Source: Complied from data from the *Nihon Keizai Shimbun*, the Securities Bureau of the Ministry of Finance, Nenpo (Annual Report). "The First Year of the Financial Supervisory Agency", and "The First Year of the Financial Services Agency."

cluding indirectly owned subsidiaries, were prohibited from operating in the stock brokerage market. The Institutional Reform Law was enforced in June 1992 based on those conditions, and mutual entry into these financial sectors became a reality.

Around the time that the debate on financial system reform was dying down, the uncovering of major financial and securities scandals shook the banking and securities industries. For the securities industry it was unveiled by a tax audit that during the financial bubble major securities companies had been compensating their largest corporate clients for losses incurred (in August 1991, total compensation by the four major securities companies and 17 second-tier and medium-sized companies had reached approximately ¥172 billion). Dealings with members of known crime syndicates and market manipulation charges also surfaced, escalating the problems into a social issue. Most of the loss compensation was done to *eigyo tokkin* accounts (discretionary accounts managed by the securities company). The commonly used methods involved arranging to have the client earn a profit on transactions disguised as bond transactions or shifting losses between corporate clients with differing fiscal year-ends to avoid reporting the loss by temporarily transferring securities with losses at book value between their accounts in a process called *tobashi*.

Since under the then existing law loss compensation for trades after the fact was not illegal, the Securities and Exchange Act was immediately amended to ban securities trading under a discretionary account and loss compensation before or after the fact. Criticism mounted that "excessive profits of securities companies due to the regulator's protection, problematic administration, and fixed rate commissions had made loss compensation possible," and it was said that "what the solution requires is not the banning of loss compensation or the punishment of securities companies, but the implementation of financial system reform itself." In September 1991, the Provisional Council for the Promotion of Administrative Reform recommended the liberalization of brokerage commissions, the promotion of new market entries, and the separation of the market surveillance organization from the Ministry of Finance. In July 1992, the authorities established the Securities and Exchange Surveillance Commission. The rest of the Provisional Council's recommendations were included in the financial Big Bang reforms that came later, contributing to the formation of a new framework for Japan's financial and capital markets.

8. The Debate on, and Enforcement of, the Act on Revision, etc. of Related Acts for the Financial System Reform (1996—2000)

The bursting of the economic bubble left deep scars on the economy. The trauma from the collapse of stock prices emerged in the form of securities scandals, while that from the collapse of land and real estate prices emerged as the nonperforming loan problem in the financial industry. The nonperforming loan problem in particular lingered without the implementation of any fundamental solution - the banking industry struggled for close to 10 years to get out from under its bad debt. During this long process, foreign companies and investors and financial transactions flowed out of the Japanese market, making the hollowing out of the financial market real. Japan's way of addressing the issue was the financial Big Bang initiative proposed by then prime minister Ryutaro Hashimoto in 1996. The goals of the initiative were to wrap up the cleanup of nonperforming loans by 2001 and rebuild the Japanese financial market into an international market comparable to the New York and London markets based on the principles of "free, fair, and

Chart II-11.   Stock Price Movement (Nikkei Dow and TOPIX) (1996–2000)

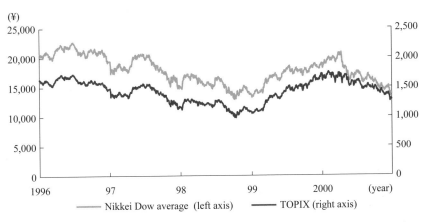

Source: Compiled from data from the *Nihon Keizai Shimbun* and the *Shoken tokei nenpo* (Annual Securities Statistics).

global."

Discussions on financial reform took place in the Securities and Exchange Council, the Financial System Research Council, the Insurance Council, the Council on Foreign Exchange and Other Transactions, and the Business Accounting Council. Those discussions resulted in recommendations to change Japan's established bank intermediation-based capital allocation system (indirect financing) to a market-based capital allocation system (direct financing). Passed in October 1998, the Act on Revision, etc. of Related Acts for the Financial System Reform, paved the way for services based on vigorous intermediation, set up a market system with special characteristics, and established a framework for trading that users could trust. Among its many revisions, the deregulation of stock brokerage commissions and the shift to the registration system of securities companies provided incentive for securities companies to reform their business models. Its elimination of the obligation to trade stocks only on exchanges, on the other hand, promoted competition between markets.

Almost at the same time as the financial Big Bang initiative was being proposed, major financial institutions experienced business and financial crises that led to bankruptcies. Among troubled banks were Hokkaido Takushoku Bank, Ltd., the Long-Term Credit Bank of Japan, Ltd., and the Nippon Credit Bank, Ltd. The list of securities companies included second-tier Sanyo Securities Co., Ltd., and one of the four major securities companies, Yamaichi Securities Co., Ltd. These companies previously would have been

Table II-11.   Schedule for Reforming the Securities Market During the Big Bang

	FY1997	FY1998	FY1999	FY2000	FY2001
I. Investment Vehicles (Attractive investment instruments)					
1. Diversity of the types of bonds					
2. Diversity of derivatives products					
3. Developing Investment Trust Products					
(1) Introduction of Cash Management Account (wrap account)					
(2) OTC sales of investment trusts products by banks					
(3) Private placement of investment trusts					
(4) Investment company type funds					
4. Review of the definition of securities			---------------->		
5. Enhancement of corporate vitality and efficient use of capital					
II. Markets (An efficient and trust framework for transactions)					
1. Improvement of transaction system on stock exchanges					
2. Improvement of OTC (JASDAQ) market system					
3. Deregulation of sales solicitations by securities firms for unlisted, unregistered stock					
4. Improvement of share lending market					
5. Improvement of clearing and settlement system			---------------->		
6. Strengthening inspection, surveillance and enforcement systems			---------------->		
7. Strengthening disclosure			---------------->		
III. Financial Intermediaries (Diverse investment services to meet client needs)					
1. Deregulating brokerage commissions					
2. Diverse activity by intermediaries					
3. Use of holding company structure					
4. Strengthening asset management					
5. Enhancing monitoring system for soundness of securities companies					
6. Entry regulations for securities companies					
(1) Licensing system reform					
(2) Enhancing mutual entry into banking, securities and trust businesses					
7. Investor protection related to exits of intermediaries from the market					
(1) Strict separation of client assets from securities companies' own assets					
(2) Enhancing the securities Deposit Compensation Fund scheme					
Review of the taxation related to securities					
Shift to the new administrative regime					

Source: Drawn from the Securities and Exchange Council's report "Comprehensive Reform of the Securities Market—For a Rich and Diverse 21st Century"

rescued by being absorbed by or merged with other major financial institutions. But there were no financial institutions with the financial strength to do so. The myth that banks could not fail was shattered, and the convoy system of securities companies came to an end. Forced into action by the crisis, the major financial institutions reorganized beyond traditional corporate lines, condensing into four major financial groups. The new groups also, furthermore, began reorganizing their affiliated securities companies from second-tier to small and medium-sized ones. Amid such major changes as the shift to a registration system and the deregulation of brokerage commissions, an information technology (IT) revolution occurred. This resulted in a rush into the market of securities companies with online brokerage businesses and other new business models, producing a change in key market players.

Chart II-12.   Stock Price Movement (Nikkei Dow average and TOPIX) (2001-2008)

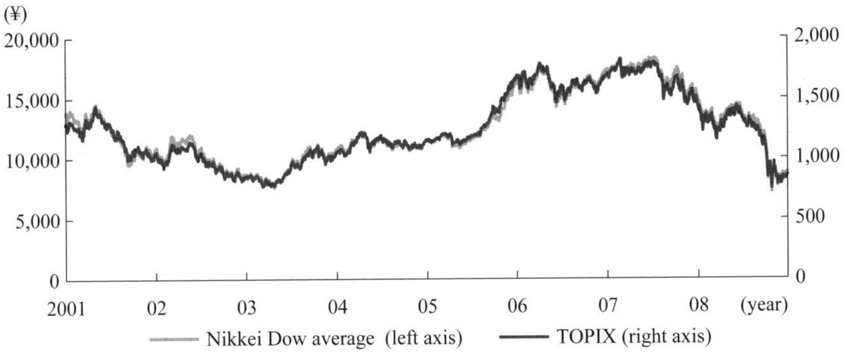

Source: Compiled from data the *Nihon Keizai Shimbun*, the *Tosho tokei geppo* (TSE Monthly Report), *Shoken tokei nenpo* (Annual Securities Statistics), and the web site of the Tokyo Stock Exchange.

9. Developments Since the Big Bang (2001-2008)

Entering the 2000s, the nonperforming loan problem reached a turning point. Prime Minister Junichiro Koizumi championed structural reform and oversaw the final clearing of this bad debt from the banking sector based on a Financial Revitalization Program in October 2002 that prioritized eliminating nonperforming loans. Because this approach threatened dangerously low levels of capital reserves at banks, a rise in bankruptcies in the corporate sector, and an increase in unemployment, the government took steps to control its adverse effects. It injected capital into banks to maintain the stability of the financial system and established restructuring mechanisms for corporations. These mechanisms included the enactment of the Civil Rehabilitation Act and of the function of the Resolution and Collection Corporation (RCC) and the setting up of the Industrial Revitalization Corporation of Japan (IRCJ).

Under the slogan of "From Savings to Investment," Japan's government also implemented policies and programs to shift to a market-based financial system with a strongly rooted securities market at its core in which a diverse range of investors would participate. The policies and programs included the Basic Policies for Economic and Fiscal Management and Reform (June 2001), the Program for Structural Reform of Securities Markets (August 2001), and the Program for Promoting Securities Markets Reform (August 2002). These policies and programs put an emphasis on the expansion and improvement of sales channels (lifted a ban on banking and securities joint branch offices and introduced a securities intermediary system); the diversification of financial instruments and services (lifted a ban on wrap accounts,

Chart II-13.   Changes in the Composition of Household Assets

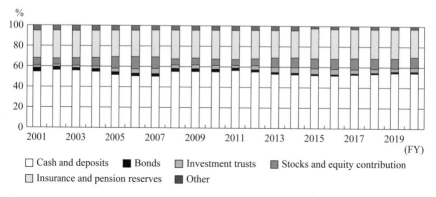

☐ Cash and deposits   ■ Bonds   ▨ Investment trusts   ▨ Stocks and equity contribution
☐ Insurance and pension reserves   ■ Other

Source: Compiled from the web site of the Bank of Japan.

Chart II-14.   Trading Amounts on TSE and Brokerage Income

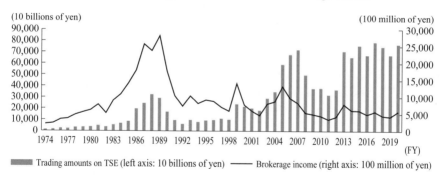

▨ Trading amounts on TSE (left axis: 10 billions of yen)   —— Brokerage income (right axis: 100 million of yen)

Source: Produced based on data from the *Tosho tokei geppo* (TSE Monthly Report), the *Tosho yoran* (TSE Fact Book), the *Shoken* and the website of the Tokyo Stock Exchange.

etc.); and the fairness and transparency of the financial business (thorough disclosure and the greater supervisory oversight of audit corporations, etc.). The authorities aimed at establishing a market that participants would have confidence in and that would attract a wide range of investors. Thanks to their reforms, the allocation of household financial assets into risk-class assets, such as equities, bonds, investment trusts, and other securities, trended upward until 2006. The reforms also, however, resulted in an increase in the number and volume of complex financial instruments and transactions that demanded a comprehensive set of regulations to ensure the thorough observance of investor protection rules and the coverage of an expanding and increasingly diversified range of investment instruments. In response, the government revised the Securities and Exchange Act, reintroducing it as the Financial Instruments and Exchange Act.

In the aftermath of the financial Big Bang, the retail securities business reform and the inter-market competition between exchanges got under way in earnest. In the retail securities business, ever since the liberalization of brokerage commissions, the level of commission income became sluggish. Therefore, leading securities companies that used to focus on the brokering business shifted their direction to adopting a marketing approach of paying greater attention to asset management in an effort to break away from being dependent on the market condition. Meanwhile, the inter-market competition was focused on attracting new listings and more transaction volume. The exchanges started targeting new listings around 2000, launching start-up company markets, and start-up companies and growth companies successively listed their shares on exchanges. In the battle for greater transaction volume, Tokyo Stock Exchange (TSE) quickly took the lead. The TSE introduced electronic stock trading and off-floor trading, strengthening its dominant position. The concentration of stock trading on the TSE, however, produced a notable decline in support for other regional stock exchanges, leading to successive reorganizations that began around 2000.

10. Changes after the Lehman Shock (2008 onwards)

Following the Lehman Shock, the outlook for global economy became increasingly uncertain, reflecting factors such as European sovereign debt crisis triggered by problems with Greek debt, trade friction between the U.S. and China, and the COVID-19 pandemic. In response to these crises, countries continued to implement massive fiscal injections and monetary easing.

In addition, the Bank of Japan has had a policy of drastic monetary easing in place since 2013 to combat deflation, purchasing not only government bonds but also ETFs and REITs. In February 2016, the central bank adopted a negative interest rate policy. Nearly 10 years have passed since the start of monetary easing, but consumer price changes have still to reach the year-on-year inflation target. Accordingly, the Bank of Japan's assets have expanded rapidly, from ¥164 trillion at the end of March 2013 to ¥717 trillion at the end of June 2021. Moreover, the assets purchased by the Bank of Japan include about ¥37 trillion in ETFs and REITs - measures still not used by central banks overseas. It has been reported that the number of companies in which the Bank of Japan is the de facto largest shareholder exceed 100 as of November 2020. Such large purchases of JGBs and ETFs continue to increase the Bank of Japan's presence in the market and raise concerns about a

Chart II-15.   Stock Price Movement (Nikkei Stock Average and TOPIX) (2010 onward)

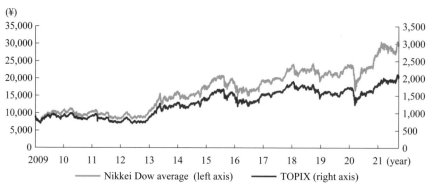

Source: Compiled from data the *Nihon Keizai Shimbun* and the web site of the Tokyo Stock Exchange.

Chart II-16.   Changes in the Central Bank Assets (at the end of March)

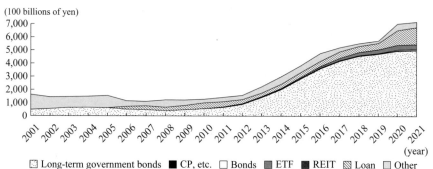

Source: Compiled from the data published on the web site of the Bank of Japan.

Chart II-17.   Transactions on Proprietary Trading Systems

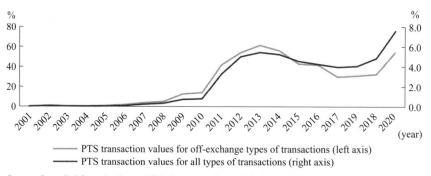

Source: Compiled from the data published on the website of the Japan Securities Dealers Association.

deterioration in the proper functioning of the market.

Corporate governance reforms have also been implemented in order to improve corporate profitability. These reforms include the introduction of the Corporate Governance Code, which outlines standards to be observed by listed companies, and the Japanese version of the Stewardship Code, which outlines the Principles for Responsible Institutional Investors, with the aim of improving corporate value and returns over the medium to long term. Since the introduction of these codes, institutional investors have publicly disclosed the results of their exercise of voting rights and engaged in dialog with investees (source: Bank of Japan website). In addition, the number of companies appointing outside directors and dissolving cross-shareholdings is also increasing.

Another change has been the increasing use of IT in securities trading, typified, for example, by high-frequency trading (HFT) and robo-advisors. In 2010, the Tokyo Stock Exchange upgraded its trading system, leading to the introduction of HFT in earnest. According to the FSA, the number of orders placed via co-location had reached 80% by March 2021. With the large-scale entry of HFT and the start of margin trading, use of proprietary trading systems (PTS) has also begun to increase. Meanwhile, changes are also evident in the asset management practices of individuals. Robo-advisor services, which use AI to automatically manage assets, were launched in Japan in 2016. The number of users has increased, mainly among those in their 20s and 30s, with assets under management for specialized firms alone in excess of ¥580 billion at the end of fiscal 2020.

CHAPTER III

The Stock Primary Market

1. New Issues of Stocks in the Primary Market

For the purpose of the Companies Act, companies are classified into corporations (*kabushiki kaisha*); general partnerships (*gomei-gaisha*); limited partnerships (*goshi-gaisha*); and limited liability companies (*godo-gaisha*). Of these, corporations have a number of advantages against the others in that (1) ownership interest in a company is divided into shares of stock; (2) investors may recoup contributed capital simply by selling their shareholdings; and (3) investors shall be held liable only to the extent of capital contributed by them (limited liability). These advantages help a corporation to raise a large amount of capital from various investors.

The shares issued by a corporation are capital securities, or narrowly defined securities, in that they represent certain claims and rights of their investors. Shareholders contribute capital in exchange for their shareholdings, which give them privileges to (1) participate in the management of the corporation (by attending general shareholder meetings and exercising voting rights that are proportionate to their shareholdings); (2) claim distribution of profits; (3) claim residual corporate assets; and (4) file derivative suits. Issued shares, unlike bonds, are not redeemable except when shares are repurchased by the corporation or upon liquidation. Because contributed equity may not usually be repaid by the corporation, shareholders wishing to monetize their holdings can only do so by selling them in the market. For the benefit of increased liquidity, stock is divided into a standard unit of shares and often represented by share certificates. On the other hand, with corporate bonds, another class of capital securities, the repayment value is backed by the issuer.

The legal framework for stocks has undergone substantial changes by a series of amendments to the Commercial Code introduced since 2001. Pursuant to the amendments that took effect on October 1, 2001, par value stock was abolished and all stocks are now issued with no par value. Accordingly, the par value-based *tan'i-kabu* round-lot system was replaced by the new, discretionary *tangen-kabu* system. Under the amendments enforced on April 1,

Table III-1.   Principal Rights of Shareholders

Rights for personal interest (rights on benefits of owing property)	Rights for common interest (rights on participating in management)
· Right to claim dividend of surplus · Right to subscribe for new shares · Right to demand distribution of residual assets · Right to request registration of name transfer · Right to request purchase of shares	· Right to exercise votes at general shareholder meetings · Right to bring representative suit · Right to convoke a general shareholder meeting · Right to demand suspension of illegal action by a director · Right to make a shareholder proposal · Right to request dissolution · Right to demand dismissal of a corporate officer · Right to request inspection, etc.

Table III-2.   Recent Amendments to the Commercial Code Relating to Equity Financing and Main Contents of the Companies Act

The amendments made in 2001 (enforced on October 1, 2001):
A revision of the system of acquiring and holding one's own shares (the ban on holding treasury shares was lifted); the abolition of the system of issuing shares with face value (under this system, all shares are issued without par value); the abolition of the requirement of net asset value (a minimum of ¥50,000 or $487.8 at the rate of ¥102.50 to the dollar); the abolition of the *tan'i-kabu* system in favor of *tangen-kabu* system; and the relaxation of the legal reserve system, etc.

The amendments made in 2001 (enforced on April 1, 2002):
The institution of the equity warrant system and the abolition of regulation of the stock option system, the electronification of corporate documents, and a revision of regulation of the classified stock (the lifting on the ban of tracking stock*), etc.

The amendments made in 2002 (enforced in April 2003):
A revision of regulation of the classified stocks, the institution of the system relating to lapses of stock certificates, and the rationalization of the procedure for reducing capital, etc.

The amendments made in 2003 (enforced on September 25, 2003):
The acquisition of one's own shares by a resolution of the board of directors under the provisions of the articles of incorporation and a revision of the method of computing a limit on interim dividends, etc.

The amendments made in 2004 (enforced on October 1, 2005):
The adoption of a system of not issuing stock certificates, the introduction of a system of issuing notices by electronic means, etc.

Amendments in conjunction with the enactment of the Companies Act in 2005 (enforced on May 1, 2006):
A revision of regulations to make the share transfer system more flexible, the rationalization of the system of retiring shares, a revision of regulations relating to issuing of share certificates, and the abolition of fractional shares, etc.

The amendments made in 2014 (enforced on May 1, 2015):
Revision of new share issuance procedure involving transfer of controlling shareholders Introduction of a cash-out method that allows a special controlling shareholder to request other shareholders to sell their shares, etc.

The amendments made in 2019 (enforced on March 11, 2021):
Founding the system of share delivery

Note: The ban on tracking stock (under this system, dividends are paid not out of the earnings of a company as a whole but out of the earnings of a specific division or a subsidiary of such company) was lifted.

2002, (1) new subscription rights/warrants were introduced, (2) the regulation of stock options was relaxed, and (3) the regulation regarding multiple classified stocks was relaxed.

The Commercial Code as amended in 2004 and the Law Revising the Act on Book Entry of Corporate Bonds and Shares etc., for Streamlining Settlement of Transactions in Stocks, etc., introduced a system allowing electronic bookkeeping for shares. As a result of the revision of the Companies Act, share certificates of public companies were dematerialized from January 2009. Transfer restrictions on any and/or all classes of stock and issuance of classified stocks subject to wholly call were put in place in May 2006, and a "cash out" system where controlling shareholders of a company may force minority shareholders to sell their shares to them was enacted in May 2015. The amended Companies Act of 2019 introduced a new stock delivery system as a way for companies to acquire other companies in exchange for their own shares (enacted in March 2021).

2. Forms of Issuing New Shares

Shares are first issued when a corporation is established. Establishment of a corporation can be roughly divided into incorporators-only establishment and by-subscription establishment. When a corporation is established only with the funds contributed to its capital stock by its promoters, this method of establishing a corporation has the advantage of its shares being fully subscribed to, but it has a drawback in that the number of shares it can issue is limited to the funds its promoters can raise. On the other hand, establishing a corporation with the capital raised by publicly offering its shares to an unspecified large number of investors is called "establishment through a public offering of shares." While a large amount of capital can be raised through this method, one major drawback is that it takes time to successfully complete the public offering, and when its shares are not fully subscribed to by investors during the public offering period, the corporation cannot be established. Under the old provisions of the Commercial Code, the par value of shares issued by a corporation at the time it was established had to be ¥50,000 or more, but this restriction was abolished—and the requirement of par value has been liberalized—by virtue of the 2001 amendment to the Commercial Code.

Even after a corporation is established, it is a general practice for the corporation to issue new shares after in order to raise funds, to transfer the control of its management to a third party, or to enhance the liquidity of its shares. Usually, the method of issuing new shares is divided into paid-in capital increase and stock splits (and gratis issues).

Issuing new shares against the payment for them by shareholders is called

Table III-3. Forms of Issuing New Shares

Payment required
Capital increase through a public offering Capital increase through a third-party allocation of new shares Capital increase through a rights offering The exercise of subscription rights/warrants
Payment not required
Stock split Merger Swap of shares Stock transfers Share delivery

Table III-4. Funds Raised by Equity Financing

(100 million yen)

Year	Rights offering		Public offering		Third party allotment		Exercise of subscription rights/warrants		Preferred stock and others		Total	
	No.	Amount	No.	Amount	No.	Amount	No.	Amount	No.	Amount	No.	Amount
1998	0	0	8	2,782	32	6,880	28	864	5	4,710	73	15,236
1999	0	0	28	3,497	75	23,473	62	2,529	25	69,894	190	99,393
2000	2	82	24	4,941	46	9,228	87	1,056	4	1,073	163	16,298
2001	3	320	18	12,015	57	4,772	85	374	5	2,161	168	19,322
2002	0	0	19	1,533	62	4,844	78	2,763	36	9,968	195	19,107
2003	2	15	35	5,672	84	2,232	121	366	74	25,322	316	33,592
2004	1	27	78	7,502	129	5,726	228	995	50	13,626	486	27,849
2005	2	37	74	6,508	150	7,781	336	1,669	45	11,678	607	27,635
2006	0	0	69	14,477	145	4,165	371	1,513	26	5,597	611	25,751
2007	1	81	60	4,570	117	6,621	347	1,650	12	7,955	537	20,796
2008	1	1	27	3,417	93	3,958	240	209	9	5,937	370	13,521
2009	0	0	52	49,668	115	7,146	169	188	28	4,740	364	61,743
2010	1	7	50	33,089	88	5,356	159	246	10	736	308	39,427
2011	0	0	45	9,678	66	3,952	171	261	7	693	289	14,584
2012	1	4	53	4,518	71	1,593	174	218	17	12,755	316	19,084
2013	1	10	114	11,137	151	3,719	350	1,904	3	1,200	619	17,970
2014	0	0	129	13,780	190	3,928	412	1,087	14	2,242	745	21,037
2015	1	1	131	9,620	187	1,636	437	815	6	7,513	762	19,583
2016	1	2	95	2,577	151	6,230	483	901	7	1,480	737	11,191
2017	2	1	116	4,242	238	8,816	526	1,926	7	613	889	15,599
2018	0	0	129	4,016	303	2,146	597	2,277	6	595	1,035	9,034
2019	0	0	93	2,198	307	9,104	572	1,431	10	1,508	982	14,241
2020	1	4	108	7,328	342	7,226	624	2,203	11	1,947	1,086	18,708

Source: Website of the Tokyo Stock Exchange.

paid-in capital increase, and a corporation can raise its equity capital by this method. Paid-in capital increase is also divided on the basis of investors to whom shares are issued into public offering, rights offering, and allotment of new shares to a third party.

By definition, a stock split, the act of splitting one share into two or more shares, does not by itself increase the assets or the capital of a corporation. However, new shares issued through a stock split play an important role. The stock split increases the number of the corporation's shares outstanding on the market, and the fall in the per share price caused thereby enhances the liquidity of shares, making it easier for the corporation to raise funds through equity financing in the future. Until 2001, there was a rule banning any stock split that reduces the value of net assets per share to less than ¥50,000, but this rule was abolished by virtue of the 2001 amendment to the Commercial Code. This step was taken because of widespread complaints among venture businesses—those that have high growth potential and whose shares are traded at high prices despite limited net assets—that on account of the restrictions against a stock split, they could not improve the liquidity of their shares. However, it was desirable to prevent share certificates from being in short supply during the period from the record date of stock split (day on which the shareholders to whom new shares are allocated are determined) to the effective date (day on which the right to new shares for shareholders goes into effect), which can disrupt the demand-supply balance and cause stock prices to fluctuate violently. Hence, it was decided that the effective date would fall on the day following the record date from January 2006.

Other cases in which a corporation is authorized to issue new shares include the exercise of new share subscription rights/warrants, a new type of warrant introduced by the April 2002 amendment to the Commercial Code; equity swaps with one's subsidiaries under the equity swap system; allocation of shares to shareholders of one's subsidiaries under the stock transfer system and the newly introduced stock delivery system.

3. Procedures for Issuing New Shares

New share issuance may be done in exchange for capital paid in by investors in the form of a public offering, third-party allotment, or rights offering.

In a rights offering, shareholders on record as of a specified record date are given subscription rights in proportion to their stockholdings. In the case of public companies, grant of subscription rights or allotment of new shares to non-shareholders are only subject to board approval. On the other hand, a third-party allotment by a private company, under the Companies Act, inprinciple, requires a special resolution at the general shareholders meeting, but it

Chart III-1. Equity Financing in 1989 by TSE-Listed Companies, by Type of Financing
(Total capital procured: ¥8,529.39 billion)

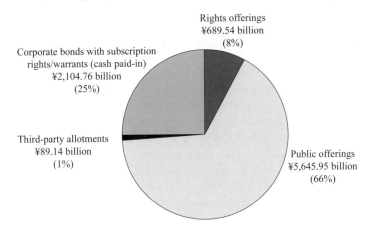

Source: Tokyo Stock Exchange, *the Tosho tokei geppo* (TSE Monthly Report)

Chart III-2. Equity Financing in 2020 by TSE-Listed Companies, by Type of Financing
(Total capital procured: ¥1,870.77 billion)

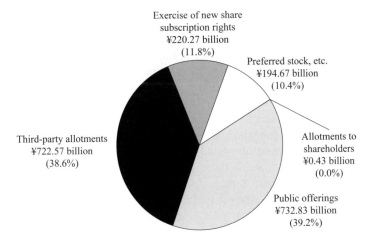

Source: Web page of the Tokyo Stock Exchange.

may be conducted by ordinary resolution when provided for in the Articles of Incorporation. A rights offering to existing shareholders is a means of capital raising that is neutral to the control of corporations, in that it does not affect proportionate ownership of the shareholders. An offering of rights at par used to be the dominant measure of equity financing, but such offering is no longer common, partly due to the elimination of par value of stocks under amendments to the Commercial Code in 2001.

Public offerings grant subscription rights to the general public. A public offering raises more capital for an issuer than an offering of rights at par, which was once prevalent along with par value stock, by the excess of the issue price over par. From the viewpoint of investors, however, it deprives investors of the opportunity to earn the premium, thereby losing their incentive to subscribe. Although public offerings declined in the 1990s, they are now a primary means of raising equity capital today.

A third-party allotment raises capital by granting subscription rights to certain third parties, including banks or business corporations with special relationships with the issuer and/or its director(s). This method is often used to bail out troubled companies, strengthen relationships with corporate partners, and form a business and capital alliance rather than simply to raise capital. Additionally, the method has recently been noted as a measure for fending off hostile takeovers. Third-party allotments cause dilution of ownership of existing shareholders. They may be approved by board resolution except when terms of rights harm the interests of existing shareholders because they are unequivocally advantageous to the grantee(s) in which case a special resolution at the general shareholders meeting will be required (advantageous issuance). An issuer pursuing a capital increase by third party capital allocation has an obligation to explain the rationality and necessity of the capital increase in its securities registration statement.

Under the revised Companies Act of 2014 that went into effect in 2015, when new share issuance by a public company involves any transfer of controlling shareholders (accounting for one-half or more of voting rights), the name and other information of the underwriter must be notified to existing shareholders. Furthermore, if there is opposition by 10% or more of voting rights, the share issuance is subject to a resolution not only by the board of directors but also by the general shareholders meeting. Thus the involvement of shareholders in share issuance was strengthened.

4. The Current State of the New Issue Market

New shares are usually issued (1) in exchange for capital contribution (equity financing in the forms of public offerings, third-party allotments, rights offer-

Table III-5. The State of Issuing New Shares by Listed Companies

(in thousands of shares)

Year	Paid-in capital increase	Rights offering	Public offering	Third party allotment	Preferred stock, conversion of a corporate bond with subscription rights/ warrants of the convertible bond type into shares, etc.	Exercise of subscription rights/warrants	Stock split	Others	Total
1980	5,900,618	1,761,008	1,619,438	311,354	2,208,818	—	3,270,677	34,846	9,206,243
1981	10,621,006	5,624,372	2,360,917	99,890	2,535,827	—	3,542,488	64,632	14,228,128
1982	4,919,006	1,932,416	1,760,389	111,822	1,102,860	11,519	4,265,996	318,347	9,503,352
1983	4,231,828	1,005,145	513,645	589,154	2,006,283	117,601	4,208,030	24,857	8,464,718
1984	5,312,713	1,170,322	778,686	319,665	2,835,670	208,370	4,033,612	169,830	9,516,159
1985	5,580,645	909,635	590,696	118,126	3,514,706	447,179	4,390,653	93,169	10,064,468
1986	4,503,842	371,191	346,883	78,308	2,831,297	876,161	3,939,802	621,924	9,065,569
1987	8,600,184	547,900	718,327	314,650	4,753,694	2,265,611	3,300,518	510,942	12,411,644
1988	9,052,096	849,464	1,286,177	169,633	4,623,233	2,123,587	4,004,200	96,212	13,152,509
1989	12,467,106	803,396	3,558,558	94,151	5,522,653	2,488,346	5,906,047	44,848	18,418,003
1990	4,733,374	758,546	1,284,250	252,593	1,859,145	578,839	8,283,600	1,632,879	14,649,854
1991	1,604,596	420,553	39,850	182,776	600,930	360,485	3,451,047	1,581,058	6,636,703
1992	766,227	244,895	2,180	190,340	139,205	189,605	1,584,403	414,121	2,764,752
1993	1,605,059	87,091	4,150	479,440	347,764	686,612	901,948	1,147,000	3,654,008
1994	1,530,474	24,152	33,360	543,846	445,479	483,635	2,330,679	1,190,447	5,051,602
1995	1,433,831	249,876	10,400	490,557	343,684	339,311	1,015,654	359,334	2,808,819
1996	2,546,611	455,200	200,883	583,427	506,753	800,348	847,835	1,873,163	5,267,610
1997	3,093,475	204,686	93,250	1,493,319	1,034,959	267,261	551,076	251,712	3,896,265
1998	3,641,490	7,707	97,137	2,380,126	1,079,024	77,295	168,263	22,696	3,832,450
1999	9,627,895		54,599	8,402,531	976,593	194,170	742,946	61,952	10,432,793
2000	3,709,565	87,140	84,200	2,621,987	835,744	80,492	1,599,465	1,158,762	6,467,792
2001	4,526,944	143,051	49,760	3,328,896	935,912	69,324	624,199	3,330,016	8,481,160
2002	4,260,986		238,268	2,719,729	546,153	756,815	692,917	1,412,881	6,366,784
2003	4,541,171	20,352	431,517	2,995,729	679,841	413,729	333,448	5,931,549	10,806,168
2004	5,659,174	18,193	516,166	1,586,466	2,404,691	1,133,656	2,975,260	24,497	8,658,931
2005	11,393,111	53,120	616,574	2,957,298	6,241,871	1,524,246	3,051,215	△13,967,015	477,311
2006	7,459,697		1,638,972	850,680	4,450,694	519,349	6,713,875	△1,201,938	12,971,634
2007	5,341,133	80,862	409,532	1,521,236	2,928,468	401,032	11,749,106	△3,504,021	13,586,219
2008	3,542,021	6,998	687,868	1,549,130	1,119,159	178,863	120,552	△542,754	3,119,819
2009	22,418,250		12,049,714	3,192,219	6,846,482	329,833	16,193,816	238,890	38,850,955
2010	10,464,418	68	7,548,008	1,935,650	835,992	144,697	877,229	△860,938	10,480,708
2011	6,391,284		2,947,644	2,283,962	839,211	320,465	1,842,238	625,267	8,645,867
2012	4,309,521	34,504	2,371,349	663,776	1,024,399	215,492	3,759,441	576,904	8,858,789
2013	5,226,016	613	1,244,084	2,058,111	1,400,302	522,905	27,099,251	△8,996,091	23,329,176
2014	4,624,642		1,422,172	657,011	1,933,058	642,391	8,841,942	△6,101,224	7,365,361
2015	3,717,412	1,560	679,898	767,728	1,797,390	470,834	7,060,155	△12,958,857	△2,181,288
2016	5,403,536	3,699	140,825	4,152,569	798,326	308,115	2,232,113	△29,020,941	△21,385,291
2017	4,747,915	1,312	320,095	2,934,439	606,853	885,214	4,836,899	△71,033,038	△61,448,223
2018	2,380,544		251,482	572,821	323,032	1,233,208	4,567,464	△26,497,834	△19,549,824
2019	4,691,381		110,331	3,895,668	59,353	626,026	6,495,653	△5,056,466	6,130,569
2020	2,955,072	6,155	338,199	1,380,132	214,293	1,016,292	7,360,701	△25,389,212	△15,073,438

Source: Tokyo Stock Exchange, *Shoken tokei nenpo* (Annual Securities Statistics) and *Tosho tokei geppo* (TSE Monthly Report).

ings, exercise of subscription rights, etc.); (2) in conjunction with stock splits (and gratis issues); and (3) for the purpose of corporate acquisitions. (Share counts are reduced when treasury stock is cancelled.) In 2020, the leading source of new shares issued by listed companies was by stock splits and gratis issues (increase of 7.36 billion shares), followed by the onerous exercise of new share subscription rights/warrants (1.38 billion shares) and the third party allotment (1.02 billion shares). The amendments to the Commercial Code in 1991 defined stock splits as a notion that encompasses stock dividends, gratis issues and reclassification of paid-in capital in excess of par into capital stock all of which were cases that did not involve payments by investors at the time of issuance of new shares.

Today, in Japan, equity financing is the leading source of new shares. Listed companies on the Tokyo Stock Exchange (TSE) raised approximately ¥1.9 trillion in equity in 2020. By contrast, equity financing, except for initial public offerings, is less used in the United States and the United Kingdom because it tends to cause earnings dilution and consequently pushes down the stock price. It should be noted, however, that over the past years, equity financing in Japan has undergone many changes. During the period of rapid economic growth, corporations mostly used the method of rights offering at par to raise equity capital, because investors did not have enough accumulation of financial assets, while issuing companies suffered a chronic shortage of funds. (Stock par value was abolished in 2001.) In those days, corporations mostly relied on bank borrowings for their funding requirements, and the stock market was a marginal marketplace for raising capital. However, as the economy slowed down after the oil shocks, the funding needs of businesses were reduced, and due in part to the necessity of securing a strong stockholder base, public offerings at market price became the prevalent means of raising equity among business corp orations. Meanwhile, the weight of rights offerings also shifted from rights offering based on par value to that based on a median of par and market values. In the second half of the 1980s, with progress in deregulation concerning debt financing, issuing of convertible corporate bonds and corporate bonds with subscription rights/warrants increased, and so did their conversion and exercise. Particularly, as banks came under pressure to meet Tier 1 capital requirements imposed by the Basel regulatory standards, they scrambled to shore up their capital base, and such issuing accounted for about half of equity financing at the time.

In the 1990s, there was a marked decline in public offerings because of stagnant stock prices, and increasing capital through public offerings remained stagnant thereafter. However, following the global financial crisis that kicked off in 2008, equity financing picked up as companies sought to shore up their weakened financial bases by public stock offerings which became active in 2009. Although significant volumes of shares have been issued through the exercise of new share subscription rights/warrants and stock splits in recent years, the overall number of issued shares has been declining, due mainly to the retirement of treasury shares.

5. New Share Underwriting

The method of issuing shares may be divided into direct offering and indirect offering, and public offering and private placement. When the issuing company itself performs the administrative procedures necessary for issuing shares and sells them to investors, this is called "direct offering (or self-offering)." Although this method helps the issuing company save the fees payable to an intermediary, it is not an easy task to perform the technically complicated procedures and sell the securities to an unspecified large number of investors. When the issuing company commissions a specialist intermediary to handle the public offering of its shares, this is called "indirect offering." The intermediary provides the issuing company with expert advice, handles the distribution of shares and performs the necessary administrative procedures on behalf of the issuing company, and takes over the shares remaining unsold after the public offering period. At present, almost all shares are offered through the indirect offering method. A "public offering" is the public solicitation of an unspecified large number of investors for the purchase of new shares, and "private placement" is the private solicitation of a specified small number of investors to purchase them. In public offerings of new shares, indirect offering through underwriting securities companies is the general rule.

In the case of an indirect offering, the issuing company concludes an underwriting agreement with a securities company. Underwriting agreements are divided into standby underwriting (the underwriting securities company commits itself to buying up the shares remaining unsold) and firm commitment underwriting (it agrees to buy up the entire issue from the start). Today, the latter has become the general practice.

When the total amount of shares offered is too large, a securities company alone cannot accept the underwriting risk involved. Therefore, a number of securities companies often get together to form an underwriting syndicate. Of these securities companies, the firm that plays the leadership role in organizing the syndicate members and in negotiating the terms and conditions of the underwriting agreement with the issuing company is called the "lead managing underwriter." And the group of securities companies that assumes no underwriting risk and only sells the securities is called the "selling group."

In a public offering or secondary distribution, it is necessary to have a strategy for balancing supply and demand. Using an over-allotment option allows the securities firm that is the lead managing underwriter of an offering

Table III-6.   Number of Lead Managing Underwriters in Shares of Securities Companies (IPOs)

(Existing stock exchanges and start-up markets in 2020)

Securities companies	Main Markets		Mothers		JASDAQ	
	No. of co.	% of total	No. of co.	% of total	No. of co.	% of total
Nomura	5	33.3	4	28.6	13	20.6
Mizuhoa	1	6.7	3	21.4	16	25.4
SMBC Nikko Securities	4	26.7	1	7.1	10	15.9
Daiwa	3	20.0	–	–	9	14.3
SBI	–	–	3	21.4	11	17.5
Mitsubishi UFJ Morgan Stanley	2	13.3	–	–	–	–
Ichiyoshi	–	–	2	14.3	3	4.8
Tokai Tokyo	–	–	–	–	1	1.6
H.S.	–	–	1	7.1	–	–
Total	15	100.0	14	100.0	63	100.0

Source: PRONEXSUS, *Kabushiki Kokai Hakusho* (White Paper on Public Listings).

Table III-7.   Flow from additional secondary distribution by over-allotment in initial public offering to syndicate cover transaction

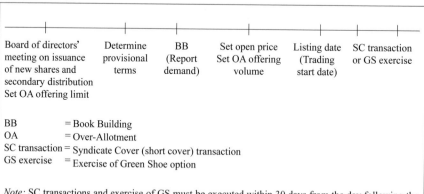

| Board of directors' meeting on issuance of new shares and secondary distribution Set OA offering limit | Determine provisional terms | BB (Report demand) | Set open price Set OA offering volume | Listing date (Trading start date) | SC transaction or GS exercise |

BB   = Book Building
OA   = Over-Allotment
SC transaction = Syndicate Cover (short cover) transaction
GS exercise   = Exercise of Green Shoe option

Note: SC transactions and exercise of GS must be executed within 30 days from the day following the date on which the period during which investors submit their applications to securities companies is completed (normally, 2 or 3 business days prior to the listing date).

to borrow shares from existing shareholders and sell them if demand is greater than the original scheduled number of shares. In Japan, lead managing underwriters of offerings have been able to use the over-allotment option based on the underlying underwriting agreement since January 31, 2002. This option allows the sales of additional shares up to 15% of the scheduled number of shares in the public offering or secondary distribution. The short position arising when the lead managing underwriter the over-allotment option is cleared differently depending on whether the price in the secondary market has risen or fallen compared with the price after the listing. When the price of the shares has fallen, the lead managing underwriter purchases the excess shares in the secondary market (syndicate cover). When the price of the shares has risen, the lead managing underwriter exercises a green shoe option (right to acquire additional shares from the issuing company or from investors who have lent shares).

6. Private Equity Market

Public offerings and other equity financing that raise capital from the general public are mostly conducted by public companies that have their shares traded on an exchange or other public market. However, that does not mean that equity financing by private companies faces special legal restriction. In fact, equity financing regulations for private companies can be said to be less strict than those for public companies. For example, the written notice of securities does not require information concerning the operating performance or financial conditions of the issuer because, unlike the securities registration statement, it is not intended to disclose information to investors. Under the Financial Instruments and Exchange Act and Cabinet Office Order, etc. currently in force, furthermore, in cases where the proceeds from a proposed offering or secondary distribution of shares (securities) are less than ¥100 million, the private company is exempt from filing a securities registration statement, and a written notice of securities is filed in its place, regardless of whether the solicitation is extended to 50 persons or more or not. Furthermore, if the proceeds from an offering do not exceed ¥10 million or fewer than 50 persons are solicited, the issuer is not, in principle, required to file a written notice of securities.

However, when viewed from the standpoint of investors, private equity investments, given the limitations on information available to them, involve higher risks. While stock prices of public companies are properly formed through market transactions, reasonable values of private stocks are not easy to determine since there are various methods to estimate private stock prices, including the net asset method of estimating based on the company's net as-

Table III-8. Criteria for Requirement to Submit Securities Registration Statement or Written Notice of Securities Under the Financial Instruments and Exchange Act, and Cabinet Office Order, etc.

		No. of Investors*	
		Less than 50	50 or more
Issue Amount	100 million yen or more	Not necessary	Securities Registration Statement
	10 million yen or greater but less than 100 million yen	Not necessary	Written Notice of Securities
	10 million yen or less	Not necessary	

Notes: 1. Under the current FIEA and Cabinet Office Order, etc. even when the number of investors solicited is less than 50, if the issuer has made an offering of the same type of security within six months previously and the combined number of investors solicited is 50 or more, the determination of whether a securities registration statement or written notice of securities is required must be made based on the total issuance amounts of the offerings.

2. In accordance with the revision of administrative orders effective April 1, 2003, issuance regulations have been liberalized as follows.

(1) Under specified condition of the number of Qualified Institutional Investors being 250 or less, etc., the number of professional investors (Qualified Institutional Investors) may be deducted from the count of 50 or more of the number of investors being solicited.

(2) In determining the issuance amount for a professional investor private equity offering in a solicitation for purchase of securities where only Qualified Institutional Investors are counterparties and there is little possibility of sales to anyone other than qualified institutional investors, equities, etc. and equity related products are to be included. In this case, regardless of the number of investors, the written notice of securities is required only for issues of 100 million yen or more (for solicitations of investor groups of less than 50, please see note 1 above).

sets, the income method based on cash flows, and the dividend discount method based on future dividend projections. Moreover, the problem with private equity investments is that the funds invested in them are not easily recoverable due to lack of liquidity. Thus investment in private equity was limited to a small number of investors, such as venture capital funds, which have the economic wherewithal to tolerate the high risks and long investment periods associated with such investments.

In order to stimulate entrepreneurial activity and foster startup businesses, streamlining the fund raising mechanism prior to going public has been discussed as a matter of priority.

The Japan Securities Dealers Association launched a public quotation system (Green Sheet system) for private equity or unlisted shares in July 1997. Securities companies became able to solicit investment in private equities for issues of OTC securities that met a certain standard of information disclosure

Table III-9.   Examples of methods of calculating stock values of private companies

1. Net assets approach
(1) Book value method 　　Price per share = Book value of net assets/Total number of issued shares (2) Adjusted book value method 　　Price per share = Book value of net assets reflecting unrealized gain and losses/Total number of issued shares (3) Market value method 　　Price per share = Market value of net assets/Total number of issued shares
2. Income approach
(1) Income capitalization method (direct return method) 　　Price per share = (Projected future net profit after tax/Capitalization ratio)/Total number of issued shares (2) DCF method 　　Price per share = Total amount of discounted present value of projected future profit/Total number of issued shares
3. Dividend discount approach
(1) Dividend discount method 　　Price per share = (Projected future annual dividends/Capitalization ratio)/Total number of issued shares (2) Gordon Growth Model method 　　Price per share = (Projected future annual dividends/(Capitalization ratio-Investment return ratio × Retained ratio)

and for which the securities companies provide publicly announced buy and sell quotes. The Green Sheet system was later dissolved at the end of March 2018, and new shareholder community system was introduced in May 2015. The Japan Securities Dealers Association introduced an equity-based crowd-funding system in May 2015 to facilitate the supply of risk finance for new and fast-growing companies. In June 2021, in response to the government's Growth Strategy and other measures to facilitate and diversify the means of financing for unlisted companies, the Japan Securities Dealers Association made recommendations for the development of the system, including a revision of the calculation method for the total issuance amount (less than 100 million yen) under the system and the removal of the maximum investment amount (500,000 yen) for specified investors (professional investors).

CHAPTER IV

The Stock Secondary Market

1. The Structure of the Stock Secondary Market

The stock secondary market on which shares are traded consists of a trading market opened on a stock exchange, a proprietary trading system (the so-called PTS) operated by private companies authorized under the 1998 amendment to the Securities and Exchange Act, and the off-exchange trading of listed stocks that was made by virtue of the same amendment, which abolished the duty to centralize securities trading on stock exchanges.

The exchange market is provided by stock exchanges, and there are four stock exchanges in Japan: the Tokyo Stock Exchange, and the Nagoya, Sapporo and Fukuoka exchanges. Stock exchanges used to be membership organizations consisting of securities companies. However, under the 2000 amendment to the Securities and Exchange Act, they were authorized to change their status as corporations. Today, the Japan Exchange Group, which owns the Tokyo Stock Exchange, and the Nagoya Stock Exchange are corporations.

Shares of listed stocks (1) that meet certain listing requirements are traded (2) during fixed trading hours (3) by auction, and (4) the stock exchanges as self-regulatory organizations manage and supervise the trading process and the business conduct of securities companies with a view to ensuring the fairness of trading.

The Tokyo Stock Exchange introduced arrowhead, the world-class, high speed trading platform in January 2010. Arrowhead was renewed to cope with dramatic changes in the market: increased bargains, concentration of order placement at a short time, and the new demand from investors.

The system for off-floor trading of shares listed on the Tokyo Stock Exchange (ToSTNeT) has a three-part structure to accommodate the diverse needs of investors: ToSTNeT-1 which processes large-lot and basket trades of listed stocks through negotiated or cross transactions; ToSTNeT-2 which concludes trades at specific prices such as the closing price several times a day; and ToSTNet-3 which handles purchases of treasury stocks. In addition, certain securities companies have opened a proprietary trading system (PTS)

Chart IV-1. Inter-market Competition in Japan

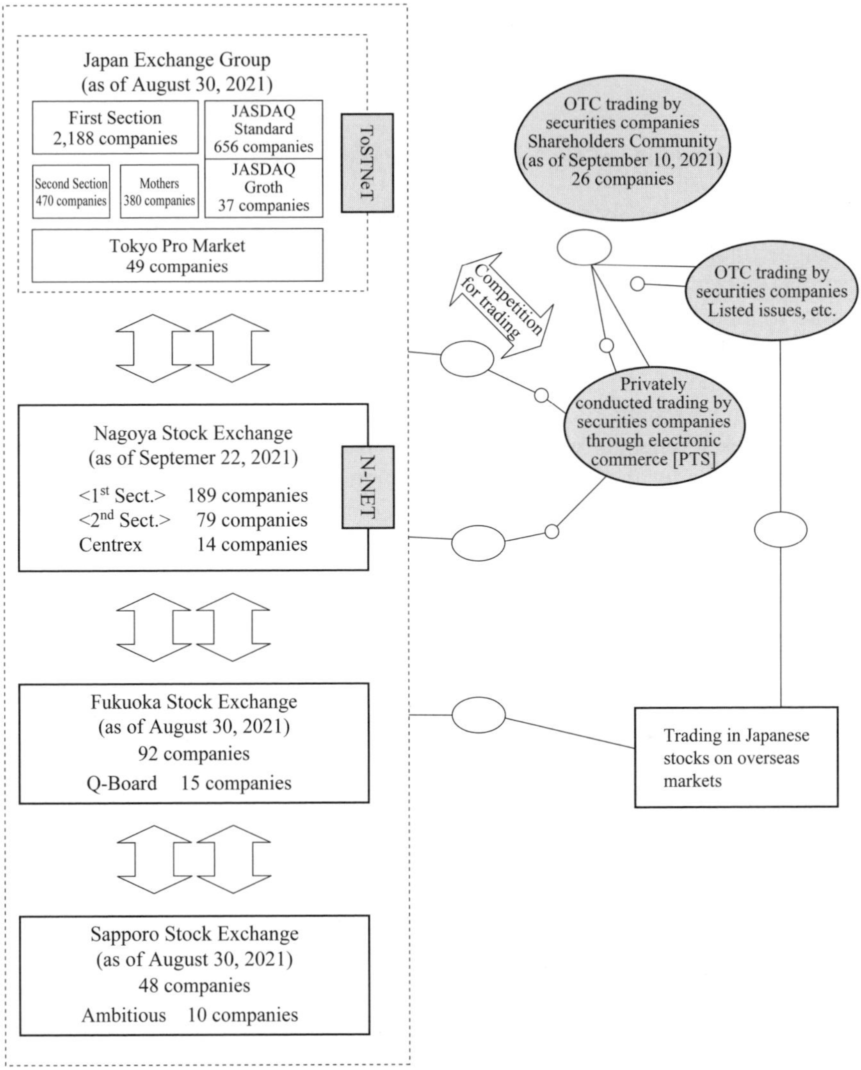

Japan Exchange Group
(as of August 30, 2021)

| First Section 2,188 companies | JASDAQ Standard 656 companies |
| Second Section 470 companies | Mothers 380 companies | JASDAQ Groth 37 companies |

Tokyo Pro Market
49 companies

ToSTNeT

OTC trading by
securities companies
Shareholders Community
(as of September 10, 2021)
26 companies

Competition for trading

OTC trading by
securities companies
Listed issues, etc.

Privately
conducted trading by
securities companies
through electronic
commerce [PTS]

Nagoya Stock Exchange
(as of September 22, 2021)

<1st Sect.>   189 companies
<2nd Sect.>   79 companies
Centrex   14 companies

N-NET

Fukuoka Stock Exchange
(as of August 30, 2021)
92 companies
Q-Board   15 companies

Trading in Japanese
stocks on overseas
markets

Sapporo Stock Exchange
(as of August 30, 2021)
48 companies
Ambitious   10 companies

on their own mainly for the purpose of matching orders received after business hours.

In addition, the Shareholder Community is a system for secondary trading of unlisted shares. This system was developed in May 2015 as an alternative to the Green Sheet market where shares of unlisted companies or not registered with the over-the-counter (OTC) market were traded over the counters of securities companies and reported to the Japan Securities Dealers Association (JSDA). The value of total transactions amounted to about ¥500 million in 2020.

2. Transaction Size of the Stock Secondary Market

As of the end of 2020, the number of companies listed on the national exchanges (including multiple listings) stood at 3,859, with 311 billion shares listed. The trading volume for 2020 was 465.8 billion shares, and the trading value totaled ¥742.4 trillion. Of these, the number of shares of the 3,753 stocks listed on the Tokyo Stock Exchange was 309.6 billion shares, with a trading volume of 465.8 billion shares and a trading value of ¥742.2 trillion. Thus, Japan's exchange tradings of shares are extremely concentrated on the Tokyo Stock Exchange, where most of the nation's companies are listed and which accounts for the majority of transactions in volume and value.

The heavy concentration of stock trading on the TSE may be explained by the fact that the stock markets have taken on a hierarchical structure, with the First Section of the TSE at the top, and many companies aim for a listing on the First Section because of its high social status and prestige. Therefore, blue-chip corporations have tended to converge on the First Section of the TSE. And as shares are actively traded in large volumes and on a highly liquid market, the externality of the order flow—trading flows to where shares are actively traded—was at work accelerating the concentration of orders.

The Second Section of the TSE, which is a market for companies, with good track-records had 476 listed stocks at the end of 2020, with a market capitalization of ¥6.8 trillion, a trading volume of 35.7 billion shares, and a trading value of ¥10.7 trillion. The JASDAQ, which became a regular stock exchange in December 2004, has two markets: The Standard market is for growing companies with a certain business scale and performance and the Growth market is for companies with unique technologies or business models and significant future growth potential. At the end of 2020, there were 704 listed stocks in total, with a market capitalization of ¥10.4 trillion, a trading volume of 29.8 billion shares, and a trading value of ¥15.5 trillion. The Second Section of the TSE and the JASDAQ market have long competed against each other in the listing of start-up companies, but the JASDAQ market has outperformed the TSE in all indicators except trading volume.

The TSE has a market for start-up companies called Mothers, with 346 listed stocks, a market capitalization of ¥9.5 trillion, a trading volume of 28.5 billion shares, and a trading value of ¥44.4 trillion at the end of 2020. Other domestic markets for start-up companies are the Centrex market of the

Table IV-1.   TSE Trading Volumes by Each Market Segment

year		2014	2015	2016	2017	2018	2019	2020
Trading volume (in thousands of shares)	First Section	612,851,073	620,005,885	593,610,396	490,384,220	406,069,774	331,759,774	368,980,635
	Second Section	36,199,273	36,580,825	25,604,041	46,368,789	30,622,268	18,408,268	35,740,358
	Mothers	23,035,432	16,053,604	16,838,945	19,187,800	14,775,667	15,957,358	28,485,961
	JASDAQ Standard	34,570,141	34,391,591	26,080,691	28,428,353	26,006,913	17,359,611	29,533,254
	JASDAQ Groth	2,448,911	2,686,382	3,634,413	3,359,757	4,158,478	2,598,980	3,097,174

Source: Japan Securities Dealers Association, Japan Exchange Group.

Table IV-2.   TSE Trading Value by Each Market Segment

year		2014	2015	2016	2017	2018	2019	2020
Trading amount (millions of yen)	First Section	576,525,070	696,509,496	643,205,780	683,218,254	740,746,041	598,213,662	671,671,658
	Second Section	7,739,865	8,266,622	6,118,938	12,744,471	11,006,506	6,188,491	10,657,529
	Mothers	34,968,861	23,059,265	29,640,306	27,408,857	23,828,660	24,904,937	44,377,305
	JASDAQ Standard	21,599,665	16,566,416	10,543,834	15,998,536	15,772,124	9,505,233	14,430,686
	JASDAQ Groth	2,272,146	1,550,819	1,591,839	1,944,079	2,468,600	1,460,462	1,108,330

Source: Japan Securities Dealers Association, Japan Exchange Group.

Table IV-3.   Trading Volume and Value by Stock Exchanges and Respective Market Share (2020)

Stock Exchanges	Trading Volume (thousands of shares)	Market Share %	Trading Value (millions of yen)	Market Share %
Tokyo	465,838	99.922	742,247,154	99.976
Nagoya	163	0.035	119,969	0.016
Fukuoka	25	0.005	26,579	0.004
Sapporo	174	0.037	35,051	0.005
Total	466,201	100	742,428,755	100

Source: Japan Exchange Group.

Nagoya Stock Exchange, the Ambitious market of the Sapporo Stock Exchange, and the Q-Board market of the Fukuoka Stock Exchange.

The TSE began a review of its market segments in the fall of 2018, and decided to reorganize the five segments into three. The transition to the new market segments of "Prime," "Standard," and "Growth" will be implemented in April 2022.

3. The Structure of Share Ownership

Following the liquidation of the financial combine *zaibatsu* (great industrial or financial conglomerates or holding companies) after the war, shares held by them were released to the stock market for distribution among individual investors. And the ratio of shares held by individual shareholders rose to 69.1% in 1949. However, as obviously not many of these individual investors could afford to hold these shares for the long haul, they liquidated their holdings soon after they had acquired them. As a result, the ratio of individual investors' shareholdings declined rapidly thereafter. Partly due to the fact that some investors had cornered these shares, groups of companies that had belonged to the former financial combine (*zaibatsu*) started cross-holding shares of one another to strengthen their group solidarity.

In the 1960s, capital transactions were liberalized following the post-war restoration efforts. However, in fear of a hostile takeover by foreign firms taking advantage of liberalized capital transactions, Japanese firms sought to build a strong shareholder base, and the ratio of the shareholdings of business corporations and financial institutions increased. Subsequently, the system of issuing shares at par value changed to one of issuing at market price, making it necessary for business corporations to maintain their share prices at a high level if only to enable them to advantageously raise funds for a capital increase. Consequently, the ratio of the shareholdings of business corporations continued to increase in the years up to 1975. Meanwhile, encouraged by the long-lasting bull market, financial institutions also continued to build their equity portfolios and increased the ratio of their stock holdings until the speculative bubble in the end of the 1980s.

Such corporate domination of the shareholdings structure brought about a material impact on the formation of stock prices. While individuals and institutional investors bought stocks as an investment to earn yields (profit-earning securities), business corporations or financial institutions bought shares on their proprietary accounts, in many cases, for the purpose of holding shares to strengthen corporate affiliations or business tie-ups as a means of gaining control of the management. Therefore, these corporations were more determined to hold such shares for the long haul (management-stake securities) without consideration to yields on investment, and yields on such shares tended to decline. As a result, prices of such shares rose to a level that was beyond the reach of individual investors who invested in shares on the basis of the yield they produced, and the ratio of stock holdings by individual investors dropped further. In addition, as individual investors had no choice but to aim at making capital gains even under such circumstances, the rate of turnover of their investments needed to be quickened. This was why individ-

Chart IV-2.　Changes in the Ratio of Shares Held by Different Categories of Investors

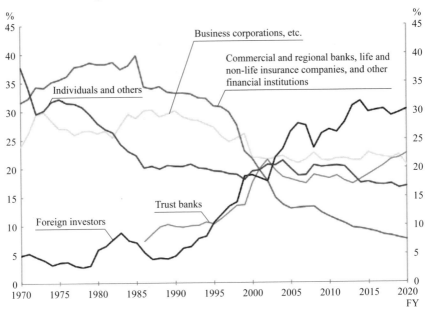

Notes: 1. Results of Trust banks are included in that of Commercial and Regional banks in and before 1985 Survey.
　　　2. Results from FY 2004 to FY 2009 include the portion of companies listed on JASDAQ, and those after FY 2010　include JASDAQ figures within Osaka Securities Exchange or Tokyo Stock Exchange.

Source: 2020 Shareownership Survey.

Chart IV-3.　Ratios of Cross-Shareholdings

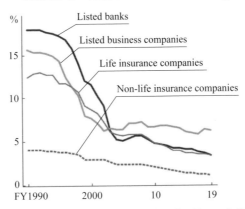

Note: Research by Nomura Institute of Capital Markets Research. Breakdown of cross-holding ratios by holding entity (by market capitalization).

Source: Nihon Keizai Shimbun Electronic Edition; July 6, 2021

ual investors took to highly speculative investment, bringing about a special structure of the stock market in this country.

However, as unrealized capital gains on stock investment shrank sharply due to falls in stock prices after the burst of the speculative bubble, holding shares was no longer an attractive investment even for corporate investors. In recent years, there has been an acceleration in the reduction of cross-share-holdings. Among other factors, this is advocated by the Corporate Governance Code, and it is also one of the listing criteria for the Prime market that the tradable share ratio should be at least 35%. In addition, companies have also felt the need to secure their cash reserves against COVID-19.

4. Stock Prices and Indicators for Investment (1)

Theoretical prices of assets such as land and stocks represent rents or dividends, as the case may be, capitalized by a certain rate of return of capital (interest rate plus risk premium). However, as only a small part of such assets is actually bought or sold, the total asset value is calculated by multiplying the total of such assets using the prices formed through such transactions. For instance, the total market capitalization on the First Section of the TSE as of September 24, 2021 was approximately ¥768 trillion, but the value of shares actually traded on that day was about ¥3.6 trillion. This indicates that the total market capitalization of the TSE is computed on the basis of share prices formed through the trading of approximately ¥3.6 trillion worth of shares. (Actually, it represents a sum total of the market valuation of all listed stocks, and the above explanation is intended to simplify the picture.)

At this stage, whether the given price of a stock is high or low is judged by comparing its dividend yield with the market interest rate then prevailing. In other words, an investment opportunity to generate better-than-average earnings, working through competition among investors who seek such investment opportunities, equalizes the dividend yield on a given stock to the market rate then prevailing. However, if an oligopoly strengthens in a given industry group and the earnings gap among companies belonging to the same industry group widens, those with higher growth potential tend to reinvest a larger portion of their profit as retained earnings. (Typical of this tendency are the former IBM and Microsoft, which had no dividends until the end of 2002.) Under such circumstances, dividend yields cannot be computed to start with, and the level of stock prices becomes irrelevant as an indicator for investment.

As highly profitable corporations increase their capital by reinvesting their earnings instead of issuing new shares, their per share profit increases and the price of their stock also rises proportionately thereto. If their stock price

Table IV-4.   Stock Splits and Changes in Divisor

Issue	Before stock split		After stock split	
	No. of shares	Stock price	No. of shares	Stock price
A	10	$20	20	$10
B	10	10	10	10
C	10	6	10	6
Total	30	36	40	26
Dow divisor	3		2.1667	
Dow scaled average	12		12	

Source: J. H. Lorie and M. T. Hamilton, The Stock Market, 1973; Japanese translation *Shoken kenkyu*, Vol. 51, 1977, pp. 73

Chart IV-4.   Stock Price and Capital Increase of Toray Industries

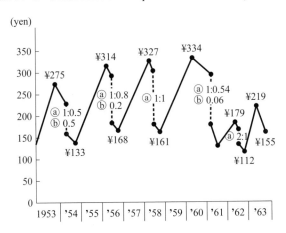

Notes: ⓐ Rights offering.
ⓑ Free distribution of shares.

$$\text{New divisor} = \text{Previous day's divisor} \times \frac{\text{Previous day's total stock price} \pm \text{total ex rights portion}}{\text{Previous day's stock price total}}$$

$$= \text{Previous day's divisor} \times \left(1 \pm \frac{\text{Total ex rights portion}}{\text{Previous day's stock price total}} \right)$$

rises too high, small investors cannot buy their shares, with the result that the marketability and liquidity of their shares suffer. Therefore, such corporations seek to recover the marketability of their shares by lowering their stock prices by means of stock split-ups or stock dividends—forms of issuing new shares that do not require payment for the new shares.

If this kind of capital management policy is adopted, such practice is bound to affect the stock price indexes. Assuming that other conditions remain unchanged, a two-for-one stock split would halve the price of such shares. However, since the number of shares a shareholder of such a corporation holds would double as a result of the two-for-one split while the stock price is halved, the total market value of the shares held by such a shareholder would not change at all. The Dow scaled average represents the average of original stock prices as seen from the standpoint of shareholders prior to the stock split. The Dow Jones Industrial Average is computed by changing the divisor each time a stock price declines due to a stock split or an issuance of new shares that does not accompany payment.

5. Stock Prices and Indicators for Investment (2)

In Japan, the Nihon Keizai Shimbun (the *Nikkei Daily*) has devised several Dow indexes (the *Nikkei average*), typical of which is the Nikkei 225. This is a price-weighted equity index, which consists of 225 leading issues listed on the TSE representing various industry groups. Whenever a stock split or dividend is reported or whenever any of the 225 issues is replaced by another, DOW indexes (the *Nikkei average*) are computed using a revised divisor. The Nikkei 225 started with a divisor of 225. Subsequently, however, the divisor has continued to decrease and dropped to 27.769 as of September 24, 2021 with the result that its multiple has risen to 8.1. This means that when the simple average of the stock prices of the 225 issues rises or falls ¥20, the Nikkei average will increase or decrease ¥162. Thus, the problem with the Dow Jones indices is that they reflect the rise or fall in the simple average of stock prices at a scale several times larger than what occurred, and can be susceptible to fluctuations in the price of scarce or highly-priced stocks because they are unweighted.

Indexes designed to remedy these shortcomings of the Dow Jones indices are market capitalization weighted indexes such as the New York Stock Exchange Composite Index, Standard & Poor's (S&P) 500 index, and the TOPIX (Tokyo Stock Price Index). TOPIX measures the free-float adjusted current market capitalization of the First Section of the TSE assuming that the market capitalization as of the base date (January 4, 1968) is 100. TOPIX has the following characteristics: (1) it covers all issues listed on the First

Chart IV-5.   Transitions in Stock Prices

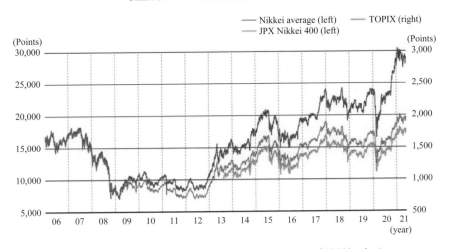

Note: The record date of JPX Nikkei 400 is August 30, 2013 (base value of 10,000 points).
Source data: Bloomberg.
Source: Japan Securities Dealers Association.

Chart IV-6.   Amounts of Trades on the TSE

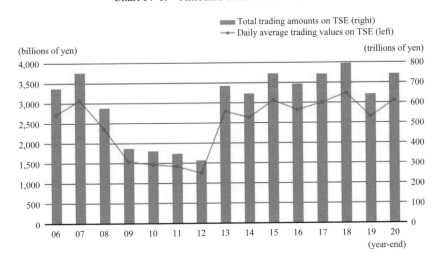

Source data: Japan Exchange Group.
Source: Japan Securities Dealers Association.

Section of the TSE and therefore reflects changes in the country's industrial structures and market trend, and is not susceptible to potential discontinuity when some issues are replaced; (2) it allows easy determination of changes in market size from the perspective of market capitalization; and (3) it is weighted by the number of shares of listed issues and is therefore not overly impacted by a rise or fall in the prices of scarce stocks or highly-priced stocks.

Although TOPIX has long played an important role as a benchmark for many institutional investors, it is not seen as a practical investment benchmark because it comprises all the issues in the First Section. The TSE is now considering a review of TOPIX, while taking into account the need to ensure its continuity as an index.

Apart from TOPIX, JPX and Nikkei have collaborated in the publication of the JPX-Nikkei Index 400 since January 2014. This index was developed with the aim of selecting issues that meet the requirements of global investment standards among listed issues, such as efficient use of capital and investor-focused management perspectives. Further more, the S&P/JPX Carbon Efficient Index, which bases its weighting of component issues by focusing on their environmental information disclosure and level of carbon efficiency, JPX and S&P have been jointly publishing since September 2018.

6. Stock Prices and Indicators for Investment (3)

As room for the discretionary implementation of capital management policy grew and diversified, the weight carried by capital gains in determining an investment policy increased and the importance of dividends or return on investment as an indicator for investment decreased. Consequently, the comprehensive yield that adds dividends to capital gains has come to be adopted as an indicator. In addition, a growing number of investors have come to value the price earnings ratio (PER), which is the quotient of the per share stock price divided by profit, i.e., a reciprocal of return on investment.

The reason behind the growing popularity of PER as an index for investment was that the concept of "growth stocks appeared" In other words, as corporations with high growth potential continued to follow financial policies that valued retained earnings and reinvestment of profit, dividend yield (a traditional index for investment) decreased, making it difficult for brokerage firms to put out buy recommendations on such shares. A phenomenon representative of this was what was known as the yield revolution—in which dividend yield fell below bond yield—that occurred in the United States in 1958. In Japan, also, a similar situation occurred in the 1960s.

In such a situation, there was a need to link the growth potential of a cor-

Chart IV-7.   Dividend Yields of TSE First Section Companies (simple average)

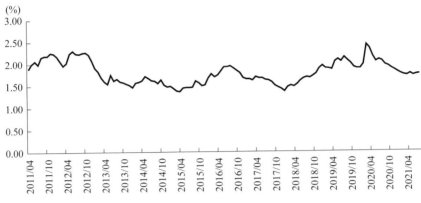

Source: Japan Exchange Group.

Chart IV-8.   Japan's "Yield Revolution"

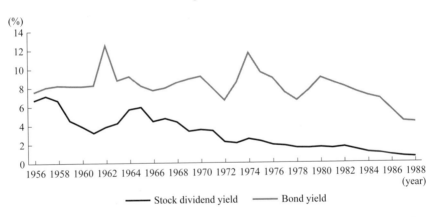

——— Stock dividend yield   ——— Bond yield

Note: Dividend yields are for dividend-paying companies on the TSE First Section. Bond yields are for general corporate bonds until 1961 and for interest-bearing NTT bonds from 1962.
Source: Tokyo Stock Exchange, statistics from Tokyo Stock Exchange Materials (1979-1988).

poration to the level of its stock price one way or another in order for broker-age firms to put out buy recommendations on such shares, and the answer was the PER. In other words, the PER shows multiples of earnings at which the underlying shares are bought and sold. Therefore, when the shares of a corporation have a high PER, it means that the market believes that the corporation has high growth potential. Actually, securities companies compare the PER of an issue with the industry average or with other issues in the same industry group to measure whether the issue is overvalued or undervalued. What is more, the PER is used not only as a stock price indicators of individual issues but also as a measure to compare the stock price level of a country with the levels of other countries. Today, it has thus become one of the typical stock price indicators.

However, while stock yield can be compared with an objective index, such as market interest rate, the PER has a drawback in that it can be compared with other indicators only relatively. For instance, as is often pointed out, the PER of the S&P 500, one of the major stock indexes of the United States, has moved between 15 and 30 since the war, but the Nikkei 225 of Japan has risen as high as 80 or more in the past. (On September 24, 2021 unconsolidated PER of the TSE First Section stood about 14.0.) It has been analyzed that the difference between the levels of the PERs of the two countries was attributable to the difference in the business accounting system (notably, the method of depreciation) and the cross-shareholding system of Japan. It is possible that these factors affected the PER level of Japan. More importantly, however, was the fact that there was no valid PER level to start with.

7. Stock Prices and Indicators for Investment (4)

While the PER shows the relationship between per share earnings and stock prices, earnings vary depending on the method used to calculate them. Particularly, depreciation expenses associated with capital investments are deducted from taxable income (which, therefore, cuts into earnings), but such investments contribute significantly to future earnings. Therefore, a stock price indicator based on earnings could sometimes mislead investors when they make an investment decision.

The price cash flow ratio (PCFR) is an indicator designed to reflect the growth potential of a corporation based on its share price. The PCFR is computed by dividing the stock price by the sum of the after-tax income and depreciation expenses for the term, minus any dividends and executive officers' bonuses. Since depreciation expenses are retained and reinvested at a later date, they are an important factor to take into account when assessing the growth potential of a corporation, as they indicate its real earnings and cash flow.

The PCFR is generally used in comparing the stock price of a corporation with the stock prices of other corporations in the same industry group and particularly in evaluating the stock prices of high-tech corporations whose future competitiveness is largely determined by the scale and components of their capital investment.

Chart IV-9. PERs of TSE First Section Companies (Simple average)

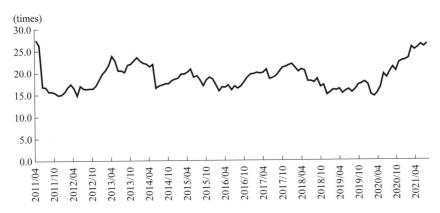

Source: Japan Exchange Group.

Chart IV-10. PBRs of TSE First Section Companies (Consolidated)

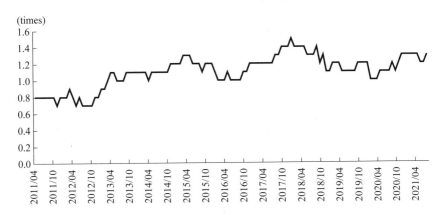

Source: Japan Exchange Group.

$$PER = \frac{\text{Stock price}}{\text{Per share after-tax income}}$$

$$PBR = \frac{\text{Stock price}}{\text{Per share net asset value}}$$

$$PCFR = \frac{\text{Stock price}}{\text{After-tax income} + \text{depreciation charges} - (\text{dividend} + \text{officers' bonus})}$$

Another frequently used indicator for investment is the price book value ratio (PBR), which shows the relationship between the net asset value owned by a corporation and its stock price. The PBR of a corporation is computed by dividing its stock price by the value of net assets per share. The net assets of a corporation represent the sum of the capital and earned surplus, etc., which is called equity capital, and they are computed by deducting liabilities (debt, etc.) from the total assets listed on the debit side of the balance sheet. In other words, it is the net assets that would remain after repaying all the debts of a corporation out of the proceeds of its assets when the corporation is dissolved at a certain point in time. Hence, the PBR is an indicator that compares the stock price of a corporation prevailing at a given time with its liquidation net asset value per share. If the PBR of any corporation falls below one (or below its liquidation net asset value per share), the stock price of such a corporation is often considered undervalued.

It is to be noted, however, that the use of the PBR as an indicator for investment is based on the assumption that it reflects the actual book value of the issue. If the actual asset value of the land and shareholdings of a corporation falls below the book value of the land and shareholdings on account of an unrealized loss, the stock price of such issue, even when its PBR is below one, cannot be considered undervalued. If such a situation arises, and the stock market functions efficiently to a certain degree, corporations will likely seek actively to merge with or acquire (M&A) another corporation. In fact, a string of corporate mergers and acquisitions did take place on the U.S. stock markets when Tobin's q (a modified version of the PBR) fell below one. The PBR of the First Section of the TSE stood at 1.28 on September 24, 2021.

8.   The Margin Trading System (1)

Shinyo torihiki (margin trading) is a system crafted on the model of the margin trading conducted in the United States and was introduced into Japan in June 1951 with a view to stimulating speculative demand for securities trading. Margin trading is a transaction in which an investor can buy a certain number of shares of a stock or sell shares which it does not own, with funds or shares borrowed from a Financial Instruments Business Operator (securities company) by depositing a margin with the Financial Instruments Business Operator. On the other hand, the Financial Instruments Business Operator that receives such an order must settle the transaction on the settlement day. As there was no adequate stock lending market or securities financing market in Japan in the early days, a securities finance company was created to help Financial Instruments Business Operators reduce their burden of having to provide cash or stock certificates for the settlement of such margin

Chart IV-11.   Outline of Margin Trading and Loans for Margin Transactions

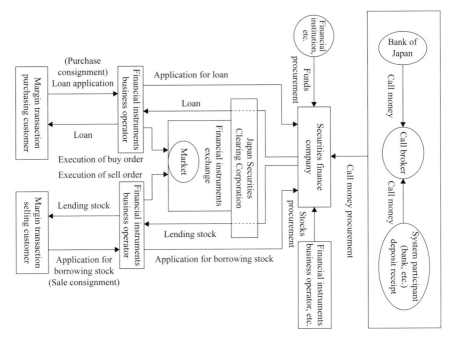

⊙Standardized margin trading (between a customer and a Financial Instruments Business Operator)
   Collateral: Shares bought (or the proceeds from the sale of shares sold)
   Margin: 30% or more of the market price of the shares bought (or sold) on margin. (When a substitute
      security is deposited, such security will have a collateral value of up to 80% or less of its
      market price.) However, the minimum amount of the margin in all cases is ¥300,000.
⊙Loans for margin transactions (between a Financial Instruments Business Operator and a securities fi-
   nance company)
   Collateral: Shares bought (or the proceeds from the sale of shares sold)
   Guarantee deposit: 30% or more of loan balance (or the lending stock balance) (When a substitute
      security is deposited, such security will have a collateral value of up to 80% of its
      market price.)
⊙Call money share collateral deposit receipt system (participating in the system are securities finance
   companies, call money dealers, companies affiliated with the deposit receipt system, financial instruments exchanges, and the Bank of Japan).
   Under this system, stock certificates pledged as collateral for a loan for margin transaction received
by a securities finance company (only such issues recognized as appropriate by the Bank of Japan) are
transferred to the account of a financial instruments exchange opened with the Japan Securities
Depository Center and the securities finance company takes in call money by pledging as collateral the
deposit receipt issued by the financial instruments exchange based on the aforesaid stock certificates.
   In other words, the system enables collateral to be used to procure the funds necessary for the loan
transaction, effectively using the stock as collateral. The deposit receipt also serves as collateral when
borrowing money from the Bank of Japan through a call money dealer.

Note: The margin rate and the ratio of collateral value above may change based on margin trading regulations.

trading. This is called the Loans for Margin Transactions.

The loan for margin transaction is where a securities finance company lends a Financial Instruments Business Operator, who is a participant of a financial instruments exchange, funds or stock certificates that are associated with margin trading issues and that are needed to settle a margin transaction, through the settlement organization of the financial instruments exchange. The securities finance company can save costs and expenses by internally offsetting applications for a loan of shares of a certain stock against those for lending shares of the same stock—more specifically, by lending the money it collects from a margin selling investor (or stock certificates it collects as collateral from a margin buying investor). When a shortage of funds develops after offsetting, the securities finance company meets the shortage by borrowing the amount of such shortage from a bank, the call market, or the Bank of Japan. When a shortage of stock certificates develops after offsetting, the securities finance company may borrow them by inviting bids from Financial Instruments Business Operators and institutional investors (see the chart on the next page). Issues for margin trading purposes are selected from among listed stocks based on standards set by the financial instruments exchange. Stocks that can be margin traded or lent for margin trading purposes can be categorized into trading issues, which can be used for both trading and loans, and loanable issues, which are used only for loans. Loanable issues are selected from the perspective of ensuring liquidity to handle speculative demand based on the number of tradable shares or the number of shareholders. Moreover, there are added restrictions on the amounts of stocks that can be borrowed.

The securities finance companies are special financial institutions on the securities market established in February 1950. They began operating loan transactions in line with the introduction of the margin trading system in June 1951. Since the role of securities finance companies on the securities market increased thereon as margin trading expanded, to strengthen their function, the government introduced a licensing system in April 1956, requiring securities finance companies to be authorized by the Minister of Finance (currently, the Prime Minister). Since then, there has been significant consolidation among securities finance companies that had been established on regional stock exchanges. As of September 30, 2021, Japan Securities Finance (JSF) alone handles loans for margin transactions as designated by each of the stock exchanges in Tokyo, Nagoya, Sapporo, Fukuoka and Osaka.

9. The Margin Trading System (2)

Based on the amendments to the Securities and Exchange Act in 1998, the restrictions on Financial Instruments Business Operators borrowing stock without going through securities finance companies and on borrowing and lending stock between themselves (the so-called stock lending market) were lifted. At the same time, the regulator approved negotiable margin trading, allowing Financial Instruments Business Operators to freely determine prices, interest rates, and contract terms between themselves and their customers. At this juncture, those margin tradings backing loans for margin transactions for which the financial instruments exchanges determine prices, interest rates, and contract terms on their markets came to be called standardized margin transactions (see Table IV-4). Negotiable margin trading became increasingly popular after they started to be used in Internet trading in Japan in 2003, and such transactions have come to account for about 20% of all margin purchase balances in recent years.

Looking at the proportion of loan balances in standardized margin stock buying balances, the dependency of Financial Instruments Business Operators on loans for margin transactions almost uniformly declined up to 1988 because of their growing ability to finance themselves primarily out of their internal reserves. However, the market's dependency on loans for margin transactions began to rise again in the 1990s, due to factors including the deterioration in the financial positions of Financial Instruments Business Operators following the burst of the economic bubble, the emergence of Internet trading, and a recovery in stock market prices starting in 1999. In 2005, the dependency of Financial Instruments Business Operators on loans for margin transactions neared the 50% mark. Since then, the dependency on loans for margin transactions has taken a downward path because of the greater diversification of financing sources for Financial Instruments Business Operators. On the other hand, looking at the balance of shares used in lending transactions, the traditionally small amount of margin sales began to rise in the latter half of the 1990s as institutionalization of stock markets became active and cases of Financial Instruments Business Operators borrowing shares from securities finance companies on their own proprietary accounts to settle buy orders increased. By 2000, the dependency of Financial Instruments Business Operators on loans for margin transactions had risen to 70%. Since then, this dependency has continued to fall because of the expanding number of sources of stock lending following the lifting of restrictions on the stock lending market.

The margin trading system and margin deposit operations of securities finance companies have changed and diversified along with the development of the securities market in Japan. The margin trading system was revised frequently to expand the number of available issues as a measure to invigorate the market, with the Second Section issues being added in December 1991 and the JASDAQ issuee in October 1997 and PTS in August 2019, added.

Table IV-5.   Comparison of Standardized and Negotiable Margin Trading

	Standardized margin trading	Negotiable margin trading
Margin deposit	30% or more of trade contract value	30% or more of trade contract value
Loan rate (negative interest)	Rate set xby the financial instruments exchange	Determined between the investor and the Financial Instruments Business Operator
Repayment due date	Up to six months	Determined between the investor and the Financial Instruments Business Operator
Eligible issues	Issues selected by the financial instruments exchange	In principle, all listed stocks
Rights processing	Method set by the financial instruments exchange	Determined between the investor and the Financial Instruments Business Operator
Financing (loan transaction)	Available	Not available

Source: Complied using data from the website of the Japan Exchange Group, etc.

Margin deposit operations have changed as well. A financing system using loanable issues for margin transactions for non-loanable issues was introduced in October 1995, and loans for margin transactions became available for the JASDAQ market in April 2004 and PTS in August 2019. Furthermore, a commercial financing system became available for Financial Instruments Business Operators that needed cash to settle their margin buying trades in negotiable margin transactions.

In addition to their licensed-based loans for margin transactions business, securities finance companies also (1) offer collateral loans for bonds and general collateral loans to Financial Instruments Business Operators or their clients, (2) run a commercial stock lending business other than the loans for margin transactions for financial instruments companies, and (3) act as intermediates in bond lending transactions.

10.   Diversification of the Securities Trading System

The basic function of the stock market is to efficiently allocate funds by finding a price at which all demands are matched with the supply available. At a stage when information technology (IT) was not fully developed, there was a need to concentrate securities trading in one place in order to achieve that purpose. In fact, a number of stock exchanges had been established in different regions to the extent that transactions in each region could be concentrated at the respective exchange, and listed securities were required to be traded

Chart IV-12. Margin Buying Balances (standardized and negotiable trading) and Loan/
Selling Balances

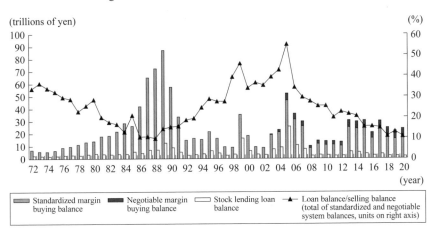

Note: Previous to 2012, figures included the margin balances of companies listed on the Osaka Securities
Exchange.
Source: Complied using data from the website of the Japan Exchange Group, etc.

Chart IV-13. Margin Selling Balances (standardized and negotiable trading) and Loan/
Stock Lending Balances

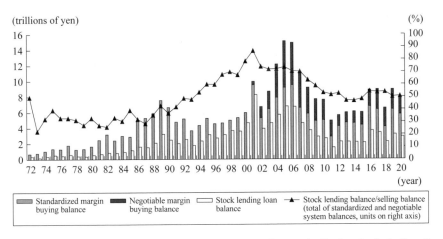

Note: Previous to 2012, figures included the margin balances of companies listed on the Osaka Securities
Exchange.
Source: Complied using data from the website of the Japan Exchange Group, etc.

Chart IV-14.   Trading Amounts of Exchange Transactions and OTC Transactions

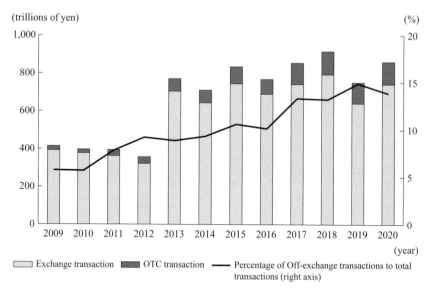

Exchange transaction   OTC transaction   —— Percentage of Off-exchange transactions to total transactions (right axis)

Source: Japan Securities Dealers Association.

Chart IV-15.   Breakdowns of OTC transactions

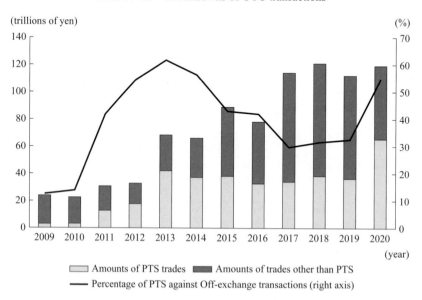

Amounts of PTS trades   Amounts of trades other than PTS
—— Percentage of PTS against Off-exchange transactions (right axis)

Source: Japan Securities Dealers Association.

on these stock exchanges. In an environment where dissemination of information, communication of orders, and processing of transactions incur costs and cannot be conducted in a timely manner, no arbitrage transaction—a practice that plays the role of eliminating a price difference—could sufficiently take place even if an opportunity arose to make a profit by taking advantage of a difference in the price of one and the same stock between stock exchanges. Under such circumstances, it became necessary to concentrate securities trading on the stock exchange to avert the occurrence of what is known as the "fragmentation of the market."

However, the securities markets have shifted to computerized trading systems thanks to the development of information technology, and stock exchanges where orders are processed manually on the trading floor have become a rarity in the world. That is, elements of securities trading, i.e. integration of trading information, transmission and execution of orders, delivery of securities, settlement, and custody, are integrated by the computer networks and processed in real time, realizing an environment in which balanced prices can be found even through a dispersed computer network installed at markets in multiple locations. The idea of market operation based on such an infrastructure of securities trading is called inter-market competition. Meanwhile, given the growing number of institutional investors in the securities market, the need for a guarantee of anonymity and for a trading system designed to minimize the market impact cost has increased, and special forms of trading, such as large-lot transactions and basket transactions, have also increased. As complex trading rules can be instituted without difficulty in a computerized trading system, a trading system capable of meeting such needs can be provided at a low cost.

These technological innovations make it difficult to distinguish the trading systems provided by private companies from those provided by the traditional securities exchanges. In the United States, the Securities and Exchange Commission (SEC) has acknowledged the similarity of functions performed by the two types of trading systems and has adopted the Alternative Trading System (ATS) and has authorized the Electronic Communication Network (ECN), a type of ATS, as a securities exchange. Also in Japan, the regulators have authorized negotiated trading in listed securities following the lifting of the ban against off-exchange securities trading and have added a Proprietary Trading System (PTS) to the types of securities business that can be handled by securities companies.

CHAPTER V

New Issues of Bonds in the Primary Market

1. Types of Bonds

The term "bonds" generally refers to debt securities issued by governments and other public entities as well as by private companies. The issuance of bonds is a means of direct financing, through which the issuer raises funds, but, unlike equity financing, the issuer has an obligation to repay the principal at maturity. Bonds are classified by type of issuer into government debt securities, municipal debt securities, government agency bonds, bank debentures, corporate bonds (industrial bonds), and foreign bonds.

Government debt securities are those issued by the national government, and they are classified as short-term bills (maturing in one year or less), medium-term notes (maturing in two to five years), long-term bonds (maturing in ten years), or superlong-term bonds (maturing in ten years or more) to distinguish an issue's term to maturity. Issuance of 10-year government bonds for retail investors (variable rate) was introduced in fiscal 2002. In January 2003, issuance of bonds designated by the Finance Minister as STRIPS bonds, whereby the principal and interest portions can be traded separately as book-entry transfer JGBs, started. In addition, the government started issuing 10-year CPI (consumer price index)-linked bonds, 5-year bonds for retail investors, 40-year fixed-rate bonds, and 3-year bonds for retail investors in fiscal 2003, 2005, 2007, and 2010 respectively.

Municipal debt securities can be roughly divided by type of funds into "public sector funds" and "private sector funds." The former are raised through fiscal loan funds and Japan Finance Organization for Municipalities, while the latter are raised in the public market or underwritten by banks and other financial institutions. Among these funds, the funds raised in public markets are divided into nationally placed municipal bonds, jointly offered local government bonds, and municipal bonds targeting local residents (mini-local bonds). While the municipal bonds underwritten by banks and other financial institutions are called bank, etc. underwritten bonds, they come in two types, funds borrowed on deeds from banks and other financial institutions or debt securities issued in the market. Government agency bonds are

Chart V-1. Types of Bonds

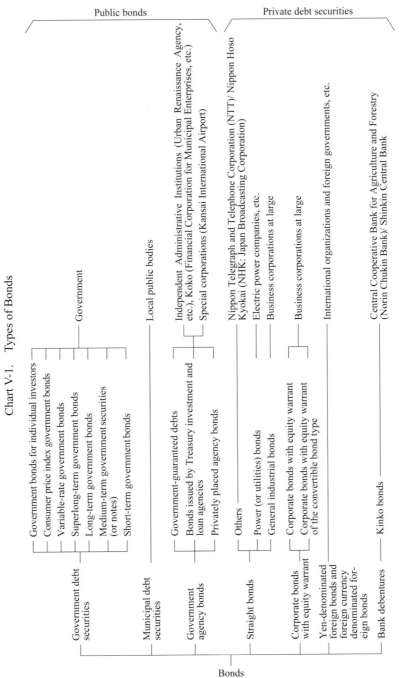

Note: Local government bonds represent debt issued under local government laws and fiscal policies. However, only those publicly placed or underwritten by banks or other financial institutions based on the issue of debt securities are included in public bonds.

debt securities issued by various government-affiliated entities, such as independent administrative agencies. Agency issues with a government guarantee are categorized as government-guaranteed bonds. On the other hand, non-guaranteed government agency bonds can be further divided into Fiscal Investment and Loan Program (FILP) agency bonds that are publicly placed bonds and privately placed bonds issued by certain special financial institutions. The three categories of debt securities mentioned above are sometimes collectively called "public bonds."

Bank debentures are debt securities issued by certain banking institutions under special laws. They are principally issued in the form and maturities of 5-year interest-bearing and 1-year discount debentures. As bank debentures and government agency bonds fall within the category of "debentures issued by a juridical person under a special Act" stipulated in Article 2, Paragraph 1, Item (iii) of the FIEA, they are sometimes called "special debts (*tokushu-sai*)." Corporate bonds are those issued by private-sector companies and are also known as industrial bonds. In addition to non-financial enterprises, banks and consumer finance companies may also issue corporate bonds. Foreign bonds are defined as debt securities issued in Japan by foreign governments and companies (non-residents).Those denominated in yen, in particular, are separately classified as yen-denominated foreign bonds.

2. Issuing Status of Bonds

With three major supplementary budgets drawn up as a response to the COVID-19 pandemic, the total amount of bond issuance in fiscal 2020 was ¥253.1 trillion, an increase of about 45% on the previous year.

If we look at the breakdown of issuance by type, total government bond issuance in fiscal 2020 was ¥221.4 trillion, accounting for about 87.5% of all public and corporate bonds. Government bond issuance had continued to increase from fiscal 2009 to fiscal 2013, driven by the financial crisis of 2008. However, issuance fell back from fiscal 2014 onwards, and the value of government bonds issued in fiscal 2019 was more subdued and in line with the level of fiscal 2001. However, in fiscal 2020, the issuance of JGBs increased by about ¥78 trillion vs. the previous year, mainly in the form of treasury bills, due to the pandemic. JGB issuance can be broken down into superlong-term government bonds (¥34.7 trillion), long-term government bonds (¥35.3 trillion), medium-term government bonds (¥64.4 trillion) and treasury bills (¥80.9 trillion).

Similar to government bonds, although municipal bonds were on a downward trend after peaking in fiscal 2013, issuance has turned up since 2019. The continuing high level is basically due to the deterioration in the fiscal

Table V-1.   The Value of Bonds Issued

(¥100 million)

FY	Total of bonds		Government bonds		Of which, Interest-bearing government bonds		Of which, 10-year interest-bearing government bond		Of which, 5-year interest-bearing government bond		Of which, 4·2-year interest-bearing government bond		Of which, Short-term discount government bonds		Of which, Government bonds for individual investors	
	No. of issues	Issue Amount	No. of issues	Issue Amount	No. of issues	Issue Amount	No. of issues	Issue Amount	No. of issues	Issue Amount	No. of issues	Issue Amount	No. of issues	Issue Amount	No. of issues	Issue Amount
1998	3,531	142,467	64	95,843	3	2,398	8	16,259	0	0	18	6,555	24	39,518	0	0
1999	2,672	141,307	80	99,807	5	2,897	10	16,920	2	1,639	18	14,487	36	48,799	0	0
2000	5,386	148,356	78	105,392	10	5,894	9	18,019	9	11,755	17	20,015	24	42,841	0	0
2001	4,651	181,531	68	144,493	11	7,392	8	20,600	7	20,425	12	19,663	24	39,596	0	0
2002	9,608	181,109	73	147,298	15	10,589	10	21,800	7	22,979	12	20,731	24	43,595	1	384
2003	13,827	196,008	79	157,797	17	12,986	11	23,000	10	23,189	12	22,185	24	47,998	4	2,967
2004	19,252	223,796	79	185,101	18	16,753	10	23,000	9	25,007	12	21,742	24	47,195	4	6,821
2005	24,485	221,001	84	180,692	20	19,579	9	23,100	10	25,718	12	22,338	24	41,907	5	7,271
2006	19,433	204,033	79	170,432	17	19,331	8	23,959	9	26,038	12	22,789	22	36,799	8	7,138
2007	12,926	173,003	63	136,504	13	17,343	5	23,533	7	25,773	12	22,041	14	22,796	8	4,662
2008	2,140	156,867	68	123,867	12	16,787	9	24,354	11	25,039	12	23,126	14	21,000	8	2,293
2009	1,507	188,807	63	156,023	11	23,141	7	28,880	7	29,621	12	29,397	18	32,899	8	1,360
2010	1,601	192,981	67	160,411	12	25,926	7	30,856	7	30,288	12	33,001	12	29,999	17	1,028
2011	1,500	196,954	72	167,283	12	26,136	8	31,360	8	31,036	12	34,514	12	29,999	20	2,426
2012	1,436	204,091	73	174,957	12	28,068	7	31,872	6	32,421	12	34,008	12	29,999	24	1,875
2013	1,458	210,040	72	180,171	10	29,349	5	33,727	8	35,216	12	36,176	12	29,999	24	3,349
2014	1,397	204,622	82	176,065	9	31,776	5	33,607	6	35,158	12	33,177	12	26,700	36	2,633
2015	1,280	199,414	78	173,670	9	34,787	4	35,519	4	32,128	12	30,766	12	25,800	36	2,137
2016	1,377	197,142	78	168,001	9	33,040	4	35,172	4	30,878	12	29,654	12	25,000	36	4,556
2017	1,409	183,344	78	155,903	9	33,172	4	33,029	4	29,336	12	28,360	12	23,800	36	3,449
2018	1,478	177,678	74	148,696	7	33,686	3	33,275	3	26,115	12	27,109	12	21,600	36	4,693
2019	1,503	174,024	78	142,985	9	30,956	4	30,195	4	25,343	12	25,775	12	21,600	36	5,248
2020	1,525	253,115	90	221,416	9	34,701	4	35,347	4	30,003	12	34,442	24	80,899	36	3,029

Source: Japan Securities Dealers Association.

FY	Municipal debt securities		Government-guaranteed debts		Bonds issued by Treasury investment and loan agencies		Straight bonds		Asset backed corporate bonds		Corporate bonds with equity warrant of the convertible bond type		Bank debentures		Yen-denominated non-resident bonds	
	No. of issues	Issue Amount	No. of issues	Issue Amount	No. of issues	Issue Amount	No. of issues	Issue Amount	No. of issues	Issue Amount	No. of issues	Issue Amount	No. of issues	Issue Amount	No. of issues	Issue Amount
1998	69	1,754	35	2,610	0	0	635	10,453	59	378	15	214	712	24,474	76	393
1999	72	2,061	40	3,325	0	0	437	7,788	126	441	23	434	688	23,304	68	1,037
2000	86	2,269	67	5,141	1	50	367	7,637	140	342	18	283	696	21,043	89	2,618
2001	90	2,225	55	4,315	24	731	333	8,172	127	394	17	283	755	16,867	41	1,308
2002	151	2,837	55	4,446	63	2,565	312	7,318	85	517	13	205	666	12,023	30	671
2003	226	4,621	95	6,898	86	2,663	353	6,993	82	200	9	77	667	9,271	39	943
2004	262	5,660	94	8,752	105	3,019	307	5,895	46	187	19	191	598	7,960	45	1,677
2005	312	6,189	94	7,002	115	4,722	335	6,904	28	354	13	113	563	8,756	47	1,592
2006	334	5,860	77	4,301	101	4,399	335	6,830	25	143	10	495	496	6,730	25	798
2007	365	5,721	79	4,298	125	4,941	425	9,401	5	153	3	30	407	6,505	78	2,647
2008	375	6,346	69	4,752	123	4,814	313	9,605	8	181	1	150	384	5,517	58	2,082
2009	418	7,361	78	4,667	164	4,735	388	10,300	2	100	3	249	347	4,180	40	1,192
2010	412	7,482	64	4,197	172	5,063	459	9,933	2	120	3	78	352	3,777	70	1,919
2011	394	6,663	61	3,331	212	5,735	394	8,277	5	200	2	33	284	3,438	76	1,994
2012	392	6,577	71	4,722	206	5,312	416	8,152	4	200	3	29	220	3,000	51	1,142
2013	421	7,069	69	5,060	212	4,678	462	8,142	1	50	10	77	121	2,618	90	2,174
2014	407	6,943	68	4,220	199	3,997	439	8,715	1	60	5	37	121	2,499	75	2,086
2015	406	6,772	68	3,146	212	4,489	348	6,941	1	50	4	166	91	2,365	72	1,816
2016	360	6,249	79	3,107	184	4,857	546	11,413	2	100	5	55	76	1,738	47	1,622
2017	362	6,101	82	3,956	210	4,814	560	10,063	2	100	1	10	76	1,330	38	1,067
2018	373	6,312	77	3,104	231	5,020	583	10,452	3	270	2	16	76	1,446	59	2,362
2019	371	6,450	49	1,803	209	4,810	704	15,759	0	0	12	9	40	1,116	40	1,092
2020	375	6,991	36	1,419	262	6,170	692	15,613	0	0	6	23	40	1,016	24	467

Note: From April 2019 onwards, the figures for general bonds other than JGBs are based on statistical data from the Japan Securities Depository Center (JASDEC).

Source: Japan Securities Dealers Association.

position of local governments, resulting in the introduction of publicly offered municipal bonds targeting local residents in fiscal 2001 and publicly offered joint local government bonds in fiscal 2003.

Issuance of straight corporate bonds has moved from a declining trend up until fiscal 2015 to an increasing trend at present, with both the number of corporate bond issues and the value of bonds issued remaining at high levels in recent years. In fiscal 2020, there were 692 issues with a value of ¥15.6 trillion, an all-time record. Since the start of 2019 there have been a number of large-scale corporate bond issues against the background of the decline in long-term interest rates. In response to the further monetary easing of monetary conditions, especially in response to the pandemic, straight corporate bonds of ¥2.5 trillion and ¥2.8 trillion were issued in July and December 2020, respectively, with another ¥2.2 trillion issued in June 2021.

The total amount of bank debentures issued in fiscal 2020 (all interest bearing) stood at ¥1.0 trillion, continuing to decline from the ¥43 trillion recorded in fiscal 1995. Backdrop to the decline includes the virtual disappearance of the long-term credit banks that had acted as suppliers of long-term capital to industry, the discontinuation of bank debenture issues by Bank of Tokyo-Mitsubishi (now the Bank of Mitsubishi-Tokyo UFJ) in March 2002, followed by Mizuho Corporate Bank (excluding debentures for asset building purposes) in March 2007 and Aozora Bank in September 2011. Among government agency bonds, issuance of government-guaranteed bonds in fiscal 2020 was ¥1.4 trillion and issuance of FILP agency bonds was ¥6.2 trillion. Back in fiscal 2000, the Government Housing Loan Corporation issued its first ¥50 billion. FILP agency bond, following the reform of the fiscal investment and loan program. Since then, FILP agency bond issuance has grown considerably. The amount of yen-denominated foreign bonds dropped sharply to ¥0.5 trillion yen in fiscal 2020.

3. Methods of Issuing Public Bonds

Government securities are issued in the public market or directly to individual investors or underwritten by the public sector. This section deals with the former two methods of issuance.

When issued in the market, JGBs are primarily sold through public auctions based on competitive bidding on price (or on yield), as the method of underwriting by syndicates was discontinued in fiscal 2006. In accordance with the terms of offering set forth by the Ministry of Finance, auction participants submit their bid prices and amounts, and they are then aggregated to determine the issue price and amount. Depending on the type of securities to be auctioned, the issue price is set either in a conventional auction, where

Table V-2. Categories of Government Securities

Maturity	Short-term government bonds		Medium-term government bonds	Long-term government bonds
	6-month	1-year	2-year, 5-year	10-year
Type of issue	Discount government bonds		Interest-bearing government bonds	
Minimum denomination	¥50,000		¥50,000	
Issuance method	Public auction BOJ switch		Public auction OTC sales (based on subscriptions to offering)	
Auction method	Price-competitive bidding Conventional style		Price-competitive bidding Conventional style	
Noncompetitive Bidding, etc.	Non-price Competitive Auctions I		Noncompetitive Bidding Non-price Competitive Auctions I Non-price Competitive Auctions II	
Transfer restriction	No		No	
Issuance frequency (FY2021 Plan)	Twice a month	Monthly	Monthly	

Maturity	Superlong-term government bonds			Individual investor government bonds	Inflation-indexed government bonds	Floating interest rate government bonds
	20-Year	30-Year	40-Year	3-year, 5-year fixed rate; 10-year floating rate	10-year	15-year (Note 1)
Type of issue	Interest-bearing government bonds					
Minimum denomination	¥50,000			¥10,000	¥100,000	
Issuance method	Public auction			OTC sales (based on subscriptions to offering)	Public auction	–
Auction method	Price-competitive bidding Conventional style		Yield-competitive bidding Dutch auction	–	Price-competitive bidding Dutch auction	–
Noncompetitive Bidding, etc.	Non-price Competitive Auctions I Non-price Competitive Auctions II		Non-price Competitive Auctions II	–	Non-price Competitive Auctions II	–
Transfer restriction	No			Yes	No	No
Issuance frequency (FY2021 Plan)	Monthly		6 times a year	Monthly	Quarterly	Not scheduled

Note: 1. There have been no additional issues of 15-year floating rate JGBs since they were first issued in May 2008.
2. There have been no additional issues of Inflation-indexed government bonds after May 2020.
Source: Based on the Ministry of Finance, *Debt Management Report* 2021, p. 39.

bonds are issued to successful bidders at their respective bid prices, or in a Dutch auction, where the issue price (yield) is set at the lowest price (highest yield) among accepted bids. Other than competitive bidding, two-, five-, and ten-year fixed rate JGBs are also offered through a noncompetitive bidding

Chart V-2.   Organization of Underwriting Publicly Offered Municipal Bonds at a Glance

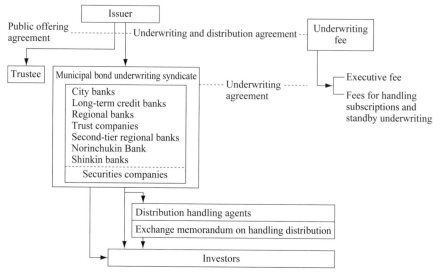

Source: Japan Local Government Bond Association.

process that facilitates small- and medium-sized bidders and through Non-price Competitive Auctions I and II reserved for special participants (20 companies are designated as of September 1, 2021). Private financial institutions handle subscriptions for individuals in offering JGBs for individuals and in offering two-, five-, and ten-year fixed rate JGBs under the new over-the-counter sales approach.

To issue municipal bonds, a local public body must prepare a budget plan that defines the use of proceeds from the proposed bond issue and obtains the approval of the local assembly. The actual issuance is also subject to consultation with the Minister of Internal Affairs and Communications (MIC) or the governor of the prefecture concerned (local bond consultation system). Even when the issuer is authorized to issue a municipal bond, the proceeds of such bonds can be used only for authorized projects - to finance a publicly run corporation, for equity contributions and loans, and to roll over maturing debts, etc. As of September, 2021, 36 prefectures and 20 cities ("designated cities") that have been designated by an ordinance of the Ministry of Internal Affairs and Communications have issued municipal bonds through public offerings. In most cases, the issuer negotiates the terms of issue with an underwriting syndicate that handles its public offering, under which the underwriting syndicate buys up whatever bonds remain unsold after the public offering. Municipal bonds publicly offered on the joint primary market (municipal bonds jointly issued by 36 local public bodies) in and after fiscal 2003 are also handled by underwriting syndicates, but the municipal bonds targeted at local residents introduced in March 2002 generally commission local financial institutions to handle the underwriting and subscription administration.

The issuance of government-guaranteed bonds is planned as part of the Fiscal Investment and Loan Program, and annual ceilings on the issue amount must be approved by the Diet. They are issued by way of either an underwriting syndicate or issued by separate and individual bidding by competing underwriters. In the former method, the terms of issue are determined based on the results of recent JGB monthly competitive bidding. In the latter, the terms are bid for competitively along with the lead managing underwriter for the offering. FILP agency bonds are also issued as interest-bearing bonds, and in issuing them, the issuing agency usually selects a lead managing underwriter which, in turn, forms an underwriting syndicate.

4. Methods of Issuing Corporate Bonds

The issuance of straight bonds had in the past been subject to strict regulations, and the corporate bond trustee system was the core of those regulations. Against the backdrop of the main bank system in Japan at the time, the banks had an extremely strong influence on individual corporate straight bond issues under the corporate bond trustee system. Even in the overall corporate bond primary market, banks had a greater voice than securities companies. However, as the role played by the corporate bond trustee system declined in the 1980s, the Commercial Code was amended in 1993 to drastically change the system, and regulations on the issuance of corporate bonds have been substantially eased.

The issuing corporation appoints managing underwriters and other underwriters that together constitute an underwriting syndicate, a bond manager or a fiscal agent, and providers of other relevant services and obtains a preliminary credit rating. When preparations are completed, the underwriting syndicate, under the leadership of managing underwriter, conducts pre-marketing in order to build a book for the bonds. Along with this process, the issue terms of the bonds are finalized and the offering begins. The book-building method is one under which the lead managing underwriter asks syndicate member companies to survey investors' interest in the bonds and then decides on the issuing terms on the basis of the findings of that survey. Previously, many issuers employed "spread pricing", a method under which investors' appetite in an issue is measured in terms of a spread over the yield of a JGB

Table V-3.   Major Corporate Bonds issue cases

Low rating bonds	Issue Amount	Interest Rate	Maturity	Rating
Jun. 2020 AIFUL CORPORATION	10 billion yen	1.00%	1 year and 6 month	BB + (JCR)
Jun. 2021 AIFUL CORPORATION	20 billion yen	0.93%	1 year and 6 month	BB + (JCR)
Perpetual subordinated bonds				
Oct. 2020 DMG MORI CO.,LTD (Note 1)	33 billion yen	(Note 2)	–	BBB (R&I)
Aug. 2021 DMG MORI CO.,LTD	30 billion yen	0.9% (Note 3)	–	BBB (R&I)
Apr. 2021 Rakuten Group, Inc. (Note 4)	1 billion euros	4.25% (Note 5)	–	BB (S&P)
Apr. 2021 Rakuten Group, Inc.	1.75 billion dollars	(Note 6)	–	BB (S&P)
Digital corporate bond (Security Tokens)				
Apr. 2021 SBI SECURITIES CO.,LTD.	100 million yen	0.35%	1 year	A − (JCR)

Note: 1. Issued in two tranches, ¥8.0 billion and ¥25.0 billion. The perpetual subordinated bonds issued by DMG Mori Seiki in 2016 were not offered to the public.
  2. The ¥8.0 billion tranche has a fixed interest rate of 1.00% until October 2023 and a floating interest rate thereafter. The ¥25.0 billion tranche has a fixed interest rate of 2.40% until October 2027 and a floating interest rate thereafter.
  3. Fixed interest rate until August 2026, floating interest rate thereafter.
  4. Rakuten's foreign currency perpetual subordinated bonds are issued to overseas investors.
  5. Fixed interest rate until April 2027, floating rate thereafter.
  6. $750 million of the bonds have a fixed interest rate of 5.125% until April 2026 and a floating interest rate thereafter. $1.0 billion of the bonds have a fixed interest rate of 6.25% until April 2031 and a floating interest rate thereafter.
  7. Prior to SBI Securities, Daiwa Securities, issued digital corporate bonds through private placement in February 2021.
Source: Japan Securities Dealers Association, The List of public and corporate bond, bonds and debentures.

or an interest rate swap with the same term, to determine the issuing rate. However, after the introduction of negative interest rate policy by the Bank of Japan in January 2016, so-called "absolute value pricing" has become more familiar, which provide absolute yield in projecting potential investor demand.

In terms of issuer ratings, the majority of issuers continue to issue bonds with high ratings; only a small proportion of bonds have low ratings, which is a characteristic of Japan. The reason can be attributed to the fact that major institutional investors limit their investment in corporate bonds to issues with ratings of A or higher. AIFUL CORPORATION attracted attention in 2019 with a BB-rated bond issue, and followed this up in June 2020 and June 2021 with ¥10 billion and ¥20 billion, respectively, of publicly offered BB+ bonds. Mitsui O.S.K. Lines' corporate bond issued in April 2021 was rated BBB, but this was a subordinated bond with a high interest rate of 1.60%.

Perpetual subordinated bonds are subordinated bonds that do not have a

Chart V-3.   Mechanism of Underwriting Corporate Bonds

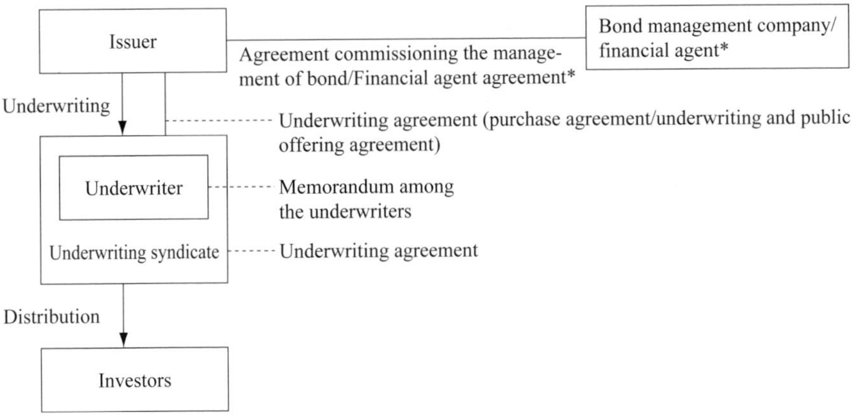

Note: *The issuer signs this agreement with a trustee company in the case of a mortgage bond.
Source: Daiwa Securities Co., *Saiken no joshiki.*

fixed maturity date and therefore have a capital like nature. DMG Mori Seiki issued perpetual subordinated unsecured bonds totaling ¥33 billion yen in October 2020 and ¥30 billion in August 2021, while Rakuten Group issued perpetual subordinated bonds totaling ¥320 billion in April 2021, one euro-denominated and two dollar-denominated.

In addition, SBI Securities' ¥100 million security token offering in April 2021 attracted attention as the first publicly offered digital corporate bond in Japan.

5. Credit-Rating Agencies and Rating of Bonds

Credit rating is a classification of credit risk, indicated by a rating symbol based on measurement of the certainty of payment of the principal of, and interest on, a bond, and it is ordinarily given by an credit-rating agency specializing in rating credit. Originally, the system developed in the bond market of the United States and is believed to have taken root during the Depression of the 1930s. It was introduced to Japan in the 1980s, and today, obtaining a credit rating has become a general practice among issuers of corporate bonds.

In assigning a credit rating to a given bond issue, a credit-rating agency investigates and verifies to see if the issuer has any collateral to back up its obligation and if it has a special financial contract and, if it has preferential or subordinated creditors, analyzes its financial position and business; determines its capacity to pay the principal of, and interest on, the proposed bond;

Table V-4.   Definitions of Credit-Rating Symbols

Rating and Investment Information, Inc. (R&I)	
Credit Rating	Definition
AAA	Highest creditworthiness supported by many excellent factors.
AA	Very high creditworthiness supported by some excellent factors.
A	High creditworthiness supported by a few excellent factors.
BBB	Creditworthiness is sufficient, though some factors require attention in times of major environmental changes.
BB	Creditworthiness is sufficient for the time being, though some factors require due attention in times of environmental changes.
B	Creditworthiness is questionable and some factors require constant attention.
CCC	Creditworthiness is highly questionable and a financial obligation of an issuer is likely to default.
CC	All of the financial obligations of an issuer are likely to default.
C	R&I believes that all of the financial obligations of an issuer are in default.

Japan Credit Rating Agency, Ltd. (JCR)	
Credit Rating	Definition
AAA	The highest capacity of the obligor to honor its obligation to its financial commitment.
AA	A very high capacity to honor its obligation to its financial commitment.
A	A high capacity to honor its obligation to its financial commitment.
BBB	An adequate capacity to honor its obligation to its financial commitment. However, this capacity is more likely to diminish in the future than in the cases of the higher rating categories.
BB	Although the capacity to honor the financial commitment on the obligation is not considered problematic at present, this capacity may not persist in the future.
B	A low capacity to honor its obligation to its financial commitment, giving cause for concern.
CCC	There are factors of uncertainty that the obligation to financial commitment will be honored, and a possibility of default.
CC	A high default risk.
C	A very high default risk.
D	In default.

Moody's Investor Service	
Credit Rating	Definition
Aaa	Obligations rated "Aaa" are judged to be of the highest quality, subject to the lowest level of credit risk.
Aa	Obligations rated "Aa" are judged to be of high quality and are subject to very low credit risk.
A	Obligations rated "A" are considered upper-medium grade and are subject to low credit risk.
Baa	Obligations rated "Baa" are subject to moderate credit risk. They are considered medium grade and as such may possess certain speculative characteristics.
Ba	Obligations rated "Ba" are judged to be speculative elements and are subject to substantial credit risk.
B	Obligations rated "B" are considered speculative and are subject to high credit risk.
Caa	Obligations rated "Caa" are judged to be speculative of poor standing and are subject to very high credit risk.
Ca	Obligations rated "Ca" are highly speculative and are likely in, or very near, default, with some prospect of recovery of principal and interest.
C	Obligations rated "C" are the lowest rated class and are typically in default, with little prospect for recovery of principal or interest.

Standard & Poor's	
Credit Rating	Definition
AAA	An obligation rated "AAA" has the highest rating assigned by Standard & Poor's. The obligor's capacity to meet its obligation to its financial commitment is extremely strong.
AA	An obligation rated "AA" differs from the highest-rated obligations only to a small degree. The obligor's capacity to meet its obligation to its financial commitment is very strong.
A	An obligation rated "A" is somewhat more susceptible to the adverse effects of changes in circumstances and economic conditions than obligations in higher-rated categories. However, the obligor's capacity to meet its obligation to its financial commitment is still strong.
BBB	An obligation rated "BBB" exhibits adequate protection parameters. However, adverse economic conditions or changing circumstances are more likely to lead to a weakened capacity of the obligor to meet its obligation to its financial commitment.
BB	An obligation rated "BB" is less vulnerable to nonpayment than other speculative issues. However, it faces major ongoing uncertainties or exposure to adverse business, financial, or economic conditions which could lead to the obligor's inadequate capacity to meet its obligation to its financial commitment.
B	An obligation rated "B" is more vulnerable to nonpayment than obligations rated "BB," but the obligor currently has the capacity to meet its obligation to its financial commitment. Adverse business, financial, or economic conditions will likely impair the obligor's capacity or willingness to meet its obligation to its financial commitment.
CCC	An obligation rated "CCC" is currently vulnerable to nonpayment and is dependent upon favorable business, financial, and economic conditions for the obligor to meet its obligation to its financial commitment. In the event of adverse business, financial, or economic conditions, the obligor is not likely to have the capacity to meet its obligation to its financial commitment.
CC	An obligation rated "CC" is currently highly vulnerable to nonpayment. The "CC" rating is used when a default has not yet occurred, but Standard & Poor's expects default to be a virtual certainty, regardless of the anticipated time to default.
C	An obligation rated "C" is currently highly vulnerable to nonpayment, and the obligation is expected to have lower relative seniority or lower ultimate recovery compared to obligations that are rated higher.
D	An obligation rated "D" is in default or in breach of an imputed promise. For non-hybrid capital instruments, the "D" rating category is used when payments on an obligation are not made on the date due, unless Standard & Poor's believes that such payments will be made within five business days in the absence of a stated grace period or within the earlier of the state period or 30 calendar days. The "D" rating also will be used upon the filing of a bankruptcy petition or the taking of similar action and where default on an obligation is a virtual certainty, for example due to automatic stay provisions. An obligation's rating is lowered to "D" if it is subject to distressed exchange offer.
NR	This indicates that no rating has been requested, or that there is insufficient information on which to base a rating, or the Standard & Poor's does not rate a particular obligation as a matter or policy.

and assigns a symbol on the basis of the findings of such investigations. Normally, any debt security with an AAA rating indicates that its issuer has the highest credit standing and is virtually free from the uncertainties of paying the principal of and interest on the obligation. The creditworthiness of a bond declines as its rating goes down, in order, from AAA to AA, A, and BBB, and a bond with any of these four ratings is called an investment-grade bond. Bonds with a credit rating of BB, B, CCC, CC, or C are called "junk bonds." As these bonds carry high credit risk, their issuer offers a high yield to attract buyers. Thus, they are called "high-yield bonds," and their primary market has developed on a relatively large scale in the United States and Europe. This type of junk bond primary market did not exist in Japan because of a policy that excluded bonds that did not meet the eligibility standards from the market. However, today no such regulations restrict the issuance of junk bonds because the eligibility standards were abolished in 1996. Nevertheless, very few BBB-rated bonds have been offered in the market despite being an investment-grade category; with the exception of a BB-rated issue (by AIFUL) in 2019.

Designated credit-rating agencies now include both domestic players, such as the Rating and Investment Information (R&I) and the Japan Credit Rating Agency (JCR), and global agencies, such as Standard & Poor's and Moody's and Fitch. In Japan, a new registration system of the credit-rating agencies replaced the conventional system based on the Act for Partial Amendment of the Financial Instruments and Exchange Act enforced in April 2010. Further, in recent years, municipal bonds and FILP agency bonds have also come to be rated.

The outbreak of the U.S. subprime loan problem raised strong doubts over the way ratings were given. To begin with, there were criticisms pointing out that credit-rating agencies tended to give generous ratings because their source of income was rating fees collected from issuers. Meanwhile, from a different perspective, ratings were acknowledged as nothing more than reference. Currently, however, ratings are used in various financial regulations and policies. Credit-rating agencies today operate under a registration system also on a global basis and are placed under administrative supervision.

6. Corporate Bond Management

A drastic reform of the conventional corporate bond trustee system was carried out by an amendment of the Commercial Code in June 1993 to clarify the basic functions of the current corporate bond administrator system. Under this amendment, the conventional name "bond trustee company" was changed to "bond management company." In addition, (1) the establishment

Table V-5.   Appointment, Power, and Liability of the Bond Manager under the Companies Act

Item	Contents	Article
Appointment and Power		
When a bond manager has to be appointed	A corporation issuing a corporate bond must appoint a bond manager. However, when the face value of a bond certificate is in excess of ¥100 million, and in such other cases as may be prescribed by an ordinance of the Ministry of Justice as one which poses no threat to the protection of bondholders, the issuer need not appoint a bond manager.	Article 702 of the New Companies Act
Qualifications for becoming a bond manager	Banks, trust companies, and equivalent financial institutions	Article 703
Matters entrusted	The bond manager will be entrusted to receive payments, to preserve rights of claim, and to take other steps necessary for the management of bonds on behalf of bondholders.	Article 702 of the New Companies Act
Duty of the bond manager	The bond manager must perform the administration of bonds in a fair and sincere manner on behalf of the bondholders ("duty of fairness"). The bond manager must manage the bonds with due care of a prudent manager to the bondholders ("duty of due care of a prudent manager").	Article 704
Power of the bond manager	The bond manager has the authority do all judicial and non-judicial acts on behalf of bondholders that are necessary to receive payments relating to the bonds or to preserve the realization of claims relating to the bonds. When the bond manager deems it necessary to take such steps, the bond manager may, with the permission of the court, investigate the status of the business and assets of the bond-issuing company.	Paragraphs 1 and 4 of Article 705
Special regulation on the power of the bond manager	When the bond manager plans to take the steps described below, it must obtain a resolution of a bondholders' meeting. (1) With respect to all of the bonds, granting extension for the payment of those bonds, or releasing, or settling liability arising from the failure to perform the obligations of those bonds (2) With respect to all of the bonds, prosecuting lawsuits, or proceeding with bankruptcy procedures, rehabilitation procedures, reorganization procedures or procedures regarding special liquidation ("lawsuit" includes court-mediated settlement) Under the Act, the bond manager has the power to take these actions without a resolution of a bondholders' meeting if the bond management agreement so prescribes.	Paragraphs 1 and 2 of Article 706 Item (viii), Article 676
Power of the bond manager in taking steps for the protection of creditors	When a bondholder wants to object to any action taken by the issuer, he/she must obtain a resolution of a bondholders' meeting, in principle, but the bond manager can express its objection on behalf of bondholders. This, however, shall not apply in cases where there is a provision to the contrary in the contract entrusting bond management.	Paragraghs 1 and 2, Article 740
Liability		
Liability (damages)	When the bond manager takes an action in violation of the Companies Act or any resolution of the bondholders' meeting, it is jointly and severally liable for damages incurred by bondholders.	Paragraph 1 of Article 710
Statutory special liability (damages)	(1) When the bond manager has received from the issuer of a bond collateral for the obligation represented by such a bond or when the issuer has taken an action extinguishing such obligation within three months prior to a default on the redemption of, or on the payment of interest on, the bond, or the suspension of payment by its issuer (2) When the bond manager has received from the issuer collateral for the obligation or repayment with respect to the credit of the bond manager (3) When the bond manager transfers its credit to a company controlling, or controlled by, such bond manager, or to another company that has a special relationship with the bond manager (4) When a bond manager who has a credit to the issuer of the bond concludes an agreement with the issuer authorizing it to dispose of the property of the issuer for the purpose of offsetting such credit, or when the bond manager concludes an agreement to take over any obligations of any company that owes a debt to the issuer. (5) When a bond manager that owes a debt to the issuer offsets such debt by taking over a credit to the issuer.	Paragraph 2 of Article 710
Exemption of debt	The bond manager is exempt from debt when it has not been derelict in its management of the bond, when it has established that any loss caused to the bondholders is not blamable to an action taken by the bond manager.	Proviso to Paragraph 2 of Article 710
Resignation of the bond manager and its liability	(1) The bond manager may resign with the consent of the bond issuer and the bondholders' meeting. (However, the bond manager must appoint in advance a successor who will take over the administration of the bonds.) (2) In case the bond manager has an unavoidable reason to resign, it may resign with permission of the competent court. (3) The bond manager may resign based of the causes prescribed in the agreement entrusting the management of the bonds. (However, such agreement must have a provision designating a succeeding bond manager that will take over the job.) *) A bond manager that resigns after the issuer has defaulted on the redemption of the bond or on the payment of interest on such bond, or that has resigned for reasons prescribed in the agreement commissioning the management of the bond within three months prior thereto, is not exempted from liability to pay damages under Paragraph 2 of Article 710.	Article 711 Article 712

Source: Compiled from the data drawn from Akihiro Sato, *Shinkaishaho de kawatta kaisha no shikumi* (The Changed Company System under the New Companies Act), Nihon Horei, 2005, pp. 179 and 181.

of a bond management company was made mandatory, in principle, and the eligibility for becoming one was restricted to banks, trust companies, and companies that have received a license under the Mortgage Bond Trust Law; (2) services to be provided by a bond management company were restricted to the management of outstanding bonds; and (3) the powers, duties, and liabilities of the bond management company were clarified. Put another way, the back-office services provided by the trust company at the time a bond is offered will not become the core services of the bond management company, and the services to be provided by the bond management company after a bond is issued are restricted to bond management.

As a result of the amendment, the possibility of a bond trustee company being involved in the issuance of corporate bonds of individual issuers has been legally removed, and the power of the conventional bond trustee system regulating individual issuers has thus come to an end. The amendment has resulted in the following changes: (1) The fee the trustee bank had been collecting was renamed "bond management fee," and it was lowered; (2) by instituting exceptional provisions with respect to the mandatory establishment of a bond management company (this applies when the face value of a bond certificate is in excess of ¥100 million), issuers can appoint a fiscal agent in lieu of a bond management company, and instances of making do with a fiscal agent have since increased.

Under the New Companies Act enforced in May 2006, a bond management company is now known as a "bond manager," and its liability and power have been expanded. More specifically, (1) under the former Commercial Code, the term "management of corporate bond" referred only to the exercise of power legally granted to the bond management company and did not include the exercise of power based on an agreement, etc., entrusting the management of bonds (contractual power); under the new Companies Act, however, the exercise of the contractual power is included in "the management of bonds" and the bond manager owes the duty of fairness and the duty of due care of a prudent manager; (2) when the agreement entrusting the management of bonds contains a provision to that effect, the bond manager may act in relation to filing a lawsuit and taking bankruptcy or rehabilitation proceedings for all of the bonds without obtaining a resolution of the bondholders' meeting; and (3) in taking steps to protect the creditors in the case of a capital reduction or a merger, the bond manager may, in principle, object to such capital reduction or merger without obtaining a resolution of the bondholders meeting.

The revised Companies Act, which came into effect in March 2021, has introduced an "assistant bond administrator" system, whereby assistant bond administrators are obliged to facilitate administrative procedures related to corporate bonds and help to protect claims. The system is applicable to bonds for which no bond administrator is established, and like the "bondholder sup-porting agent" system founded by the Japan Securities Dealers Association in 2016, it can be played by financial institutions as well as lawyers and legal firms familiar with bankruptcy affairs.

7. Corporate Bonds with Subscription Rights/Warrants and Structured Bonds

Subscription rights/warrants give their issuer an obligation to either issue new shares or transfer shares in its treasury at a predetermined price to the rights/warrants holder upon the exercise of their rights/warrants within a pre-scribed period.

Corporate bonds with subscription rights/warrants are divided into those that in effect correspond to convertible bonds and those with undetachable warrants. Corporate bonds with subscription rights/warrants correspond to the former and refer to bonds (1) from which the rights cannot be detached or separately transferred, (2) whose issue value is equal to the amount of money payable upon the exercise of the rights, and (3) for which the exercise of the subscription rights/warrants is always based on the contribution in kind of the corporate bonds (debt equity swap). Except in the case of a stock split, the conversion price is fixed at the time of its issue. In certain cases, howev-er, the conversion price of rights may be revised downward when the price of its underlying stock falls. Among these cases, bond issued under the condi-tion that the conversion price can be adjusted downward with a frequency of one or more times every six months are called "corporate bonds with sub-scription rights/warrants with adjustable conversion price (MSCBs: moving strike convertible bonds)." Because of market concerns about this type of "death spiral" financing, however, few of these types of bonds have been is-sued recently. On the other hand, as corporate bonds issued with detachable warrants are deemed a concurrent offering of corporate bonds and equity warrants, only those with undetachable warrants are included in the defini-tion of "corporate bonds with subscription rights/warrants." In such case, the money to be paid upon the exercise of subscription rights/warrants should be paid additionally, and the bond remains outstanding.

"Structured bond" is the name popularly given to a bond structured with derivatives. In recent years, various types of structured bonds have been is-sued. The underlying assets for derivatives embedded in structured bonds in-clude equities, interest rates, foreign exchanges and credit risks. Nikkei 225 Index-linked Bond is a form of structured bonds, which incorporates Nikkei 225 options trading, a form of derivative component exposed to equities-re-lated risks. In general, when the Nikkei 225 index rises, the deal generates a

Table V-6. Kinds of Structured Bonds

[Variable Cash Flow Bonds]

Step-up Bond: A bond issued initially with a coupon rate that is lower than the going rate then prevailing and that rises after the lapse of a certain period. By its very nature, the issuer often issues such a bond with a call option.

Step-down Bond: A bond issued initially with a coupon rate that is higher than the going rate then prevailing and that declines after the lapse of a certain period.

Deep-Discount Bond: This bond carries an interest rate lower than the going rate throughout its life, but it is issued at an under-par price to help its holders make up for the lower coupon by a redemption gain.

Reverse Floater Bond: The coupon rate of this bond falls when the interest rate rises, and the coupon rate rises when the interest rate declines. This is a kind of derivative bond using interest rate swap.

[Index Bonds]

Stock, interest rate, or bond-index-linked bond: These are bonds whose redemption principal is linked to the Nikkei average, whose coupon rate is linked to the Nikkei average, whose coupon rate is linked to the interest swap rate, or whose redemption principal is linked to the Japanese government bond futures price.

Exchange Rate Index Bond: Most of these dual-currency bonds are divided into those with a principal and coupon in yen that are redeemable in a foreign currency and into reverse dual-currency bonds with a principal and coupon redeemable in yen that carry a coupon in a foreign currency. As the amount of principal is normally larger than the coupon, dual-currency bonds carry a larger risk of exchange rate fluctuation.

[Bonds with Options]

Exchangeable Bonds (EB): Issuers of this bond may at their discretion pay redemptions with a pre-fixed number of shares of another company. For the purchaser, this means the sale of a put option, and under this arrangement, the coupon increases by as much as the option premium.

Other Bonds with Options: Included in this kind are callable bonds (the issuer can call the bond in advance of its maturity at the discretion of the issuer); puttable bonds (its holder can demand redemption in advance of its maturity); and knock-in, dual-currency bonds (a dual-currency bond with an exchange-rate option).

Source: Compiled on the basis of the data drawn from the website of Hephaistos Investment Research (http://hephaistos.fc2web.com/bond_guide/shikumi_sai.html) (Japanese) and the website of The Central Council for Financial Services Information

higher return; but when it falls, the options is exercised, causing a loss, and the bond price falls below its par value. A corporate bond with a clause to convert it into shares of another company ("exchangeable bond" or EB) is a bond that incorporates a stock option of the target company. In general, when the stock price of such corporation rises, the deal generates a higher return because the holder can acquire the option fee, but when the price of its stock falls, the option is exercised, and the holder has to accept the share at a lower price and suffers a loss. However, unlike in the case of a bond linked to the Nikkei average, the holder can hold the share until its price recovers.

CHAPTER VI

The Secondary Markets for Bonds

1. Trading of Bonds

Bonds are circulated by two different methods: (1) trading on a market operated by a financial instruments exchange, and (2) negotiated transaction between an investor and a securities company or other market intermediary. The former is referred to as an exchange transaction and the latter as an over the-counter (OTC) transaction. OTC transactions account for the majority of transactions on the bond secondary market.

The trading volume of public and corporate bonds in the secondary market (including JGB basket trades from May 2018; the same applies here in Section 1 below) was only ¥58 trillion in fiscal 1975, but continued to grow thereafter, hitting the ¥10 quadrillion level in fiscal 2007. Although trading volume decreased to ¥7.7 quadrillion in fiscal 2010 due to the impact of the Lehman Shock and other factors, it has recently increased significantly due to the shift from general collateral repos to repurchase repo transactions, and has reached ¥30 quadrillion in fiscal 2020.

Looking at the bond trading volume by bond type, trading of JGBs account for over 90% of all trading. The government has continuously been issuing massive amounts of JGBs, resulting in a large increase in those outstanding in the market and driving the expansion of the bond secondary market.

This trend has been continuing. Between fiscal 2010 to 2020, the trading volume of JGBs increased by ¥22,908 quadrillion, while the overall increase for all public and corporate bonds was ¥22,857 quadrillion. As such, government securities outweigh by far other categories of bonds in overall fixed income trading volume. The dominance of government debts stems most likely from the difference in liquidity, which in turn is mainly because government debts are considered risk free in Japan and attract funds for various investment needs.

For the sake of development of secondary markets for bonds in Japan going forward, it is important that bonds other than JGBs are traded actively. Recognizing the need to vitalize the corporate bond market, which plays an important role in corporate finance, the Japan Securities Dealers Association

Chart VI-1. Annual Amount of Purchasing and Selling of Bonds (Face Value Basis) and Share of OTC Trades

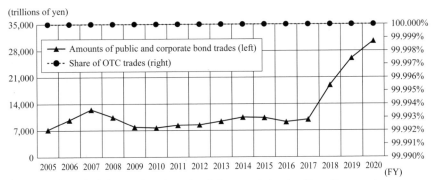

Notes: 1. Figures include *gensaki* trades and exclude corporate bonds with equity warrants.
2. The purchase price is, in principle, based on original face value, but government bond basket transactions from May 2018 onwards are based on execution price.
Source: Compiled from statistics on the Japan Securities Dealers Association website (OTC trading volume of public and corporate bonds; OTC trading volume by bond type) and the Japan Exchange Group website (transaction volume and value)

(JSDA) issued, in 2009, a report titled, "Toward Vitalization of the Corporate Bond Market" that organized the issues faced by the country's corporate bond market and also proposed specific measures to create a more efficient corporate bond market with higher transparency and liquidity. The report went on to state that vitalization of the Japanese corporate bond market would be an important factor in Japan's new economic growth strategy and that the public and private sectors should actively cooperate in advancing the measures.

Some of the specific initiatives taken by the JSDA are described later in this Chapter.

2. Participants in the Secondary Bond Market

Looking at the OTC bond market by type of investor or transaction party, trading is dominated by bond dealers, such as securities companies. OTC trading of public and corporate bonds requires dealers to promptly cope with a broad range of trading requirements from investors. However, the large number of bonds and the wide variety of available transaction forms make it difficult to quickly find a matching counterparty for certain transactions. Therefore, in most bond transactions, securities companies or dealer banks act as the counterparty, buying or selling as principal against clients' needs to

Chart VI-2.   Bond Trading volume by Bond Type

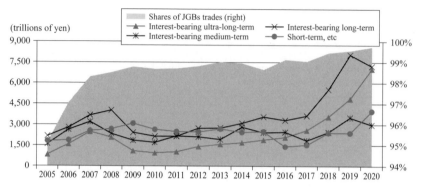

Note: Figures include *gensaki* trades (excluding JGB basket transactions from May 2018) and exclude corporate bonds with equity warrants.
Source: Compiled from statistics on the Japan Securities Dealers Association website (OTC trading volume of public and corporate bonds; OTC trading volume by bond type)

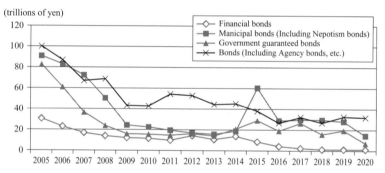

Note: Figures include *gensaki* trades and exclude corporate bonds with equity warrants.
Source: Compiled from statistics on the Japan Securities Dealers Association website (OTC trading volume of public and corporate bonds; OTC trading volume by bond type)

facilitate smooth transactions. Furthermore, securities companies, etc. trade bonds on a proprietary basis, which adds to overall dealer trading volumes. Following bond dealers, entities grouped as "others" account for the next largest share of the total volume. This group includes the Bank of Japan, which functions as the underwriting agent for JGBs and also buys and sells a range of debt securities as part of its open market operations Buying and selling by non-residents has risen in recent years, aggressively trading short-term government bonds such as treasury bills, as well as long-term and superlong-term bonds. Their purpose of investing in the Japanese bond market is more as a means to make investment in the yen rather than in bonds. In addition,

Table VI-1. Trends in Bond Transactions by Investor Type

(Figure on the top line is the total of buy and sell; figure on the lower line is the net of buy and sell and negative figure denotes selling on balance)

(¥10 billion)

	FY2011	FY2012	FY2013	FY2014	FY2015	FY2016	FY2017	FY2018	FY2019	FY2020
City (commercial) banks	46,511 (−1,997)	40,150 (−2,861)	18,599 (−2,837)	25,407 (−2,630)	12,709 (−973)	6,085 (1,064)	10,231 (2,209)	9,135 (352)	10,077 (158)	12,401 (3,259)
Regional banks	5,891 (1,020)	5,765 (644)	4,140 (482)	4,550 (303)	3,480 (51)	2,525 (−80)	1,640 (−60)	1,561 (16)	1,484 (308)	1,606 (518)
Trust banks	24,789 (8,252)	22,294 (8,109)	16,800 (5,478)	14,175 (1,298)	10,861 (561)	10,000 (299)	10,074 (516)	10,582 (423)	12,234 (882)	13,792 (1,964)
Agriculture-related banking institutions	3,356 (2,221)	3,099 (2,126)	1,764 (779)	1,307 (486)	1,000 (232)	975 (240)	980 (325)	1,026 (230)	1,038 (286)	1,245 (408)
Other banking institutions	5,448 (2,346)	4,266 (2,602)	3,475 (2,016)	2,636 (790)	2,128 (806)	1,631 (578)	733 (155)	613 (109)	545 (140)	706 (244)
Life and property casualty insurance companies	4,583 (1,896)	4,826 (1,631)	4,256 (1,387)	2,704 (908)	1,956 (507)	1,555 (404)	1,507 (371)	1,701 (406)	1,880 (563)	2,256 (728)
Investment Trusts	2,885 (2,100)	3,108 (2,309)	4,318 (3,165)	4,372 (3,045)	3,961 (2,284)	2,139 (416)	2,159 (240)	2,498 (381)	2,912 (519)	3,634 (733)
Public employees mutual aid associations	277 (166)	299 (213)	210 (151)	114 (54)	115 (15)	84 (5)	86 (7)	82 (3)	65 (5)	109 (−32)
Corporations	1,003 (922)	1,203 (1,093)	1,281 (1,104)	696 (630)	320 (256)	81 (40)	98 (75)	144 (94)	180 (109)	160 (120)
Entities not domiciled in Japan	36,902 (14,891)	34,131 (15,997)	34,799 (16,300)	35,730 (20,103)	37,609 (21,575)	36,466 (21,814)	34,992 (21,208)	40,444 (24,486)	45,376 (23,929)	54,653 (27,909)
Others	52,719 (−31,408)	58,930 (−30,369)	62,355 (−26,367)	60,975 (−23,756)	61,742 (−24,673)	56,869 (−22,866)	48,849 (−24,303)	46,837 (−26,216)	44,075 (−26,870)	70,883 (−37,612)
Bond dealers	179,035 (−570)	164,805 (−1,172)	162,073 (−661)	187,339 (−223)	142,679 (−446)	116,243 (−465)	117,185 (28)	111,706 (34)	111,933 (10)	101,576 (−135)
Total (including other investors)	369,000 (1,253)	348,505 (1,432)	318,446 (2,222)	344,034 (1,984)	281,281 (557)	236,550 (1,490)	230,135 (881)	228,532 (474)	233,583 (336)	265,029 (−799)

Note: Excludes trades of corporate bonds with equity warrants, other than *gensaki* bonds.
Source: Compiled from statistics on the Japan Securities Dealers Association website (OTC trading volume of public and corporate bonds; OTC trading volume by bond type)

with the difficult investment environment recently, city banks, in pursuit of profit, are vigorously engaging in proprietary bond trading and also reselling municipal and other bonds underwritten by themselves. It should also be noted that trust banks have traditionally allocated large shares of assets under management or administration, including pension assets, to bonds.

As measured in terms of difference between selling and buying transactions, almost all business categories were net buyers of bonds in fiscal 2018 and 2019, except "others". The reason why "others" is constantly and signifi-cantly oversold is that primary JGBs issued by auction are settled via the Bank of Japan and reported as sales by the central bank. In fiscal 2020, gov-ernment bond issuance increased significantly due to two supplementary budgets in response to the pandemic. This drove a sharp rise in the net sale amount in the "others" category but also a large increase in the net value in many categories, including city banks and non-residents. According to the JGB issuance plan for fiscal 2021, issuance is expected to be lower than in fiscal 2020. However, since issuance remains at historically high levels, the net buying trend in all categories except "others" is expected to continue.

3. Over-the-counter Bond Transactions

Depending on where transactions take place, the circulation of bonds may be broadly divided into exchange transactions and over-the-counter (OTC) transactions.

An overwhelming majority of bond transactions takes place over the coun-ter rather than on exchanges. This is due to the following reasons: (1) there are so many issues of bonds that it is practically impossible to list all of them on exchanges; (2) due to the wide variety of bond transaction forms and other specifications that different buyers and sellers require, it is difficult to in-stantly locate a matching counterparty for a particular transaction; (3) corpo-rate investors, who account for the bulk of the bond trading volume, tend to trade in large lots and often carry out complex transactions involving more than one issue; and (4) tax on bond interest varies according to the tax pro-files of bondholders. Due to these reasons, bond transactions, in general, do not lend themselves to trading on exchanges, where the terms of transactions need to be standardized. Bonds are more efficiently traded over the counter, where trades are executed based on the terms individually negotiated be-tween buyers and sellers.

Unlike exchange markets, where all orders for a particular instrument are concentrated in a single marketplace, OTC trading, in essence, is a decentral-ized, free transaction process based on one-to-one negotiation between the parties that is conducted over the counter at individual securities companies, etc. In that sense, it may be said that the counter of each securities company is a market in itself and that there are as many OTC markets as there are se-curities companies.

A wide variety of transactions may be executed over the counter once an investor and a securities company agree on their terms. Private placement bonds as well as publicly offered bonds may be traded, and the delivery and settlement procedures are to be agreed upon between the buyer and the seller.

Table VI-2.   Bond Trading by Market

(¥10 billion)

		Government securities	Corporate bonds with subscription rights/ warrants	Others
FY2011	Stock Exchanges	0	40	0
	Over the counter	829,983	46	10,773
FY2012	Stock Exchanges	0	30	0
	Over the counter	842,314	45	9,760
FY2013	Stock Exchanges	0	27	0
	Over the counter	936,753	24	9,230
FY2014	Stock Exchanges	0	8	0
	Over the counter	1,039,157	11	11,273
FY2015	Stock Exchanges	0	30	0
	Over the counter	1,025,087	20	14,432
FY2016	Stock Exchanges	0	18	0
	Over the counter	921,027	31	7,335
FY2017	Stock Exchanges	0	6	0
	Over the counter	983,609	13	8,717
FY2018	Stock Exchanges	0	4	0
	Over the counter	1,889,240	11	8,141
FY2019	Stock Exchanges	0	3	0
	Over the counter	2,596,532	8	7,979
FY2020	Stock Exchanges	0	4	0
	Over the counter	3,052,768	7	5,090

Notes: 1. The figures for exchange trading volume are double those actually reported by exchanges to account for both buy and sell sides of transactions.
   2. OTC trading volume includes *gensaki* trades (including JGB basket transactions (execution amount basis) from May 2018)
Source: Compiled from statistics on the Japan Securities Dealers Association website (OTC trading volume of public and corporate bonds; OTC trading volume by bond type) and the Japan Exchange Group website (transaction volume and value)

The transaction price can also be decided between the two parties, often in reference to the prices of other relevant financial instruments.

In OTC trading, a securities company, etc. first buys bonds that a client offers to sell and then resells them to another client afterward. When a client wants to buy bonds, it sells them out of its own inventory or tries to get them from other brokers. These types of transactions, in which a securities compa-

Table VI-3. Breakdown of Major Bond Categories, by Outstanding Balance and Number of Issues

(¥1 trillion, No. of issues)

		Government securities	Municipal bonds (public offering)	Government-guaranteed bonds; FILP agency bonds	Straight bonds	Corporate bonds with subscription rights/ warrants	Bank debentures (interest bearing and discount)
FY2011	No. of Issues	449	2,525	1,634	2,658	21	1,272
	Outstanding balance	781	52	64	62	1	15
FY2012	No. of Issues	470	2,655	1,772	2,709	17	1,163
	Outstanding balance	814	55	66	60	1	14
FY2013	No. of Issues	476	2,805	1,916	2,823	18	900
	Outstanding balance	848	57	69	60	0	12
FY2014	No. of Issues	493	2,917	2,021	2,863	22	789
	Outstanding balance	873	58	69	59	0	12
FY2015	No. of Issues	497	3,008	2,151	2,828	24	526
	Outstanding balance	901	59	69	57	0	11
FY2016	No. of Issues	506	3,059	2,244	2,961	26	428
	Outstanding balance	927	60	68	60	0	10
FY2017	No. of Issues	512	3,100	2,370	3,070	23	366
	Outstanding balance	948	60	68	60	0	9
FY2018	No. of Issues	516	3,152	2,505	3,269	17	364
	Outstanding balance	966	61	68	62	0	8
FY2019	No. of Issues	520	3,193	2,475	3,556	25	235
	Outstanding balance	978	62	67	70	0	7
FY2020	No. of Issues	536	3,261	2,624	3,769	23	223
	Outstanding balance	1,065	62	68	76	0	6

Note: Outstanding balance figures are in trillions of yen. The aggregation method has been partially changed since April 2019.
Source: Compiled from statistics on the Japan Securities Dealers Association website (issuance and redemption amount of public and corporate bonds)

ny takes part in a transaction as the client's counterparty, are generally referred to as "principal transactions" and make up a significant proportion of trades in the bond market.

4. Reference Statistical Prices (Yields) for OTC Bond Transactions (1)

As OTC bond trading is a negotiated process between a securities company, etc. and a client, it is difficult for a third party to discover the price at which a transaction is consummated. Publication of prices and other information concerning OTC bond transactions not only helps efficient and orderly trading of bonds but is also of critical importance from the standpoint of investor protection by promoting the formation of fair prices and facilitating investors' access to trading at the best possible price. Publication of bond prices is thus indispensable for the development of bond markets.

With a view to providing investors, securities companies, and others with reference information, the JSDA instituted the System for Dissemination of Reference Statistical Prices (Yields) for OTC Bond Transactions, which publishes (mid price between buy and sell quotes) quotes for publicly offered bonds that meet certain criteria. The system was originally instituted in August 1965 by the Bond Underwriters Association of Japan for publishing OTC Quotes for Industrial Debentures and was succeeded by the Tokyo Securities Dealers Association, the predecessor of the JSDA, which began the system for dissemination of OTC quotations of bonds in March 1966. The initiatives were implemented with a backdrop of social necessity to promote the formation of fair prices and efficient and orderly trading for JGBs, issuance of which had been resumed after the war with a view to contributing to public interest and investor protection. The system has since undergone many

Table VI-4.   The System for Dissemination of Reference Statistical Prices (Yields) for OTC Bond Transactions

1. Outline
(1) Purpose
To publish quotations reported by member companies appointed by the Japan Securities Dealers Association to be used as reference by member companies of the association and their clients in trading bonds over the counter between them.
   Note: In August 1965, the Bond Underwriters Association started publishing quotations on OTC industrial bonds. Subsequently, the Tokyo Securities Dealers Association started publishing OTC bond quotations in March 1966, and improvements have been made on several occasions thereafter.

(2) Calculation of Reference Statistical Prices (Yields) for OTC Bond Transactions
The JSDA receives reports from its member companies affiliated with the system (13 securities companies as of December 31, 2021) on quotations of trades with a face value of approximately ¥500 million as of 3:00 p.m. each trading day. The JSDA computes the reference prices (yields) of a given issue on the basis of an arithmetic average of quotations on issues with respect to which it has received reports from five or more member companies.

Table VI-5.   History of System for Dissemination of Reference Statistical Prices (Yields) for OTC Bond Transactions

	Kinds of selectable issues	No. of selected issues
March 1966 Over-the-counter quotes announced · Date of announcement (Thursday of each week)	Government securities, municipal bonds, government-guaranteed bonds, coupon bank debentures, corporate bonds, telegraph and telephone (TT) coupon bonds subscribed to by subscribers, discount TT bonds, and such other bonds as may be recognized by the Japan Securities Dealers Association (JSDA)	No. of issues announced: 280 (as of May 12, 1966)

January 1977
· Announcement of bench-mark and standard quotes (Benchmark quotes are announced every day except Saturday. Standard quotes are announced once a week on Thursday.)
	(1) Benchmark quotes (for institutional investors) are selected from such bonds whose volume of trading correctly reflects the movement of the market.
	(2) Standard quotes (for small-lot investors) are selected from one of government securities, municipal bonds, special debts, bank debentures, corporate bonds, and yen-denominated foreign bonds, other than those listed in (1) above in terms of maturities and interest rates.
		(1) Benchmark quotes:
		  Issues announced: 14
		  (as of January 31, 1977)
		(2) Standard quotes:
		  Issues announced: 77
		  (as of January 27, 1977)

August 1978
· Announcement of bench-mark and standard quotes (bid and ask quotations are announced). (Benchmark quotes are announced every day except Saturday. Standard quotes are announced once a week on Thursday.)
	The same as above.	(1) Benchmark quotes:
		  Issues announced: 19
		  (as of August 31, 1978)
		(2) Standard quotes:
		  Issues announced: 137
		  (as of August 31, 1978)

January 1992 · Standard quotes on OTC bonds are announced daily.	One of the government securities, municipal bonds, government-guaranteed bonds, bank debentures, corporate bonds, and yen-denominated foreign bonds that are not listed is selected in terms of kinds, maturities, and interest rates.	Issues announced: 298 (as of January 31, 1992)
April 1997 · No. of selectable issues was sharply increased (the new system started operating.)	Publicly offered but unlisted bonds (with a remaining life of one year or longer) that maintain a fixed interest rate throughout their life and redeem their principal in a lump sum were selected.	Issues announced: 1,746 (as of May 1, 1997)
December 1998 · The duty to concentrate its trading on the exchange market was abolished.	Publicly offered bonds (with paid-in principal, interest, and redemption money all paid in yen) are selected.	Issues announced: 2,867 (as of December 1, 1998)
August 2002 · Name of system changed to "Reference Statistical Prices (Yields) for OTC Bond Transactions." In addition to average values, highs, lows and medians are announced.	The same as above.	Issued announced: 4,198 (as of August 1, 2002)
December 2013 · Decision made to revise the calculation method for corporate and other bonds and announce quotes earlier.	The same as above.	Issued announced: 7,931 (as of December 2, 2013)
November 2015 · Start of operation of revised system	The same as above.	Issued announced: 8,257 (as of November 2, 2015)
May 2018 · Change of last announcement date due to the shortened settlement period (T+1) of JGBs.	The same as above.	No. of issues announced: 9,345 (as of May 1, 2018)
July 2020 · Change of last announcement date due to the shortened settlement period (T+2) of non-JGB bonds.	The same as above.	No. of issues announced: 10,423 (as of July 13, 2020)

Note: Selected issues reported on and after August 5, 2002, were transferred to the System for Dissemination of Reference Statistical Prices (Yields) for OTC Bond Transactions.

changes and improvements in response to the changing environment surrounding the bond market. During that period, the number of published issues has ballooned from about 300 when the system was introduced to approximately 11,100. In August 2002, the JSDA changed the name of the data from Standard Quotes on OTC Bonds to Reference Statistical Prices (Yields) for OTC Bond Transactions to clearly indicate that the data is offered as a reference for OTC bond transactions. At the same time, the system was enhanced by publishing high, low, and median values of quotes in addition to the average, which had previously been the only data available.

Since the system started publishing bond quotes 50 years ago, its use has evolved from the original purpose of providing price references for OTC bond trading in Japan. In addition to that role, it has become widely used for mark to market valuation for financial reporting and tax accounting purposes and the valuation of collateral for different types of transactions. The expansion of usage required an even greater degree of confidence in the system. As a result, in 2013 a review was made of the quotation system primarily with regard to publishing reference statistical prices (yields) for corporate straight bonds. The new system arising from that review began operation in November 2015.

5. Reference Statistical Prices (Yields) for OTC Bond Transactions (2)

To provide reference information on bond prices, the JSDA publishes Reference Statistical Prices (Yields) for OTC Bond Transactions each business day based on the values of quotations for trades with a face value of roughly ¥500 million reported as of 3:00 p.m. by members designated by the JSDA (hereinafter referred to as "Designated-Reporting Members"). With calls made to further increase the reliability and stability of this publication system, however, the JSDA made some revisions to the system, primarily to the matters relating to corporate bonds. The new system was implemented in November 2015.

Major enhanced elements in the new system are as follows.

(1) Stricter designation standards for Designated-Reporting Members: Recognizing the need to appoint members with the capability to report appropriate quotations that reflect movements of the corporate bond market as Designated-Reporting Members in order to increase reliability of Reference Statistical Prices (Yields) for OTC Bond Transactions, stricter designation standards, such as the member's trading volume of corporate bonds, etc. must be within the top 20, were added.

(2) Enhancement and reinforcement of guidance and management structure at the JSDA: To ensure that proper reporting is made by Designated-Re-

Chart VI-3.   Illustrated Flow of Procedure up to the Publication of Reference Statistical Prices (Yields) for OTC Bond Transactions

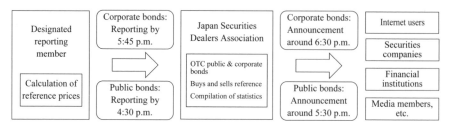

Table VI-6.   Designation of Designated-Reporting Members

The Japan Securities Dealers Association screens members intending to become Designated-Reporting Members based on the following designation standards to specify Designated-Reporting Members.
(1) The member understands the purport of the System for Dissemination of Reference Statistical Prices (Yields) for OTC Bond Transactions and intends to become a Designated-Reporting Member.
(2) The member is well versed in the operations for OTC bond trades.
(3) The member has in place an organizational structure and staffing required for properly executing the operation for reporting quotations.
(4) Other matters set forth by the JSDA.
*For further details on screening standards, please see the website of the JSDA.

porting Members, the JSDA performs checks to detect (i) any inappropriate quotations for each business day and (ii) any problems with the reporting framework of each Designated-Reporting Member.

(3) Revised calculation method for Reference Statistical Prices (Yields) for OTC Bond Transactions: When the reported corporate bond quotations are relatively dispersed and there is a major movement on the market, quotations that deviate significantly from the average quote may actually be more appropriate, and because abnormal values are eliminated in the checking performed in (2), it was decided that truncating the highest and lowest values of reported quotations, which was previously done mechanically, would no longer be performed.

(4) Pushing back the time of reporting deadline and the time of announcement: In consideration of the voices from non-reporting members raising the need to push back the reporting deadline for bond quotations in order to make reports, the deadline for trade reporting and that for announcement were pushed back by 75 minutes and 60 minutes respectively.

(5) Promoting better understanding of Reference Statistical Prices (Yields) for OTC Bond Transactions: It was decided that more easy-to-understand explanations on the characteristics of the Reference Statistical Prices (Yields)

Table VI-7.   Revisions to Reference Statistical Prices (Yields) for OTC Bond Transactions

Revision measures	Outline	Revisions to bonds applicable to reporting
(1) Stricter designation standards for Designated-Reporting Members	Added the following specific standards in acknowledging that the member is "well versed in the operations for OTC bond trades." · A Designated-Reporting Member that reports quotations on corporate bonds, etc. shall be ranked within the top 20 in terms of the bond trading volume. · However, reporting may be made for bond trades for which the member serves as the lead managing underwriter.	Corporate bonds, TMK bonds, yen-denominated foreign bonds
(2) Enhancement and reinforcement of guidance and management structure at the JSDA	· Adoption of a process to check the reported quotations (including warnings issued to Designated-Reporting Members) every business day · Adoption of a process to check the reporting systems of Designated-Reporting Members · Setting self-regulatory regulation of prohibiting information exchange, etc. relating to quotation standards between Designated-Reporting Members	All debt securities
(3) Revisions to the method of calculating reference statistical prices for OTC bond transactions	· Removal of the step to cut off the highest and lowest quotations reported	Corporate bonds, TMK bonds, yen-denominated foreign bonds
(4) Pushing back the time of reporting deadline and the time of announcement	· Pushed back the time of reporting deadline by 1 hour and 15 minutes to 5:45 p.m. · Pushed back the time of announcement by about 1 hour to 6:30 p.m.	Corporate bonds, TMK bonds, yen-denominated foreign bonds
(5) Promoting better understanding of reference statistical prices (yields) for OTC bond transactions	· Easier-to-understand explanations on the nature, etc. of reference statistical prices (yields) for OTC bond transactions, such as the possible deviation from actual trade prices, on the JSDA website, etc.	All debt securities

for OTC Bond Transactions should be posted on the JSDA website, etc., such as the fact that the Reference Statistical Prices (Yields) for OTC Bond Transactions referred to the middle rate of bid and ask, and therefore some discrepancy between data and actual transaction price could be seen.

6. Reporting & Announcement System of Corporate Bond Trading

Recognizing the importance of increasing transparency of information on corporate bond prices and securing reliability through providing bond trading data in an aim to vitalize the corporate bond market, the JSDA decided to publicize actual trading prices of corporate bond trades on the OTC market from November 2015.

This new initiative is composed of the JSDA's system to receive reporting on transaction prices, etc. from member securities companies and the system to disclose the reported transaction prices, etc.

(1) System of reporting corporate bond transactions: JSDA's Self-Regulatory Rules set out reporting requirements on each securities company (a member of JSDA) that participate in a bond transaction on one side or the other. Reporting is required for the following bonds: (i) that were publicly offered or sold in Japan, (ii) that were in Japan, (iii) of which the principal, interest, and redeemed principal are yen-denominated (excluding short-term corporate bonds and corporate bonds with subscription rights/warrants). Transactions subject to reporting include the followings: (i) transactions that are reported every business day (trades with a face value of ¥100 million or above) and (ii) transactions that may be reported on a monthly basis if notified to the JSDA (trades with a face value of less than ¥100 million; provided, however, that transactions with a face value of less than ¥10 million may be omitted from reporting).

(2) System of publicizing corporate bond transactions: The JSDA announces information on bond trades on its website on the business day following the day on which reports on trades are received from securities company. Items announced are: (i) contract date, (ii) issue code, (iii) name of issue, (iv) due date, (v) coupon rate, (vi) trading value (whether the face value is ¥500 million or above, or not), and (vii) unit price (traded price per face value of ¥100 yen), and (viii) buy or sell (whether the counterparty of securities company is abuyer or seller). In addition to bonds with an issue rating of AA or higher, from April 2021, bonds with an issue rating of A (excluding A minus) and an issue amount of 50 billion yen or more (excluding subordinated bonds and bonds with a remaining maturity of 20 years or more) has been adopted as the bonds to be announced.

When certain conditions apply, the announcement of such corporate bond transaction is suspended.

(3) Periodical verification: The JSDA has decided to periodically verify the impact, etc. of the implementation of the system of publicizing corporate bond transaction information on the liquidity of corporate bonds and to consider revising the system if needed.

Chart VI-4.   Illustrated Flow of Reporting & Announcement of Corporate Bond Trading

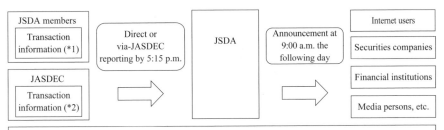

(*1) Transactions processed (or approved) by the system between 3:00 p.m. on the previous business day and 3:00 p.m. on the day.
(*2) Trade reporting data transmitted to the settlement reconciliation system between 4:45 p.m. on the previous business day and 4:45 p.m. on the day.

Chart VI-5.   Information announced

○Announced on December 1, 2021
Trade contract date: November 30, 2021

Issue code	Issue name	Redemption date	Coupon rate	Trading type	Transaction volume (face value basis) of ¥500 million or above	Transaction volume (face value basis) of less than ¥500 million	Contracted unit price (¥)	[Reference] Reference Statistical Prices (Yields) for OTC Bond Transactions (Average Prices)
000039023	XX Industries 3	2027/09/20	1.9	Sell	*		102.△△	102.09
000039023	XX Industries 3	2027/09/20	1.9	Buy		*	102.× ×	102.09
000039023	XX Industries 3	2027/09/20	1.9	Sell		*	102.●●	102.09

Chart VI-6.   Example of suspension of announcement and removal of suspension of announcement

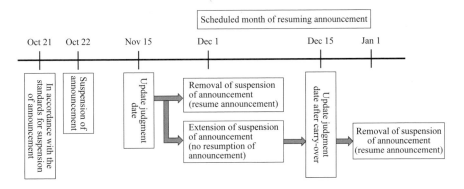

7. Book-Entry Transfer System for Bonds

In the past, investors held bonds in various forms—more specifically, in physical certificates issued by the issuers; in registered form, where bondholders are registered on the registry at the registrar designated for the issue; and as book-entry JGBs, where physical certificates are deposited with the BOJ so that trades can be settled by book-entry transfers (within the system established in 1980) among the accounts of brokers and other system participants (account management institutions).

However, with the increasing bond trading volume, it was evident that the current management measures of bondholders' ownership by means of certificates, which needed to be physically delivered, or registered bonds, whose transfer required amendment in records of bond-specific registries, would encounter a capacity bottleneck in terms of settlement procedures, and that the book-entry transfer system for JGBs had several shortcomings. The situation indicated that the settlement procedures for bonds were in need of review. There was a growing perception that Japan urgently needed to renovate the existing system to create a safer and more efficient infrastructure that would

Chart VI-7.   Structure of Book-Entry Transfer System for Bonds

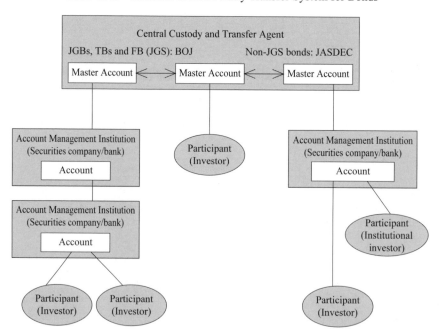

Table VI-8.   Bonds under Custody and Book-Entry Transfer Volume

(No. of transactions, millions of yen)

		Increase: Under-writing new issues	Decrease: Redemptions and retirement by purchase	Transfer	Number of participating issues (at fiscal year-end) Account balance
FY2011	No.	26,664	35,619	439,867	60,701
	Amount	32,955,046	30,589,808	156,713,049	252,439,190
FY2012	No.	27,326	33,476	471,798	58,486
	Amount	33,558,410	33,213,581	143,537,681	252,784,020
FY2013	No.	26,726	31,642	437,387	55,595
	Amount	34,446,614	34,030,438	135,561,923	253,200,196
FY2014	No.	25,761	32,082	465,813	54,294
	Amount	33,410,427	34,831,065	158,293,806	251,779,558
FY2015	No.	25,722	30,604	524,130	53,825
	Amount	31,146,061	32,462,918	204,529,981	250,462,702
FY2016	No.	27,401	28,040	349,226	58,288
	Amount	41,737,175	35,052,475	131,163,539	257,147,401
FY2017	No.	28,345	27,238	287,072	63,087
	Amount	34,276,788	34,479,534	140,831,156	256,944,654
FY2018	No.	28,885	26,163	289,272	68,826
	Amount	36,439,329	31,520,591	145,921,506	261,863,392
FY2019	No.	26,765	26,564	318,896	74,569
	Amount	37,743,822	31,844,372	146,798,435	267,762,842
FY2020	No.	21,821	25,775	300,113	77,900
	Amount	41,438,860	31,240,061	127,984,617	277,961,641

Note: The JGB book-entry system began on January 10, 2006.
Source: Compiled from Japan Securities Depositary Center website (Book-Entry Transfer System for Corporate Bonds)

make the country's securities markets globally competitive. Against this background, the securities settlement system reform law was enacted in June 2002, and, pursuant to its provisions, the existing legislation for book-entry transfer was later amended and renamed the Act on Book Entry of Corporate Bonds and Shares with objectives including the complete dematerialization of securities, the shortening of settlement cycles, and the reduction in settlement risk. The amended law provided for the legal framework of new book-entry transfer systems for corporate and government securities. On the basis

Table VI-9.   Reforms of Bond Delivery and Settlement System

Month/Year	Changes implemented
April 1994	Delivery versus payment (DVP) of government bonds through the Bank of Japan network starts.
April 1977	System of T+3 government bond rolling settlement starts.
October 1999	System of T+3 general bond rolling settlement starts.
January 2000	Real-time gross settlement (RTGS) of government bonds starts.
January 2003	Act on Book Entry of Corporate Bonds and Shares (stipulating paperless trading in bonds, etc.) is enforced. Paperless trading in government bonds starts.
May 2004	DVP trading in bonds other than government bonds starts.
May 2005	Trading in government bonds through a settlement organization starts.
January 2006	Paperless issuance of and paperless trading in bonds other than government bonds starts.
April 2012	Shortening of settlement of JGBs starts. (T+2)
May 2018	Shortening of settlement of JGBs starts. (T+1)
July 2020	Shortening of settlement of retail JGBs and general bond transactions starts. (T+2)

of that framework, the BOJ renovated the existing JGB book-entry system in January 2003, and the Japan Securities Depository Center (JASDEC) started operating a new central custody and book-entry transfer system for securities, including nongovernment bonds in January 2006.

The book-entry transfer systems have a multitier, tree-like structure. On the top tier of the system are the "Transferring Institutions" – the Bank of Japan for government bonds and the JASDEC for other eligible securities. The second tier consists of a number of "Account Management Institutions" (such as securities companies etc. that directly hold accounts in the Transferring Institutions). Under each Account Management Institution are other securities companies etc. and investors that hold accounts in the Institution. Bond ownership is managed through the registration or recording in the "Transfer Account Book" managed by Transferring Institutions and Account Management Institutions. In principle, all bonds under the book-entry transfer system are incorporated into the system at the time of issuance. With the entire issue being dematerialized, none of those book-entry bonds may be withdrawn over their life in the form of either physical certificates or registered bonds.

The previously mentioned Securities Settlement System Reform Law also provided measures to abolish the Corporate Bond Registration Law following the setup of the book-entry transfer systems.

8. Bond Yield and Terms of Issuance

Those who raise funds (fund raising party) by issuing bonds look for the lowest possible cost. On the other hand, investors who buy bonds choose issues that offer the highest possible return within the range of tolerable risk. In theory, the issue terms of a new bond (subscriber's yield to maturity) are determined at a certain level where opportunities for arbitraging its subscriber's yield to maturity and the secondary market yield (yield to maturity) of outstanding issues of a nature similar to that of the bond are balanced. When such a point of balance is achieved, it is said that "issue terms that adequately reflect the secondary market conditions have been established." Important conditions for efficient arbitrage to occur include the following: the outstanding balance and trading volume of comparable bonds are sufficiently large, new bonds are issued regularly, and the secondary market yields of comparable bonds are available for reference at the time of pricing new issues. It can be said that in the Japanese bond market yields at the issue of bonds have come into line with yields of comparable bonds as the amount of new issues of the bonds and secondary trading volume of such bonds increased.

More specifically, while JGBs had been issued through the underwriting syndicate program for smooth and stable financing, the proportion of bond issuance through competitive bidding that more closely reflect market conditions has steadily increased under a market-oriented national debt management policy, replacing the previous emphasis on non-competitive, syndicated underwriting, where issue terms were based on the official discount rate or other benchmarks. Currently, in principle, all government bonds (excluding those for retail investors) are issued through auctions (the syndicated underwriting program for JGBs was discontinued in March 2006).

The market-oriented transition of bond issuance has also been witnessed in pricing spreads among bonds with different credit qualities. For example, yields at the issue of government-guaranteed bonds and local bonds are determined in reference to the yield at issue of 10-year JGBs issued earlier in the month. From time to time in the past, the spreads of issues among the three classes of bonds deviated from market spreads. In recent years, however, as investors started to focus more on differences in credit quality, the spreads of issues among the three classes have increasingly tended to move more in line with credit spreads prevailing in the market. Another case in point that demonstrates the increased market orientation in bond issuance is that a growing portion of government-guaranteed bonds is now issued through a competitive bidding process (as individual issues). Investors are also showing an increasing tendency to differentiate corporate bonds based on credit ratings by rating agencies, ESG initiatives and other factors. In re-

Chart VI-8. Changes in Issue Terms (Yields) of Bonds

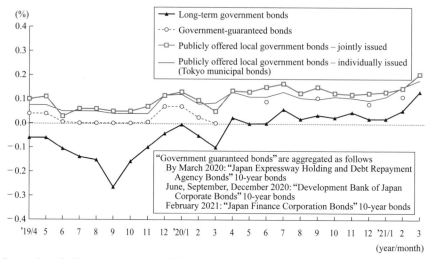

Source: Compiled from statistics on the Ministry of Finance website (JGB auction results) and the Japan
Securities Dealers Association website (list of Bond Issues).

Chart VI-9. Changes in the Difference in Issue Terms and Secondary Market
Yields between Publicly Offered, Jointly Issued Municipal Bonds and
Government-Guaranteed Bonds

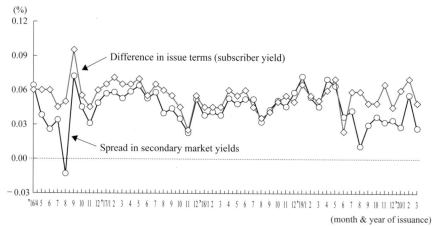

Notes: 1. Spread in secondary market yields is the difference in reference prices of OTC traded public and
corporate bonds (average value: simple interest) on the day prior to the term determination date of
jointly issued local government bonds and of government guaranteed bonds (10-year long-term).
2. Difference in issue terms (subscriber yield) is jointly issued local government bonds minus
government guaranteed bonds (each 10-year bonds).
Source: Compiled from statistics on the Japan Securities Dealers Association website (Issuing, Redemption
and Outstanding Amounts of Bond, Reference Statistical Prices (Yields) for OTC Bond Transactions)

sponse to this, many issuers go through a premarketing process to identify and estimate investors' demand and determine the terms of issue accordingly.

9. *Gensaki* Market for Bonds (1)

A repurchase agreement (*gensaki* transaction) (a conditional purchase or sale) is a form of trading between a seller and a buyer of bonds whereby the seller (or the buyer) agrees to repurchase (or resell) the securities at an agreed-upon price at a stated time. When the holder of bonds sells them to a buyer under an agreement to buy them back (a *gensaki* sell transaction), the holder can raise funds temporarily. When the counterparty buys bonds from a seller under a repurchase agreement to sell them back to the seller (a *gensaki* buy transaction), the buyer can earn a certain amount of interest by investing funds for a short period. When a securities company, etc. acts as an intermediary and arranges a repurchase agreement (*gensaki* transaction) by introducing a buyer which wants to invest idle cash in bonds to a seller which wants to raise funds by selling bond holdings, such a deal is called a brokered repurchase agreement. When a securities company, etc. that is in need of short-term cash sells bonds out of its inventory to an investor under a repurchase agreement, it is called a proprietary repurchase agreement. As the repurchase (or resale) price includes an amount equivalent to a return on investment or financing charge based on an agreement by the buyer and seller, the price does not usually tally with the market price of the bond prevailing at the time of its repurchase (or resale).

Despite some annual fluctuation, *gensaki* transactions have maintained a significant level of trading volume because they conveniently meet the short term funding and cash management needs. The outstanding balance of *gensaki* transactions reached almost ¥50 trillion at the end of fiscal 2007, compared with ¥7 trillion in the latter 1980s. Although there have been some dips in the balance since then due primarily to the effects of the global financial crisis, the balance has turned upward since 2010. After the settlement period for government bond transactions was compressed (to T+1) in May 2018, trading volume and outstanding balance of *gensaki* transactions have increased sharply in line with the shift from general collateral repos to repurchase repo transactions. The trading volume in fiscal 2020 and the outstanding balance as of the end of fiscal 2020 exceeded ¥28 quadrillion and ¥140 trillion, respectively.

Previously, the overwhelming majority of *gensaki* transactions were for short-term government securities (Treasury Bills (TBs) and Financing Bills (FBs)), supported by the increasing trading activity of TBs and FBs, which have maturities and credit quality more suitable for *gensaki* transactions

Chart VI-10.   Working Mechanism of Bond Lending (secured with cash deposit)

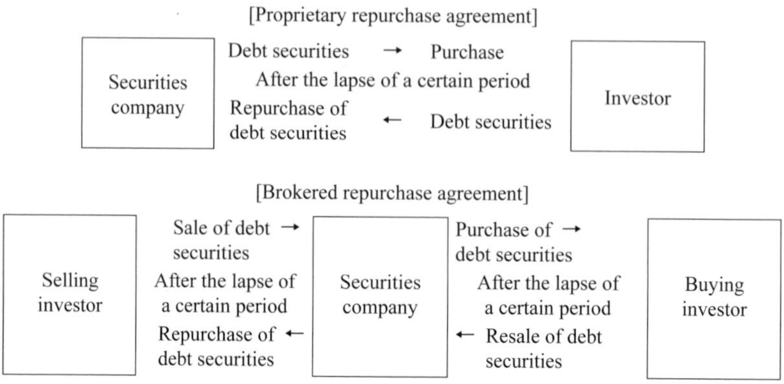

[Proprietary repurchase agreement]

| Securities company | Debt securities → Purchase
After the lapse of a certain period
Repurchase of ← Debt securities
debt securities | Investor |

[Brokered repurchase agreement]

| Selling investor | Sale of debt → securities
After the lapse of a certain period
Repurchase of ←
debt securities | Securities company | Purchase of →
debt securities
After the lapse of a certain period
← Resale of debt securities | Buying investor |

Table VI-10.   Turnover and Balance of Bond Repurchase Agreements (*Gensaki*)

(¥10 billion, %)

FY	Turnover of bonds (A)	Turnover of repurchase agreements (B)	B/A	Balance of repurchase agreements
2011	840,802	471,756	56.1	2,538
2012	852,118	503,564	59.1	2,354
2013	946,008	627,538	66.3	2,641
2014	1,050,441	706,429	67.3	3,079
2015	1,039,539	758,277	72.9	3,053
2016	928,393	691,841	74.5	3,344
2017	992,339	762,223	76.8	4,024
2018	1,897,392	1,668,849	88.0	11,642
2019	2,604,519	2,370,929	91.0	15,635
2020	3,057,865	2,792,828	91.3	14,841

Notes: 1. Figures include government bond basket transaction from May 2018.
2. Fiscal year-end balance (March 31st)
Source: Compiled from statistics on the Japan Securities Dealers Association website (OTC trading volume of public and corporate bonds; OTC trading volume by bond type; monthly outstanding amounts of conditional sale and purchase of bonds (*gensaki* transactions) by investor type)

Table VI-11. Balance of Bond Repurchase Agreements, by Major Investor Group

(¥10 billion)

	FY2011		FY2012		FY2013		FY2014		FY2015		FY2016		FY2017		FY2018		FY2019		FY2020	
	Selling balance	Buying balance	Selling balance	Buying balance	Selling balance	Buying balance	Selling balance	Buying balance	Selling balance	Buying balance	Selling balance	Buying balance	Selling balance	Buying balance	Selling balance	Buying balance	Selling balance	Buying balance	Selling balance	Buying balance
Trust banks	0	97	0	13	0	0	0	2	0	0	0	0	0	0	1,715	1,396	1,895	1,537	1,638	1,386
Other banking institutions	0	111	0	86	0	56	3	4	0	0	5	0	0	0	1,843	776	2,179	1,136	2,423	1,035
Investment Trusts	0	143	0	206	0	84	0	33	0	0	0	0	0	0	0	27	0	14	0	26
Corporations	0	82	0	50	0	31	0	25	0	4	0	3	0	3	0	2	0	2	0	1
Entities not domiciled in Japan	616	1,200	511	1,293	588	1,759	865	1,951	754	2,228	572	2,373	882	2,988	1,175	2,995	1,818	4,254	1,329	3,888
Others	121	288	70	196	55	122	99	188	66	46	384	55	151	119	820	1,392	1,731	1,844	1,731	2,256
Bond dealers	1,800	618	1,772	511	1,998	588	2,111	876	2,233	774	2,383	914	2,991	913	6,088	5,054	8,012	6,846	7,719	6,250
Total	2,538	2,538	2,354	2,354	2,641	2,641	3,079	3,079	3,053	3,053	3,344	3,344	4,024	4,024	11,642	11,642	15,635	15,635	14,841	14,841

Source: Compiled from statistics on the Japan Securities Dealers Association website (OTC trading volume by bond type; monthly outstanding amounts of conditional sale and purchase of bonds (*gensaki* transactions) by investor type)

compared to other instruments in the secondary market. More specifically, these short-term government securities dominated the market because in 1986, (1) the government introduced public auction for TBs on the basis of the principle that the government securities must be absorbed by private-sector market participants, and (2) the BOJ stopped reselling FBs that it had underwritten in the secondary market, shifting this operation back to the *gensaki* market, and in 1999 (3) the government introduced public auction for FBs on the basis of aforementioned principle. Subsequently, the issuance of both TBs and FBs has been regular and of large volume.

Although the *gensaki* market developed primarily against the backdrop of this expansion of the short-term government securities market, interest-bearing JGBs have taken center stage in recent years, partially because of the massive overall issuance of government bonds.

10. *Gensaki* Market for Bonds (2)

In an effort to modernize and strengthen the international competitiveness of Japan's money market, the *gensaki* market underwent a reform to improve its functions as a repo market that facilitates the need for both short-term financing and bond borrowing, and thus what came to be called new *gensaki* transactions started in April 2001. Up to that point, *gensaki* transactions were

Chart VI-11.   Working Mechanism of the New *Gensaki* Transaction System

1. Start of transaction

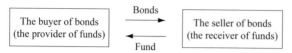

- Purchase money for bonds
  The market price of the bonds prevailing at the time a deal is struck ÷ (1 + haircut rate) × number of bonds traded

2. Control of credit risk during the life of the agreement

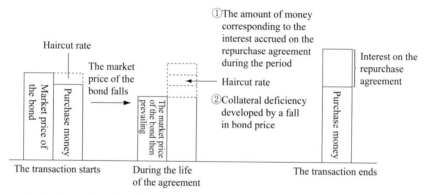

- Credit given to the seller of the bonds by the buyer of the bonds (the provider of funds) = ① + ②
- In the case referred to above, the buyer of the bonds can demand collateral (cash and/or bonds) of the seller, the value of which is equal to the credit given him (margin call).

3. End of transaction

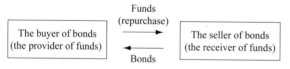

- Money to repurchase the bonds is necessary for the seller at the time the transaction is consummated.
- The money of the buyer is needed to purchase the bonds at the time the transaction started + interest accrued on the repurchase agreement.

bought and sold much like the transactions commonly known as repo trades in the U.S. and Europe but had various shortcomings that cried out for reform. In particular, the *gensaki* market did not have functional risk management facilities or standard rules for dealing with counterparty default. Therefore, measures were taken to establish new *gensaki* transactions, on the basis of conventional ones, in accordance with global standards through the development and expansion of various mechanisms including risk management.

The newly introduced provisions for risk management and other purposes (clauses in the repurchase agreement) may be summed up as follows:

(1) Risk control clause:

The amount of collateral (bonds) shall be adjusted flexibly so as not to cause a shortage of collateral on account of a fall in the price of bonds submitted as collateral.

(i) Application of the ratio for computing the purchase/sale value of bonds (the haircut clause): mechanism is established to ensure that the unit price used in the repurchase agreement is lower by certain rate than the market price of the bonds at the time of execution, so that there is no shortfall in collateral even if the market value of the bonds experiences some decline during the trading period.

(ii) Application of a margin call clause (collateral management, etc.): A mechanism is established to ensure that the amount of credit extended is maintained by adjusting collateral so that the market value of the bonds is consistent with the amount of collateral (i.e.; the buyer has the right to require the seller to put up collateral if the market value of the bonds declines.)

(iii) Application of repricing: In a case in which the market price of the underlying bonds falls sharply from that which prevailed at the time of the repurchase agreement, the parties to the agreement agree to cancel the agreement and renegotiate a new agreement on the basis of the price then prevailing, on terms and conditions identical to those of the agreement thus canceled.

(2) Substitution of underlying bonds:

Under this clause, the seller of bonds can replace the underlying bonds with other bonds with the consent of the buyer, allowing the seller to use the underlying bonds if necessary.

(3) Institution of a netting-out system:

If the other party goes into default for any reason, such as bankruptcy, the value of all transactions covered by the agreement will be reassessed based on market prices, and the difference between claims and obligations will be settled.

11. Bond Lending

When investors have shorted bonds (or sold bonds that they do not own) and failed to buy them back before the settlement date, they turn to bond lending services to borrow bonds to deliver. When the collateral is cash, bond lending

Chart VI-12.   Trading Mechanism of Repurchase Agreements

[Proprietary repurchase agreement]

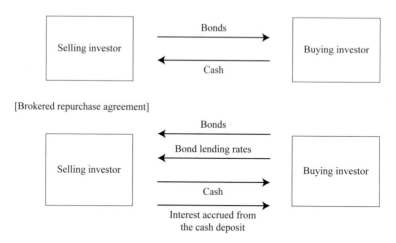

[Brokered repurchase agreement]

Table VI-12.   The Balance of Bond Lending Transactions, by Type of Collateral (on the basis of delivery and face values)

(¥10 billion)

End of	Bonds lent				Bonds borrowed			
	Secured transactions	Secured by cash deposit	Unsecured transactions	Total	Secured transactions	Secured by cash deposit	Unsecured transactions	Total
2011	8,296	8,286	207	8,503	8,296	8,286	207	8,503
2012	8,239	8,200	227	8,467	8,239	8,200	227	8,467
2013	10,085	9,984	267	10,352	10,085	9,984	267	10,352
2014	10,483	10,310	322	10,805	10,483	10,310	322	10,805
2015	9,680	9,454	450	10,130	9,680	9,454	450	10,130
2016	12,316	12,178	428	12,744	12,316	12,178	428	12,744
2017	13,093	12,903	806	13,899	13,093	12,903	806	13,899
2018	5,536	5,370	846	6,382	5,536	5,370	846	6,382
2019	5,589	5,419	1,160	6,749	5,589	5,419	1,160	6,749
2020	5,232	5,041	1,040	6,273	5,232	5,041	1,040	6,273

Note: Breakdowns of bond lending transactions have been published since January 1997. A partial revision was made to the calculation method in January 2009.
Source: Compiled from statistics on the Japan Securities Dealers Association website (bond borrowing and lending transactions - list)

is also used to procure or invest money on a short-term basis similar to *gensaki* transactions. Bond lending services enable investors to execute sell position even if they do not own bonds (short sell), which could lead to improvement of bond market liquidity.

Bond lending was instituted by the lifting of the practical ban on bond short selling in 1989. Traditionally, market participants had refrained from shortselling bonds because of concerns over potential repercussions on brokers' and financial dealers' financial soundness and the potential impact on bond pricing. This ban, however, was lifted to help encourage active market making in cash bonds, and arbitrage between cash bonds and futures. Bond lending was introduced as a means to locate bonds for delivery. Initially, cash collateral bond borrowing and lending was restricted in light of potential conflicts with the *gensaki* market and other considerations, and, subsequently, most transactions were uncollateralized. However, with credit fears rising, the bond lending market remained stagnant and cash collateral bond borrowing and lending transactions were effectively deregulated in 1996 in order to invigorate the market.

When viewed from a legal standpoint, a bond lending transaction is deemed to be a contract for a loan for consumption. A borrower borrows bonds for the purpose of consumption and, when due, the borrower has only to return bonds identical in kind and quantity with those originally borrowed. Bond lending transactions may be broadly classified into "secured transactions" and "unsecured transactions" depending on whether they are collateralized or not. Secured bond lending transactions may be further divided into "cash-collateralized transactions" and "securities-collateralized transactions" by the type of collateral being pledged. Cash-collateralized transactions used to borrow specific bond issues are called SC *torihiki* (specified collateral trades), while those without such specifications that mainly aim for financing and cash management are termed GC *torihiki* (general collateral trades). The size of the bond lending market (in terms of the balance of outstanding loans) has generally been on the rise since cash-collateralized transactions were deregulated in 1996. The market has grown from approximately ¥34 trillion at the end of fiscal 1996 (including approximately ¥17 trillion in cash-collateralized transactions) to ¥139 trillion at the end of fiscal 2017 (including approximately ¥129 trillion in cash-collateralized transactions). At the end of fiscal 2020, the market had fallen to around ¥63 trillion (including approximately ¥50 trillion in cash-collateralized transactions), reflecting the recent trend toward increased usage of *gensaki* transactions.

CHAPTER VII

Investment Trusts

1. Overview

An investment trust is a financial instrument that raises money from plural number of investors in order to establish a large fund that it invests in regarding a variety of assets, such as stocks and bonds, under the management of an investment specialist, and the profits earned through that investment are then distributed among the investors in proportion to their contributions.

An investment trust allows investors to indirectly enter various asset markets even with a small amount of money as well as to enjoy the benefits of scale economies and efficient diversified investment that are generated through a joint investment with other investors, also allowing them to take advantage of information analysis and investment sophistication gained by having the investment managed by specialists. The repayment of the principal of an investment trust is not guaranteed, because its earnings depend upon its performance. There are a variety of investment trusts depending on investment instruments and methods, including one that is similar to deposit and savings accounts and another that is like derivatives trading in that it aims at achieving higher earnings by assuming higher risks.

The overall structure of the Japanese investment trust system is stipulated in the Act on Investment Trusts and Investment Corporations. Regulations concerning the actions of investment trust management companies, the key players in the management of investment trusts, are defined in the Financial Instruments and Exchange Act. Investor protection is also provided by self-regulatory rules established by The Investment Trusts Association, Japan (JITA), an approved self-regulatory organization under the Financial Instruments and Exchange Act.

Investment trusts play a major role in making investments for the general public and have the economic benefit of helping companies to raise money by bringing the funds of the general public to the securities market. They also perform the function of contributing to the reasonable determination of prices in the securities markets as an institutional investor.

Chart VII-2 shows the growth of the total net assets of publicly offered in-

Chart VII-1.   Investment Trust Concept

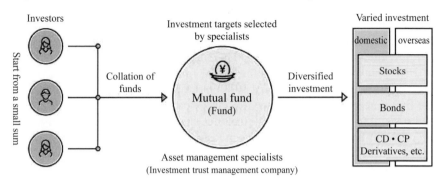

Source: The Investment Trusts Association, Japan.

Chart VII-2.   Trend of Total Net Assets of Publicly Offered Investment Trusts and Their Positions

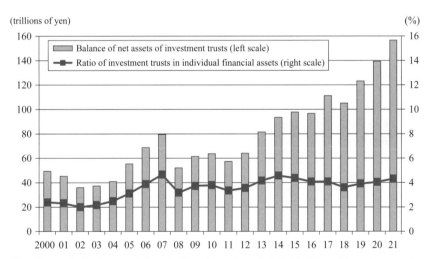

Note: Figures for 2021 are as of the end of June (percentages in individual financial assets are as of the end of May).

Source: Balance of net assets of investment trusts: the Investment Trusts Association, Japan; ratio of investment trusts in individual financial assets: Bank of Japan "Flow of Funds Accounts".

vestment trusts over the past 20 years in Japan. The outstanding balance declined after the burst of the bubble economy but rebounded temporarily around 2005 along with the recovery of the stock market encouraged by a heightening of investment awareness among the people of the country in an ultralow-interest-rate environment. The outstanding balance fell again, a drop of 35% year on year, following the global financial crisis in 2008. Nevertheless, it hit the bottom in January 2009 and topped the ¥100 trillion level for the first time in May 2015. The COVID-19 pandemic hit in March 2020, but had generally little impact on the balance throughout the course of the year. As of the end of 2020, Japan accounted for only 2.4% of the net assets total of the world's publicly offered open-ended investment trust of more than $57.4 trillion (¥5,920 trillion), a small share compared with Japan's approximately 5.9% share of the world gross domestic product (GDP). This suggests that there is high growth potential for investment trusts in Japan, so it is expected that investment trusts will grow as a core product to accelerate the shift from "saving" to "asset-building" in the future.

2. History of Investment Trusts

A product of the investment trust, a collective investment scheme, has proved popular in various forms around the world since its inception in the U.K. in the late nineteenth century.

In Japan, investment trusts existed before World War 2; however, the current system started with the implementation of the Securities Investment Trust Act in June 1951, taking the form of unit-type stock investment trust (contractual type). It was not naturally generated from demands from investors as in the U.S. and Europe but was politically introduced for a supply-and-demand adjustment of stocks substantially released as a result of the break-up of the zaibatsu financial combines (democratization of securities) and in order to raise money for revivifying industries during the postwar period, when there was a severe lack of funds.

The Securities Investment Trust Act was partially amended in 1967 after the securities crisis, to establish the code of conduct for investment trust management companies; to clarify the fiduciary duty of investment trust management companies to beneficiaries (persons who process operations for others in trust are required to act only for the benefit of the others); and to adopt and strengthen provisions on prohibited activities. In 1995, a major reform was conducted, mainly for the purpose of advancing deregulation and greater disclosure.

The drastic amendments to the law made in 1998 were associated with implementation of the Act on Revision, etc. of Related Acts for the Financial

Table VII-1.   History of the Investment Trust in Japan (Post-war)

System	Products	Marketing	Management
The Securities Investment Trust Act was implemented (1951)	Investment trusts were launched in the form of unit-type investment trusts (1951)	Investment trusts became available at securities companies	Assets were invested mainly in domestic stocks
	Open-type investment trust was launched (1952)		
Investment trust management business was separated from securities companies (beginning operations in 1960)	Bond investment trusts were established (1961)		The weight of domestic bonds substantially increased (1961)
The Securities Investment Trust Act was amended to add provisions for the duty of loyalty of investment trust management companies to beneficiaries and the duty of disclosure, etc. (1967)			
		The marketing of foreign investment trusts in Japan was liberalized (1972)	Foreign securities began to be included in assets of investment trusts (1970)
Investment trust management companies entered the investment advisory business (1984)	The medium-term government bond investment trusts were established (1980)		
Foreign companies entered Japanese investment trust management business (1990)			
Bank affiliates entered investment trust management business (1993)	MMFs were established (1992)	Investment trust management companies started to sell investment trusts directly (1993)	
Investment trust reform was determined (1994) Reform was implemented in 1995	Nikkei 300 Exchange Traded Fund was established (1995)		Investment restrictions were deregulated, including utilization of derivatives for purposes other than hedging (1995)
Act on Revision, etc. of Related Acts for the Financial System Reform was implemented (1998)	Private placement investment trusts were launched (1999)	Banks and insurance companies started to sell investment trusts (1998)	
The Act on Investment Trusts and Investment Corporations was implemented (2000)	Corporation type investment trusts were established (2000)		Target of investment trusts expanded to a variety of fields, including real estate (2000)
Portfolio valuation method of bond investment trusts shifted to market value accounting (2001)	Real estate investment trusts were established (2001)	The Act on Sales, etc. of Financial Instruments was implemented (2001)	Some MMFs' net asset value fell below their principle amount (2001)
Defined contribution pension plaus started (2001)	In-kind contribution ETFs were listed (2001)	Sales of investment trusts started at post offices (2005)	
The Financial Instruments and Exchange Act was implemented (2007)			Target of investment trusts was expanded to commodities (2008)
			ETF purchases by BOJ began (2010)
Launch of NISA (2014)	Monthly distribution investment trusts are popular		Implementation of credit risk regulations (2014)
		FSA promotes customer-first business practices (2017)	MMF balances go to zero on negative interest rates (2017)
	ESG investment trusts are popular	Introduction of Critical Information Sheet (2021)	

Source: Materials prepared by Mr. Koji Sugita (modified by the author)

System Reform. As a result of the amendments, the corporation type investment trust, the mainstream in the U.S. and Europe, was introduced in Japan, where only the contractual type had existed, deregulating the establishment of new funds by changing from an approval system to a filing system, and allowing investment trust management companies to outsource the management of the fund to outside companies. Distribution channels were also expanded to financial institutions, and banks became able to distribute investment trusts. Disclosure was enhanced by obligating investment trusts to meet disclosure requirements under the Securities and Exchange Act.

In 2000, investment objects were expanded to those other than securities. This allowed investment trust management companies to establish the "real estate investment trust." The law was renamed "the Act on Investment Trusts and Investment Corporations," deleting the word "Securities." Amendments were made to include additionally the duty of due care of a prudent management (investment fund management companies are required to give instructions on asset management of investment trusts as good managers) in the rules of conduct for investment trust management companies.

In 2006, in relation to the enactment of the Financial Instruments and Exchange Act (implemented at the end of September 2007), the Act on Investment Trusts and Investment Corporations was amended to relegate provisions on the rules of conduct for investment trust management companies. Further, in 2014, risk regulations on managed assets were also introduced.

In recent years, NISA (Nippon Individual Savings Account, a small-amount investment tax exemption scheme) and defined contribution pensions systems, such as iDeCo, as well as wrap accounts haven been developed. The investment trust industry, being well aware of the expectations that its products and services will be utilized and developed in a healthy manner, requests the distributers to be fully compliant with customer-first business practices.

3. Forms of Investment Trusts

Investment trusts are broadly classified into the contractual type and the corporation type.

Contractual Type (Investment Trust)

Contractual type investment trusts take such legal form as a trust or a common fund; in Japan the contractual type investment trust takes the legal form of a trust and is subclassified into investment trusts with investment instructions from trustors and those without investment instructions from trustors.

An investment trust with investment instructions from trustors involves

Chart VII-3.   The Operating Structure of Investment Trusts with Instructions from Trustors

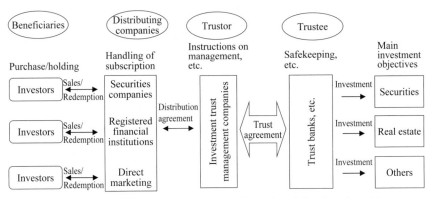

Source: Partially adjusted flowchart from the Investment Trusts Association, Japan's report on "Investment Trusts in Japan 2014."

Chart VII-4.   Operating Structure of Corporation Type (Investment Corporation) Investment Trusts

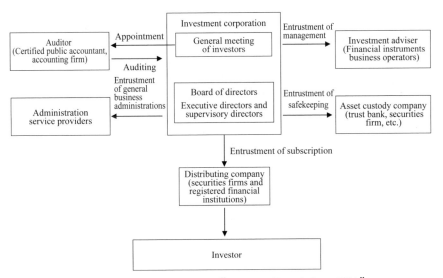

Source: The Investment Trusts Association, Japan, "Investment Trusts in Japan 2014."

three players: the trustor, the trustee, and the beneficiary. The trustor is an asset management company (investment trust management company) registered with the Financial Services Agency. It carries out product development, prepares a trust deed and files it with the authorities, and provides investment instructions to a trustee (it has the authority to outsource the investment instructions to outside companies). The trustee is a trust company or a bank concurrently engaging in the trust business of holding and administrating assets under investment trusts according to a trust agreement. Investors obtain the position of beneficiary by accepting a beneficiary certificate and receive the profits arising from investment management as dividends or by redeeming the certificate. This structure is illustrated in the figure on the right.

In the case of an investment trust without investment instructions from trustors, the trustee enters into a trust agreement with two or more investors and combines their funds into a trust asset, which is then invested mainly in specified assets excluding securities and held and administrated by the trustee without instructions from the trustors.

Corporation Type (Investment Corporation)

The corporation type is operated in a legal form that is similar to a corporation. In Japan, an investment corporation with a corporate veil is established and operated by officers who are appointed by an investors meeting, but it must entrust its business, such as asset management, custody of the fund's assets, general business administration, and the handling of subscriptions, to outside companies. Investors obtain the position of shareholder by accepting share certificates (investment certificates) issued by the investment corporation and receive the profits arising from the investment management as dividends. Chart VII-4 illustrates such a structure.

Both the contractual type and the corporation type of investment trusts in the world include the open-end type and the closed-end type. Which type they are grouped into depends on the claims of investors to redeem issued certificates. The open-end type accepts the beneficiary's request and redeems the certificates at market price by selling trust assets, while the closed-end type does not accept the beneficiary's request to redeem the beneficiary's certificates. The latter ensures liquidity by listing its issued certificates. In Japan, contractual type investment trusts are principally of the open-end type, while corporation type investment trusts, in particular, real estate investment trusts, are of the closed-end type.

4. Investment Trust Products

The total net assets of broadly defined investment trust products amounted to

Chart VII-5.   Overview of Investment Trusts (total net assets, number of funds)
As of June 30, 2021

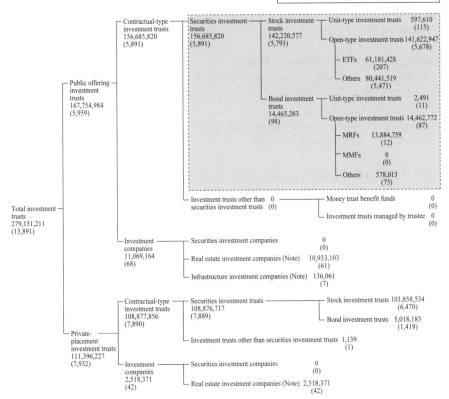

Note: Figures on real estate investment companies and infrastructure investment companies are from the previous month.
Source: The Investment Trusts Association, Japan.

¥279 trillion in Japan as of the end of June 2021. They are classified by a variety of methods.

Public Offering of Investment Trusts and Private Placements of Investment Trusts

A public offering of investment trusts is offered to 50 or more unspecified investors, while a private placement is sold to Qualified Institutional Investors or specified investors stipulated in the Financial Instruments and Exchange

Act or to fewer than 50 investors. Establishment of a private placement was made possible by the 1998 amendment to the Investment Trust Act. It has the margin to freely design products only with the approval of the investors, because a private placement is subject to less-rigid investment restrictions than a public offering. Therefore, privately placed funds attract the attention of large investors, in particular institutional investors, and rapidly increase in volume as funds invested in by variable annuities, etc.

Stock and Bond Investment Trusts
The Japanese tax laws define stock investment trusts as funds that hold even a small number of stocks, and bond investment trusts are funds that invest not in stocks but only in bonds. Bond investment trusts include funds that invest mainly in long-term bonds and Money Reserve Funds (MRF) that invest in short-term money market vehicles.

Unit-Type and Open-Type Investment Trusts
Unit-type investment trusts are funds that do not allow additional subscriptions after having accepted funds in principal value only during their initial subscription period, while open-end investment trusts are funds that do accept additional subscriptions at market value after their establishment. In Japan, investment trusts were launched in the form of the unit type, which was similar to savings instruments, in 1951; however, open-end investment trusts have currently become a mainstream, just as in overseas markets.

Classification by Investment Object
The Investment Trusts Association, Japan, offers a product classification according to the object of investment of the funds, so that investors can select funds easily. The prospectus of each funds must clearly describe into which classification the fund fall.

Exchange Traded Funds (ETF)
Among open-type funds, funds whose net asset value fluctuates closely with various indexes, including the stock indexes, and whose units are listed on exchanges and traded like stocks are called ETF. (In the U.S., actively managed ETFs also exist.) They are formed by the in-kind contribution of stocks by designated participants and others, and the units/shares of many ETFs can be exchanged for the component stocks held in a timely manner. This creates arbitrage opportunities with the component stocks, a mechanism that keeps the gap between the traded prices of the fund on the exchange and the indexes targeted by the fund within a small range.

5. Sale of Investment Trusts

The subscription and sale of investment trusts had been practiced only by securities companies in Japan since the establishment of investment trusts in 1951. (Some investment trust management companies started direct marketing in the 1990s.) The entries of financial institutions, including banks, in 1998 and some post offices in October 2005 expanded the distribution network rapidly. The share of publicly offered investment trusts sold through financial institutions was once over 40%, but as of June 2021, this has declined to 21%. On the other hand, the share of privately placed investment trusts was almost 50% from the beginning, and has been as high as 80% in recent years. In contrast, investment trust management companies saw weak growth in direct marketing, partially due to the exit of large companies related to securities companies (as such companies absorbed the sales).

Investment trusts were generally sold on an over the counter basis from distributing companies and through sales agents. Recently, the number of online transactions has also grown. According to a JSDA survey in 2021, 20.6% via securities company, and 9.9% via financial institution, of respondents said that they used internet to place orders to buy or sell investment trusts.

Distributing companies are subject to the Financial Instruments and Exchange Act, Act on Sales, etc. of Financial Instruments and the regulations of the Japan Securities Dealers Association, and they are obliged to comply with the rules on sales of the Investment Trusts Association, Japan. For example, they must comply with the suitability rule, which requires distributing companies not to engage in inappropriate solicitation activities in light of customers' knowledge, experience, investment purpose, and assets and to assume "accountability" for risk factors, including market and credit risk, and for important portions in the structure of transactions and to maintain the "duty of sincerity to customers" not to conduct "prohibited activities" at the time of sale, such as providing conclusive evaluations. Depository institutions, such as banks, shall be required to take measures to prevent customers from mistaking investment trusts for deposits at the sale of investment trusts, including explaining that they are not covered by the deposit insurance system. As a part of the enhancement of accountability at the implementation of the Financial Instruments and Exchange Act in 2007, the "duty to deliver documents prior to the conclusion of a contract" was introduced. For investment trusts, the requirement is satisfied by delivering the eligible prospectus. Furthermore, "Critical Information Sheets" to help customers compare products with investment risk for the advancement of "customer-first business practices" were introduced from 2021.

The sales commission for investment trusts, which had been determined

Chart VII-6. Breakdown of Total Net Assets of Publicly Offered Stock Investment Trusts by Distribution Channel (As of June 30, 2021)

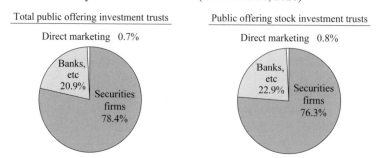

Chart VII-7. Changes in Composition of Total Net Assets of Publicly Offered Investment Trusts by Distribution Channel

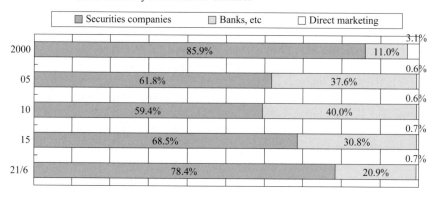

Chart VII-8. Changes in Breakdown of Total Net Assets of Overall Private Placement Trusts by Distribution Channel

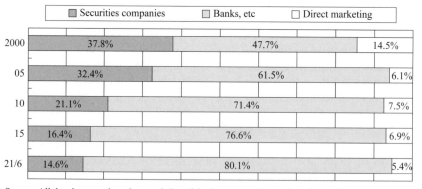

Source: All the above are based on statistics of the Investment Trusts Association, Japan.

by the fund, was liberalized in Japan as a result of amendments to the business rules of the Investment Trusts Association, Japan, in 1998. At present, different companies can charge different commissions even for the same fund. There have also been reductions in commissions and a diversification of commission systems.

6. Investment Management of Investment Trusts

Investment trusts invest mainly in "specified assets" defined by the Order for Enforcement of the Act on Investment Trusts and Investment Corporations. (As of September 2019, the specified assets consist of 12 types of assets, including securities, real estate, and rights associated with derivatives trading.) Funds investing mainly in securities are called securities investment trusts.

Chart VII-9 shows the distribution of assets under the management of publicly offered securities investment trusts as of June 2021. Reflecting an improvement in stock market conditions, the ratio of stocks is high while the ratio of bonds is declining due to low interest rates. Moreover, blue-chip stocks are being given preference in the selection of the domestic stocks included in the funds, such as electric, information and communications stocks.

In operating business activities, investment trust management companies, which invest their assets according to the investment policies described in the prospectus of funds, are subject to the Special Provisions Concerning the Investment Management Business of the Financial Instruments and Exchange Act. They assume the duty of sincerity to customers and the duty of loyalty and the duty of due care of a prudent management to the beneficiaries; they also are prohibited from undertaking following activities: (1) transactions between the investment trust management company and its directors/executive officers; (2) transactions among funds under management (excluding certain portions); (3) transactions for the purpose of its own benefit or the benefit of a third party by taking advantage of the changes in price of specific financial instruments resulting from such transactions; (4) transactions whose terms are different from those of ordinary transactions and that affect adversely the benefits of beneficiaries; (5) transactions of securities and other transactions for its own account by using the information for investment management; and (6) cases in which an investment trust management company or some third party provides beneficiaries or a third party with compensation to offset a loss or increase profit. As firewalls it is prohibited to execute unnecessary transactions in light of the investment management policy to promote profits of other businesses or of the parent company, subsidiaries, etc.. Additionally, the Investment Trust Act imposes a restriction on investment trust management companies prohibiting them from giving instructions to acquire stocks

Chart VII-9. Distribution of Assets of Investment Trusts in Japan (as of June 30, 2021, total publicly offered securities investment trusts)

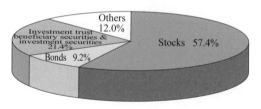

Chart VII-10. Breakdown by Industry Group of Domestic Stocks Held by Investment Trusts (publicly offered stock investment trusts as of the end of June 2021)

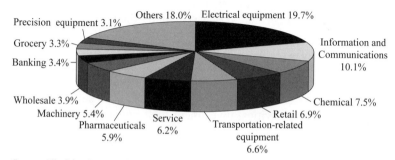

Source: All of the charts on this page are based on data from the Investment Trust Association, Japan.

of the same issuing company when the number of stocks held by all investment trusts managed by the given investment trusts management company exceeds 50% of the total number of outstanding stocks of that same issuing company. The Investment Trusts Association, Japan, has self-regulatory rules concerning investment instruments and investment methods in addition to those concerning credit risk regulations.

The Investment Trust Act stipulates that an investment trust management company exercises the rights of shareholders, including voting rights, on portfolio stocks. Investment trust management companies disclose their basic policies and the results of the exercise of voting rights on their websites. Additionally, in accordance with Japan's Stewardship Code formulated in 2014, activities to promote engagement by listed companies are also under way.

Table VII-2. Exercise of Voting Rights for Domestic Stocks at General Shareholders Meetings by Investment Trust Management Companies (One year until June 2020)
— Voting on Items Proposed by Companies, Total for 71 Companies that Invest in Domestic Stocks —

Name of proposal		For (A)	Against (B)	Abstain (C)	Blank mandate (D)	Total Against and Abstain (E) (B)+(C)	Total number of proposals (E) (A)+(E)+(D)	Percentage of votes against, etc. (E)/(F) %
Proposal about Establishment of Organs	Election and Dismissal of Directors (*1)	343,917	40,733	659	0	41,392	385,309	11%
	Election and Dismissal of Company auditors (*1)	50,937	8,658	18	0	8,676	59,613	15%
	Election and Dismissal of Accounting Auditors	1,203	14	2	0	16	1,219	1%
Proposal about Remuneration for Officers	Remuneration for Officers (*2)	16,364	1,520	16	0	1,536	17,900	9%
	Payment of Retirement benefits for Retired Officer	1,210	1,658	2	0	1,660	2,870	58%
Proposal about Capital policy (except for Proposal about Articles of Association)	Disposal of surplus	32,302	945	55	0	1,000	33,302	3%
	Reorganization related (*3)	690	24	0	0	24	714	3%
	Introduction/update/abolition of takeover defense measures	167	1,661	1	0	1,662	1,829	91%
	Other capital policy proposal (*4)	1,091	73	0	0	73	1,164	6%
Proposal about Articles of Association		10,256	368	3	0	371	10,627	3%
Total of Other proposals		205	60	0	0	60	265	23%
Total		458,342	55,714	756	0	56,470	514,812	11%

*1 Revision of executive compensation, issuance of stock options, introduction/revision of performance-based compensation system, officer bonus, etc.
*2 Merger, business transfer/acquisition, share exchange, share transfer, company split.
*3 Purchase of treasury shares, decrease in statutory reserve, capital increase by third-party allotment, capital decrease, share consolidation, issuance of class shares, etc.
Source: Compiled by the author from data of the Investment Trusts Association, Japan.

7. Customer Base of Investment Trusts

The chart on the right shows the breakdown of investment trust beneficiaries (in terms of value) in Japan. Over 30% of investment trust assets are held by households, and nearly 40% by financial institutions, followed by insurance companies and pension funds. Compared to the U.S., households and insurance companies and pension funds account for less proportion. Purchase from private pensions remains low profile, while financial institutions are active buyers of private placement investment trusts. Meanwhile, the holding ratio of the BOJ has increased as the central bank expanded its ETF purchase.

The penetration of investment trusts into household financial assets is low. A 2021 survey that was conducted by the Japan Securities Dealers Association indicates that only 10.1% of the adult population holds investment trusts. That ratio is extremely down from the level of more than 16% in 1988 during the bubble economy. The penetration shows a sign of recovery after reaching the bottom of 6.1% in 2003. By age group, the holding rate of investment trusts is almost 15% for people aged 55 or more, while it is only 0 to 10% for people in their 20s. It is noticeable that the holding rate is extremely low in young people. Although not shown in the chart, the average penetration of investment trusts among households in the U.S. is 46%, with 54% within Generation X (40-55 years), 44% within Baby Boomers (56-74 years), and as high as 47% within the younger generation of Millennials (under 39 years). (as of 2020) It is desired also in Japan that enhancing the individual-type defined-contribution pension plan, including NISA, Junior NISA, Dollar-Cost Averaging NISA and iDeCo, will drive an increase in the holding of investment trusts among the younger age groups.

According to a 2020 Investment Trust Association survey, the average total amount of investment trust purchases was ¥3.62 million. In terms of the number of subscribers, 38.5% of subscribers spent less than ¥1 million, 20.1% spent between ¥1 million to ¥3 million, while 10.2% spent more than ¥10 million (non-applicable responses were 10.2%).

Many investors had previously answered that there was no specific investment purpose for their purchase investment trusts ("saving up in case of illness or disaster" is a typical and somewhat vague response). Recently, however, more and more people are giving "post-retirement living expenses" as their reason for buying investment trusts.

In the U.S., the majority of individuals buy investment trusts for their retirement. In many cases, Americans continuously purchase the trusts via accounts for defined contribution pension plans, including the 401k. (This results in a higher holding rate among the young and middle-aged groups.) In contrast, many buyers do not have any specific purpose in Japan. In many

Chart VII-11.   Breakdown of Holders of Investment Trusts (as of the end of 2020)

Japan   (Reference) U.S.

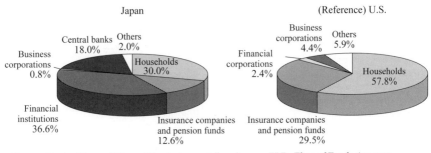

Source: Bank of Japan, "Flow of Funds Accounts".   *Source:* FRB, *Flow of Funds Accounts.*

Table VII-3.   Profiles of Individual Investors Holding Investment Trusts (2021)

Investment trust holding ratio by age			Investment trust holding ratio by annual income	
	Male	Female		
Aged 20 to 24	2.9%	2.3%	Less than ¥1 million	5.7%
Aged 25 to 29	7.3%	4.7%	¥1 million or above, less than ¥2 million	8.5%
Aged 30 to 34	10.6%	7.5%	¥2 million or above, less than ¥3 million	9.4%
Aged 35 to 39	12.8%	7.2%	¥3 million or above, less than ¥4 million	11.7%
Aged 40 to 44	12.1%	10.4%	¥4 million or above, less than ¥5 million	13.1%
Aged 45 to 49	11.5%	8.3%	¥5 million or above, less than ¥7 million	16.8%
Aged 50 to 54	6.9%	6.0%	¥7 million or above, less than ¥10 million	20.4%
Aged 55 to 59	18.6%	12.0%	¥10 million or above	32.7%
Aged 60 to 64	15.1%	11.0%		
Aged 65 to 69	17.0%	10.2%		
Aged 70 to 74	14.3%	11.4%		
Aged 75 to 79	15.2%	7.8%		
Aged 80 to 84	15.2%	5.6%		
Aged 85 to 89	3.2%	5.3%		
Aged 90 or above	0.0%	3.3%		
Overall average: 10.1%				

Note: 7,000 respondents overall.
Source: JSDA "Nationwide Survey (on individuals) concerning Securities Investment Trusts)" FY2021
  issue

cases, they do not make monthly payments into investment trusts; rather, they invest a good sum of money at one time, and this is estimated to be largely dependent on the movement of the securities markets.

Table VII-4.   Purpose of Purchasing Financial Instruments by Individual Investors

Japan		(Reference) U.S.A.	
Living expenses after retirement	70.0%	Funds after retirement	75%
Saving in case of possible illness or accident	60.9%	To prepare for emergencies	6%
Education funds for children	30.4%	Supplementary to current revenue	5%
No particular purpose, but having financial assets makes me feel more secure	18.6%	Education funds	5%
Funds for purchasing durable consumer goods	18.4%	Funds to purchase house or other large item	4%
Funds for travel and leisure	14.3%	Reduction of taxable income	3%
Funds for acquiring a house or extending it (including land)	12.0%	Others	2%
Funds for children's marriage	4.1%		

Source: Japan: Central Council for Financial Services "Survey of household finances; Household survey
of 2 or more people 2020" Multiple answers allowed up to 3
U.S.A.: ICI "Profile of Mutual Fund Shareholders" 2020 Single answer responses to survey on
"Primary Purpose of Owning Mutual Funds"

8.   Disclosure of Investment Trusts

Until 1997, disclosure of investment trusts was covered not by the Securities
and Exchange Act but by the framework defined in the Securities Investment
Trust Act (now the Act on Investment Trusts and Investment Corporations).
Following the deregulation of the establishment of funds, in which the filing
system replaced the approval system, as a result of the enforcement of the
Act on Revision, etc. of Related Acts for the Financial System Reform in
1998, the Securities and Exchange Act (now the Financial Instruments and
Exchange Act) was applied to investment trusts the same as to stocks, etc.
Therefore, publicly offered investment trusts are now subject to both the Investment Trust Act and the Financial Instruments and Exchange Act in terms
of disclosure. Details of disclosure are summarized as follows.

Issuance Disclosure

The Financial Instruments and Exchange Act requires investment trust management companies to make a disclosure at the time of offering by filing the
"securities registration statement" with the competent authority (for public
inspection) and by delivering the "prospectus" to individual investors at the
time of subscription. Given the unique characteristics of the way in which investment trusts are sold (while offering for subscription of stocks is made
only at initial public offering and capital increases, and at other times, investors purchase issued stocks on the secondary market, investment trusts are
continuously offered after establishment of funds by initial subscription), the

Table VII-5.   Publicly Offered Securities Investment Trusts Disclosure System of Japan

	Statutory disclosure				Voluntary disclosure
	Disclosure for supervisory authorities and for public inspection		Individual disclosure for investors		Public disclosure for investors
	FIEA	Act on Investment Trusts and Investment Corporations	FIEA	Act on Investment Trusts and Investment Corporations	The Investment Trusts Association, Japan Rules, etc.
Issuance Disclosure (Disclosure at offering)	Securities Registration Statement Amendment of Securities Registration Statement	Registration on the contents of the agreement	Prospectus (Summary prospectus) (Detailed prospectus)	Document summarizing the contents of the agreement (may be indicated in the prospectus)	Define the Guidelines on Preparation of Prospectus
Periodic Disclosure (disclosure while under management)	Annual Securities Report Semi-annual Securities Report Extraordinary Report	Financial report (investment report)		Financial report (investment report) (Summary financial report) (full-version financial report)	Monthly disclosure of MMF, MRF and timely disclosure on the website of each investment management company

Source: Created by Mr. Koji Sugita

prospectuses were split into two volumes to "provide investors with information in an easy-to-understand manner" in 2004. That is, the two volumes consist of a "summary prospectus," which distributing companies are required to deliver in advance to all investors entering into contracts, and a "detailed prospectus," which distributing companies deliver to investors when requested.

As issuance disclosure, the Investment Trust Act requires investment trust management companies to "notify the details of the basic terms and conditions" to the competent authority and to "deliver documents describing the details of the basic terms and conditions" to the investors. Descriptions in the prospectus are substituted for the latter.

Periodic Disclosure

In terms of disclosure after the establishment of investment trust funds, pursuant to the Financial Instruments and Exchange Act investment trust management companies are required to file their "securities report" to the compe-

Table VII-6.   Major Items in Summary Prospectus (Explanatory Document) of Publicly Offered Investment Trust

Items recorded	Contents recorded
(Items recorded on the front page, etc.)	
(1) Name of fund and product category	Name of the fund indicated on the securities registration statement and product category in the Guidelines Concerning Product Categories set forth by the Investment Trusts Association, Japan.
(2) Information on investment trust management company, etc.	Name of investment trust management company, date of establishment, paid-in capital, total net asset value of investment trusts managed, website address, telephone number, name of trustee, etc.
(Items recorded in the main text)	
(1) Fund objective and characteristics	Fund characteristics and investment focus based on the basic investment policy, investment attitude, etc. provided in the agreement; Matters reflecting the fund characteristics, e.g., fund structure, investment method, investment process, investment restrictions, and distribution policy; If investment management is outsourced, the name of the investment manager and the content of outsourcing
(2) Investment risks	Factors underlying fluctuations in standard price, risk management system, comparison with other assets
(3) Investment performance	(i) Transition of standard prices and net assets in the last decade—standard prices illustrated using a line graph; net assets illustrated using a bar or area graph (ii) Transition of distributions in the last decade (iii) Status of core assets—top 10 portfolio issues, ratio by industry, ratio by asset type, etc. (iv) Transition of annual earnings ratio in the last decade—illustrated using a bar graph. For funds with benchmarks, also indicate the percentage changes of benchmarks
(4) Procedure, commission, etc.	(i) Subscription memo (purchase price, application procedure, trust period, taxes, etc.) (ii) Fund costs (commission at purchase, partial redemption charge, investment management cost (trust fees) and allocation thereof, other expenses, taxes
(5) Additional information	If there is a need to provide explanations on fund characteristics and risks in a greater detail (e.g., for fund of funds, use of structured bonds and derivatives), the details

Source: Cabinet Office Order on Disclosure of Information on Regulated Securities and the JITA Rules on Preparation of Summary Prospectus.

tent authority after the end of each accounting period (for public inspection). (Semi-annual securities reports are also filed when funds settle accounts once a year.)

As for periodic disclosure, pursuant to the Investment Trust Act investment trust management companies are required to deliver their "financial report" to individual investors. In 2014, it was decided that the financial report would be made available in two phases based on an approach similar to having two volumes of prospectuses as described above: a summary financial report issued to all beneficiaries and a financial report (full version) publicized on the website of the management company and issued to beneficiaries upon request.

In addition, the Investment Trusts Association, prescribes in its self-regulatory rules a requirement for each investment trust management company, to make a timely disclosure on its website, to post and this disclosure is performed at least monthly for each fund.

9. Services and Products Based on Investment Trusts

Cash Management Account

This is a combination of the securities trading accounts of securities companies and money reserve funds (MRFs), open-end bond investment trusts for the account, via auto transfer. Recently, the MRFs can be replaced with bank accounts in some cases. The account invests its remaining idle monies, including the interest on bonds, dividends on stocks, and proceeds from the sale of securities in MRFs and also offers such services as payment on the acquisition of securities, cash advance on ATMs, and securities-backed loans. The account was established in October 1997 on the model of the CMA (Cash Management Account) funds developed in 1977 by Merrill Lynch in the U.S. The Investment Trusts Association, Japan, imposes rules on MRFs on investment management, including one stipulating that investments should be made to financial instruments with high credibility and with a short term up to maturity in light of liquidity and security.

Wrap Account

A wrap account is a product that securities companies, etc. bundle and for which they offer a set of asset management services, including the determination and rebalancing of asset allocation and the selection of individual issues and management reports, only in exchange for annual fees to customers' balance of assets (no commission resulting from trading). Wrap accounts, which invest their assets in investment trusts only, were commercialized following liberalization of sales commissions for investment trusts in 1998 and after obtaining permission to engage in the discretionary investment management business by securities companies. Wrap accounts are also commercialized to offer asset management services with individual issues, such as

Chart VII-12.   Outline of a Securities General Account

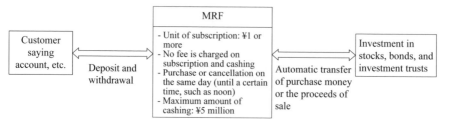

Source: Author of chapter.

Chart VII-13.   Flow of Wrap Account Service (example)

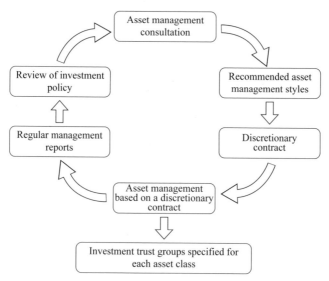

Source: Information compiled by reference to Daiwa Securities website etc.

stocks, as a result of the complete liberalization of brokerage commissions in October 1999.

Defined Contribution Pension Plans (e.g., Japanese 401k, iDeCo)

Partially backed by the increasing mobility of the employed and a deterioration in the financial positions of DB (defined benefit) corporate pensions, DC (defined contribution) pension plans offering high portability began to be offered in 2001. The participants in corporate DC plans invest their company contributions (contributions to the reserves by employees have been permitted since 2012), and participants in individual-type DC plans (referred to as "iDeCo") invest their own distributions in investment instruments, including investment trusts, deposits and savings, and insurance, at their own responsibility. Their performances are reflected in future receivable pensions. Many investment trust companies offer low-cost funds exclusively for individual-type defined-contribution pension funds.

Variable Annuities
Variable annuities, which were launched in full scale in 1999, are products offered by insurance companies. Just as with the defined contribution pension plans, variable annuities also invest premiums from policyholders in investment trusts, and receivable pension amounts are determined by their performance. In addition to securities companies, banks have also begun selling these products.

10. Foreign Investment Trusts

The sale of foreign investment trusts created under foreign laws in foreign countries was liberalized in 1972. Initially, foreign investment trusts were subject to regulations that they should be invested mainly in foreign-currency-denominated assets and that a weighting of yen-denominated assets was limited to below 50% of the total assets, in consideration of the effect on domestic investment trusts. However, foreign private placement investment trusts were introduced into Japan, as foreign investment trusts were not subject to the Securities Investment Trust Act. At that time, private-placement investment trusts had yet to be recognized in Japan.

As a result of amendments to the Investment Trust Act in 1998, foreign investment trusts became subject to the same regulations as Japanese investment trusts was under the revised act. Namely, the amendments required foreign investment trust management companies to file the same notification as Japanese investment trusts did at the sale of foreign investment trusts in Japan and allowed Japanese courts to issue an order to prohibit or stop the sale of foreign investment trusts if inappropriate investment management of foreign investment trusts impairs the profits of domestic investors and if there is an urgent necessity to prevent further losses to investors. It was also permitted to introduce yen-denominated funds into Japan, and currently the same tax system as Japanese investment trusts is applied to foreign investment trusts. The disclosure system is also in line with Japanese and foreign investment trusts, including preparation and delivery of a prospectus and financial reports. The Japan Securities Dealers Association has "selection criteria of foreign investment trust beneficiary certificates" in the "rules concerning for-

Table VII-7.   Total Net Assets of Foreign Investment Trusts in Japan (¥100 million) and Their Ratio to Total (Public Offering) Investment Trusts

Year-end	Total net assets of foreign investment trusts (A)	Total net assets of domestic investment trusts (B)	Total (C)	(A)/(C)
2000	36,084	493,992	530,076	6.8%
01	41,426	452,807	494,233	8.4%
02	47,147	360,160	407,307	11.6%
03	54,427	374,356	428,783	12.7%
04	62,411	409,967	472,378	13.2%
05	79,670	553,476	633,146	12.6%
06	87,104	689,276	776,380	11.2%
07	82,427	797,606	880,033	9.4%
08	51,473	521,465	572,938	9.0%
09	59,306	614,551	673,857	8.8%
10	58,800	637,201	696,001	8.4%
11	52,358	573,274	625,632	8.4%
12	57,839	640,600	698,439	8.3%
13	61,290	815,200	876,490	7.0%
14	62,893	935,045	997,938	6.3%
15	54,248	977,562	1,031,810	5.3%
16	53,540	966,415	1,019,955	5.2%
17	60,913	1,111,920	1,172,832	5.2%
18	54,143	1,051,592	1,105,735	4.9%
19	62,094	1,231,723	1,293,817	4.8%
20	65,735	1,394,311	1,460,046	4.5%
21/6	68,183	1,566,858	1,635,041	4.2%

Note: The total net assets of domestic investment trusts are the total net assets of publicly offered invest-ment trusts in Japan.

Source: Total net assets of foreign investment trusts and domestic investment trusts were taken from the Japan Securities Dealers Association and the Investment Trusts Association, Japan, respectively.

eign securities transactions" to set the requirements for foreign funds to be available in Japan.

Table VII-7 shows the trend of total net assets of foreign investment trusts sold in Japan for the recent 20 years. The total net assets had been dependent on the effects of exchange rates, etc. Sales of foreign investment trusts surged in Japan after 1997, reflecting a higher demand for high-yield foreign bonds and a tendency toward a weaker yen during the continued ultralow interest rate. The ratio of foreign investment trust assets to total investment trust as-sets, including domestic investment trusts, was above 13% in 2004. After that, the growth in sales of overseas registered investment trusts came to a halt due to the recovered popularity of domestic stock funds and an increase

Chart VII-14. Breakdown of Total Net Assets of Foreign Investment Trusts in Japan by Product Category

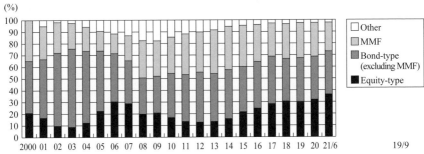

Source: Compiled by the author based on materials disclosed by the Japan Securities Dealers Association.

Chart VII-15. Breakdown of Total Net Assets of Foreign Investment Trusts in Japan by Presentation Currency

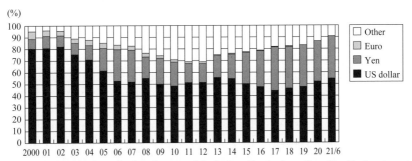

Source: Compiled by the author based on materials disclosed by the Japan Securities Dealers Association.

in monthly dividend paying type funds registered in Japan. Recently, total net assets have fallen below ¥7 trillion yen, and the pace of expansion has been slower than that of domestic investment trusts. By product, as shown in the figure on the right, stock investment trusts increased for a time after 2004 when stock prices recovered globally, and real estate and alternative funds classified in the "others" category also increased. However, broadly-defined bond funds, including MMFs, have continued to be mainstream. Looking at foreign investment trusts by country of establishment, Luxembourg investment trusts enjoyed an overwhelming share of the market in the past, but Cayman investment trusts have increased their share since around 2005. At the end of March 2021, Cayman, Luxembourg, and other investment trusts accounted for 54.5%, 33.8%, and 11.7% in terms of total net assets, respectively.

CHAPTER VIII

The Derivatives Market

1. Futures Trading

"Futures trading" refers to an agreement to buy or sell a specific amount of a commodity or financial instrument at a particular price on a stipulated future date. The history of futures trading is said to be as old as that of commodities trading. However, it is generally believed that the precursor of today's fully developed futures market emerged in Japan as the account-balancing trading in rice (the rice market) conducted in Osaka in the Edo period (1603–1868). This was a method that made it possible for parties to consummate a transaction by organizing one-on-one negotiated transactions in such a way as to enable them to settle the difference without delivery of the underlying commodity or financial instrument and is considered the beginning of Japan's futures trading. By inheriting this tradition, stock futures were traded by settling the difference in the form of forward transactions on the stock exchange in Japan in prewar years. After the war, forward transactions were prohibited by the General Headquarters (GHQ) of the Supreme Commander for the Allied Powers (SCAP) in Japan in order to curb speculative transactions, but some claim that it was partly revived in the form of margin trading with individual investors on the stock market.

In 1972, the Chicago Mercantile Exchange started trading in currency futures. The Chicago Board of Trade started trading in futures on fictitious bonds called benchmark issues in 1974, and the Kansas City Board of Trade started trading in stock index futures in 1982. And these types of futures trading spread to other countries around the world, including the introduction of trading in securities futures in Japan. Long-term government bond futures trading that started on the TSE in 1985 was the first financial futures trading conducted in Japan. More products emerged in quick succession: the OSE's "Osaka Stock Futures 50 (OSF50)" in 1987; the OSE's Nikkei 225 futures contracts trading and the TSE's TOPIX futures trading in 1988; and the Tokyo Financial Exchange Inc. (TFX)'s Japanese yen short-term interest rate futures, U.S. dollar short-term interest rate futures, and yen-dollar currency futures in 1989.

Table VIII-1.   Years in Which Major Financial Futures of the World Were Listed

Year	Other countries	Japan
1972	Currency futures (mark-dollar and yen-dollar) (CME)	
1976	TB futures (CME)	
1977	Treasury bond futures (CBOT)	
1981	Eurodollar interest rate futures (CME)	
1982	S&P 500 futures (CME); T-note futures (CBOT); U.K. government bond futures and pound interest rate futures (LIFFE)	
1984	FTSE 100 futures (LIFFE)	
1985		Long-term government bond futures (TSE)
1986	French government bond futures (MATIF), Nikkei average futures (SIMEX)	
1987	Japanese government bond futures (LIFFE)	
1988	CAC40 futures; PIBOR (Paris interbank offered rate) futures (MATIF); BUND futures (LIFFE)	Nikkei 225 futures (OSE); TOPIX futures (TSE)
1989	Euroyen interest rate futures (SIMEX)	Euroyen short-term interest rate futures (TIFFE)
1990	Euromark interest rate futures (LIFFE); Nikkei average futures (CME); DAX futures and BUND futures (DTB)	
1991	Interbank interest rate futures (BM&F)	
1992	USD/RUB currency futures (MICEX)	
1996	Euroyen interest rate futures (LIFFE); NASDAQ 100 futures (CME); KOSPI 200 futures (KSE)	
1997	E-mini S&P 500 futures (CME)	
1998	EURIBOR futures (LIFFE), Euro STOXX 50 futures (EUREX)	
1999	E-mini NASDAQ 100 futures (CME)	
2000	CNX Nifty Index futures (NSE)	
2001	Single stock futures (LIFFE), FTSE China A50 (SGX)	
2004	VIX index futures (CFE)	
2005	RTS stock price index futures (RTS)	
2006		Exchange FOREX margin contracts (TFX)
2008	Russell 2000 futures (ICE)	Nikkei 225 mini futures (OSE)
2010	CSI 300 futures (CFFEX)	
2019	Micro E-mini S&P 500 futures (CME), Micro E-mini Nasdaq 100 futures (CME)	

Note: BM&F: Brazilian Mercantile and Futures Exchange (presently BM&F BOVESPA), CBOT: Chicago Board of Trade, CFE: CBOE Futures Exchange, CFFEX: China Financial Futures Exchange, CME: Chicago Mercantile Exchange, DTB: Deutsche Terminbörse (presently Eurex), ICE: ICE Futures U.S., KSE: Korea Stock Exchange (presently KRX), LIFFE: London International Futures and Options Exchange (presently ICE Futures Europe), MATIF: Marché à Terme International de France (presently Euronext Paris), MICEX: Moscow Interbank Currency Exchange (presently Moscow Exchange), NSE: National Stock Exchange of India, RTS: Russian Trading System (presently Moscow Exchange), SIMEX: Singapore International Monetary Exchange (presently SGX), TSE: Tokyo Stock Exchange; OSE: Osaka Securities Exchange (presently Osaka Exchange), TFX: Tokyo Financial Futures Exchange (presently Tokyo Financial Exchange).

In English, "futures contracts" are transactions that are traded on the exchange, however while a futures contract can be transferred to a third party, a margin has to be deposited to provide against non-performance of the contract. Whereas a "forward contract" is a transaction between parties that cannot be transferred to a third party, and does not require a deposit of a margin. Transactions in currency or short-term interest-rate futures are forward contracts often negotiated between a bank and its client, and they are called forward-exchange agreements (FXA) or forward-rate agreements (FRA). Along with swap trading, these two types of transactions played a leading role in boosting the derivatives markets around the world in the 1990s.

2. Bond Futures Trading

Trading in securities futures (Government National Mortgage Association [GNMA] certificates) started in 1974 in the United States. Trading in 10-year government bond futures started on the Tokyo Stock Exchange in 1985 with the backup that they were issued in massive amounts. This was the first financial futures trading in Japan. In 1988, superlong-term (20-year) government bond futures (discontinued in 2002, but resumed in 2014) were listed on the Tokyo Stock Exchange, and trading in U.S. Treasury bond futures, which had the largest trading volume in the world, started on the Tokyo Stock Exchange in 1989. With the trading in medium-term (5-year) government note futures that started on the Tokyo Stock Exchange in 1996, Japan had finally developed a product mix comparable to that of other countries.

Bond futures are generally traded on the basis of a fictitious issue called a benchmark issue whose price is assumed to indicate the level of yield curve then prevailing. Therefore, the price of bond futures is formed in the belief that the prices of individual bonds are above the yield curve of the benchmark issue or above a yield curve that runs parallel to it. Because a seller can choose an issue just as in a regular settlement, the seller chooses the most reasonably priced issue at that point in time, but the price of the issue to be delivered is computed by multiplying the price of the benchmark issue by a conversion factor prescribed by the exchange.

One of the characteristics of the bond futures trading conducted in Japan is that issues are traded in units with a total par value of ¥100 million, about 10 times as large as that of other countries. (This compares with $100,000 in the case of treasury bond futures traded on the Chicago Board of Trade, or 100,000 Eurodollars in the case of BUND futures traded on the EUREX.) This is due to the fact that in cash bond transactions, bonds whose value falls short of ¥100 million are treated as a fraction of a trading unit. As bond fu-

Table VIII-2.   Trading Mechanism of Bond Futures

	Medium-term JGB futures	Long-term JGB futures	Superlong-term JGB futures
Trading object	Medium-term JGB Standardized 3%, 5-year residual	Long-term JGB Standardized 6%, 10-year residual	Superlong-term JGB Standardized 3%, 20-year residual
Delivery object	Interest-bearing 5-yr. govt. notes with a remaining life of 4 yrs. to 5 yrs. and 3 mos.	Interest-bearing 10-yr. govt. notes with a remaining life of 7 to 11 yrs.	Interest-bearing 20-yr. govt. bonds with a remaining life of 19 yrs. and 3 mos. to 20 yrs.
Contract month	3 contract months from March, June, September, December	3 contract months from March, June, September, December	3 contract months from March, June, September, December
Delivery date	20th of March, June, September, December	20th of March, June, September, December	20th of March, June, September, December
Final trading day	5 business days prior to the delivery date	5 business days prior to the delivery date	5 business days prior to the delivery date
Trading hours	8:45-11:02, 12:30-15:02, 15:30–5:30 the following day	8:45-11:02, 12:30-15:02, 15:30–5:30 the following day	8:45-11:02, 12:30-15:02, 15:30–5:30 the following day
Trading unit	¥100 million in par value	¥100 million in par value	¥100 million in par value
Price asked	¥0.01 per par value of ¥100	¥0.01 per par value of ¥100	¥0.01 per par value of ¥100
Daily price limit	Standard: Base price ±¥2.00 Maximum: Base price ±¥3.00	Standard: Base price ±¥2.00 Maximum: Base price ±¥3.00	Standard: Base price ±¥4.00 Maximum: Base price ±¥6.00
Circuit breaker mechanism	In a futures trading, if following a buy (sell) order for the central contract month placed (or contracted) at the upper (lower) price limit, there is no trade execution at a price outside the price range from the upper (lower price) limit to the immediately executable price range (for medium-term and long-term JGB futures, last traded price plus or minus 0.1 yen, for superlong-term JGB futures, last traded price plus or minus 0.3 yen) for one (1) minute, trading is suspended for 10 minutes.		

Table VIII-3.   Transition in Bond Futures Trading

	Medium-term JGB futures		Long-term JGB futures		Superlong-term JGB futures	
	No. of deals	No. of contracts	No. of deals	No. of contracts	No. of deals	No. of contracts
2017	0	0	8,190,265	96,251	1,602	62
2018	0	0	10,304,257	110,589	3,434	162
2019	0	0	9,611,513	78,887	1,957	312
2020	0	0	7,148,071	68,770	1,648	28
2021	0	0	8,187,093	105,539	1,055	46

Source: Website of the Japan Exchange Group (JPX).

tures trading is usually compared with that of other countries in terms of the number of contracts, futures traded in Japan tend to be underestimated.

It is said that another characteristic of the bond futures market of Japan is that it is concentrated in trading in long-term government bond futures. This is likely to be related to the fact that the maturities of government bonds, though to a lesser extent than before, tend to be primarily in 10-year issues. Yet this stands in contrast with the U.S. and Germany where medium-term bond futures trading maintains liquidity.

Since the mid-1990s, however, the concentration of cash government bond trading on the benchmark issue, which was a phenomenon peculiar to Japan, has eased. Since the end of March 1999, the practice of designating a government bond as a benchmark issue has been discontinued, with 10-year government bond futures assuming the role played by benchmark issues. Among new products, contract for difference (CFD) futures on mini-long-term government bonds, which are one-tenth the amount of normal bonds, were listed on the Tokyo Stock Exchange from the end of March 2009, but trading accounts for less than 1% of long-term government bond futures.

3. Stock Index Futures Trading

The first stock index futures contract was listed in the United States in 1982. In Japan, the Osaka Securities Exchange started trading Osaka Stock Futures 50, a futures contract for a basket of 50 stocks, in 1987. That product was followed in 1988 by the listing of Nikkei 225 futures on the Osaka Securities Exchange and TOPIX futures on the Tokyo Stock Exchange. Nikkei 300 futures were listed on the Osaka Securities Exchange in 1994. In 1998, High-Tech 40, Financial 25, and Consumer 40 stock index futures started to be traded on the Osaka Securities Exchange and sector index futures contracts for three industries, electric appliances, transportation equipment, and banks, were listed on the Tokyo Stock Exchange. The Tokyo Stock Exchange launched S&P/TOPIX 150 stock index futures in 2001, while three futures contracts based, respectively, on the MSCI Japan, the FTSE Japan, and the Dow-Jones Industrial Average indices were listed on the Osaka Securities Exchange (OSE) in 2002. RN (Russell Nomura) Prime Index futures commenced trading on the OSE in 2005, followed by Nikkei 225 mini-futures on the OSE in 2006, and the TOPIX mini, TOPIX Core30, and TSE REIT index futures on the TSE in 2008. In 2010, the OSE introduced the Nikkei Stock Average Dividend Point Index and the TSE introduced TOPIX and TOPIX Core30 dividend indexes, while the Tokyo Financial Exchange launched Nikkei 225 equity margin contracts. In 2012, the OSE began trading Nikkei Stock Average Volatility Index futures and NY Dow Jones Industrial Average

Table VIII-4.   Trading Mechanism of Stock Index Futures

	Nikkei 225 mini futures	Nikkei 225 futures	TOPIX futures
Trading object	Nikkei stock average	Nikkei stock average	TOPIX
Contract month	Jun & Dec: Nearest 10 contract months Mar & Sept: Nearest 3 contract months Other months: Nearest 3 contract months	Jun & Dec: Nearest 10 contract months Mar & Sept: Nearest 3 contract months	5 months in the Mar, Jun, Sept & Dec quarterly cycle
Trading unit	Nikkei stock average × 100	Nikkei stock average × 1,000	TOPIX × ¥10,000
Price asked	Units of ¥5 in Nikkei stock average	Units of ¥10 in Nikkei stock average	Units of 0.5 points in TOPIX
Maturity	On the 2nd Friday of Mar, Jun, Sept, or Dec	On the 2nd Friday of Mar, Jun, Sept, or Dec	On the 2nd Friday of Mar, Jun, Sept, or Dec
Final trading day	One business day prior to the delivery date	One business day prior to the delivery date	One business day prior to the delivery date
Trading hours	8:45–15:15, 16:30–5:30 the following day	8:45–15:15, 16:30–5:30 the following day	8:45–15:15, 16:30–5:30 the following day
Daily price limit	Standard: Base price ± 8% 2nd Expansion: Base price ± 12% Maximum: Base price ± 16%	Standard: Base price ± 8% 2nd Expansion: Base price ± 12% Maximum: Base price ± 16%	Standard: Base price ± 8% 2nd Expansion: Base price ± 12% Maximum: Base price ± 16%
Circuit breaker mechanism	If, following a contract or buy (sell) order for the central contract month for a futures trading placed at the upper (lower) price limit, there is no trade execution for one (1) minute because of a fall (rise) of over 10% of the price limit range from the upper (lower) price limit, trading is suspended for 10 minutes.		

Table VIII-5.   Transition in Stock Index Futures Trading

	Nikkei 225 mini futures		Nikkei 225 futures		TOPIX futures	
	No. of deals	No. of contracts	No. of deals	No. of contracts	No. of deals	No. of contracts
2017	219,518,050	683,633	23,054,495	413,373	24,392,610	665,711
2018	273,327,463	1,279,710	26,193,823	426,448	26,224,277	534,861
2019	237,577,721	500,550	22,527,189	335,127	26,345,546	561,087
2020	321,718,519	365,751	27,171,013	304,922	27,702,276	514,650
2021	224,009,276	245,947	18,073,552	319,752	23,309,732	421,213

Source: Website of the Japan Exchange Group (JPX).

futures. In 2014, CNX Nifty futures and JPX Nikkei Index 400 futures, and in 2016, TSE Mothers and Taiwan Capitalization Weighted Stock Index futures were listed on the Osaka Exchange, followed by FTSE China A50 Index futures in 2017. Prior to all these domestic listings for Nikkei 225 futures, the Singapore International Monetary Exchange (SIMEX, now SGX-DT) started trading SIMEX Nikkei 225 futures in 1986, followed in 1992 by dollar- and yen-denominated Nikkei 225 futures on the Chicago Mercantile Exchange (CME).

Out of many futures contracts based on a variety of Japanese stock indexes or listed on different exchanges, the OSE Nikkei 225 futures are the most actively traded, while the TOPIX futures, Nikkei 225 mini-futures, and SGX Nikkei 225 futures contracts, are quite liquid, creating a rather unique situation in which there is more than one contract having good liquidity among the stock index futures.

Since June 1989, the last trading day falls, as is the case with the United States, one business day prior to maturity, and the final settlement price is decided on the basis of a special quotation (SQ) that is computed on the basis of the opening prices of component issues on the date of maturity. In addition to a three-stage daily price limit, the stock exchanges in Japan have instituted a system temporarily suspending trading called the circuit breaker system in order to control price fluctuations for domestic stock index futures trading. This does not exist in the cash market and is different to restrictions on changes in stock prices.

4. Financial Futures Trading

Currency futures trading started in the United States in 1972, and Eurodollar short-term interest rate contracts were the first interbank futures listed on a U.S. exchange, in 1982. In Japan, Euroyen futures, Eurodollar short-term interest rate futures (trading was suspended in 1998), and Japanese yen-U.S. dollar currency futures (contracts were delisted in 1992) were simultaneously listed on the Tokyo International Financial Futures Exchange in 1989. These contracts were followed by the TIFFE/TFX listings of dollar-yen futures in 1991; 1-year Euroyen futures in 1992 (trading was suspended in 1998); Euroyen LIBOR futures in 1999; 5-year and 10-year yen swap futures in 2003 (trading was suspended in 2007); and Exchange FOREX margin contracts (Click 365) on U.S. dollars, Euros, UK pounds, and Australian dollars in 2005. In 2009, the TFX listed overnight (O/N) uncollateralized call rate and general collateral (GC) spot-next (S/N) repo rate interest futures, and added margin contracts for Nikkei stock average, FTSE 100, and DAX indexes (Click 365) on the TIFFE (TIFFE was renamed the Tokyo Financial Ex-

Table VIII-6.   Trading Mechanism of Financial Futures

	3-month Euroyen interest rate futures	USD-JPY exchange FOREX margin contracts	Nikkei 225 margin contracts
Trading unit	Principal ¥100 million	US$10,000	Nikkei stock average × 100
Indicating method	100 minus rate of interest (%, Act/360 day basis)	Yen equivalent per U.S. dollar	Yen equivalent per stock price index
Price asked	0.005 (¥1,250)	0.01 (¥100)	¥1 (¥100)
Contract month	Mar, Jun, Sep, Dec, cycle (20 contract months traded at any one time)	No	No
Final trading day	Two business days prior to the third Wednesday of the contract month	No	No
Final settlement day	Business day following the final trading day	No	No
Settlement method	Settlement of differences (the final settlement price is equal to ¥100 less TIBOR rounded off at the fourth decimal places)	Making up differences	Making up differences
Daily price limit	No	No	No
Trading hours	8:45–11:30, 12:30–15:30, 15:30–20:00	Monday 7:10 a.m. to 6:55 a.m. the following day Tuesday to Thursday 7:55 a.m. to 6:55 a.m. the following day (1 hour each during U.S. Daylight Savings Time)	Friday 7:55 a.m. to 6:00 a.m. the following day 8:30 a.m.–6:00 a.m. the following day (5:00 a.m. during U.S. Daylight Savings Time)

Table VIII-7.   Transition in Financial Futures Trading

	3-month Euroyen interest rate futures		USD-JPY exchange FOREX margin contracts		Nikkei 225 margin contracts	
	No. of deals	No. of contracts	No. of deals	No. of contracts	No. of deals	No. of contracts
2017	1,545,861	134,560	10,478,227	537,737	5,722,311	237,114
2018	1,423,666	102,874	8,363,218	534,564	4,266,773	218,858
2019	855,250	58,550	5,352,811	523,692	5,254,459	200,762
2020	263,657	15,656	7,181,607	398,555	10,701,148	167,049
2021	74,206	6,080	6,326,876	373,916	9,730,043	45,919

Source: Website of the Tokyo Financial Exchange.

change (TFX) in 2007) in 2010.

Financial futures trading in the United States began with futures and futures options on commodity exchanges while European countries introduced financial futures exchanges for these products. In Japan, futures and options on bonds and stocks are traded on the stock exchanges, while interbank interest rate and currency futures and options are traded on the TFX, a separate market established by some banks and securities companies.

On the TFX, trading has been concentrated from the start in yen short-term rate futures, with little trading in other futures. To increase the liquidity of those financial futures, the market-making system was introduced for dollar short-term rate futures and yen-dollar currency futures in 1990, dollar-yen currency futures in 1991, and options on yen short-term rate futures in 1992. However, their liquidity did not improve much.

Meanwhile, in 1996 TIFFE introduced a TIFFE-SPAN (Standard Portfolio Analysis of Risk) system on the basis of which the amount of margin commensurate with the risks involved is computed. Moreover, in an effort to stimulate financial futures trading, it linked the prices of its products to those of the London International Financial Futures and Options Exchange (LIFFE) and extended its trading hours in the same year. It made efforts to stimulate trading by introducing the night-trading system for dollar-yen currency futures in 1997. Since 1995, however, TIFFE/TFX's business, which had grown during the first half of the 1990s, has been decreasing on account of the extremely low interest rate climate. Meanwhile, trading of Click 365, which was listed with an eye to the expansion of foreign exchange margin transactions, and trading of Click Stock 365, which is linked with Nikkei average stock prices, have established a presence.

5. Options Trading

Options trading refers to an agreement to trade the right to buy or sell a specific amount of a commodity or a financial instrument at a fixed price (the exercise price) within a specified period in the future. The right to become the buyer is called a call option, and the right to become the seller is called a put option.

The history of options trading goes back to antiquity. According to Aristotle, the first known option trading was written by Thales (ca. 620–ca. 555 BC), a Greek philosopher, on the sale of an olive press. The Chicago Board Options Exchange (CBOE) established in 1973 is the first fully developed options trading market. This provided a method that made it possible for parties to consummate a transaction by organizing one-on-one negotiated transactions in such a way as to enable them to settle the difference without deliv-

Table VIII-8.   Years in Which Major Financial Options of the World Were Listed

Year	Other countries	Japan
1973	U.S. options on individual stocks (CBOE)	
1974	U.S. options on individual stocks (AMEX, PHLX, PCX)	
1978	U.K. options on individual stocks (LTOM)	
1982	Currency options (PHLX), T-bond futures options (CBOT)	
1983	S&P 100 options; S&P 500 options (CBOE); S&P 500 futures options (CME)	
1984	Currency futures options (CME), FTSE 100 options (LIFFE)	
1987	Pound interest rate futures options (LIFFE), options on French individual stocks (MONEP)	
1988	French government bond futures options (MATIF); CAC40 options (MONEP); BUND futures options (LIFFE)	
1989		Bond OTC options (OTC); Nikkei 225 options (OSE); Nikkei 225 options (OSE); TOPIX options (TSE)
1990	Options on individual German stocks (DTB); Euroyen interest rate futures options (SIMEX); Euromark interest rate futures options (LIFFE); DAX options and BUND futures options (DTB)	Long-term government bond futures options (TSE)
1991		Euroyen short-term rate futures options (TFX)
1992	Nikkei average futures options (SIMEX)	
1994	JGB futures options (SIMEX)	
1997	KOSPI 200 options (KSE)	Options on individual stocks (TSE, OSE)
1998	EURIBOR futures options (LIFFE), Euro STOXX 50 options (EUREX), TAIEX options (TAIFEX)	
2000	U.S. options on individual stocks (ISE)	
2001	Nifty options (NSE), SENSEX options (BSE)	
2006	VIX index options (CBOE)	
2013	Nifty Bank option (NSE)	

Note: AMEX: American Stock Exchange (presently NYSE MKT), BSE: Bombay Stock Exchange, CBOE: Chicago Board Options Exchange, CBOT: Chicago Board of Trade, CME: Chicago Mercantile Exchange, DTB: Deutsche Terminbörse (presently EUREX), ISE: International Securities Exchange, KSE: Korea Stock Exchange (presently KRX), LIFFE: London International Futures and Options Exchange (presently ICE Futures Europe), LTOM: London Traded Options Market (presently ICE Futures Europe), MATIF: Marché à Terme International de France (presently Euronext Paris), MONEP: Marché des Options Négociable de Paris (presently Euronext Paris), NSE: National Stock Exchange of India, PHLX: Philadelphia Stock Exchange (presently Nasdaq OMX PHLX), PCX: Pacific Exchange (presently NYSE Arca), SIMEX: Singapore International Monetary Exchange (presently SGX), TAIFEX: Taiwan Futures Exchange,TSE: Tokyo Stock Exchange, OSE: Osaka Securities Exchange (presently Osaka Exchange), TFX: Tokyo International Financial Futures Exchange (presently Tokyo Financial Exchange).

ery of the underlying commodity or financial instrument, similar to a futures trading, and is considered to have been the groundbreaking event in the history of options trading.

The options trading started by the CBOE in 1973 spread to other financial instruments, such as currency options trading, bond options trading, and bond futures options trading, in 1982; stock index options trading, and stock index futures options trading in 1983; and to currency futures options trading in 1984. And it has since spread to major financial markets worldwide. In Japan, OTC bond options trading (trading in bonds with options) was introduced in April 1989. The Osaka Securities Exchange introduced Nikkei 225 options in June, the Tokyo Stock Exchange introduced TOPIX options in October, and the Nagoya Stock Exchange introduced Options 25 in October 1989 (discontinued in 1998). The Tokyo Stock Exchange introduced long-term government bond futures options in 1990, and the Tokyo International Financial Futures Exchange (TIFFE) introduced yen short-term rate futures options in 1991. In addition, the Osaka Securities Exchange introduced Nikkei 300 options in 1994, and both the Tokyo Stock Exchange and the Osaka Securities Exchange introduced options on individual stocks in 1997. In 1998, the Osaka Securities Exchange introduced three industry-specific stock index options (High-Tech 40, Financial 25, and Consumer 40). In 2015 it introduced Nikkei 225 Weekly options.

Listed options are traded on exchanges. While they can be transferred to a third party, the seller is required to deposit a margin with the exchange to provide against defaults on the contract. OTC options trading is a one-on-one transaction, and it cannot be transferred to a third party, but the seller is not required to deposit a margin. Unlike stock options and stock index options, many of the currency or interest rate options are traded with banks or securities companies on the OTC market.

6. Bond Options Trading

Treasury bond (T-bond) options trading (on the Chicago Board Options Exchange) and T-note options trading (on the American Stock Exchange) started simultaneously in 1982 constituted the first trading in listed bond options. And T-bond futures options were traded on the Chicago Board of Trade for the first time in 1982. In Japan, the first bond options trading was started on the OTC market in the name of "trading in bonds with options" in April 1989. Trading in long-term government bond futures options started in 1990, and trading in medium-term government note futures options (discontinued in 2002) started in 2000, both on the TSE.

Unlike bond futures trading, which is conducted on the basis of a bench-

Table VIII-9.   Trading Mechanism of Bond Options Trading

	OTC bond options	Long-term government bond futures options	Medium-term government bond futures options
Trading object	All debt securities other than convertible bonds and warrant bonds	Call options or put options on long-term government bond futures	Call options or put options on medium-sterm government bond futures
Contract months	Free	March, June, September, December cycle (nearest two contract months traded at any one time), other months (up to nearest two contract months)	March, June, September, December cycle (nearest two contract months traded at any one time), other months (up to nearest two contract months)
Final trading day	—	The last trading day of the month immediately preceding Mar, Jun, Sep, and Dec.	The last trading day of the month immediately preceding Mar, Jun, Sep, and Dec.
Delivery date	Within one year and 3 months from the date of contract	Business day following the trading day	Business day following the trading day
Trading unit	¥100 million in par value	One contract on long-term JGB futures	One contract on medium-term JGB futures
Price asked	—	¥0.01 per par value of ¥100	¥0.01 per par value of ¥100
Option exercise price	Free	± 10 prices at ¥0.5 intervals, additional prices set according to price movement in underlying futures	± 10 prices at ¥0.5 intervals, additional prices set according to price movement in underlying futures
Daily price limit	—	Standard: Base price ± ¥2.10 Maximum: Base price ± ¥3.00	Standard: Base price ± ¥2.10 Maximum: Base price ± ¥3.00
Circuit breaker mechanism	—	When circuit breaker mechanisms are in place for the underlying futures contracts	When circuit breaker mechanisms are in place for the underlying futures contracts
Method of exercising the right	Free	American option	American option

mark issue, OTC bond options are traded on the basis of individual issues, such as government bonds, corporate bonds, or foreign bonds. Because they are traded on the OTC market, bond options agreements cannot be transferred to a third party (most of the transactions are for government bonds). As with government bond futures trading, bond options are traded in units of ¥100 million in par value. Because their life (from the date of contract to the date of delivery) is restricted to a maximum period of one year and three months, and as they cannot be resold to a third party, contracts usually run a relatively long period—six months or one year.

By contrast, long-term government bond futures options are available in

Table VIII-10.   Transition in Bond Options Trading

	OTC bond options		Long-term government bond futures options		Medium-term government note futures options	
	Trading value	Outstanding price	No. of deals	No. of contracts	No. of deals	No. of contracts
2017	1,644,695	12,226	861,714	20,995	–	–
2018	2,145,579	29,494	783,545	7,720	–	–
2019	2,188,984	17,990	631,807	4,411	–	–
2020	1,805,445	23,852	323,210	3,710	–	–
2021	1,447,264	20,158	193,708	4,994	–	–

Source: The websites of the Japan Exchange Group (JPX) and the Japan Securities Dealers Association (JSDA).

the form of listed American options (the option can be exercised any day during its life), and their trading mechanism is similar to that of long-term government bond futures. Whereas long-term government bond futures have only three contract months with a maximum period of nine months, long-term government bond futures options offer up to four contract months with a maximum period of six months. In addition, compared with OTC bond options, transactions in long-term government bond futures and long-term government bond futures options are concentrated in those with a short remaining life.

In Western countries where options trading has long been conducted, investors are quite familiar with the system. However, in Japan, where there is no custom of options trading, investors utilize options trading less often than futures trading. Particularly, the amount of long-term government bond futures options trading is far smaller than that of long-term government futures trading. This is because investors' interest is concentrated in outright transactions that deal only in options, and covered transactions are not made in conjunction with underlying assets (namely, long-term government bond futures). On the other hand, in conducting OTC bond options trading, investors follow the strategy of combining underlying assets with covered call or target buying.

7. Stock Index Options Trading

Trading in listed options on individual stocks started in 1973 on the Chicago Board Options Exchange (CBOE). In 1983, the CBOE introduced S&P 100 options (the first stock index options). The Chicago Mercantile Exchange (CME) listed S&P 500 futures options (the first stock index futures options

Table VIII-11.   Trading Mechanism of Stock Index Options

	Nikkei 225 options (Weekly)	TOPIX options
Trading object	Call options or put options on Nikkei stock average	Call options or put options on TOPIX
Contract months	Jun and Dec contracts are nearest 16 months, Mar and Sept contracts are nearest 3 months, other contract months are 6 months (Weekly Options are nearest 4 weekly contracts)	June and Dec contracts are nearest 10 months, Mar and Sep contacts are nearest 3 months, other contracts months are nearest 6 months
Trading unit	Nikkei stock average × 1,000	TOPIX × ¥10,000
Price asked	¥50 or less: ¥1; over ¥50 up to ¥1,000: ¥5; over ¥1,000: ¥10	0.1 points for prices up to 20 points, 0.5 points for prices over 20 points
Maturity	On the 2nd Friday of the delivery month	On the 2nd Friday of the delivery month
Final trading day	One business day prior to the delivery date	One business day prior to the delivery date
Trading hours	9:00–15:15, 16:30–5:30 the following day	9:00–15:15, 16:30–5:30 the following day
Option exercise price	Initially, ±8 strike prices at ¥250 intervals; ±8 strike prices at ¥125 intervals for closest 3 contract months when less than 3 months remaining	Over-4 month contracts: ±6 prices at 50-point intervals (if 4 months, same as 4 months or less), contracts of 4 months or less: ±9 prices at 25-point intervals
Method of exercising the right	European option	European option
Daily price limit	Normal: 4, 6, 8 or 11% according to the base price 1st Expansion: Base price +3% 2nd Expansion: 1st Expansion +3%	Normal: 4, 6, 8 or 11% according to the base price 1st Expansion: Base price +3% 2nd Expansion: 1st Expansion +3%
Circuit breaker mechanism	Possible interruption in connection with the actuation of the circuit breaker mechanism for Nikkei 225 futures trading	Possible interruption in connection with the actuation of the circuit breaker mechanism for TOPIX futures trading

ever) and the New York Stock Exchange (NYSE) listed the New York Stock Exchange Composite Stock Index futures options in 1983. In Japan, a series of stock index options have been listed—the Nikkei 225 stock index options on the Osaka Securities Exchange in June 1989, Options 25 on the Nagoya Stock Exchange in September of the same year (discontinued in 1998), and the TOPIX options on the Tokyo Stock Exchange in 1989. In 1994, the Nikkei 300 stock index options were introduced on the Osaka Securities Exchange (discontinued in 2010). Three industry-specific stock index options (High-Tech 40, Financial 25, and Consumer 40, discontinued in 2002) were also introduced on the Osaka Securities Exchange in 1998, and S&P/TOPIX

Table VIII-12.   Transition in Stock Index Options Trading

	Nikkei 225 options		Nikkei 225 Weekly options		TOPIX options	
	No. of deals	No. of contracts	No. of deals	No. of contracts	No. of deals	No. of contracts
2017	32,594,768	2,083,846	493,801	2,229	259,384	76,958
2018	35,502,311	1,909,369	601,555	1,605	179,262	69,113
2019	29,763,572	1,546,360	697,579	628	238,319	99,876
2020	28,666,550	1,253,114	634,770	1,088	306,978	78,589
2021	24,187,070	1,102,485	735,201	9,413	431,916	82,066

Source: Website of the Japan Exchange Group (JPX).

150 options (discontinued in 2002) were listed on the Tokyo Stock Exchange in 2001. In 2015, the Osaka Exchange introduced weekly options for the Nikkei 225 options. Meanwhile, trading in the Nikkei average futures options started in 1992 on the Singapore International Monetary Exchange (SIMEX, or the present SGX-DT).

In Japan, listed stock index options (the Nikkei 225 options) are most actively traded on the Osaka Securities Exchange. Unlike stock index futures, other stock index options are scarcely traded in Japan.

A comparison of the trading mechanisms of the Nikkei 225 options, the TOPIX options, and the SGX's Nikkei average futures options shows that while domestically traded stock index options are based on cash stock options, the Nikkei average futures options traded on the SGX are based on futures options. Another difference in the trading mechanisms is that the Nikkei 225 options and SGX's Nikkei average futures options offer long-term options. Meanwhile, in computing the amount of margins, all exchanges have adopted the method of netting margins in accordance with risks called Standard Portfolio Analysis of Risk (SPAN) developed by the Chicago Mercantile Exchange, and there is no significant difference among them. In addition, when the circuit breaker mechanism is tripped in stock index futures trading, options trading is also halted.

8. Securities Options Trading

Options on individual stocks were first listed on the Chicago Board Options Exchange in 1973, with call options. In 1977, put options were also listed on the same exchange. While the options on individual stocks were first listed and then stock index options were listed in other countries, in Japan stock index options were introduced in 1989 first and equity options on 20 individual stocks were listed afterward on the Tokyo Stock Exchange and the Osaka Se-

Table VIII-13.   Trading Mechanism of Securities Options

	Marketable securities options (OSE)
Trading object	Call options or put options on domestically listed marketable securities
Contract month	Nearest two contract months + nearest two months from March, June, September and December
Delivery date	5th day from the exercise of the right
Maturity	On the 2nd Friday of the delivery month
Final trading day	One business day prior to the delivery date
Trading unit	The trading unit of the underlying stock
Price asked	16 stages from ¥0.1 to ¥5,000 depending on the price of the underlying security
Option exercise price	± 2 prices at 16 stages from ¥25 to ¥5 million depending on the price of the underlying stock, with additional prices available afterwards based on market
Daily price limit	The value derived by taking the base price of the security for the option trade on the designated market as of the trade date and multiplying it by 25%
Position limit	Set for each eligible security
Trading hours	9:00–11:35, 12:30–15:15
Method of exercising the right	European option

Table VIII-14.   Transition in Securities Options Trading

	OSE Securities Options	
	No. of deals	No. of contracts
2017	915,787	78,082
2018	869,163	24,713
2019	1,226,146	29,129
2020	1,347,612	44,223
2021	2,032,945	28,011

Source: Website of the Japan Exchange Group (JPX).

curities Exchange in 1997 (seven of them were listed on both exchanges). Since then, option trading has been extended to all listed securities along with a name change to "securities options." On March 24, 2014, the derivatives market on the Tokyo Stock Exchange was merged with the derivatives market on the Osaka Exchange, and individual securities options trading on the Osaka Exchange was integrated with the marketable securities options trading on the Tokyo Stock Exchange as of that date.

Soon after the Chicago Board Options Exchange was established, the advisability of introducing securities options to Japan was considered. However, it is said that their introduction was postponed for more than 20 years for fear that they might compete with margin trading, a major source of income for small- to medium-sized securities companies.

The mechanism of trading in marketable securities options is basically identical to that of stock index options but differs from that of stock index options trading in that the securities certificate underlying an option must be delivered to the buyer and that the final settlement price is decided on the basis of the closing price of the underlying securities.

Although it was thought that securities options might compete with margin trading, they were not as actively traded. This is because there is no tradition of trading in options in Japan, investors are not familiar with options trading, and, unlike their Western counterparts, few individual investors are interested in options trading. Options are traded in combination with their underlying assets. In Japan, capital gains earned from trading underlying equities and from securities options are subject to separate taxation. However, investors are not allowed to offset gains and losses between these two categories. This is believed to have discouraged individual investors from participating in securities options trading. In other countries, brokers and dealers are granted preferential treatment for their market-making in relatively illiquid securities options. In a similar move, the Osaka Securities Exchange and Tokyo Stock Exchange introduced the Securities Options Market-Maker Program and TSE Securities Option Supporter system, respectively. These actions, however, have not resulted in any significant increase in the trading of these options in Japan.

9. OTC Derivatives Trading

The market on which derivatives trading achieved remarkable growth around the world in the 1990s was not the exchanges but the OTC market. Particularly, spurred by the financial liberalization, the interest rate swap trading that started in 1982 has spread not only to banking institutions, but also to business corporations and has come to play the leading role on the derivatives market. As statistics on derivatives trading conducted on the exchanges have been well kept, it was easy to follow changes occurring in their trading, but because there was no organization that kept track of the derivatives trading conducted on the OTC market, it was extremely difficult to find out how it was doing. To remedy the situation, the Bank for International Settlements (BIS) decided to investigate, beginning in 1995, the derivatives markets along with—and on the occasion of—the triennial investigation of the for-

Table VIII-15.   OTC Trading in Securities Derivatives

Trading status (notional principal, ¥100 million)

Number of transactions	Total		Forward trading		Forward trading in OTC index, etc.		OTC options trading		OTC index swaps trading	
FY2016	5,165,442	−12.5%	1,874	0%	3,899,978	76%	237,830	5%	1,025,760	20%
FY2017	5,590,496	8.2%	1,182	0%	3,369,999	60%	244,985	4%	1,974,330	35%
FY2018	15,800,873	182.6%	2,375	0%	10,105,159	64%	360,779	2%	5,332,560	34%
FY2019	26,977,566	70.7%	3,870	0%	19,456,439	72%	2,628,363	10%	4,888,894	18%
FY2020	35,593,111	31.9%	7,310	0%	30,931,296	87%	3,454,510	10%	1,199,995	3%

Trading value	Total		Forward trading		Forward trading in OTC index, etc.		OTC options trading		OTC index swaps trading	
FY2016	2,122,106	−11.4%	85,368	4%	161,615	8%	1,525,389	72%	349,733	16%
FY2017	2,645,609	24.7%	91,602	3%	171,760	6%	1,901,057	72%	481,190	18%
FY2018	3,967,378	50.0%	195,294	5%	319,906	8%	2,086,395	53%	1,365,783	34%
FY2019	3,870,469	−2.4%	201,334	5%	356,499	9%	1,879,968	49%	1,432,668	37%
FY2020	3,596,332	−7.1%	231,454	6%	563,143	16%	1,347,410	37%	1,454,324	40%

Term-end balance	Total		Forward trading		Forward trading in OTC index, etc.		OTC options trading		OTC index swaps trading	
FY2016	550,874	29.9%	13,178	2%	10,053	2%	297,890	54%	229,753	42%
FY2017	486,476	−11.7%	21,387	4%	8,454	2%	242,686	50%	213,949	44%
FY2018	523,759	7.7%	15,922	3%	7,142	1%	281,099	54%	219,596	42%
FY2019	435,003	−16.9%	22,947	5%	10,484	2%	196,774	45%	204,798	47%
FY2020	545,296	25.4%	13,178	2%	10,053	2%	297,890	55%	224,175	41%

Brokering status (notional principal, ¥100 million)

Number of transactions	Total		Forward trading		Forward trading in OTC index, etc.		OTC options trading		OTC index swaps trading	
FY2016	1,478,041	97.6%	1,081	0%	1,700	0%	18,789	1%	1,466,471	99%
FY2017	3,093,610	109.3%	1,034	0%	2,223	0%	25,273	1%	3,065,080	99%
FY2018	28,605	−99.1%	1,545	5%	1,625	6%	17,558	61%	7,877	28%
FY2019	27,169	−5.0%	1,435	5%	1,502	6%	15,442	57%	8,790	32%
FY2020	26,546	−2.3%	1,352	5%	1,877	7%	14,256	54%	9,061	34%

Trading value	Total		Forward trading		Forward trading in OTC index, etc.		OTC options trading		OTC index swaps trading	
FY2016	652,753	−14.8%	73,469	11%	120,653	18%	205,505	31%	253,125	39%
FY2017	894,615	37.1%	117,021	13%	185,121	21%	193,597	22%	398,876	45%
FY2018	701,479	−21.6%	186,539	27%	131,695	19%	145,707	21%	237,534	34%
FY2019	662,435	−5.6%	194,539	29%	126,692	19%	138,033	21%	203,169	31%
FY2020	661,200	−0.2%	212,315	32%	194,683	29%	137,872	21%	116,328	18%

Note: Figures next to annual total amounts represent percentage changes from the previous fiscal year. Percentages in parentheses elsewhere represent the ratio to the total for the year under the respective transaction types.

Source: Compiled based on the data available on the JSDA website.

eign exchange markets from 1986 to grasp the state of trading in derivatives on the OTC market worldwide.

According to a survey of the Japanese OTC derivatives market conducted in April 2019, the daily average notional value of OTC interest rate derivatives traded in Japan (excluding FS swaps) was $135.2 billion, representing an increase of 142% from the previous survey in April 2016 (the results compare against a daily global total of $6.501 trillion and an increase of 143%). By contract type, interest rate swaps were $129.9 billion (up 174%) (overnight index swaps: $11.4 billion, others: $118.5 billion), interest rate options were $4.6 billion (down 40%) and FRAs were $800 million (down 8%). The total notional value of the outstanding OTC derivatives contracts of financial institutions in Japan as of the end of June 2019 stood at $55.1 trillion, up 8% from June 2016, relative to a total of $524 trillion and a 4% decrease worldwide. Looking at the breakdown of the total by contract type, interest rate swaps increased by 4% to account for 78.0% (compared with 81.6% in the 2016 survey), interest rate options increased by 61% to account for 11.2% (compared with 7.6% in 2016), and FRAs increased by 8% to account for 10.7% (compared with 10.8% in 2016).

At the G20 Pittsburg Summit in 2009, it was agreed that all OTC derivatives contracts standardized by the end of 2012 should be settled through central clearing organizations. In Japan, Japan Securities Clearing Corporation (JSCC), which belongs to the Japan Exchange Group (JPX), began clearing and settlement of CDS in July 2011, followed by clearing of interest rate swaps starting in October 2012. JSCC settles ¥70 trillion to ¥100 trillion worth of yen-denominated interest rate swaps, which account for 90% of all interest rate swaps, on a monthly basis.

10. Credit Derivatives Trading

"Credit derivatives trading" refers to trading in credit risks involved in loans and corporate bonds in the form of swaps and options. While conventional derivatives trading bought or sold market risks, credit derivatives trading deals in credit risks. Credit risks trading may be characterized as trading in guarantees in that it not only deals in guarantees against default but also provides a variety of products that cover the risk of declining creditworthiness caused by a deterioration of business performance.

Credit derivatives are traded largely in three typical types: credit default swaps (CDS), total return swaps (TRS), and credit-linked notes (CLN). A CDS is a type of options trading that guarantees the credit risks involved in a loan, and when the borrower defaults on a loan underlying the CDS the damage caused by such default is guaranteed. CDS derives its name from the

Table VIII-16.   Credit Derivatives Trading in Japan

(Outstanding balance of notional principal; US $ million)

	OTC trading	Credit default swap			Total return swap			Credit spread product			Credit-linked notes			Other products		
	Total	Total	Sell	Buy	Total	Sell	Buy	Total	Sell	Buy	Total	Issue	Purchase	Total	Sell	Buy
June 2011	1,157,661	1,151,538	579,602	571,934	278	266	12	0	0	0	5,642	4,915	727	204	136	620
Dec. 2011	1,116,847	1,111,618	553,655	557,963	195	182	13	0	0	0	4,649	4,068	581	386	199	575
June 2012	1,105,389	1,098,891	547,638	551,253	209	196	13	0	0	0	6,038	3,933	2,105	252	107	418
Dec. 2012	1,047,913	1,040,915	529,454	511,462	473	374	99	0	0	0	6,302	3,510	2,792	226	93	282
June 2013	1,061,005	1,055,262	536,826	518,436	542	143	399	130	65	65	4,868	1,838	3,030	203	86	68
Dec. 2013	853,899	848,494	427,571	420,923	455	119	336	0	0	0	4,815	1,815	3,000	132	75	187
June 2014	785,138	778,255	389,898	388,358	367	123	244	0	0	0	5,999	2,316	3,683	514	455	145
Dec. 2014	710,060	703,689	356,398	347,292	261	104	157	0	0	0	5,664	2,471	3,193	444	394	133
June 2015	563,687	552,855	280,527	272,330	4,415	2,260	2,155	0	0	0	6,144	2,864	3,280	270	221	117
Dec. 2015	518,641	507,140	261,156	245,986	4,313	2,101	2,212	0	0	0	6,967	3,591	3,376	223	173	57
June 2016	510,693	505,278	255,136	250,141	5,414	2,054	3,360	0	0	0	(9,209)	(4,784)	(4,425)	(384)	(384)	(59)
Dec. 2016	441,444	437,525	219,801	217,721	3,918	1,522	2,396	0	0	0	(9,071)	(5,340)	(3,731)	(353)	(353)	(50)
June 2017	411,471	406,931	203,595	203,335	4,537	1,804	2,733	0	0	0	(8,862)	(6,291)	(2,571)	(138)	(138)	(49)
Dec. 2017	381,682	375,022	187,255	187,769	6,656	2,802	3,854	0	0	0	(9,410)	(6,548)	(2,862)	(159)	(159)	(50)
June 2018	382,030	377,141	189,032	188,108	4,812	2,091	2,721	82	82	0	(10,438)	(7,465)	(2,973)	(262)	(262)	0
Dec. 2018	384,498	380,788	189,823	190,965	3,707	1,647	2,060	0	0	0	(10,156)	(7,265)	(2,891)	(342)	(342)	0
June 2019	391,418	387,741	194,000	193,741	3,683	2,174	1,509	0	0	0	(10,133)	(7,098)	(3,035)	(445)	(445)	0
Dec. 2019	416,496	411,549	207,163	204,390	4,947	2,390	2,557	0	0	0	(9,785)	(6,691)	(3,094)	(562)	(562)	0
June 2020	481,306	473,848	241,711	232,137	7,459	2,547	4,912	0	0	0	(9,062)	(5,986)	(3,076)	(620)	(620)	0
Dec. 2020	510,502	506,011	259,276	246,734	4,495	1,950	2,545	0	0	0	(8,469)	(5,134)	(3,335)	(925)	(797)	0
June 2021	534,398	525,860	270,351	255,509	8,546	4,627	3,919	0	0	0	(7,824)	(4,710)	(3,114)	(645)	(645)	0

Note: Figures for "credit-linked notes" and "other products" that had been included in credit derivatives were excluded from the scope of the survey from 2016 onwards. Data shown is for reference purposes only.

Source: Compiled based on the data on chronological coefficients in Bank of Japan, "*A Survey of Regular Market Reports Concerning Derivatives Trading.*" (http://www.boj.or.jp/en/statistics/bis/yoshi/index.htm/)

form in which the payment of a premium is swapped. Next, a TRS is a deal that swaps the total profit or loss (coupon and evaluated profit or loss) with the market rate, and it is used when the holder of a credit cannot sell it. And a CLN is a deal that links credit risks to a bond issued by the issuer of the underlying notes. Therefore, it may be said that a CLN is a CDS based on a bond instead of a guarantee. A CLN is redeemed in full on maturity unless the company designated in the contract defaults on its obligations, but when the company defaults the CLN is redeemed at a reduced value prior to maturity. While a CDS is concluded under the assumption that the guaranteeing company has an adequate capacity to guarantee, a CLN is guaranteed by the purchase of a bond. Therefore, a CLN has the advantage in that it can be concluded regardless of the credit standing of the investor.

According to the data published by the Bank of Japan, the total notional value of outstanding credit derivatives in Japan was accelerating in growth from 2003 on, increasing by a factor of 83 from the end of December 2002 to the end of June 2011. However, the value declined almost constantly and was down to half or less of its peak by the end of June 2015. The notional value of outstanding credit derivatives has also been on a decrease in the U.S. after hitting a peak in 2008, but the degree of decline has not been as significant as that of Japan. During the period from 2008 when the nominal value of outstanding credit derivatives recorded its peak in the U.S., the outstanding balance of credit derivatives in Japan doubled over a period of three years from then. However, the outstanding balance halved from the end of June 2011 to the end of June 2015, reflecting erratic movements on the market. After touching bottom in December 2017, the balance has continued to increase thereafter.

CHAPTER IX

The Securitized Products Market

1. What Is a Securitized Product?

A company pool the income-generating assets separately from its balance sheet into a special-purpose vehicle (SPV), and the SPV issues a security backed by the cash flow to be generated by such assets and sells the security to investors. This method is called "securitization." The security issued through such a process is generally called a "securitized product." Business enterprises use their assets—such as auto loans, mortgage loans, leases receivable, business loans and such claims as loans to corporations, and commercial real estate—as collateral to back up their securitized products. As defined by the Act on Securitization of Assets, intellectual property (such as copyrights and patents) also can be securitized.

When viewed from the standpoint of asset holders, securitization of assets has the advantage of enabling them to use the proceeds of the assignment or sale of such assets that they obtain at the time of issue in exchange for cash flows that may be generated by the assets over a future period of years. In other words, asset holders can monetize uncertain future cash flows into current income. In addition, in case any holder of a piece of less-liquid commercial real estate wants to issue a security by putting up such real estate as collateral, such asset holder may easily sell the security by issuing it in small denominations to attract a larger number of small investors, thereby increasing liquidity.

When viewed from the standpoint of investors, securitized products give them an additional choice of investments that have a new character. More specifically, a security backed by a piece of real estate gives them an opportunity to invest in real estate that otherwise they cannot afford to buy outright with a small sum of money. Second, as asset holders can issue different classes, or tranches, of securities ("the senior/subordinated structure") at one and the same time with varying levels of credit risks, they offer investors the opportunity to purchase a security that meets their needs. The issuers of asset-backed securities—Security 1 to Security N in Chart IX-1—simply tailor their terms of issue to best suit the needs of Investor 1 to Investor N, instead

Chart IX-1.   Conceptual Chart of Securitized Products

At the time a securitized product is issued

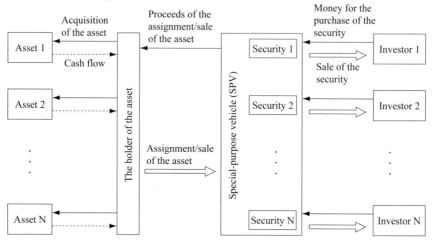

After the securitized product has been issued

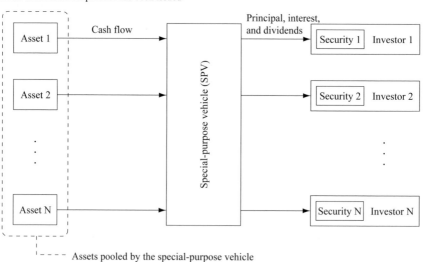

of making them uniform. For instance, by issuing securities with different characters—differentiation of the order of priority for the payment of interest and redemption of principal or granting credit-enhancing conditions (credit enhancement)—the scope of choice for investors can be enlarged. By adding such new wrinkles, investors can restructure their portfolios into more efficient ones.

2. Basic Mechanism of Issuing Securitized Products

Generally, many of the securitized products are issued through the mechanism described below. First, the holder ("originator") of assets such as mortgage loans and accounts receivable that are to be securitized assigns them to a SPV. By doing so, such assets are separated from the balance sheet of the originator and become assets of the SPV, which becomes the holder of the assets. An SPV may take the form of a partnership, a trust, or a special-purpose company (SPC). An SPC established under the Act on Securitization of Assets is called *tokutei mokuteki kaisha* (TMK, or a specific-purpose company). To ensure bankruptcy remoteness (no impact even if the company, etc., held by the SPC goes bankrupt), an overseas SPC is generally set up as a subsidiary through what are called charitable trusts under U.S. and U.K. laws using what is termed a "declaration of trust," and the domestic SPC established as a subsidiary of the overseas SPC. In terms of originators, the entity responsible for the debt is called the original obligor.

The next step is to formulate the terms of issue of the securitized product to be issued by the SPV. If the originator opts for the trust method, it issues beneficiary certificates like those of a trust company. If it chooses the SPC method, it issues the kinds of securities decided upon by the SPC to provide securitized products to investors, but it does not have to issue them on one and the same terms of issue. In short, it can design each type (tranche) of security with a different character by differentiating the order of priority with respect to the payment of interest and redemption of principal, by varying maturities, or by offering the guarantee of a property and casualty insurance company. By adding such variation, the originator can issue securities that meet the diverse needs of investors. In the order of priority for payment, such securities are called "senior securities," "mezzanine securities," or "subordinated securities."

When the originator plans to sell its securitized products to an unspecified large number of investors, it should make them readily acceptable to investors by offering them objective and simple indicators (credit ratings) for independently measuring the risks involved. In addition, there are other players involved in different processes of securitized products, such as servicers, who

Chart IX-2.   Example of General Working Mechanism for Issuing Securitized Products

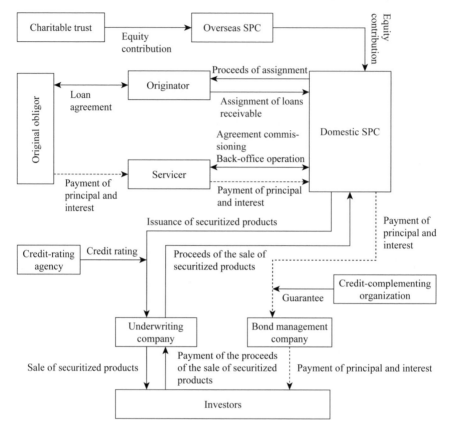

manage assets that have been assigned to an SPV and securitized and also re-cover funds under commission from the SPV, and bond management compa-nies, which administer the securitized products (corporate bonds) purchased by investors. Firms that propose such a mechanism for securitizing assets and that coordinate the issuing and the sale of such products are called "arrang-ers," and securities companies and banks often act as arrangers.

3. Description of Major Securitized Products

Securitized products are divided into several groups according to the types of assets offered as collateral and the characters of the securities issued. Those belonging to the group of products that are backed by real estate and the

Table IX-1.   Classification of SPVs

Types	SPVs established under basic laws	SPVs established under special laws
Corporation type	Special-purpose company (SPC) Domestic: − Corporation (Companies Act) Overseas: − SPC (foreign governing law)	Specific-purpose company–TMK (Act on Securitization of Assets) Investment corporation (Act on Investment Trusts and Investment Corporations)
Trust type	General trust (Trust Act and Trust Business Act)	Specific-purpose trust (SPT) (Act on Securitization of Assets) Investment trust (Act on Investment Trusts and Investment Corporations)
Partnership type	Silent partnership (Commercial Code), general partnership (Civil Code)	Silent partnership, general partnership (Act on Specified Joint Real Estate Ventures)

Source: Prepared by the author from various materials.

claims collateralized by it are residential mortgage-backed securities (RMBS), commercial mortgage-backed securities (CMBS), and real estate investment trusts (REIT). RMBSs are issued in retail denominations against a portfolio that pools home mortgage loans. The first securitized product based on residential mortgage loans was the residential mortgage loan trust launched in 1973. However, this product failed to attract the attention of both issuers and investors because of too much limitation. Nevertheless, as the scheme based on SPC became available thereafter, thanks to the enforcement of the SPC Law, the volume of this type of issue has increased since 1999. Although bonds backed by housing loans that have been issued by the Japan Housing Finance Agency since 2001 were not issued through an SPC, they may be included among the RMBSs. CMBSs are backed by loans given against the collateral of commercial real estate (office buildings, etc.). The mechanism of issuing them is almost the same as that for RMBSs. The REIT that became available by virtue of enforcement of the Act on Investment Trust and Investment Corporation in May 2000 is an investment trust in that it can only invest in assets backed by real estate.

Another group consists of asset-backed securities (ABS, narrowly defined), such as accounts receivable, leases receivable, credits, auto loans, and consumer loans, etc. Sales of these products began to increase in the latter half of 1990s following the enforcement of the Specified Claims Law in June 1993. As these collateralized assets are a collection of relatively small assets and can be dispersed, they are highly suitable for securitization. What is more, as the laws governing the products have since been developed, they are securitized more extensively than the real-estate-backed group.

Table IX-2.   Description of Major Securitized Products

Underlying claims	Securities issued	Originator	Governing laws	Basic scheme
Housing loans receivable	Residential mortgage-backed securities	Banks, Other banking institutions	Act on Securitization of Assets, Trust Act, Trust Business Act, Financial Instruments and Exchange Act	A banking institution that holds mortgage credits assigns them to an SPC; the SPC, in turn, issues a bond backed by such credits or entrusts them to a trust bank, which, in turn, issues beneficiary certificates backed by them.
	Japan Housing Finance Agency bonds backed by housing loans receivable (RMBS)	Japan Housing Finance Agency	Act on the Japan Housing Finance Agency, Independent Administrative Agency Financial Instruments and Exchange Act	Housing loans receivable held by the Japan Housing Finance Agency are given in trust to a trust bank, and a specified corporate bond backed by the beneficiary certificates of a trust is issued at that time through an SPC.
Commercial mortgage credits and rental revenues	Commercial mortgage-backed securities (CMBS)	Business corporations, Banks, Other banking institutions	Act on Securitization of Assets, Trust Act, Trust Business Act, Financial Instruments and Exchange Act	The originator assigns the commercial mortgage credits and rental revenues, etc., to an SPC; the SPC, in turn, issues a bond backed by such credits or entrusts them to a trust bank, which, in turn, issues beneficiary certificates backed by them.
Real estate	Real estate-specific joint venture products	Authorized or registered firms	Act on Specified Joint Real Estate Ventures	An equity contribution is invited from a large number of retail investors, and the funds thus pooled are jointly invested in real estate by taking advantage of the scheme of a voluntary association, an anonymous association, or a real estate investment trust.
	Real estate investment trusts (REIT)	Owners of property purchased by an investment trust	Act on Investment Trusts and Investment Corporations Financial Instruments and Exchange Act	An investment corporation issues units of investment and purchases a piece of real estate and real estate loan claims with the proceeds of such units in accordance with instructions given by a management company.
Mortgage loans receivable created on land, buildings, and superficies	Mortgage securities	Mortgage securities companies	Mortgage Securities Act Financial Instruments and Exchange Act	Mortgage securities are issued by registering mortgage loan receivables of the mortgage securities company, and jointly held equity in mortgage securities is sold to investors.
Fiscal Loan Fund receivables	Fiscal Loan Fund loan-backed securities	Government	Act on Securitization of Assets, Financial Instruments and Exchange Act	The government entrusts the loan receivables from its Fiscal Loan Fund to a trust company. Beneficiary certificates issued on the loans are then sold to an SPC, which issues securities with the loans as the underlying assets.
Leases receivable, credit card receivables, and installment credit accounts and notes receivable	Asset-backed securities (ABS, ABCP)	Business corporations	Act on Securitization of Assets, Trust Act, Trust Business Act, Financial Instruments and Exchange Act	A business corporation that holds lease credits assigns them to an SPC; the SPC, in turn, issues a bond backed by such credits or entrusts them to a trust bank, which, in turn, issues beneficiary certificates backed by them.
General loans	Collateralized loan obligations (CLO)	Banks	Act on Securitization of Assets, Trust Act, Trust Business Act, Financial Instruments and Exchange Act	A banking institution that holds general loans assigns them to an SPC; the SPC, in turn, issues a bond backed by such loans or entrusts them to a trust bank, which, in turn, issues beneficiary certificates backed by them.
Bonds	Collateralized bond obligations (CBO)	Banks and other bondholders	Act on Securitization of Assets, Trust Act, Trust Business Act, Financial Instruments and Exchange Act	The banks and other bondholders that hold a number of bonds assign them to an SPC; the SPC, in turn, issues a bond backed by such credits or entrusts them to a trust bank, which, in turn, issues beneficiary certificates backed by them.

Other securitized products are called collateralized debt obligations (CDO), which are securities issued against the collateral of general loans, corporate bonds, and credit risks of loans that are held by banking institutions. For instance, loans to small and medium-sized business enterprises that are securitized may be considered CDOs. And CDOs are subdivided into collateralized loan obligations (CLO) and collateralized bond obligations (CBO). Moreover, since the eligibility requirements for issuing commercial paper (CP) were abolished in 1996, an increasing number of business corporations have come to use asset-backed commercial paper (ABCP) as a form of securitized product.

4. The Size of the Market

In 2011, the Bank of Japan started to publish the outstanding balance of securitized products, tracing back to data as of the end of fiscal 2007. Until then, a part of the outstanding balance of securitized products had been disclosed as "credit liquidation-related products." According to these statistics, the balance of securitized products outstanding as of the end of fiscal 2020, stood close to ¥41 trillion. When compared with that of stocks and beneficiary certificates of investment trusts (¥1,568 trillion), loans by private financial institutions to corporations and government entities (¥957 trillion), industrial bonds (¥94 trillion) and bank debentures (¥ 6 trillion), their share of privatesector financing as a whole is still not very large. In contrast, a similar balance (of ABS and mortgage-related combined) in the United States, which is considered the most advanced nation in securitizing claims, stood at about ¥1,400 trillion at the end of fiscal 2021. The total issuance amount came to ¥440 trillion, reflecting the extraordinary size of the market compared to the Japanese one.

The scale of the securitized products market that stood at a mere ¥400 billion at the end of fiscal 1989 increased sharply thanks to the enforcement of the Specified Claims Law in 1993 (repealed in 2004), the Special Purpose Companies Law in 1998 and the Act on Securitization of Assets, which is a revised version of the Special Purpose Companies Law, in 2000. This also suggests that assets that can be used as collateral have diversified and that asset securitization has found a growing number of applications. Looking back, the issuance of securities backed by installment credits, which was made possible by the enactment of the Specified Claims Law, was the engine of growth of the market. As these assets have short maturities and can be readily pooled for diversification, they carry relatively low risks and can be easily securitized, and such attributes have been a factor in expanding the scale of the market for them. Since 2000, the securitization of mortgage loans, as well

Chart IX-3. The Balance of Securitized and Claims Liquidation-Related Products

(trillions of yen)

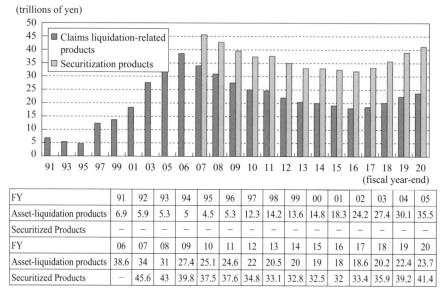

FY	91	92	93	94	95	96	97	98	99	00	01	02	03	04	05
Asset-liquidation products	6.9	5.9	5.3	5	4.5	5.3	12.3	14.2	13.6	14.8	18.3	24.2	27.4	30.1	35.5
Securitized Products	–	–	–	–	–	–	–	–	–	–	–	–	–	–	–
FY	06	07	08	09	10	11	12	13	14	15	16	17	18	19	20
Asset-liquidation products	38.6	34	31	27.4	25.1	24.6	22	20.5	20	19	18	18.6	20.2	22.4	23.7
Securitized Products	–	45.6	43	39.8	37.5	37.6	34.8	33.1	32.8	32.5	32	33.4	35.9	39.2	41.4

Source: Complied on the basis of the data drawn from *Nichigin shikin junkan-tokei* (Flow-of-Funds Statement of the Bank of Japan).

Table IX-3. Changes in Composition of Collateralized Assets, etc.

(trillions of yen)

	2008	2010	2012	2014	2016	2018	2020	Ratio to net operating income
Asset backed bonds (ABB)	13.8	13.9	14.1	14.1	14.9	16.5	18.8	45.4
MBS issued by JHFA	7.6	9	10.6	11	12.1	13.6	15.1	36.5
ABB backed by real estate properties	4.4	3.4	2.2	1.7	1.8	2.2	2.5	6.0
Other ABB	1.8	1.4	1.3	1.3	1	0.8	1.2	2.9
ABCP	3.9	2.4	2.3	1.8	1.7	1.5	1.8	4.3
Trust beneficiary rights	25.4	21.2	18.4	16.9	15.4	17.9	20.8	50.2
Of which backed by housing loans	9.7	8.6	7.7	7.7	7.6	9.5	11.3	27.3
Of which backed by loans to companies and governments	3.7	2.7	1.9	1.7	1.7	1.5	2.2	5.3
Of which backed by accounts receivable	5.2	5.4	5.1	3.6	1.7	1.2	0.7	1.7
Of which backed by lease and consumer credits	5.6	3.8	2.8	2.9	3.6	4.5	5.1	12.3
Total	43	37.5	34.8	32.8	32	35.9	41.4	100.0

Source: Complied based on the data from *Nichigin shikin junkan-tokei* (Flow-of-Funds Statement of the Bank of Japan).

as of loans to business corporations and the government, has expanded dramatically. This may be explained by the fact that, pressed by the need to raise the capital adequacy ratio in compliance with the Basel Accords, banks have sought to unload loan assets from their balance sheets. After reaching a peak in fiscal 2006, the volume of securitized products fell back as the economy weakened in the wake of the subprime loan crisis. It has, however, started to recover again since.

"Securitized products" are defined as the total of asset-backed securities, asset-backed commercial paper (ABCP) and trust beneficiary interests. Residential mortgage-backed securities (RMBS) issued by the Japan Housing Finance Agency (JHF; formerly, Housing Loan Corporation) account for 80% of asset-backed securities. Looking at the underlying assets of trust beneficiary interests that account for nearly half of the total outstanding balance, nearly 50% are mortgage loans while almost 25% are leases & credit receivables.

5. Primary Market for Securitized Products

As the bulk of securitized products are issued in private placement transactions between the parties concerned, it is difficult to accurately grasp the size of the primary market of securitized products. However, the Japan Securities Dealers Association (JSDA) currently compiles and publishes the "Securitization Market Trends Survey" conducted jointly with the Japanese Bankers Association based on information on issuance trends of securitized products received voluntarily from arrangers of securitized products and others. According to the Securitization Market Trends Survey, securitized products issued in Japan in fiscal 2020 reached just over ¥5 trillion. Although securitized product issuance reached a peak of ¥9.8 trillion in fiscal 2006, it went through a period of decline under the impact of the weakening economy kicked off by the subprime loan crisis. However, it has been on a recovery trend over the last few years.

Looking at the trend by the type of asset pledged as collateral, while residential mortgage loans and shopping credits have exhibited a recovery trend, other assets have declined—a result that reflects the differences in the types of underlying assets. Residential mortgage loans account for an increasing percentage of the underlying assets used as collateral, a trend that has not changed over the past few years. This trend reflects that lending banks are actively securitizing mortgage loans of their own origination and that the issuance of RMBS by the Japan Housing Finance Agency has remained at a high level. Shopping credit saw a steep rise between fiscal 2012 to 2020 to jump almost fivefold, now accounting for 30% of the

Chart IX-4. Securitized Products Issuance

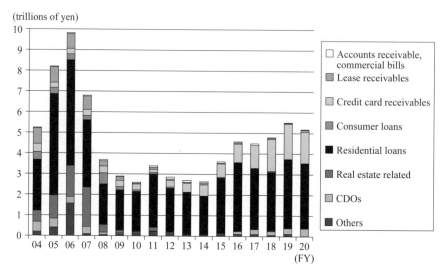

Source: Compiled from "Securitization Market Trends Survey Report" by the Japan Securities Dealers
  Association.

Chart IX-5. Breakdown of Collateralized Assets

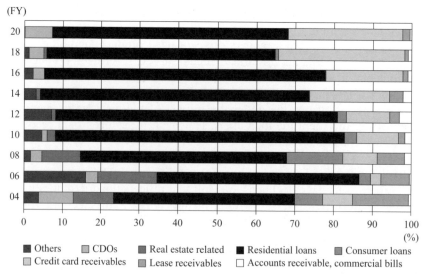

Source: Compiled from "Securitization Market Trends Survey Report" by the Japan Securities Dealers
  Association.

underlying assets used as collateral.

According to the data on issuance compiled by the JSDA, the total value of publicly offered asset-backed corporate bonds had steadily increased since 1997, the year in which the association started tracking the data. After hitting a peak of ¥0.52 trillion in fiscal 2002, however, the total declined, falling to ¥50 billion in fiscal 2019, with no bonds issued at all in 2020. The popularity of privately placed asset-backed corporate bonds is thought to be the result of considerations with regard to investor protection framework, taxes, and disclosure cost.

Now turning to other characteristics of securitized products issued, pass-through repayments accounted for 8% or more of the overall repayment methods, followed by installment and lump-sum repayments.

In terms of ratings, 80% or more is rated AAA. The remaining portion consists of long- or short-term AA-, A-, and a few BBB-rated instruments. No issuance below BB can be seen since 2017.

6. Secondary Market for Securitized Products

With the exception of beneficiary certificates of real estate investment trusts (REITs) and infrastructure funds to be discussed later, trading in securitized products is not concentrated in stock exchanges. As is the case with the secondary market for bonds, securitized products and their transactions are too complex and varied to lend themselves to exchange trading. Hence this has led to the dependence on an over-the-counter interdealer market as the secondary market for their trading. In this section, we will overview the present state of the interdealer market of securitized products by using primarily the data on "TMK bonds" (which are publicly offered corporate bonds issued by a corporation established based on the Act on Securitization of Assets. And asset-backed bonds, which is an item for statistics for the primary market, includes the portion of the issuer established for funds raising purposes based on the Companies Act.) published by the JSDA, which is in a position to obtain data on interdealer transactions.

Data on the trading amounts of TMK bonds compiled by the JSDA on the basis of reports from member securities companies for the years prior to 1998 are not available. According to these reports, the trading amount of TMK bonds peaked in 2014, but is on an overall declining trend albeit with frequent fluctuations. A comparison of TMK trading amounts with those of other bonds in 2020 shows that TMK bond trading amounted to nearly ¥50 billion, and those of corporate straight bonds and utility bonds stood at ¥10.8 trillion and ¥2.4 trillion, respectively. Although these issues constitute only a part of the whole universe of securitized products, it is evident that the

Chart IX-6.   The Amount of TMK Bonds Traded

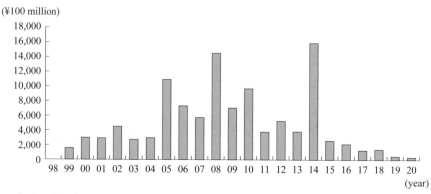

(¥100 million)

Source: Compiled from "Trading Volume of Over-the-Counter (OTC) Bonds" by the Japan Securities Dealers Association.

Chart IX-7.   Changes in launch spread (Average) of Japan Housing Finance Agency MBS (Monthly Bonds)

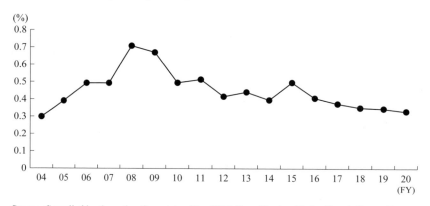

(%)

Source: Compiled by the author from data of the JSDA Securitization Market Trends Survey Report.

trading amounts remain quite limited. The number of securities companies that offer them is quite limited, and their liquidity is considerably low. On the other hand, a large number of securities companies make a market in RMBS issued by the Japan Housing Finance Agency, the bonds are classified as FILP agency bonds for statistical purposes, and their market seems to have a certain degree of liquidity.

As their trading market is yet to attain maturity, it is difficult to precisely

Chart IX-8.   Claims Liquidation-Related Product Holding Ratio

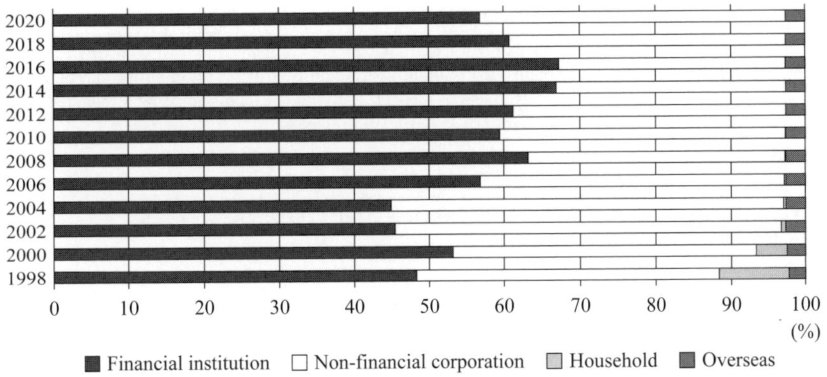

Source: Complied on the basis of the data drawn from *Nichigin shikin junkan-tokei* (Flow-of-Funds Statement of the Bank of Japan).

measure their secondary market yields, and they have to be substituted with yields at issue. Measured in terms of yields at issue, the most highly liquid JHF bonds are traded at a higher yield than government-guaranteed bonds. Reinvestment risk occasioned by early mortgage loan repayment in addition to the expected redemption period and the availability of a government guarantee may be a factor behind this. While the spread of these two bonds can slightly widen at times, it is generally stable at no more than 0.4% in recent years.

According to the balance of financial assets and liabilities of the Flow-of-Funds Accounts of the Bank of Japan, the current holders of credit liquidation-related products (securitized products) are almost entirely made up of non-financial corporations (less than 40%) and financial institutions (60%). In 1990, households were the primary holders. Since then, however, holdings by households have declined consistently, and currently stand at zero. During this time, financial institutions increased their holdings of securitization-related products and have become the primary holders.

7. Primary and Secondary Markets for the Beneficiary Certificates of Real Estate Investment Trusts

On September 10, 2001, the Japan Building Fund Investment Corporation and the Japan Real Estate Investment Corporation listed their certificates on the Tokyo Stock Exchange and became the first public real estate investment

Table IX-4.   The Listing Requirements of the Tokyo Stock Exchange

Item	Listing requirements
Eligibility for becoming an asset management company	The investment trust management company, the trust company for an investment trust without instruction by trustor, or an entity that otherwise manages assets of a REIT applying for listing must be a member of the Investment Trusts Association, Japan.
Ratio of real estate to the total value of assets managed	The ratio of real estate is expected to be 70% or higher.
Ratio of real estate and related assets and liquid assets to the total assets under management	The ratio of real estate is expected to be 95% or higher.
Total net asset value	Expected to increase to ¥1 billion or more by the time of listing.
Total asset value	Expected to increase to ¥5 billion or more by the time of listing.
Auditor's opinion	(a) The securities report for the two immediately preceding terms are fair and accurate and contain no false statements. (b) The audit reports for the two immediately preceding terms contain the remarks "unqualified opinion" or "qualified opinion with an exception."
No. of units listed	Expected to increase to 4,000 or more by the time it is listed.
Major beneficiaries or investors	The total number of units owned by major beneficiaries or investors is expected to be 75% or less of the total units listed.
No. of beneficiaries or investors	Their number (except major beneficiaries or investors) is expected to increase to 1,000 or more at the time of listing.

Source: Compiled on the basis of the data drawn from the website of the Tokyo Stock Exchange.

Table IX-5.   Statistics Relating to REITs Listed on the Tokyo Stock Exchange

Calendar year	No. of issues listed	Capital contribution (¥100 million)	Total net Assets (¥100 million)	Total liabilities (¥100 million)	Total assets (¥100 million)
2009	42	39,624	40,202	40,947	81,514
2010	35	36,239	39,090	41,360	80,842
2011	34	37,925	41,097	44,321	85,636
2012	37	42,444	45,789	47,654	93,679
2013	43	53,762	57,387	57,595	115,252
2014	49	61,521	65,407	64,601	130,328
2015	52	66,287	73,483	70,504	144,336
2016	57	72,797	82,955	77,972	161,431
2017	59	78,199	88,498	82,772	171,889
2018	61	83,928	95,837	89,193	185,544
2019	64	90,001	102,099	94,788	197,499
2020	62	95,595	108,121	101,194	209,891

Source: Compiled from "Real Estate Investment Trusts" by Investment Trusts Association, Japan.

trusts (REITs) in Japan. These real estate investment trusts owe their creation to the amendment of the Securities Investment Trust Act enforced in November 2000, which made it possible to form trust funds through a real estate investment trust scheme. In addition, the Tokyo Stock Exchange instituted a rule granting a special exception to the securities listing regulations in favor of real estate investment trust certificates and enforced it on March 1, 2001. By March 31, 2020, the number of listed issues had increased to 62.

The basic mechanism of REITs is this: investment corporations or investment managers called investment trust management companies pool funds of investors, invest such funds primarily in real estate, and distribute the investment income (including rent income) to investors. The three types of securities defined in the Act on Investment Trusts and Investment Corporations—beneficiary certificates of investment trusts with instruction by trustor, beneficiary certificates of investment trusts without instruction by trustor, and investment securities of investment corporations—may also be issued by real estate investment trusts. The first type of trust is managed by a trust company that holds the assets in custody in accordance with instructions given by the management company. The second type is managed by a trust bank in accordance with its own judgment. And the third is commissioned to a management company by the investment corporation that holds the assets. All of the certificates of the REITs listed on the Tokyo Stock Exchange are investment securities issued by investment corporations.

One of the advantages investors can derive from REITs is that they are able to invest in real estate with a small amount of money, and they can enjoy liquidity in freely trading their investments in the market. Another is that REITs offer diversification to their investment portfolio. REIT dividends may be expensed provided that a REIT meets certain requirements, including distributing more than 90% of its income to its certificate holders.

One problem that the managers of REITs have to address is the possibility of a conflict of interests between investors and the manager of a REIT with respect to any investment of its assets commissioned to a third party. In other words, it is feared that the management company may force the REIT to buy a piece of real estate held by its stockholders at a high price. To avoid the occurrence of such a situation, it is desirable to require the REIT to fully disclose information concerning its investments. And investors should consider getting involved in the management of investment corporations through a general meeting of investors.

8. Listed Infrastructure Funds

In April 2015, the Tokyo Stock Exchange (TSE) established an infrastructure fund market for listing funds that invest in infrastructure properties. The infrastructure funds handled on this market hold infrastructure properties and attain a cash flow that arises when lending the assets to operators. It is on the infrastructure fund market that the securities issued as underlying instruments of the cash flow are traded.

The structure of infrastructure funds is basically similar to that of REIT. While the listing rules for the infrastructure fund market are generally based on the framework for the REIT market, there is a key difference in that the policy for selecting operators who borrow and operate the infrastructure properties is included in the rules.

There have been listed only six issues on the infrastructure fund market by March 31, 2019. In addition, all listed issues hold solar power generation facilities as underlying assets and have issued securities. This is likely due to the projection that a solar power plant would be a highly stable source of profits given that power companies buy power at fixed prices following the enforcement of the Act on Special Measures Concerning Procurement of Electricity from Renewable Energy Sources by Electricity Utilities ("Feed-in Tariffs (FIT) Act") in 2011.

Properties that support the livelihoods of people, including electricity and gas facilities, water supply facilities, railroads and roads, can be the underlying assets of infrastructure funds. One of the reasons why infrastructure funds have been drawing attention is because earnings generated by such infrastructure properties are considered to be relatively less vulnerable to economic changes. This makes it possible for infrastructure funds to also maintain stable profits. While currently in Japan all funds pertain to solar power plants, it is anticipated that infrastructure funds that invest in other types of properties will emerge going forward.

The total number of shares issued for the seven issues combined amounted to approximately 630,000 shares, with a market capitalization of approximately ¥160 billion as of December 2019. Daily trading volume stood at nearly 4,000 shares from March to August 2021 for the seven issues listed at the time. The trading volume is also on the rise, drawing attention for further developments in the future.

In infrastructure investment, the terms greenfield and brownfield are used. The former signifies a field that has not been touched by human hands, reflecting a type of investment made where nothing exists. Meanwhile, the latter refers to a state in which human intervention has already been made, reflecting an investment in an existing infrastructure facility.

Chart IX-9.   Structure of Infrastructure Funds

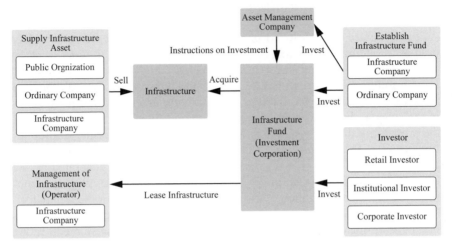

Source: Website of the Japan Exchange Group, Inc.

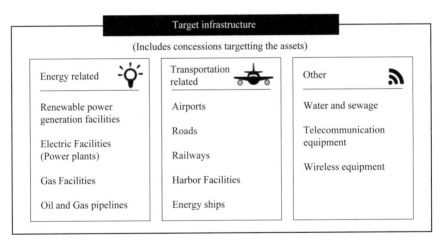

* Right to operate public facilities (concession) refers to the right to operate the public facility, which collects charges for usage that can be outsourced to a private business operator while the ownership of the facility remains with the public entity.
Source: "Infrastructure Funds" Section on the website of the Japan Exchange Group, Inc.

9. Risks and Credit Enhancement of Securitized Products

As the structure of securitized products is complex, credit rating is widely used as a criterion for making an investment decision. And in order to package assets into a securitized product that merits a high credit rating, a device for controlling various risks has to be built into the product. The substance of risks varies depending on the kind of underlying assets and the participants in the scheme, but one thing in common among them is the default risk, or the probability that the issuer may fail to pay its interest or principal promptly when due. The default risk of a securitized product is largely divided into two kinds: the risk of changes occurring in the cash flow generated by the underlying assets (bad debt or arrears) and the risk of bankruptcy of parties involved in the securitization of assets (the debtor, the SPC, or the originator).

The risk involved in the cash flow may be reduced by taking various credit-enhancing measures. Unlike general corporate bonds, whose credit rating is determined by the credit risk of their issuers, the credit rating of a securitized product must be based on the results of examinations of assets underlying each product. The arranger who underwrites and markets the securitized product and the originator negotiate with a credit-rating agency to obtain a high rating. There are various credit-enhancing measures to choose from for different schemes employed for issuing a securitized product, but they may be largely divided into two: an external credit-enhancing measure that utilizes external credit (such as banking institutions) and an internal credit-enhancing measure that gives the structure of the security the function of enhancing its credit. There are two methods of external credit enhancement: indirect and direct. The former complements cash flows from underlying loan assets, and the latter complements that of a securitized product. The indirect method has a drawback in that it cannot eliminate risks associated with a servicer or any other party involved in securitization. As a means of enhancing internal credit, a senior subordinated structure is commonly used. In Japan, however, the subordinated securities are often held by the originator because, among other reasons, there are few investors who are willing to purchase them.

A large part of the risk of changes in cash flows from underlying assets can be covered by credit enhancing measures. However, the risk of bankruptcy of the parties involved in securitization is a serious problem. As assigned claims and receivables of a bankrupt originator are typically subject to bankruptcy proceedings, investors carry the risk of nonpayment of their principal and interest. Therefore, it is important to check whether there is any risk in the business of any party concerned or whether the party is shielded from the risk of other parties concerned. Risks are complexly intertwined, and they are summed up in Table IX-7.

Table IX-6.   Main Credit Enhancing Measures

Credit enhancement (external)	Recourse of the originator	The originator owes recourse to a certain part of the assets sold to the SPC. Off-balance sheet accounting may not be authorized depending on the extent to which the originator owes such recourse.
	Credit default swaps	The purchaser of a swap pays a certain amount of money in premium in exchange for a guarantee of credit risk of a specified claim.
	Guarantee, insurance by financial institutions	A property and casualty insurance company provides insurance covering the entire default risk is issued securities.
Credit enhancement (internal)	Spread account	The balance of funds remaining after deducting the amounts paid to the investors and fees from the cash flow of the underlying assets is deposited in a spread account to be used as compensation money in case of default.
	Over collateral	The credit standing of securities is enhanced by selling such part of the underlying assets whose value is in excess of the amount of the securities issued to the special purpose vehicle (SPV).
	Senior/subordinated structure	By designating part of the securities issued as subordinated debt, the credit standing of the rest of the issue is enhanced.

10. The Enactment of Securitization-Related Laws

The existing legal system of Japan is built around business-specific laws, and the regulatory system of financial instruments is vertically divided along the lines of business-specific laws. As these laws contain many provisions regulating or banning business activities outright, it was pointed out that to spur the development of new business, such as the securitization of assets, the existing laws had to be amended, and new laws must be enacted.

As regards the securitization of assets, pioneered by the Mortgage Securities Act introduced in 1931, the Specified Claims Law was enacted as an independent law in 1993. Since the enforcement of this law, the legal infrastructure has been developed steadily. Under and thanks to the Specified Claims Law, the liquidation and securitization of assets classified as specified claims, such as leases receivable and credit card receivables, started. Thereafter, various laws were enacted to help the banking institutions meet the capital adequacy standards imposed by the Basel Committee on Banking Supervision and to encourage the securitization of their assets to deal with the bad loan problem that had become serious since the turn of the decade of the 1990s.

Under the Special-Purpose Company (SPC) Law and the Act on Securiti-

Table IX-7.   Typical Risks of ABS

Overall risks of ABS	Outline	Measures necessary to avoid risks
Credit risk	There is a risk of a failure to generate an expected cash flow due to a default of the originator.	A review of credit-enhancing measures is needed. In the case of an underlying asset that consists of many credits, steps must be taken to diversify such underlying assets.
Prepayment risk	If the issuer redeems the security ahead of its maturity, the investors will be exposed to prepayment risks.	It is necessary to develop techniques such as a collateralized mortgage obligation (CMO) and a security with a period of deferment that adjusts the relationship between the underlying assets and the cash flow generated by the security issued thereby.
Liquidity risk	When the funds flow out rapidly from the market, the holder cannot sell the security in a timely manner because the liquidity of the securitized product is not adequate, and the holder is thus exposed to a liquidity crunch.	The development of a secondary market for trading ABSs is a must. Also, the subordinated security shoud be traded widely among the investors.
Risks of the parties concerned	Outline	Measures necessary to avoid risks
Originator's risk	Once the claims of the originator sold to the SPC are recognized as part of the bankruptcy estate, the investors have the risk of forfeiting their right to receive the payment of the principal and interest of the security.	It is necessary to ensure that the transfer of the claims is not for securing a loan but is their true sale. The assets must be separated from the balance sheet. Transaction must have the conditions necessary for counteracting against a third party.
Servicer risk	The commingling risk: A servicer of receivables that went bankrupt may mingle the funds it had received before it went bankrupt with its own funds without remitting them to the SPV.	The designation of a backup servicer capable of putting up excess collateral is needed. Payment of remittances received from debtors must be made directly into the account of the SPV. Management of a lock-box account must be conducted.
SPC risk	Bankruptcy remoteness must be established so that the SPC of an asset securitization scheme itself will not go bankrupt or will not be affected by the bankruptcy of other companies.	The substance of business must be clearly defined, and an SPC in which the originator has no equity interest must be founded by establishing a charitable trust. The commencement of bankruptcy proceedings must be averted by making the charitable trust its beneficial shareholder.

Table IX-8.   Chronology Relating to the Securitization of Assets

Month & Year	Changes implemented
Aug. 1931	The Mortgage Securities Act is enacted.
June 1973	Housing loan companies raise funds by offering beneficiary certificates of housing loan claim trusts.
Sept. 1974	Housing loan companies raise funds by offering mortgage-backed securities.
Jan. 1988	The Law Concerning the Regulation of Mortgage-Backed Securities Business is enforced.
Apr. 1992	The Law Concerning the Regulation of Business Relating to Commodity Investment (the Commodity Fund Law) is enforced.
Apr. 1993	The Securities and Exchange Act designates beneficiary certificates of housing loan claim trusts as securities.
June 1993	The Law Concerning the Regulation of Business Relating to Specified Claims, etc. (the Specified Claims Law) is enforced.
July 1993	The ban on the issuance of CPs by nonbanks is lifted.
Apr. 1995	The Act on Specified Joint Real Estate Ventures is enforced.
Apr. 1996	As a method of liquidizing assets under the Securities and Exchange Act, the issuance of asset-backed securities (ABS and ABCP) is authorized, making it possible to issue them other than under the Securities and Exchange Act.
June 1997	Beneficiary certificates of general loan claim trusts (including loans secured by real estate) are designated as securities under the Securities and Exchange Act.
Feb. 1998	The Securities Investment Trust Act is amended (and the ban on corporation type investment trusts and privately placed investment trusts is lifted).
Apr. 1998	A total plan for the liquidation of land and claims is announced.
Sept. 1998	The Act on Securitization of Specified Assets by Specified Purpose Companies (the SPC Law) is enforced.
Oct. 1998	The Law Concerning Exceptions to Requirements under the Civil Code for the Perfection of Assignment of Receivables and Other Properties (the Perfection Law) is enforced.
Jan. 1999	A statement of opinion on establishing accounting standards for financial instruments is published. (The financial component approach to conditional transfer of financial assets is adopted.)
Feb. 1999	The Act on Special Measures Concerning Claim Management and Collection Business (the Servicer Law) is enforced.
May 1999	Act on Issuance, etc. of Bonds for Financial Corporations' Loan Business (the so-called Nonbank Bond Law) is enforced.
May. 2000	The SPC Law is amended to the Act on Securitization of Assets (Revised SPC Law), the assets subject to liquidation is expanded.
Nov. 2000	The Act on Investment Trusts and Investment Corporations (the revised Securities Investment Trust Act) is enforced, expanding the assets that can be securitized to real estate, etc.
Sept. 2001	The revised Act on Special Measures Concerning Claim Management and Collection Business is enforced.
Dec. 2004	The Trust Business Act is amended, and the system requiring trust companies of the management type to register is launched.
Dec. 2004	The Specified Claims Law is repealed.
Oct. 2005	The Special Provisions of Assignment of Obligations was amended to the Act on Special Provisions, etc. of the Civil Code Concerning the Perfection Requirements for the Assignment of Movables and Claims.
May 2006	The Companies Act is enforced.
Dec. 2006	The Trust Act is amended and provided for business, personal, and purpose trusts.
Oct. 2007	The Financial Instruments and Exchange Act is enforced.
Nov. 2011	Revised Act on Securitization of Assets is enforced.
Apr. 2018	Revised Financial Instruments and Exchange Law is enforced.
June 2023	Revised Company Law is scheduled to be enforced.

zation of Assets enacted as the revised SPC Law, structures incorporating SPVs, including specific-purpose companies (TMK) and specific-purpose trusts (SPT), may be used for securitizing specified assets designated in the provisions of the said laws (real estate, designated money claims, and beneficiary certificates issued against such assets in trust) in the form of asset-backed securities (such as senior subscription certificates, specified corporate bonds, and specified promissory notes, etc.). Under the SPC Law, the system of disclosing an asset liquidation plan and individual liquidation projects was introduced, in addition to the disclosure requirements on the disclosure of information on securities under the Securities and Exchange Act (currently the Financial Instruments and Exchange Act).

In 1998 the Act on Special Provisions, etc. of the Civil Code Concerning the Perfection Requirements for the Assignment of Movables and Claims was enacted as a law prescribing exceptions to requirements under the Civil Code for the perfection of the assignment of receivables and other properties, and it was amended in 2005. The Civil Code provides the legal requirements for the assertion of the assignment of nominative claims (claims with named creditors) against obligors or third parties. Designated claims were transferable, but the provisions of the Civil Code had been a major hurdle standing in the way of securitizing them. And the Perfection Law set forth simple procedures for the perfection of such interests.

The Act on Special Measures Concerning Claim Management and Collection Business, enacted to account for exceptions to the provisions of the Attorney Law, allows accredited corporations to provide the services of administering and collecting debts. Under the Act on Special Measures Concerning Claim Management and Collection Business, a debt collection company may be established to provide a bad debt collection service without conflicts with the Attorney Law. The Act on Issuance, etc. of Bonds for Financial Corporations' Loan Business conditionally lifted the ban imposed on nonbanks on the issuance of corporate bonds and CPs for the purpose of raising capital for lending operations and on ABSs.

As a result of the revision of the Securities and Exchange Act based on the Act on Revision, etc. of Related Acts for the Financial System Reform and the enforcement of the Financial Instruments and Exchange Act, beneficiary certificates of and trust beneficiary interests in assets that are deemed eligible for securitization by the provisions of the Act on Securitization of Assets and mortgage certificates under the Mortgage Securities Act are now legally considered securities. Furthermore, pursuant to the enactment of the Act on Investment Trusts and Investment Corporations as revised, real estate was included in eligible assets, which paved the way for the issuance of REIT securities. Since then, the scope of eligible assets has been expanded, and the infrastructure funds emerged.

CHAPTER X

Financial Instruments Exchange, etc. (1)

1. The Function of the Financial Instruments Exchanges

The basic function of a financial instruments exchange is to establish a market and concentrate supply and demand of marketable securities in a single market to enhance the liquidity of securities, to help form fair prices that reflect supply and demand, and to promptly publish the prices thus formed. The purpose of a financial instruments exchange is to establish a market for trading securities and executing exchange derivatives trading and to run the market in such a way as to facilitate fair and efficient trading in the public interest and for the protection of investors. The basic mission of the financial instruments exchange is to provide a fair and transparent market. The market established by a financial instruments exchange has the function of providing a marketplace that enhances the liquidity of financial instruments and helps form fair prices so as to provide investors with an environment in which investors can conduct investment activities free from anxiety, raise funds smoothly by issuing securities, and hedge risks by executing exchange derivatives trading among other activities. Furthermore, prices formed on an exchange can serve as a base for assessing the asset value of securities among others and price indexes serve as an important indicator of economic and business trends. Because financial instruments markets operated by exchanges perform an important role in supporting the economy of the nation, a license must be obtained from the prime minister to open an exchange, and the operation of that exchange is placed under supervision according to the Financial Instruments and Exchange Act.

Stock exchanges were conventionally required to be membership organizations under the Securities and Exchange Act. An amendment of that law that went into effect in 2000, however, allowed stock exchanges to change their legal status to that of a corporation. Starting with Osaka in 2001, the Tokyo, Nagoya, and JASDAQ exchanges became corporations. The enforcement of the Financial Instruments and Exchange Act in 2007 provided for the establishment of an exchange holding company, self-regulatory organization, etc. Given this law, in the same year, the Tokyo Stock Exchange Group, Inc.

Chart X-1. The Function of the JPX-operated Financial Instruments Exchanges

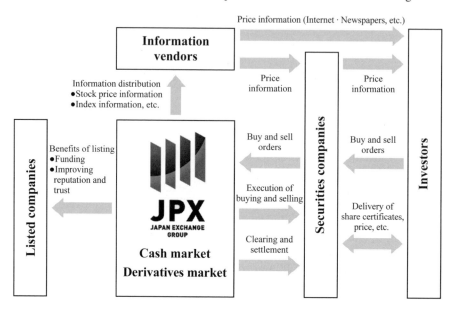

Chart X-2. Overview of Comprehensive Exchange

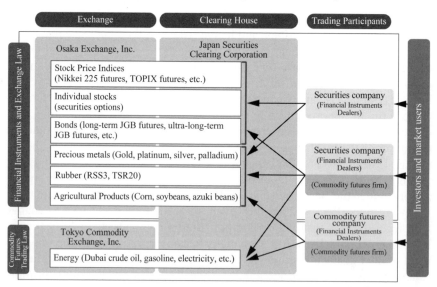

As of August 31, 2021

was established as a holding company of the Tokyo Stock Exchange and a self-regulatory organization. The establishment of a holding company was prompted by potential conflicts of interest between the public role of an exchange as an operator of self-regulating operations and the for-profit orientation of an exchange as a corporation, where exchanges sought to reinforce the independence of their highly public function to ensure self-regulation of the market. Furthermore, against the backdrop of intensifying competition among markets across borders resulting from the advancement of financial transaction systems, in 2013, the Tokyo Stock Exchange Group and the Osaka Securities Exchange combined their operations to increase the appeal and convenience of their markets and to enhance their global competitiveness, forming the Japan Exchange Group (JPX).

In 2019, JPX acquired Tokyo Commodity Exchange (TOCOM), and in 2020 it transferred trading in precious metal futures and other commodities from TOCOM to Osaka Exchange (OSE), which specializes in derivatives, and integrated clearing organizations under its umbrella to create a comprehensive exchange for trading a wide range of products from financial instruments to commodities.

2. Footsteps of Markets

When the stock exchange resumed trading after WW2, the exchange market was a single market. With the Japanese economy entering a period of high growth and the demand for capital from small and medium-sized enterprises increasing, the OTC transactions executed outside the stock exchange rapidly evolved into a marketplace for so-called "collective transactions". It became necessary to institutionalize the marketplace to encourage the development of the SMEs and to protect investors. In 1961, the Tokyo, Osaka and Nagoya Stock Exchanges set up Second Sections that have with more relaxed listing standards than the conventional market, thereby absorbing many of the shares which had previously been traded OTC. This is the origin of the First Section and the Second Section of the TSE. Previously, new listing companies were due to be designated on the Second Section. However, with the initial listing of Nippon Telegraph and Telephone Corporation (NTT) in 1986, part of designation standards was revised, enabling certain companies with a large number of listing shares and likelihood for exceptionally favorable shareholder base to be designated on the First Section. In 1996, with the objective of clarification, the standards for listing directly on the First Section were formalized, which required a certain number of listing shares and the shareholder base conformable to the First Section designation standards.

Amid Japan's high economic growth, the Japan Securities Dealers Associ-

Table X-1.   History of the TSE's First and Second Sections

Apr. 1949	Stock Exchange reopened
Oct. 1961	The Second Section of the market opened in Tokyo, Osaka and Nagoya Establishment of listing criteria for shares designated to be listed on the First Section and those re-designated to be listed on the Second Section
Nov. 1986	Revision of regulations concerning the listing of NTT shares • Certain companies with a large number of listing shares and the likelihood for exceptionally favorable shareholder base could be directly designated as First Section stocks.
Nov. 1996	Standards for listing directly on the First Section formalized for clarification purposes • Number of listing shares, shareholder base (conformable to the First Section designation standards), etc.

Table X-2.   History of the JASDAQ

Nov. 1983	New over-the-counter (OTC) market launched.
Dec. 1998	The JASDAQ market defined as an OTC securities market (in parallel with other exchange markets).
Dec. 2004	Stock exchange license acquired by JASDAQ and by the Securities and Exchange Act its name changed to the JASDAQ Securities Exchange.
Aug. 2007	The NEO market established.
Oct. 2007	JASDAQ, NEO, and Hercules markets merged, forming the new JASDAQ market.
July 2013	The businesses of TSE and OSE combined, with the TSE continuing to operate JASDAQ.

Table X-3.   History of the Mothers

Nov. 1999	Mothers launched.
May 2002	Listing criteria reviewed: • Newly establish delisting criteria regarding sales. • Newly establish listing screening standards and delisting criteria regarding market capitalization, etc.
Dec. 2006	The first phase of a comprehensive listing system improvement program undertaken. • Require new applicants to obtain a letter of recommendation from the managing underwriter.
Nov. 2007	The second phase of a comprehensive listing system improvement program undertaken. • Abolish provisions for moving from main exchange to Mothers market (clarify Mothers' position as a start-up market), etc.
Nov. 2009	Steps taken to improve confidence in market taken. • Newly establish "appropriateness of business plan" as a listing criteria. • Newly establish stock price related delisting criteria, etc.
Mar. 2011	Further steps to improve confidence in and stimulate market taken. • Require listed companies to be audited by an audit firm registered with exchange. • Newly establish requirement to choose whether to stay on Mothers after 10 years. • Introduce listing screening policy in line with market concept (confirm appropriateness of business plan).

ation (JSDA) introduced the OTC Registration System in 1963 to provide a marketplace to secure funding for those companies that lack listing opportunities on the exchange markets. The OTC Registration System was reorganized into the new OTC Stock Market in 1983 and served to complement the conventional stock exchanges as a capital market for growth and start-up companies. After the revision of the Securities and Exchange Act in 1998, the OTC Stock Market was redefined that exists in parallel with other exchange markets in its own right. In 2004, it became the JASDAQ Securities Exchange, which was subsequently merged with the OSE-operated Hercules in 2010. Following the management integration of the TSE and the OSE, the exchange has been operated as the TSE JASDAQ market since July 2013.

In 1999, the TSE established a market of start-ups called Mothers to provide listing opportunities for emerging companies in their start-up growth phase. This new market offered improved protection for investors through enhanced disclosure requirements, while allowing companies with high growth prospects to get listed even if they had negative net worth or suffered pretax losses. Subsequently, after a set of scandals among some of the listed companies, the screening criteria for listing were tightened to improve investor protection. Consequently, in 2011, the TSE undertook a review of the Mothers' listing system and implemented measures to increase confidence and stimulate activity in the market. Among those measures, the exchange added the requirement for listed companies to be audited by an audit firm registered in JICPA's Company Audit Firm Resister. The TSE also changed its listing screening policy to one of evaluating whether the business plans of companies seeking to list were achievable in the long term.

3. Review of TSE market segment

As of September 2021, TSE operates four markets for general investors: the First Section, the Second Section, Mothers and JASDAQ (Standard and Growth). This market structure reflects the fact that when TSE and OSE merged in 2013, they maintained their respective structures so as to minimize the impact on listed companies and investors. In recent years, however, it has become evident that there is room for improvement in certain areas. Accordingly, in 2018, TSE canvassed opinion on various issues related to market structure and the future direction of the market. Specifically, market participants raised the following points: (1) many investors find the concept of each market segment unclear and confusing; (2) the market is not fully fulfilling its expected role in terms of incentivizing listed companies to sustainably increase their corporate value, and (3) there is no index that functions properly as a benchmark investable index.

Chart X-3.   Major Issues regarding TSE Cash Equity Market Structure

1. Ambiguous market concept impairing convenience of investors & losing attractiveness
✓ Concerns that market concept of the 2nd Section, Mothers, and JASDAQ overlap and confusing
✓ Concerns that market concept of the 1st Section is unclear, and the growth of TOPIX-linked passive investment is affecting price formation of issues with relatively low liquidity

2. Insufficient incentives for listed companies to sustainably grow and increase corporate value
✓ Concerns that listing criteria for "step-up" to the 1st Section is not functioning sufficiently to incentivize growth
✓ Concerns of insufficiency of market participation by institutional investors Mothers and JASDAQ and of the disclosed information of start-up companies

3. There is no index available that is not only good for investment but also well representing the whole market
✓ TOPIX, widely used by investors as a benchmark is comprised of all stocks listed on the 1st Section
✓ Few investors use JPX Nikkei 400 nor TOPIX 500 as a benchmark stocks

For the Japanese economy to continue growing, it is imperative and urgent that listed companies increase their corporate value over the medium-to-long term and many start-up companies grow

Chart X-4.   Restructuring the Market Segments with a clear market concept

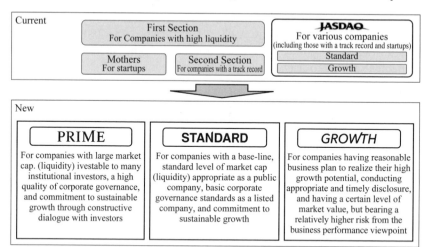

Based on these issues, TSE has been reviewing the segments of the market. On April 4, 2022, the market is scheduled tobe reorganized into three new segments: Prime, Standard, and Growth, in order to provide a market that incentivizes sustainable growth and mid-to long-term corporate value creation of listed companies and attracts various types of investors, both domestic and foreign.

Listing requirements for each new market segment set quantitative and qualitative criteria for liquidity, corporate governance and others in accordance with each market concept. In principle, the same criteria shall apply to both initial listing and listing maintenance for each segment, and therefore listed companies will be required to comply with the standards of the initial listing criteria on a continuous basis after listing. Each market segment is independent, and thus are no special lowered requirements for transfer between segments, as is the case so far. Therefore, when a listed company changes its market segment, it is required to undergo a new examination based on the same criteria as the initial listing criteria of the market segment to which it is changing, and to comply with those criteria.

In addition to the abovementioned review of market segments, TOPIX, currently comprised of all companies listed on the First Section, will also be reviewed with the aim of further improving not only how well it represents the market but also its functionality as an investable index.

4. Initial Listing System

The TSE imposes initial listing requirements on each market segment from the viewpoint of investor protection and examines listing applications to see whether they satisfy the listing requirements. TSE's initial listing criteria for each market segment comprise quantitative (formal) and qualitative (eligibility) requirements and the TSE examines applications from companies wishing to be listed based on consultation and their submitted documents.

Prime Market: In terms of the formal requirements, "tradable share market capitalization of at least ¥10 billion" which ensures the basis for ample liquidity so that a variety of institutional investors can invest in a company with confidence; "tradable share ratio of at least 35%" which is the basis for ensuring an effective foundation for constructive dialogue with institutional investors; either ¥2.5 billion profit (total of previous two years) or sales of at least ¥10 billion and notional market capitalization of at least ¥100 billion which are the basis for a stable and excellent revenue/financial base. In terms of the qualitative requirements, criteria are set from the viewpoint of corporate continuity, profitability, corporate governance, and effectiveness of internal control systems.

Table X-4.   Initial Listing Criteria (Quantitative Requirements)

Items		Prime Market	Standard Market	Growth Market
Liquidity	Number of Shareholders	800 or more	400 or more	150 or more
	Tradable Shares	20,000 units or more	2,000 units or more	1,000 units or more
	Market capitalization of the tradable share	JPY 10 billion or more	JPY 1 billion or more	JPY 0.5 billion or mor
	Market Capitalization	JPY 25 billion or more	—	—
Governance	The number of tradable shares	35% or higher of the listed stocks	25% or higher of the listed stocks	25% or higher of the listed stocks
Operating results	Revenue base	The applicant company satisfies either of the following a. or b.:Aggregated profits over the last two years are JPY 2.5 billion or more Net sales over the last year are JPY 10 billion or more and market capitalization is estimated to be JPY 100 billion or more at time of listing	Total profits over the last year are JPY 0.1 billion or more	—
Financial conditions		The amount of consolidated net assets is JPY 5 billion or more and amount of unconsolidated net assets is a positive figure	The amount of consolidated net assets is a positive figure	—
Public Offering		—	—	500 trading units or more
Others		Years of Business Operation, False Statements or Adverse Opinions, etc., Audit by a Listed Company Audit Firm, Establishment of a Shareholder Services Agent, Share Unit, Classes of Stock, Restriction on Transfer of Shares, Handling by the Designated Book-Entry Transfer Institution, etc.		

Notes: 1. No. of shareholders means the number of shareholders who own one or more units of shares.
2. The number of "tradable shares" is the number of shares after deducting from the number of listed shares the shares owned by shareholders, directors, etc., who own 10% or more of the listed shares, treasury (if they own their own shares), domestic common banks, insurance companies, and business corporations, and other shares deemed fixed by the Exchange.
3. The amount of profits is the amount derived by adding or subtracting net income attributable to minority interests in subsidiaries to/from the amount of current profit (loss).
4. An audit firm that is registered in the registry of listed company audit firms based on the Registration System for Listed Company Audit Firms of the Japanese Institute of Certified Public Accountants (including audit firm which is subject to quality control reviews by the Japanese Institute of Certified Public Accountants).

Table X-5.   Initial Listing Criteria (Qualitative Requirements)

Prime Market	Standard Market	Growth Market
【Corporate Continuity and Profitability】 The applicant company is operated continuously and has a stable and excellent revenue base.	【Corporate Continuity and Profitability】 The applicant company is operated continuously and has a stable revenue base.	【Appropriateness of Disclosure of Corporate Information, Risk Information, etc.】 The applicant company is in a position to appropriately disclose its business details and risk information, etc.
【Soundness of Corporate Management】 The applicant company carries out its business fairly and faithfully.	【Soundness of Corporate Management】 The applicant company carries out its business fairly and faithfully.	【Soundness of Corporate Management】 The applicant company carries out its business fairly and faithfully.
【Effectiveness of Corporate Governance and Internal Management System】 Corporate governance and internal management systems are appropriately established and functioning.	【Effectiveness of Corporate Governance and Internal Management System】 Corporate governance and internal management systems are appropriately established and functioning.	【Effectiveness of Corporate Governance and Internal Management System】 Corporate governance and internal management systems that are commensurate with the size and maturity of the company are appropriately established and functioning.
【Appropriateness of Disclosure of Corporate Information, etc.】 The applicant company is in a position where it is able to disclose its corporate information appropriately.	【Appropriateness of Disclosure of Corporate Information, etc.】 The applicant company is in a position where it is able to disclose its corporate information appropriately.	【Reasonableness of the business plan】 The applicant company has established a rational business plan and built a business foundation necessary to execute the business plan or has a rational plan to do so.
Other matters deemed necessary by the Exchange from the viewpoint of public interest or investor protection		

Standard Market: The formal requirements include a "tradable share market capitalization of at least ¥1 billion" as the basis for appropriate liquidity for smooth trading by general investors; "a tradable share ratio of at least 25%" to ensure minimum publicness as a listed company; and "profit at least ¥0.1 bn. in the most recent year" as the criterion for a stable revenue base. In terms of the qualitative requirements, similar to the Prime Market, there is the perspective of corporate continuity and profitability. However, while the Prime Market requires a stable and excellent revenue base, the Standard Market only requires a stable revenue base.

Growth market: In terms of formal requirements, the minimum liquidity requirement for a company to be investable for general investors is a "tradable shares market capitalization of at least ¥500 million;" "a tradable share ratio of 25% or more" for ensuring a minimum publicness as a listed company and "public offering of at least 500 units at initial listing" as a necessary fund raising to achieve growth.

To widely accept start-up companies to the capital market, there are no criteria related to pase business performance or financial position (profit and net assets). In terms of qualitative requirements, companies are required to demonstrate reasonable business plan to realize high growth and to have ability to conduct appropriate disclosure.

5. Listing Administration Systems

With a view to carrying out the proper administration of listed securities and to protecting investors, stock exchanges have instituted various rules relating to the administration of listings and have sought to ensure the effectiveness of these rules by requiring issuers to commit to observe these in the listing agreement they sign at the time of listing. TSE's listing requirements include rules for timely disclosure of important corporate information, a code of corporate conduct requiring companies to adhere to appropriate behavior, and the delisting of securities.

Rules Requiring Timely Disclosure of Corporate Information: To ensure the formation of fair market prices and to foster the sound development of a financial instruments market, it is extremely important for listed companies to make proper disclosure in a timely manner of information concerning important corporate matters that may influence the investment decision-making of investors, the very basis on which stock prices are formed.

TSE requires listed companies to disclose important corporate information, such as corporate decisions, events, and financial results, in a timely manner. The timely disclosure requirements are fundamentally the same through all the market segments, but the only Growth Market requires companies to disclose "business plans and matters relating to growth potential" on a continuous basis.

Code of Corporate Conduct: The Tokyo Stock Exchange has introduced a code of corporate conduct. The multifold purposes of requiring proper conduct by listed companies are to raise awareness of their role as members of the financial instruments market, to ensure greater transparency by enhancing the disclosure of corporate information, and to achieve the proper operation of investor protection measures and market functions.

Continued listing criteria; delisting criteria: Under the new market segments each market has its own continued listing criteria based on the respective concept and listed companies are required to comply with these criteria on a continuous basis. If a company is in breach of the criteria and fails to remedy this within the required period, the company will be delisted. In addi-

Table X-6.   Outline of Code of Corporate Conduct of the Tokyo Stock Exchange

Matters to be observed (if a listed company violates a provision regarding these matters, it may be subject to measures enforced by the TSE)	Matters desired to be observed (listed companies are expected to make efforts to observe them)
• Matters to be observed regarding third-party allotment • Prohibition of stock split, etc., that could cause turmoil in the secondary market • Matters to be observed pertaining to issuance of MSCB, etc. • Duty to exercise of voting rights in writing, etc. • Duty to carry out framework improvement to facilitate exercise of voting rights for listed foreign companies • Duty to secure an independent director/auditor • Duty to explain the reasons for implementing or not implementing the Corporate Governance Code • Duty to appoint a board of directors, an audit board or committee, and an accounting auditor • Duty to select a certified public accountant or public audit firm to provide the audit certificate of the accounting auditor • Duty to carry out necessary structural development of a system for ensuring the appropriateness of business • Matters to be observed pertaining to introduction of takeover defense measures • Matters to be observed pertaining to disclosure of MBOs, etc. • Matters to be observed pertaining to significant transactions, etc., with controlling shareholders • Audit by an audit firm placed on the TSE's Listed Company Audit Firm Register • Prohibition of insider trading • Exclusion of anti-social forces • Prohibition of behavior destructive to the functioning of the secondary market or the rights of shareholders	• Efforts toward the shift to and maintenance of the desired investment unit level • Efforts toward unification of trading unit • Respect for the principles of the Corporate Governance Code • Securing management structure that includes independent directors • Framework improvement to enable proper functioning of independent directors/auditors • Provide information on independent directors/auditors, etc. • Framework improvement to facilitate exercise of voting rights • Delivery of documents to shareholders owning stock without voting rights • System improvement for prevention of occurrence of insider trading • Development of system, etc. for excluding anti-social forces • Development of systems and structures to properly respond to changes in accounting standards, etc. • Fair provision of supplementary explanatory materials on details of account settlement

tion to these criteria, there are other criteria common to all the markets. To the existing listed companies the continued listing criteria shall not apply strictly but do in a relaxed manner for the timebeing as the transitional treatment. Howeber, to receive this treatment, companies must disclose a plan and the progres for meeting the full requirements.

When any stock is in danger of falling within the purview of the delisting criteria the stock shall be put on the watch list to notify general investors. When any stock actually falls within the purview of the delisting criteria, the stock shall be put on the liquidation list to publicize the information and allow the trading of such stock to continue for a specified period (ordinarily one month). After this period, the stock shall be delisted.

Table X-7.   Continued Listing Criteria

Item		Prime Market	Standard Market	Growth Market
Liquidity	Number of Shareholders	800 or more	400 or more	150 or more
	Number of tradable shares	20,000 units or more	2,000 units or more	1,000 units or more
	Market capitalization of the tradable share	JPY 10 billion or more	JPY 1 billion or more	JPY 0.5 billion or more
	Trading Value	Daily average trading value: JPY 20 million or more	Monthly average trading volume: 10 units or more	Monthly average trading volume: 10 units or more
Governance	Tradable share ratio	35% or higher	25% or higher	25% or higher
Financial conditions	Amount of Net Assets	The amount of net assets is a positive figure.	The amount of net assets is a positive figure.	The amount of net assets is a positive figure.
Market Capitalization		—	—	JPY 4 billion or more (applicable after 10 years from initial listing)

Note: Improvement period is generally one year. (Standard Market and Growth Market trading criteria is 6 months.)

Table X-8.   Delisting Criteria

Item	
Failure to Meet Continued Listing Criteria	lack of entrustment to a shareholder services agent
Suspension of bank transactions	restrictions on transfer of shares
bankruptcy/rehabilitation/reorganization proceedings	conversion to a wholly-owned subsidiary
suspension of business activities	ceasing to be subject to the book-entry transfer operation of a designated book-entry transfer institution
inappropriate merger, etc.	inappropriate restrictions on shareholders' rights
impairment of sound transactions with a controlling shareholder	acquisition of all shares
Delay in Submission of Securities Report or Quarterly Securities Report	acquisition by request for sale of shares, etc.
False Statement or Adverse Opinion, etc.	share consolidation
Securities on Alert, etc.	involvement of anti-social forces
Violation of Listing Agreement, etc.	others (cases where delisting is deemed appropriate for public benefits or investor protection)

6. The Corporate Governance Code

Outline of the Corporate Governance Code: The TSE formulated the Corporate Governance Code "(the Code"), a set of key principles that contribute to the realization of effective corporate governance of listed companies, which has been applied to the listed companies since June 2015.

The Code consists of a three-layered structure of general principles, principles, and supplementary principles, and adopts the "comply-or-explain" approach. Implementation of each principle is not uniformly required. However, if there is a principle that is not implemented due to the individual circumstances of the company, the company is required to provide an appropriate explanation of the reasons for this and the status of implementation of alternative measures. The Code has been formulated on a principles-based approach. Although there are no clear definitions of terms, it is expected that those involved will interpret the Code and respond to it appropriately in accordance with the intention and spirit of the Code. All listed companies are requested to document their status of adoption of the Code in a Corporate Governance Report. The reports are to be made available for public inspection on the websites of the relevant stock exchanges, etc.

Apart from the Corporate Governance Code, which is a code of conduct for listed companies, the Stewardship Code has been formulated for institutional investors, and it is expected that the two will work together to promote the sustainable growth of listed companies based on constructive dialogue with institutional investors. In addition, in 2018, as an annex to both codes, the "Guidelines for Dialogue between Investors and Companies" was formulated, which summarizes matters that are expected to be discussed intensively

Chart X-5. Two codes and dialogue guidelines

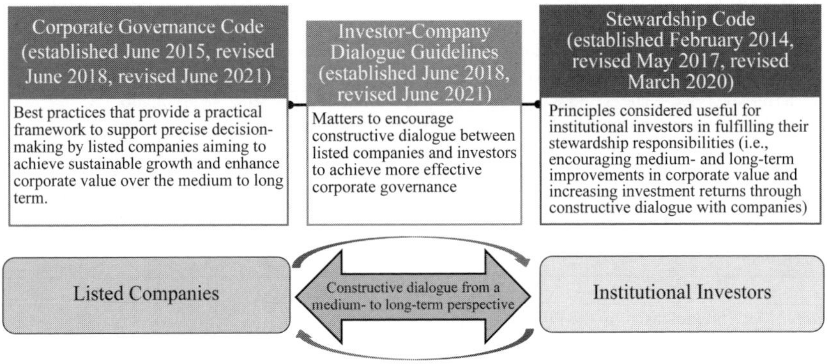

Chart X-6. Overview of the Corporate Governance Code

【1. Securing the Rights and Equal Treatment of Shareholders】
Companies should take measures to fully secure rights and equal treatment of shareholders.

➤ Securing the substantial Rights and Equal Treatment of Shareholders
⇒Measures for giving shareholders sufficient time to consider the agenda of general shareholder meetings (early delivery of convening notices, electronic exercise of voting rights, english translation of notice of convocation, etc.)
➤ Description of capital policies
⇒Basic policy, takeover defense measures and changes in controlling rights, necessity and rationale for large-scale dilution, and cross-shareholdings* etc.
  *Cross-shareholdings: disclosure of policy for reducing cross- shareholdings, explanation of the objective and rationale for shareholding based on an examination of economic rationale, establishment and disclosure of standards for the exercise of voting rights

【2. Appropriate Collaboration with Stakeholders Other Than Shareholders】
Companies should recognize that their sustainable growth is brought about as a result of contributions made by a variety of stakeholders, including employees, customers, business partners, and local communities, and should endeavor to appropriately cooperate with these stakeholders.

➤ Appropriate response to issues surrounding sustainability, including social and environmental problems
➤ Ensure diversity in the company's core human resources (women, foreigners, mid-career hires)

【3. Ensure Appropriate Information Disclosure and Transparency】
Listed companies are required to appropriately disclose financial and non-financial information in compliance with the relevant laws and regulations, and should also proactively engage in providing other information, thereby providing information that is easy for users to understand and highly useful.

➤ Enhancement of Information Disclosure
⇒Business strategies, Plan, basic principle on corporate governance, policy and procedure of nomination and remuneration of directors, English disclosure, and activities for sustainability

【4. Responsibilities of the Board】
In order to promote sustainable corporate growth and enhance earnings power and capital efficiency, the board should appropriately fulfill the following roles and responsibilities:
  (1) Setting the broad direction of corporate strategy;
  (2) Establishing an environment where appropriate risk-taking by the senior management is supported; and
  (3) Carrying out effective oversight from an independent and objective standpoint

➤ Use of independent/external directors
⇒At least one-third of the directors (prime Market listed companies) or two of the directors (other market isted companies) to be those who are qualitied to contribute to sustainable growth, exclusive meetings for independent directors, lead independent directors, proper involvement in nomination and compensation, etc.
➤ Ensuring the effectiveness of the board of directors and the audit & supervisory board
⇒Evaluation of effectiveness of the board of directors, management of directors' meetings (distribution of materials, matters to be discussed, etc.), access to information (streamlining of the company's support system, provision of opportunities for training, etc.)

【5. Dialogue with Shareholders】
In order to contribute to sustainable growth, companies should engage in constructive dialogue with shareholders.

Source: Materials released by the Financial Services Agency.

in the dialogue between companies and investors.

Revision of Corporate Governance Code: The Corporate Governance Code was revised in 2018, and again in June 2021. The three main points of the 2021 revision are the enhancement of the function of the board of directors, ensuring diversity in the core human resources of the company, and addressing issues related to sustainability. In the new market segmentation, all of the revised general principles, principles, and supplementary principles apply to companies listed on the Prime Market and Standard Market, and only the general principles apply to companies listed on the Growth Market. However, considering that the Prime Market is a segment focused on constructive dialogue with global investors, the revised principles and supplementary principles also include a requirement for a higher level of governance for companies listed thereon.

7. The Stock Trading System (1)

Most of the transactions on the stock exchanges are effected during the trading sessions. In the case of the Tokyo Stock Exchange, the trading hours are divided into two sessions: the morning session, from 9:00 a.m. to 11:30 a.m., and the afternoon session, from 12:30 p.m. to 3:00 p.m.

There are mainly two types of orders: a limit order, by which a customer limits the acceptable price, and a market order, which is executed immediately at the price available in the market without restrictions or limits. Limit orders can be made in such increments as ¥1 or ¥10, with the allowable price increments being determined according to the price range of the stock. Particularly for some highly liquid issues, more minute units of pricing are set for the purpose of improving contract prices and easing the wait until contract, and currently orders can be made even in increments of ¥0.1 (when the price is ¥1,000 or below). The allowable price for a limit order is restricted to a fixed price range based on the closing price of the previous trading day, which also controls any sharp movement in stock prices.

Trading of shares on the exchange floor is conducted in accordance with the price-priority rule (under which a buy/sell order with the highest/lowest bid/offer price takes precedence over the others) and the time-priority rule (when there is more than one order offering or bidding at the same price, the order placed the earliest takes precedence over others) and by either the *Itayose* method (single-price auction using an order book) or the *Zaraba* method (continuous auction).

Itayose **method:** The *Itayose* method is a system that is used to determine the opening or first price when trading commences or resumes on the floor. All buy and sell orders for a given issue are matched according to the price-

Table X-9.   Methods of Concluding Transactions

Itayose method			Zaraba method		
A memo (on a board) about an order received at the time an opening price is decided			A memo (on a board) about a *Zaraba* order for a given issue received		
(Asked price)	(Price)	(Bid price)	(Asked price)	(Price)	(Bid price)
H(2) I(4)	Market Quotation	K(1) M(3)		Market Quotation	
○○○	¥503		○○○	¥503	
○○○	¥502	T(1)	○○○	¥502	
○○	¥501	P(5) N(2)	○D(2) C(4)	¥501	
G(1) F(1) E(1)	¥500	A(4) B(3) C(2) D(1)	B(3) A(3)	¥500	
S(2)	¥499	○○○		¥499	F(3) G(2)○
R(4)	¥498	○○○		¥498	○○○
	¥497			¥497	○○○

Notes: 1. Alphabetical letters represent securities companies.
2. Figures given in parentheses represent the number of trading units, each consisting of 100 shares.
3. ○○○ are blanks to be filled with securities companies bidding or asking prices and the number of trading units.
4. In the case of the *Itayose* method, all bid and asked prices are considered to have been proposed simultaneously (simultaneous outcry).

The *Itayose* Method

a. First, a sell order for 600 shares at a market-asked price without limit (200 shares by securities company H and 400 shares by securities company I) is matched against buy orders for 400 shares at a market-bid price without limit (100 shares by securities company K and 300 shares by securities company M). At this point, 200 shares at a market-asked price without limit are left unmatched.

b. Then, assuming that the opening price will be ¥500, the remaining unfilled sell orders for 200 shares at a market-asked price without limit and those for 600 shares at an asked price of ¥499 or less (200 shares by securities company S and 400 shares by securities company R) are matched against buy orders for 800 shares at a bid price of ¥501 or more (500 shares by securities company P and 200 shares by securities company N and 100 shares by securities company T). As a result, sell orders for 1,200 shares at an asked price and buy orders for 1,200 shares at the bid price are matched.

c. Lastly, a sell order for 300 shares at an asked price of ¥500 (100 shares by securities company E, 100 shares by securities company F, and 100 shares by securities company G) are matched against buy orders for 1,000 shares at a bid price of ¥500 (400 shares by securities company A, 300 shares by securities company B, 200 shares by securities company C, and 100 shares by securities company D). However, there are only 300 shares offered for sale at an asked price of ¥500, while there are buy orders for 1,000 shares at a bid price of ¥500. In such cases, all the sell orders for 300 shares at an asked price of ¥500 are matched against the buy orders for 100 shares each from securities company A, B, and C (for a total of 300 shares) at an asked price of ¥500. As a result, the opening price is decided at ¥500, and orders for a total of 1,500 shares are consummated at such price.

The *Zaraba* Method

a. When the contents of an *Ita* (board) are as shown in the chart, a buy order of securities company M for 200 shares at a bid price of ¥500 can be consummated by matching the sell order of securities company A for 200 shares out of its original sell order for 300 shares.

b. When securities company N places a buy order for 1,000 shares at a bid price without limit, it can be consummated by matching it against the remaining 100 shares offered for sale by securities company A at an asked price of ¥500 and a sell order of securities company B for 300 shares at an asked price of ¥500 and then a sell order of securities company C for 400 shares at an asked price of ¥501 and a sell order of securities company D for 200 shares at an asked price of ¥501.

c. If securities company K places a sell order for 500 shares at an asked price of ¥499, a contract can be concluded by matching it against a buy order of securities company F for 300 shares at a bid price of ¥499 and a buy order of securities company G for 200 shares at a bid price of ¥499.

d. As a result, the following trading agreements can be concluded

Selling securities company	Buying securities company	Contracted price	No. of shares
Securities company A	Securities company M	¥500	200 shares
Securities company A	Securities company N	¥500	100 ″
Securities company B	Securities company N	¥500	300 ″
Securities company C	Securities company N	¥501	400 ″
Securities company D	Securities company N	¥501	200 ″
Securities company K	Securities company F	¥499	300 ″
Securities company K	Securities company G	¥499	200 ″

e. In such a manner, asked and bid prices are offered without interruption during the session hours, and when buy orders (sell orders) are matched against sell orders (buy orders), trading agreements are concluded.

priority rule to find a single price that clears all market orders and meets certain other conditions.

Zaraba **method:** The *Zaraba* method is a system by which, following the establishment of the opening price by the *Itayose* method, trades are executed in a continuous auction, in principle, through the end of a session. Through this method, a newly placed buy/sell order is matched against the existing sell/buy order that has the highest precedence based on price priority and then on time priority in order to determine the execution price.

8. The Stock Trading System (2)

While most of the transactions are effected during the trading sessions, stock exchanges introduced complementary off-auction trading systems in the second half of the 1990s to accommodate need of executing block trades or basket trades.

During the initial period that followed the introduction of these systems, the systems were used solely for executing cross transactions (buy and sell orders by the same trading participant) due in part to the restriction that required orders to be placed via fax. However, the Tokyo Stock Exchange automated its off-auction trading system to improve efficiency and convenience with the introduction of ToSTNeT in June 1998 and expanded its trading system by adding new classes of transactions.

After that, in January 2008, further classes of transactions were added and trading hours were extended, making the market independent from trading sessions. Regarding single stock trading and basket trading, in August 2020 and May 2021, various measures were put in place to improve the system in line with the diversification of the transaction needs of investors, for instance through the expansion of the range of settlement dates that can be specified.

ToSTNeT, the off-auction trading system of the Tokyo Stock Exchange, accommodates the following four types of transactions: single-stock trading, basket trading, closing-price trading, and off-floor corporate share repurchases.

Single-Stock Trading: Under the single-stock trading system, investors can effect transactions in an individual stock issue at a price within plus-minus 7% (¥5 when 7% of the price is less than ¥5) of the last price of the issue on the floor or some other reference price as specified.

Basket Trading: The basket-trading system enables investors to trade baskets of a minimum of 15 stocks worth at least ¥100 million in aggregate value within plus-minus 5% of the value of the basket based on the last prices of the component issues on the floor or some other reference prices as specified.

Closing-Price Trading: Under the closing-price trading system, off-auc-

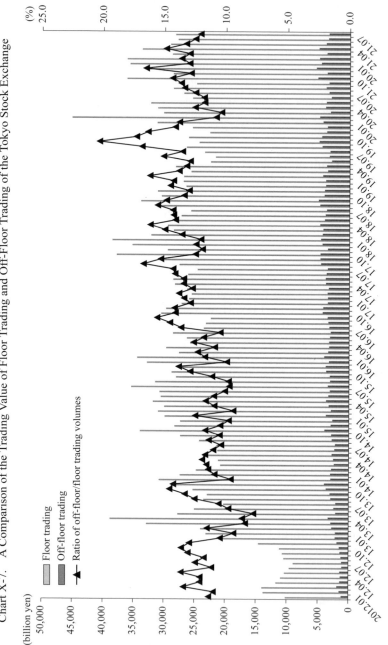

Chart X-7.   A Comparison of the Trading Value of Floor Trading and Off-Floor Trading of the Tokyo Stock Exchange

Floor trading
Off-floor trading
Ratio of off-floor/floor trading volumes

tion orders of investors are matched, in principle, based on time priority before the morning and afternoon sessions and after the afternoon sessions at the closing prices of the preceding session (i.e., the closing prices of the previous day, those of the morning session, or those of the afternoon session) or some other reference prices as specified.

Off-Auction Corporate Share Repurchases: Orders for share buyback are executed before the morning session at the previous day's closing prices or some other reference price as specified. Buyers eligible for the facility are limited to listed companies that intend to repurchase their own shares.

9. The Clearing and Settlement System (1)

Securities trading executed on the exchanges is cleared and settled through the Japan Securities Clearing Corporation (JSCC). Since January 2003, when JSCC was established all the clearing and settlement for securities trading carried out at each exchange have been unified under the JSCC.

The main functions performed by the JSCC are (1) to assume obligations, (2) to net shares and funds to transfer, (3) to instruct book-entry transfer, and (4) guarantee settlement.

(1) Assuming obligations: Upon the execution of a transaction on a stock exchange, the JSCC assumes the obligations of both the buyer and the seller against the other party (for the seller to deliver the securities sold and for the buyer to make payment for them) and, at the same time, acquires claims corresponding to both obligations. Thus, the JSCC takes up the role as the counterparty for claims and obligations. It helps enhance the efficiency of settlement operations on the part of clearing participants (those who are qualified for handling clearing and settling securities transactions through the JSCC) because the JSCC is the single settlement counterparty.

(2) Netting: The JSCC mutually offsets (nets) volumes bought and sold, and proceeds and payments, and settles the net balance. This streamlines fund payments and securities transfers required in the settlement procedures.

(3) Book-entry transfer instructions: The JSCC, after determining the settlement amount through netting, instructs the Japan Securities Depository Center, the settlement organization, to make transfers of securities, and the Bank of Japan or the fund settlement bank designated by JSCC to make the transfer of funds.

(4) Making settlement guarantees: Even in the case of a clearing participant failing to settle a trade, the JSCC performs and guarantees the settlement as the settlement counterparty against any other clearing participant. Thanks to this settlement guarantee, parties can trade securities without being concerned about the settlement default risk on the part of the original trade coun-

Chart X-8.　Delivery and Settlement Using JSCC (Exchange Transactions)

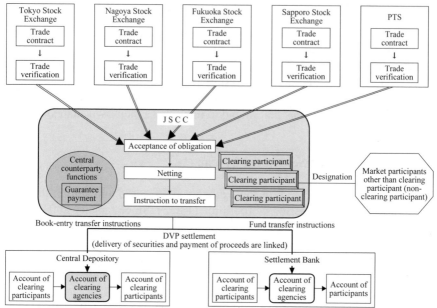

* The Clearing Agency is referred to as the Central Counter Party (CCP). It stands between the buyer and seller and acts as the settlement counterparty for both parties.

* Transactions by non-clearing participants (market participants other than clearing participants) are settled by clearing participants designated in advance by the non-clearing participants.

terparties.

Since its inception, the JSCC has expanded the scope of its clearing and settlement services, adding on offering services for securities traded on proprietary trading systems (PTSs) in 2010. After the global financial crisis, moreover, the regulatory reform of OTC derivatives trading has advanced around the world, with each country obliged to clear and settle standardized OTC derivatives trading through a central clearing house (central counterparty clearing).

The JSCC commenced clearing and settlement services for credit default swaps (CDS) transactions in July 2011 and for interest rate swaps in October 2012. In October 2013, the JSCC merged with the Japan Government Bond Clearing Corporation and thereby added OTC JGB transaction clearing and settlement services. Then, alongside the transformation of Japan Exchange Group into a comprehensive exchange, the merger of JSCC and the Japan Commodity Clearing House in July 2020 enabled the start of clearing services for commodity derivatives transactions, including precious metals.

Chart X-9. Delivery and Settlement Using JSCC (OTC Derivatives Transactions)

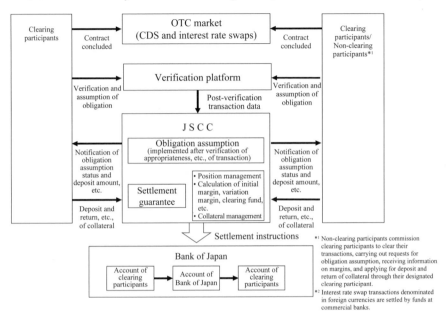

10. The Clearing and Settlement System (2)

With a view to eliminating the risk involved in the settlement of transactions in shares (and other securities handled by the Japan Securities Depository Center), in general, and the risk of a default in the payment of the principal, in particular, after the delivery of underlying securities, the JSCC has introduced a delivery-versus-payment system (DVP settlement system).

DVP settlement links the exchange of securities and funds, whereby securities are delivered on the condition that payment is made and vice versa. This ensures that the transaction does not fail even if payment default occurs.

DVP settlement by JSCC takes place on the third business day counting from the trade date (T+2) for transactions of shares and convertible bonds with new share reservation rights (CB) issues handled by the Japan Securities Depository Center on exchanges and PTS where obligation is assumed.

Under the DVP settlement system, a buyer basically cannot take delivery of shares until such time as payment from them (via fund transfer) has been verified. This, however, could undermine the overall efficiency of settlement, including payment and delivery between clearing participants and customers.

Chart X-10.   DVP Settlement Timetable

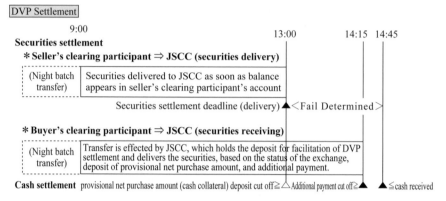

Note: The receiving of securities by the buyer's clearing participant is carried out in a way that eliminates the risk of principal default versus the cash payer JSCC through nonperformance of obligations or of delivery of collateral.

Chart X-11.   The DVP Scheme (normal settlement)

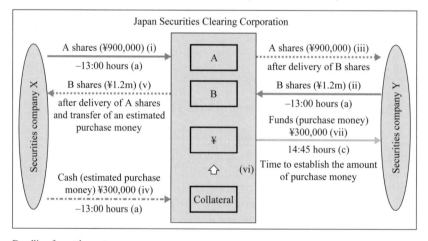

Deadline for settlement:
   a. Deadline for the delivery of securities and the deposit of the estimated purchase money
      (cash collateral): 13:00
   b. Deadline for the payment of purchase money: 14:15
   c. Time for the receipt of purchase money: 14:45
  (i)   Securities company X delivers A shares while (ii) securities company Y delivers B shares to JSCC by 13:00.
  (iii) Securities company Y can receive A shares after delivering B shares to JSCC.
  (iv) Securities company X deposits the estimated purchase money to JSCC by 13:00.
  (v)   Securities company X can receive B shares after (i) and (iv) have been executed.
  (vi) JSCC appropriates the estimated purchase money for the payment relating to funds settlement at the time the amount of the purchase money is finalized.
  (vii) Securities company Y receives the funds (purchase money) at 14:45.

Therefore, JSCC has established a mechanism for early receipt of securities. It allows the buy-side clearing participant to receive securities prior to the completion of funds settlement on deposit of cash or securities equivalent to the value of the securities to be received as collateral.

Also, in the event that a sell-side clearing participant should fail to deliver a security by the settlement deadline on the settlement date (known as a "fail"), the JSCC will carry over the delivery of and payment for the securities to the following day, with delivery and payment settlement netted off against delivery and payment of securities scheduled for that day.

However, since settlement is in principle due on the settlement date, there are mechanisms in place to prevent repeated fails, such as late payment penalties against clearing participants if a fail occurs or a buy-in (right of a participant who has suffered a fail to request compulsory purchase and delivery of the securities concerned).

11. The Book-Entry Transfer System for Stocks, Etc.

Administration of shareholder ownership rights, etc. of listed companies is performed by the book entry transfer system of the Japan Securities Depository Center, Inc. (JASDEC), the central depository for shareholder ownership rights, and transfer accounts set up by securities firms, etc. which are account administrators. Previously, administration was carried out on the premise of the existence of share certificates, etc.; now this is done electronically since share certificates were dematerialized in January 2009 through the digitization of the share certificates.

Securities eligible for the book-entry transfer system for stocks, etc., include stocks listed on domestic public exchanges; convertible-type corporate bonds (CB); investment units, such as real estate investment trusts (REIT); and preferred shares of cooperative financial institutions, subscription rights/warrants, beneficiary certificates of exchange-traded funds (ETFs), Japanese depositary receipts (JDR), and others.

The features and functions of the book-entry transfer system for stocks, etc., are as follows.

(1) Shareholders' ownership rights are administrated based on the records of the transfer account book, with transfers of shares being processed through the transfer account. (2) Account administrators inform JASDEC of the identification of beneficiary shareholders, including their names and addresses along with their share ownership data. JASDEC then compiles the information to periodically report to respective issuers (general shareholder notification). (3) Issuing companies produce their records of voting rights for general meetings of shareholders and retained earnings distributions based on a reg-

Chart X-12.   Relationships Among Participants, JASDEC and Issuers in the Book-Entry Transfer System for Stocks, etc.

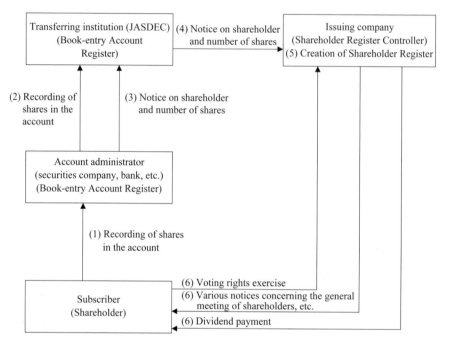

ister of beneficiary shareholders drawn up from the general shareholder notification. (4) Minority shareholders, etc., can exercise their rights by applying to JASDEC to have a notification sent to the issuer verifying their shareholdings, duration of ownership, and other particulars (individual shareholder notification). They can then exercise their rights for a limited period of time following receipt of the notification.

The main benefits that are expected from transition to the electronic book-entry transfer system include:

(1) shareholders can eliminate the risks of loss, theft, or forgery of certificates that are held at their own risk, and they also do not need to submit certificates to the issuer for replacement in the event of a corporate name change or change in the share trading unit; (2) issuers can save costs associated with issuance, such as printing costs and stamp duties, as well as those associated with corporate reorganization (such events as corporate mergers, exchanges of shares, and stock transfers) for collecting old certificates and distributing new ones; and (3) securities companies can reduce the risks and costs associated with the storage and transport of certificates.

Table X-10. Major Changes in the System Before & After Implementation of Electronic Share Certificate System

	Central Depository and Book-Entry Transfer System (before dematerialized)	Book-Entry Transfer System (current)
Share certificates	• Share certificates • Share certificates deposited with JASDEC are centrally stored at JASDEC and issued upon request • Share certificates outside the Book-Entry System are kept individually by owners	• No share certificates
Attribution of rights	• Presumption of rights on stock by ownership of share certificates (outside the Book-Entry System) • Party recorded in the account register is regarded as the owner of share certificates	• Presumption of rights regarding stocks recorded in the book-entry account register
Form of shareholder management	• Managed by shareholder register (outside the Book-Entry System) • Managed by substantial shareholder register (within the Book-Entry System) • Name-based aggregation of shareholders is performed by the shareholder register controller	• Uniformly managed by shareholder register • JASDEC performs name-based aggregation and notifies the shareholder register controller
Transfer of stocks	• Issuance of share certificates (outside the Book-Entry System) • Account transfer (within the Book-Entry System)	• Account transfer

12. Computerized Trading and Clearing Systems of the Financial Instruments Exchange (Stock Exchange) (1)

The following is a summary of the electronic stock trading system and the settlement and clearing system that maintain the stock market.

In the cash market of the Tokyo Stock Exchange (TSE), the stock trading system processes stocks, corporate bonds with subscription rights/warrants, etc. (convertible bonds), and other transactions during the trading sessions and the off-auction ToSTNeT market. Orders from a trading participant are mainly entered through the trading participant's in-house system or through a direct connection to the TSE's trading system.

The computerization of securities trading at the TSE started with CORES (Computer assisted Order Routing and Execution System) (the old stock trading system) that was introduced to the Second Section in January 1982. The current stock trading platform consists of arrowhead, renewed in November 2019 for enhanced functionality and improved performance, and the

Chart X-13.   System Integration Schedule of Japan Exchange Group, Inc.

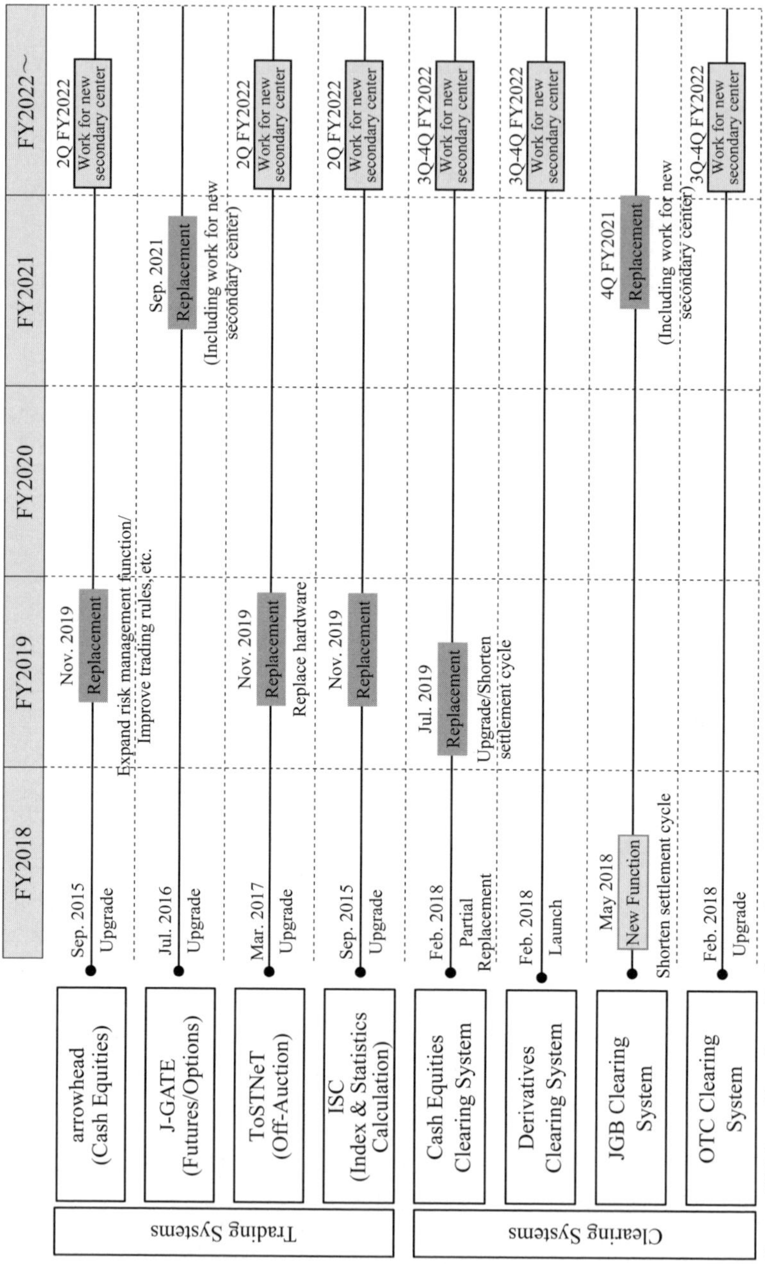

		FY2018	FY2019	FY2020	FY2021	FY2022~
Trading Systems	arrowhead (Cash Equities)	Sep. 2015 Upgrade	Nov. 2019 Replacement (Expand risk management function/Improve trading rules, etc.)			2Q FY2022 Work for new secondary center
	J-GATE (Futures/Options)	Jul. 2016 Upgrade			Sep. 2021 Replacement (Including work for new secondary center)	
	ToSTNeT (Off-Auction)	Mar. 2017 Upgrade	Nov. 2019 Replacement (Replace hardware)			2Q FY2022 Work for new secondary center
	ISC (Index & Statistics Calculation)	Sep. 2015 Upgrade	Nov. 2019 Replacement			2Q FY2022 Work for new secondary center
Clearing Systems	Cash Equities Clearing System	Feb. 2018 Partial Replacement	Jul. 2019 Replacement (Upgrade/Shorten settlement cycle)			3Q-4Q FY2022 Work for new secondary center
	Derivatives Clearing System	Feb. 2018 Launch				3Q-4Q FY2022 Work for new secondary center
	JGB Clearing System	May 2018 New Function (Shorten settlement cycle)			4Q FY2021 Replacement (Including work for new secondary center)	
	OTC Clearing System	Feb. 2018 Upgrade				3Q-4Q FY2022 Work for new secondary center

Source: IT Master Plan, Japan Exchange Group, April 2021

ToSTNeT system.

With the basic policy of enhancing three features—reliability, convenience and processing capacity—arrowhead was renewed in order to accommodate the further development of electronic trading, a continuing increase in the number of orders, and other changes in the market environment as well as to respond better to risks that the development of electronic trading can create on the market. The ToSTNeT system was also renewed with the basic policy of expanding the processing capacity and increasing convenience.

The market information system, which had been serving the role of disclosing marketing information, was integrated into arrowhead when arrowhead was renewed in 2015.

The Japan Exchange Group, Inc. (JPX) commenced operations in January 2013. In July 2013, it amalgamated the cash equity markets of the TSE and OSE while also integrating the stock and CB trading system of the OSE into the TSE's arrowhead and ToSTNeT systems.

The settlement and clearing system for stocks and CBs is designed to support delivery and other operations for the settlement and clearing of transactions executed on the TSE and other markets. Since January 2003, the JSCC has acted as the cross-market clearing organization for all domestic exchanges. Also in terms of the settlement and clearing system, the OSE's system was integrated into the TSE's platform in November 2014. The system was upgraded in July 2019 in line with the shortening of the settlement period for stocks and other securities.

The data for this process from trading participants, etc., is passed through the TSE's dedicated network arrownet.

13. Computerized Trading and Clearing Systems of the Financial Instruments Exchange (Stock Exchange) (2)

The following is a summary of the trading system and the settlement and clearing system that support the derivatives market.

The derivatives trading system is a system for entering and matching orders, preparing transaction reports, and inquiring into the state of the order book, etc., of the derivatives market of the OSE. The system processes futures, options, and other transactions during the trading sessions and the off-auction market. Orders from a trading participant are mainly entered through the trading partner's in-house system or through a direct connection to the TSE's trading system.

The OSE's trading system for derivatives, J-GATE, has the same functions and transaction formats as the systems used by major overseas markets. In introducing the system which began operation in February 2011, the OSE re-

Chart X-14.   Image Diagram of Japan Exchange Group's System (as of April 2021)

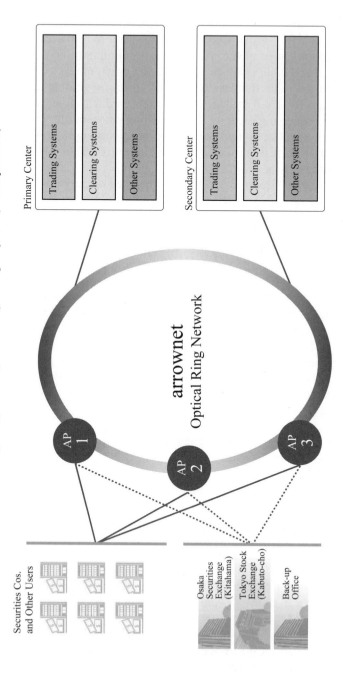

Primary Center

Trading Systems

Clearing Systems

Other Systems

Secondary Center

Trading Systems

Clearing Systems

Other Systems

arrownet
Optical Ring Network

AP 1

AP 2

AP 3

Securities Cos.
and Other Users

Osaka Securities Exchange (Kitahama)

Tokyo Stock Exchange (Kabuto-cho)

Back-up Office

Source: IT Master Plan, Japan Exchange Group, April 2021

viewed the complex transaction system peculiar to Japan to address the shift among investors to algorithmic and other advanced and diversified trading methods.

Following the launch of JPX in January 2013, the derivatives markets of the TSE and the OSE were amalgamated on the OSE market in March 2014, with the trading systems integrated into J-GATE. The J-GATE network was also consolidated into arrownet in September 2014.

In July 2016, the system was updated with NASDAQ's Genium INET Trading as the base with a view to further increasing stability and reliability as well as promoting liquidity. In September 2021, the system was updated to enable the addition of flexible products and functions, and to further improve system reliability and convenience.

Although the OSE had been using the OSE clearing system while the TSE used the JSCC clearing system, the clearing organizations were integrated into the JSCC in July 2013 and all margin operations relating to derivates trading have since been processed on the JSCC clearing system. Subsequently, in November 2014, clearing and settlement operations were also integrated into the JSCC clearing system. In February 2018, partial replacements were made for the settlement and clearance function for futures options transactions.

In July 2020, following the merger of the Tokyo Commodity Exchange (TOCOM) and its clearing organization, the Japan Commodity Clearing House (JCCH), clearing and settlement operations for commodity derivatives were integrated into the JSCC clearing system.

CHAPTER XI

Financial Instruments Exchange, etc. (2)

1. An Outline of the OTC Stock Market

(1) What is OTC trading?

In addition to shares traded on stock exchanges, shares are also traded over the counter. As only those listed issues that meet certain listing standards may be traded on exchanges, shares that are not eligible for exchange trading need to be traded elsewhere, outside exchanges. Such shares are traded between securities companies serving as brokers/dealers or between customers and brokers/dealers over the counter in negotiated transactions known as "over-the-counter (OTC) transactions." While trading and other activities of listed shares are regulated by the relevant stock exchanges, OTC stock trading executed through securities companies is regulated by the "Rules Concerning Over-the-Counter Securities" of the Japan Securities Dealers Association (JSDA) and by other rules.

OTC transactions include transactions in unlisted shares (including unlisted shares issued by listed companies); transactions effected in the OTC securities market; and off-exchange transactions in exchange-listed shares.

(2) An Outline of the OTC Stock Market

As OTC trading becomes active, information about quotes and prices is exchanged among securities companies and distributed to investors, and the market becomes more organized. After the war, OTC trading remained active even after the reopening of stock exchanges. In 1961, actively traded OTC issues were moved to the Second Section of the stock exchanges, but stocks continued to be actively traded over the counter to such an extent, in fact, that an OTC stock market, an organized market where OTC securities that meet the registration requirements of the JSDA are traded, was launched in February 1963.

As solicitation for investments was restricted in the early years, the OTC stock market was generally characterized as a market for the liquidation of stock holdings. To remedy the situation, the legal framework was enhanced by the 1971 amendment to the Securities and Exchange Act, and, in 1983, the

Table XI-1.   A Brief History of the OTC Market

1945	Group trading in shares emerges spontaneously after the war.
1949	A system of trading in OTC-authorized issues is launched in June under the rules of the JSDA.
1961	The stock exchanges create the Second Section, into which OTC-authorized issues are absorbed, and the OTC authorizing system is terminated.
1963	The OTC registration system is launched in February.
1976	The OTC market broker, Japan OTC Securities, Inc., is established.
1983	A new OTC Stock Market (the JASDAQ market) is launched in November.
1991	The JASDAQ system comes into operation.
1992	The Prohibited Acts Rule is applied to the JASDAQ market.
1997	The green sheet system is launched.
1998	The JASDAQ market becomes the OTC securities market for the purpose of the Securities and Exchange Act (currently, the Financial Instruments and Exchange Act).
2001	Japan OTC Securities changes its name to JASDAQ, Inc., and takes charge of the market.
2004	The JASDAQ market becomes a securities exchange in December and the OTC securities market is closed.
2005	Green sheet issues become "to-be-handled securities" for the purpose of the Securities and Exchange Act in April, and the regulations of insider trading are applied to green sheet issues.
2008	The Phoenix issue system is spun off from the green sheet system into an independent system.
2015	Equity Crowdfunding Scheme and Shareholders Community System are established in May.
2018	The Green Sheet system is abolished in March.

OTC stock market was defined as a market that complements exchange markets and was reorganized drastically into the JASDAQ market for trading shares of mid-tier small-to-medium sized enterprises with reasonable track records. The JASDAQ market has since grown larger as a market for emerging companies, and it was redefined as an "OTC securities market" under the Securities and Exchange Act in 1998. But the designation of "OTC securities market" exists only in law following the upgrading of the JASDAQ market into the JASDAQ Securities Exchange in December 2004.

Because a need arose for trading unregistered or unlisted stocks also outside the JASDAQ market, the JSDA established the green sheet system in July 1997, Following the abolishment of the green sheet at the end of March 2018, JSDA created the crowd funding system for equities along with the shareholders community system in May, 2015.

2. OTC Securities, Etc.

(1) Unlisted/Unregistered Issues

Issuers of unlisted or unregistered stocks are not required by law to disclose their corporate information, and, in principle, JSDA rules prohibit securities companies from soliciting investment in such issues. This is because soliciting the investing public, including individual investors, for an order to buy or sell a security on which no pertinent corporate information is available would subject the public to significant risks and cause various problems from the standpoint of the protection of investors, and such self-regulatory rules have been in place for a long time.

However, brokers/dealers may accept unsolicited orders for such issues and trade them with customers as OTC securities in negotiated transactions. The rules pertaining to such transactions (including those prohibiting them from accepting market orders or affecting when-issued or margin trading) are contained in the Rules Concerning Over-the-Counter Securities of the JSDA.

The April 2004 amendment to the Securities and Exchange Act authorized a company to issue an equity product in private placements limited to qualified institutional investors. Under this amendment, securities companies are allowed to solicit only Qualified Institutional Investors for the purchase of such shares on the condition that they do not resell their holdings to anyone other than Qualified Institutional Investors.

(2) OTC-handled Securities

Securities whose issuers regularly disclose specified corporate information in the form of an Explanatory Note on Business Conditions are considered to carry less risk than other unregistered issues. And the rules of the JSDA define them as "over-the-counter-handled securities," regarded as candidate securities to be eligible for solicitation.

An Explanatory Note on Business Conditions is a type of disclosure material required by the JSDA and prepared in accordance with the format for the "corporate information" section of a securities report pursuant to the Financial Instruments and Exchange Act. It shall be accompanied by annual financial statements with an audit report that includes the opinion of certified public accountants or persons with equivalent designation that the company's financial statements are unqualified or qualified in light of the provisions of the Financial Instruments and Exchange Act or in conformity with those of the Companies Act. Such explanatory note shall also contain forward-looking statements as to the outline of the company's business plan, its feasibility, and other aspects. In the case of a company in compliance with periodic disclosure requirements, a securities report or a securities registration statement

Chart XI-1.   Relationships Between OTC Securities and Listed/Registered Issues

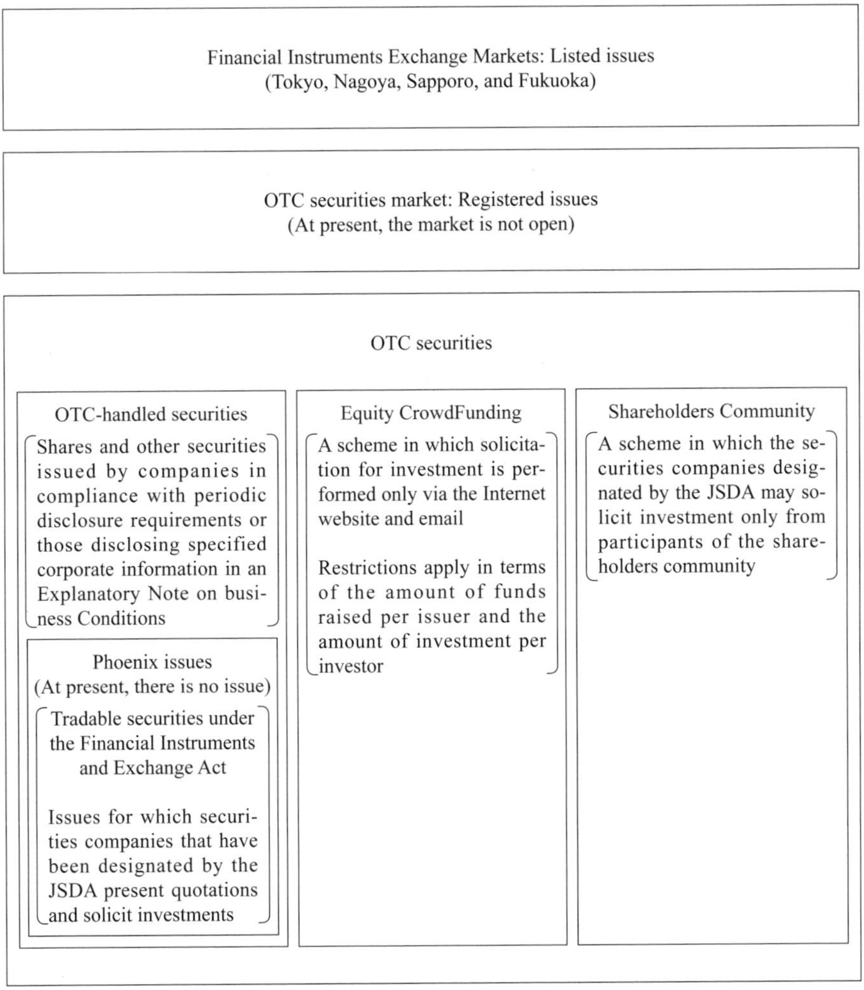

Financial Instruments Exchange Markets: Listed issues
(Tokyo, Nagoya, Sapporo, and Fukuoka)

OTC securities market: Registered issues
(At present, the market is not open)

OTC securities

OTC-handled securities	Equity CrowdFunding	Shareholders Community
Shares and other securities issued by companies in compliance with periodic disclosure requirements or those disclosing specified corporate information in an Explanatory Note on business Conditions	A scheme in which solicitation for investment is performed only via the Internet website and email Restrictions apply in terms of the amount of funds raised per issuer and the amount of investment per investor	A scheme in which the securities companies designated by the JSDA may solicit investment only from participants of the shareholders community

Phoenix issues
(At present, there is no issue)

Tradable securities under the Financial Instruments and Exchange Act

Issues for which securities companies that have been designated by the JSDA present quotations and solicit investments

---

with an unqualified or qualified opinion of the auditor can be substituted for the Explanatory Note on Business Conditions.

At present, the ban on solicitation for the purchase of OTC-handled securities is partially lifted for primary or secondary offerings of securities on the condition that the transfer of such shares is restricted for two years based on an agreement among the issuer, securities companies, and investors and that the issuer publishes an Explanatory Note on Business Conditions. The ban is fully lifted for unlisted securities of listed companies based on the condition that the issuer publishes an Explanatory Document on Securities Information, etc.

3. OTC securities transactions for the purpose of transferring management control, etc.

(1) Transactions in OTC securities for the purpose of transferring management control, etc.

As described previously, securities companies are prohibited in principle from soliciting investment for OTC securities under JSDA rules. On the other hand, business succession has recently become a social challenge for non-listed companies. Based on these circumstances, the ban on solicitation of investment for trading OTC securities for the purpose of transferring management control, etc., including business succession, was lifted in August 2019.

Transactions of OTC securities for the purpose of transferring management rights, etc. refer to a series of transactions in OTC securities, or an intermediary service thereto, aimed at both acquiring a majority of the voting rights of all shareholders of the issuing company and enabling the purchaser or a person designated by the purchaser to take office as the representative of the issuing company.

The principal requirements for such transactions are that securities companies must obtain consent from the issuing company concerning the attributes of prospective buyers and shall tell prospective buyers that they have the right to carry out a pre-trade inspection of the issuer.

(2) Solicitation for investment in OTC securities for professional investors who can assess corporate value

The ban on solicitation of investment in OTC securities was lifted in November 2020 to professional investors who can assess corporate value, etc. in order to facilitate the supply of risk funding to new growing companies.

"Solicitation for investment in OTC securities for professional investors who can assess corporate value" refers to allowing securities companies handling private placements (small private placements) and soliciting investment from large-scale investors (corporate venture capital, overseas funds, etc.) who are capable of assessing corporate value on their own under certain conditions.

The main requirements for such solicitation of investment are that securities companies obtain written representations and affirmations from their customers that they are solely responsible for their own assessment of corporate value and that securities companies provide the customers with information about the issuers.

Table XI-2.   Article 3-2 of the Rules Concerning Over-the-Counter Securities of the JSDA's Self-Regulatory Rules

Main contents of the investment solicitation for transaction of Over-the-Counter Securities for the purpose of transferring management control, etc.

1 . Can investment solicitation for transaction of Over-the-Counter Securities for the purpose of transferring management control, etc.
2 . To obtains the consent for the attributes, etc. of the customer who is subject to investment solicitation related to purchase from the issuer
3 . Due diligence
  • The issuer cooperates with the Due diligence
  • To explains for the candidate for purchase that Due diligence is possible
  • To provides a summary of the Due diligence results to the another customer who is subject to investment solicitation through the securities companies, etc. when the candidate for purchase investigates
4 . Confirmation before transaction/Prior explanation
  • To confirms before transaction that there is the prospect that the purpose of transferring management control, etc. set forth, etc. before transaction
  • To explain in advance that transaction is not executed when there is no prospect that the purpose of transferring management control, etc. set forth, etc.
5 . Reports to the JSDA before and after

Table XI-3.   Article 4-2 of the Rules Concerning Over-the-Counter Securities of the JSDA's Self-Regulatory Rules

Main contents of the investment solicitation for Acquisition of Over-the-Counter Securities which is made to professional investors who can evaluate the corporate value

Association members
1 . Can conduct investment solicitation for Over-the-Counter securities to professional investors who are able to evaluate the corporate value on their own responsibility
2 . Must obtain written representations and warranties from customers that they will evaluate the corporate value of the issuing company on their own responsibility and will make an investment based on such evaluation.
3 . Must provide following information of the company
  • The company profile
  • Business description
  • Financial information
  • In the case of private placemnts, future perspective
4 . Reports to the JSDA before and after

4. Equity Crowdfunding (1)

(1) What is Equity Crowdfunding?

The term "crowdfunding" is a coined word composed of "crowd" and raising funds or "funding." It refers to the practice of funding start-ups and growth companies by asking a large number of people to each contribute a small

Chart XI-2.   Concept Diagram of Equity Crowdfunding

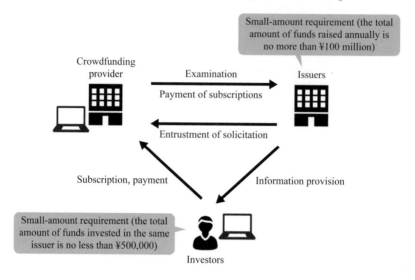

Table XI-4.   JSDA's Self-Regulatory Rules
Key components of the Rules Concerning Equity Crowdfunding Operations

1 . Solicitation for investments conducted by members of the JSDA (securities companies and Type I Small Amount Electronic Subscription Handling Agents) under the equity crowdfunding scheme is permitted as an exception to the prohibition of investment solicitation relating to unlisted stocks.
2 . Examination of issuers and measures to eliminate antisocial forces
3 . Indication of equity crowdfunding deals on the website
4 . Issuance of document prior to conclusion of contract
5 . Request for letter of intent from investors purchasing unlisted stocks for the first time under the equity crowdfunding scheme
6 . Small-amount requirements (total amount of funds raised per issuer: less than ¥100 million a year; investment per investor for one issuer: no more than ¥500,000 a year)
7 . Prohibition of simultaneous use of solicitation method other than the Internet (e.g., telephone and face-to-face contact)
8 . Conclusion of an agreement to the effect that the issuer provides proper information on a periodical basis to investors after the completion of handling of investment under the equity crowdfunding, and confirmation of information provision
9 . Establishment of an operation management system
10. Reporting and publication of monthly results

amount of money, often performed via Internet-mediated registries.

With the use of the Internet, crowdfunding makes it possible to raise funds, even on a small scale, at low cost and over a wide range by collecting a small amount of money from a large number of contributors. Thus crowdfunding, primarily the purchase-type and lending-type, has rapidly become a popular option for raising funds in the last few years. Given the circumstances, an equity crowdfunding system was introduced in May 2015 with a view to promoting provision of risk money to start-ups and growth companies and enabling such companies to raise capital by issuing OTC securities.

The equity crowdfunding scheme may be used only by securities companies and intermediaries specializing in small-amount equity crowdfunding (Type I Small-Amount Electronic Public Offering Service Operators) that are registered as Type I Financial Instruments Business Operators.

(2) Small Amount Requirements and Prohibition of Concurrent Use of Unspecified Solicitation Methods

In light of the nature of the equity crowdfunding scheme of raising a small amount of funds from each of a large number of investors, certain restrictions apply in the equity crowdfunding system. The amount of funds raised per issuer must be less than ¥100 million per year and the amount of funds contributed per investor to an issuer must not exceed ¥500,000 per year. In addition, considering that investment frauds involving unlisted stocks and corporate bonds continue to take place, the method of solicitation for investment is limited to using (i) the website and (ii) email assuming the use of the aforesaid website, and solicitation by telephone and visits by securities companies, etc. are prohibited.

(3) Examination of Issues and Issuers

In handling OTC securities using the equity crowdfunding scheme, securities companies, etc. may handle such issues as deemed proper after careful examinations of issuers, the nature of their business, financial standing, appropriateness of business plan, intended use of funds, etc. in accordance with their internal rules. Securities companies, etc. also enter into a contract with each issuer to the effect that the issuer is not an antisocial force, and must not use an equity crowdfunding scheme if it is recognized that an issuer corresponds to an antisocial force.

5. Equity Crowdfunding (2)

(4) Provision of Information via Website and Receipt/Delivery of Documents

While using the equity crowdfunding system, securities companies, etc. must provide information on issuers and fund raising as well as on risks, etc. specific to the acquisition of OTC securities issued by the issuers (such as no obligation to provide disclosure comparable to that prescribed by the Financial Instruments and Exchange Act or to the timely disclosure required by stock exchanges) via the website for perusal by investors.

Furthermore, in order to receive confirmation from investors purchasing OTC securities for the first time under the equity crowdfunding scheme of their understanding of risks, commission, etc. involved and of making the investment based on their judgment and responsibility, securities companies, etc. must provide advance explanations of these matters, request a letter of intent from each investor, and deliver the document prior to conclusion of contract containing at minimum the matters to be informed via the website concerning individual issues for every investment handled.

(5) Periodical Subsequent Information Offering by Issuer

Securities companies, etc. must have an agreement with each respective issuer that it shall regularly provide appropriate information on its business after the completion of equity crowdfunding.

(6) Reporting and Announcement of Investment Status

Securities companies, etc. must report the status of investments made under the equity crowdfunding scheme on a monthly basis to the JSDA, and the JSDA publishes the information reported.

(7) Business Control Measures by Securities Companies

Securities companies, etc. must formulate internal rules and put in place an business control measures necessary for properly carrying out equity crowdfunding in conformity with laws and regulations and their self-regulatory rules. In addition, securities companies, etc. are required to prepare an outline of their equity crowdfunding procedure and publish it on the company's website to enable investors to view the information.

When a securities company etc. violates laws and self-regulatory rules and is ordered to improve its business control measures, the securities company can not be engaged in equity crowdfunding until the ordered improvements, etc. are completed.

Chart XI-3. Provision of information/receipt of written document on equity-based crowdfunding (conduct by offer handling agent)

> 1 . To investors: Obligation to disclose information on website
> 1) Information on issues and issuers
> 2) Information on financing
> 3) Risk information
> 4) Other

> 2-1. To subscribing investors: Obligation to issue document prior to conclusion of a contract
> 1) Information on issues and issuers
> 2) Information on financing
> 3) Risk information
> 4) Other
> 2-2. To investors subscribing for the first time: Obligation to receive a confirmation note
> - a document containing the contents of pre-contract document must be delivered to the investors, and a confirmation note must be secured stating that investors understand the risks and details of the transaction and that they carry out the transaction at their own discretion and responsibility.

Offer period

> 3 . To investors who become shareholders: Obligation to provide information
> - The issuer regularly provides appropriate information on the business to investors who have become shareholders
> - The handing agent signs an information provision contract with the issuer in advance to confirm that the information is actually being provided.

After the offer period is closed

Table XI-5. Handling of Equity Crowdfunding

As of December 31, 2021

	Number of registered firms (companies)	Number of deals handled (deals)	Amount of financing (¥1,000)
2016	—	—	—
2017	3	18	514,740
2018	3	59	1,470,395
2019	3	54	951,590
2020	6	100	2,179,624
2021	5	159	3,736,570

6. Shareholders Community (1)

(1) What Shareholders Community is

The JSDA established the Shareholders Community System in May 2015 as a system for unlisted stock trading and fund-raising in place of the Green Sheet system that was abolished at the end of March 2018.

Shareholders Community was established as a mechanism in which a securities company creates a shareholders community by OTC issue and accepts investments only from investors that proactively declare and participate in the community. Since the scope of solicitation and trading is limited to participants of the Shareholders Community, and thus the distribution is limited the System is not subject to the application of insider trading regulations.

(2) Designation and Cancellation of Designation of Operating Members

In order for a securities company to create and operate a shareholders community, it must register with the JSDA and receive designation as an operating member. The JSDA may decide not to grant designation if the securities company is found to be in violation of law or self-regulatory rules.

Cancellation of designation as an operating member is normally based on a notification submitted by the operating member. It may cancel the designation altogether or suspend the designation for a certain period of time even without the aforesaid notification if, however, the JSDA finds that an operating member is in violation of law or self-regulatory rules, etc.

(3) Development of business management system

Operating members and securities companies intending to become operating members must formulate internal regulations and put in place an business management system necessary for properly operating shareholders communities. In addition, operating members are required to prepare an outline of their shareholders community operating method, etc. and publish this outline.

(4) Prohibition of Solicitation for Participation in a Shareholders Community and of Solicitation for Investment

Operating members may not solicit investors who are not shareholders community participants to participate in a shareholders community or to make investments in principle. However, if an investor falls under any of the following categories: (1) shareholder of the issuer (2) officer or employee of the issuer (3) former shareholder or former officer or employee (4) relative of an officer or employee, or (5) officer or employee of a group company of the issuer, the operating members can conduct solicitation regarding participation in the shareholders community.

Chart XI-4.   Basic Mechanism of Shareholders Community

No solicitation for investment to investors who are not participants

Solicitation for investment to participants in the shareholders community is OK

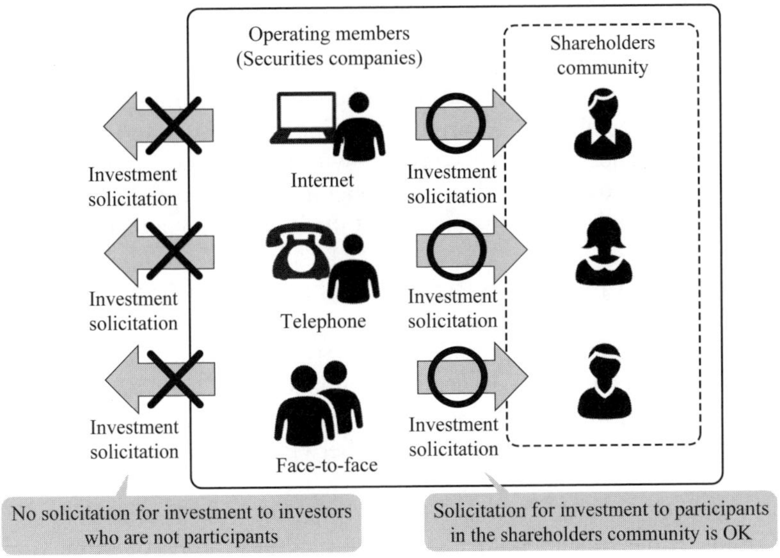

Table XI-6.   Major Components of the JSDA's Self-Regulatory Rules regarding Shareholders Community

1 . Securities companies construct a shareholders community for an unlisted stock. Investors intending to invest in the unlisted stock participate in the shareholders com-munity.
   • Assumed principal participants include officers and employees and their families of the issuer; shareholders and business partners of the issuer; and users and customers of the issuer's business.
2 . Securities companies structuring and operating a shareholders community receive designation by the JSDA as operating members.
3 . Solicitation for investment is allowed only toward investors who participate in a shareholders com-munity.
   • Solicitation for participation in a shareholders community is allowed only toward the executives and employees of the issuer and the issuer's shareholders and other company-related persons.
   • Only limited information is available to investors who are not participants in the shareholders community.
4 . Examination of issuers and measures to eliminate antisocial forces
5 . Investors participating in a shareholders community are provided with financial statements, busi-ness reports and other information based on the Companies Act in regard to the issuer.
6 . Issuance of document prior to conclusion of contract
7 . Investors who participate in a shareholders community for the first time are requested to submit a letter of intent.
8 . Establishment of an operation management system
9 . Weekly reporting and public disclosure of trades

7. Shareholders Community (2)

(5) Examination of Issues and Issuers

In handling OTC securities for which a shareholders community is to be created, operating members may strictly examine each issuer and verify the nature of their business, etc. in accordance with their internal rules and handle only such issuers as they find proper. Operating members shall enter into a contract with each issuer to the effect that the issuer is not an antisocial force.

(6) Provision of Information Regarding Shareholders Community Issues and Receipt/Delivery of Documents

Operating members are to provide investors with the necessary information on shareholders community issues in accordance with their level of involvement in the shareholders community (participation/declaration of participation in the shareholders community or otherwise; request for information or otherwise).

Furthermore, in order to receive confirmation from investors executing OTC transactions of shareholders community issues for the first time on their understanding of risks, commission, etc. involved and of making the investment based on their judgment and responsibility, operating members must provide advance explanations of these matters, request a letter of intent from each investor, and deliver the document prior to conclusion of contract containing at minimum the risks specific to such OTC transactions and other matters (e.g., no disclosure obligation comparable to the disclosure prescribed in the Financial Instruments and Exchange Act or to the timely disclosure required by stock exchanges is imposed) concerning individual issues, and explain the contents thereof.

(7) Handling of private placements, etc. of shareholders community issues

Operating members may not solicit investors who are not shareholders community participants to make investments in issues of a shareholder community in principle. However, small private placements may be made to investors who are not participants in a shareholders community on condition that they participate in the shareholders community and acquire the shareholders community issue. In this case, even if they have not yet joined the shareholders community, they shall be deemed to be participants, and the provisions of (6) Provision of Information Regarding Shareholders Community Issues shall apply.

(8) Withdrawal from and Dissolution of Shareholders Community

Operating members shall perform the withdrawal procedure when notified by

Chart XI-5.   Provision of information and delivery/receipt of documents related to shareholders community issues (by operating members)

1 . For all investors: Disclosure obligation/provision of information
1) Name of issue
2) URL of issuer's website (or telephone number, if the issuer does not have a particular website)
3) Benefits for shareholders (shareholder incentives)
4) If handling an offering, private placement or secondary distribution, the fact thereof and the application period
5) Type of business of the issuer
6) Location of the issuer's head office
7) Outline of the issuer's business
8) Whether or not the issuer is obliged to submit a securities report

2 . For investors who request information: Provision of information
1) Public information on the issuer
2) Unpublished information on the issuer where the issuer has consented to provide
3) Information on previous contracts

3-1. For investors who have applied to participate in a shareholders community: Obligation to provide information
1) Basic information on the issuer (business year, timing of annual general meeting of shareholders, and record date of voting rights of annual general meeting of shareholders)
2) Method of receiving information on issuers or inspecting such information
3-2. For investors participating in a shareholders community for the first time: Obligation to secure a confirmation note
- a document containing the contents of pre-contract document must be delivered and explained to the investors, and a confirmation note must be secured stating that investors understand the risks and details of the transaction and that they carry out the transaction at their own discretion and responsibility.

4 . For investors who execute transaction in shareholders community issues: Obligation to issue pre-contract documents
1) Issue pre-contract documents
2) Convey to participants that they may request explanations on the contents of the specified documents and materials (see 5)

5 . For investors participating in a shareholders community: Obligation to provide information and make it readily accessible
1) Securities Registration Statement, Annual Securities Report, Quarterly Securities Report, Amendment Report
2) Without the above, Financial statements and business report* provided foe in the Companies Act Information conforming to "Business risks, etc." and "Overview of stock administration of the submitting company" of the Annual Securities Report and (if handling an offering, etc.) information conforming to "Securities information" of the Securities Registration Statement
3) Other information recognized as necessary by the operating member
*Non-public companies are requested to comply with the requirements that public companies are obligated under the Companies Act in preparing these documents

Table XI-7.   Handling of Shareholders Community

As of December 31, 2021

	Number of operating members (companies)	Number of portfolio issues (issues)	Trading amount (¥1,000)
2015	2	11	71,149
2016	3	13	441,599
2017	3	16	551,013
2018	5	20	499,065
2019	6	19	500,798
2020	6	21	2,497,624
2021	7	29	1,182,991

a participant of the shareholders community of the participant's intent to withdraw or when there are other reasons as prescribed in the handling guide.

If an operating member's designation is cancelled by the JSDA, the operating member must immediately dissolve all shareholders communities it operates.

(9) Special provisions related to intermediary services for delisted issues
With respect to issues that become shareholders community issues after delisting from a stock exchange, securities companies other than the operating member of the shareholders community may solicit sales to customers on the condition that they act as intermediaries, etc., for the operating member.

8.   TOKYO PRO Market

The TOKYO PRO Market is a market for professional investors now operated by the Tokyo Stock Exchange (TSE). Its origin is the TOKYO AIM, which was founded jointly by the TSE and the London Stock Exchange (LSE) in June 2009. TOKYO AIM, Inc., was originally operated as a partnership (ownership: TSE 51%; LSE, 49%). In March 2012, however, the TSE acquired LSE's stake and merged Tokyo AIM with the TSE in July 2012. TOKYO AIM is operated under the professional investor market system provided for by the enactment of the December 2008 revision of the Financial Instruments and Exchange Act (FIEA).

Placing orders on traditional exchanges is not limited to any special category of investor. The professional investor market system, conversely, restricts trading to specified investors and nonresidents. Where fund procurement is limited to professional investors, securities registration statements are

Table XI-8. Overview of TOKYO PRO Market Listing System

Disclosure language	• Japanese or English
Listing criteria	• No quantitative criteria
Subject of evaluation	• J-Adviser (Conducts review and check on listing eligibility on behalf of the exchange)
Period from listing application to listing approval	• As a general rule, ten (10) business days • (provided, however, that there is a check procedure by the exchange to J-Adviser 30 business days prior to application)
Audit certification	Latest one (1) year
Internal control report	Optional
Quarterly disclosure	Optional
Investors	• Professional investors (Note) and non-residents *Note:* Professional investor refers to:

	Specified investors (*Tokutei Toushika*)	Qualified Institutional Investors (e.g., financial institutions); National government; Bank of Japan
	Specified investors (*Tokutei Toushika*) (may shift to general investors)	Listed companies and corporations with paid-in-capital of no less than ¥500 million
	"Deemed" specified investors	Corporations other than specified investors Individuals who meet specified requirements (total net worth/total financial assets expected no less than ¥300 million and with experience of one year or more in trading financial assets)

Chart XI-6. Role of J-Adviser

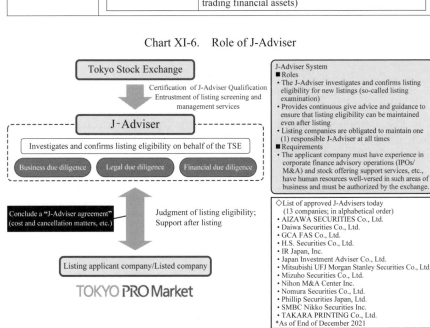

not required, and issuers need only make public financial information, etc. (called specified securities information), using the format and method stipulated by the TSE. Companies already listed on the exchange, moreover, need not submit annual securities reports and need only make public financial information, etc. (issuer information), using the TSE-stipulated format and method. The submission of internal control system reports and quarterly disclosure is voluntary. By premising requirements on the fact that only professional investors—those capable of analysis and making investment decisions—will invest in the market, the cost burden of issuing has been reduced in comparison with traditional stock exchanges.

The statutory penalties for falsifying financial information, etc., and for insider trading apply as much to the professional investor market system on the report of possession of large volume and tender offer systems. The page on the right shows details of how the TOKYO PRO Market aims to provide a flexible but disciplined market system for issuers and investors through the J-Adviser system (approved adviser system) within the previously mentioned legal framework. This operational method, which has the J-Adviser system at its core, has been drawn substantially from the Nomad (Nominated Adviser) system of the LSE's Alternative Investment Market (AIM). Under the system, specialists in corporate finance, etc., who have been approved as J-Advisers are required to guide a company through the admission process and to fulfill a duty to provide advice and instruction on timely disclosure and other regulatory matters following listing.

As of December 31, 2021, the TOKYO PRO Market had 13 J-Advisers and 47 listed companies.

9.   Market Making Scheme in the ETF Market

The TSE introduced a market-making scheme (hereinafter referred to as the "scheme") in the ETF (Exchange Traded Funds) market on July 2, 2018 to improve the liquidity of ETFs. Under the scheme, market makers who are designated by the exchange place constant orders on the basis of continuous quote obligation as prescribed, thereby enabling investors to trade on a timely basis at appropriate prices. The scheme covers all ETFs except leveraged/inverse ETFs. Market makers select at least five stocks and display quotes for these.

Continuous quote obligation and incentives

Market makers can earn incentives in exchange for placing constant orders on the basis of continuous quote obligations as prescribed. There are three types of quote obligations: 1) the number of issues for continuous quoting, 2)

Table XI-9.   Overview of ETF Market Making Incentive Scheme

Category	Item	Description
Target	ETFs excluding Leveraged/Inverse ETFs	• ETNs and Leveraged/Inverse ETFs are not included in this scheme.
Qualifications	Prop Desk of TSE Trading Participant Or Registered Low Latency Trader	• Prop Deskof TSE Member Firm (Type 1 Financial Instruments/Foreign Securities Broker) • Agency (Registered as Low Latency Trader) Either can sign up as an ETF Market Maker. The firm must apply through a TSE trading participant to sign up as an agency market maker. • Dedicated Virtual Server is needed.
Obligation (Continuous Quote Obligation)	(1) Number of ETFs for Continuous Quoting	• Must show quotes for at least the number of ETFs designated
	(2) QuotingTime	• At least 80% of the time during continuous auction. Exempt from obligation during trading halts or Special Quote periods.
	(3) Spread & Minimum Quantity	• Depends on type of ETF
Incentives	1. Proportional to TradingValue	• Price rate differs by liquidity (Average Trading Value).
	2. Waiver of Access Fee	• Access fee is partially waived for eligible issues.
	3. Waiver of Virtual Server Fee	• Server fee is partially waived when continuously quoting at least the number of ETFs designated.

Source: Tokyo Stock Exchange, Inc.

Table XI-10.   Continuos Quoting Obligation and Delivers a of number of Incentives

As of October 1, 2021

Type	Issue	Maximum Bid-Ask Spread (whichever is larger)	Minimum Quantity (one leg)
A	ETFs tracking Nikkei 225, TOPIX, or JPX Nikkei 400	20 bps OR 2 ticks	JPY 30 mil.
B	ETFs tracking domestic stocks or REITs	50 bps OR 3 ticks	JPY 10 mil.
C	Foreign index ETFs	50 bps OR 3 ticks	JPY 5 mil.
D	Selected foreign index ETFs	80 bps OR 4 ticks	JPY 5 mil.

Source: Tokyo Stock Exchange, Inc.

Chart XI-7.   Quote Display Sample

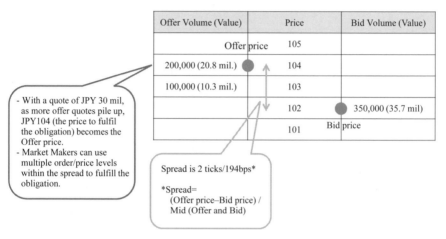

Offer Volume (Value)		Price	Bid Volume (Value)
Offer price		105	
200,000 (20.8 mil.)		104	
100,000 (10.3 mil.)		103	
		102	350,000 (35.7 mil)
		101	Bid price

- With a quote of JPY 30 mil, as more offer quotes pile up, JPY104 (the price to fulfil the obligation) becomes the Offer price.
- Market Makers can use multiple order/price levels within the spread to fulfill the obligation.

Spread is 2 ticks/194bps*

*Spread=
(Offer price–Bid price) /
Mid (Offer and Bid)

Source: Tokyo Stock Exchange, Inc.

quoting time period, and 3) spread and minimum quantity. By fulfilling all, a market maker can obtain incentives proportional to trading value and partial exemptions on transaction costs. While incentives proportional to trading value are set higher for less liquid/newly listed ETFs, none will be payable for issues with a daily trading volume in excess of ¥5 billion. This is to encourage more participants in the market making of less liquid issues.

The constant orders placed by the market makers on the basis of continuous quote obligations lead to a narrowing of spreads and an increase in volumes for a number of issues on an ongoing basis in the auction market, thereby providing an environment that is conducive to trading for investors.

Sponsored ETF Market Making Scheme

While the TSE scheme offers one-size-fits-all obligations and incentives across the board to ensure equal treatment of each ETF in the same category, a sponsored ETF market making scheme is also being implemented which enables asset managers to set their own additional quote obligations and incentives for market makers. It is expected to encourage more market makers to sign up for issues that are harder to trade in and bringing in higher level of quote obligations, leading to more liquidity in such ETFs.

CHAPTER XII

Financial Instruments Business (Securities Business)

1. Overview of Financial Instruments Business Operators (Securities Companies) (1)

The Financial Instruments and Exchange Act (FIEA), a comprehensive overhaul of the former Securities and Exchange Act, was fully enforced in September 2007. The FIEA defines the four financial instruments businesses: the Type I Financial Instruments Business, Type II Financial Instruments Businesses, the Investment Advisory and Agency Business, and the Investment Management Business. Securities companies are required to be registered as Type I Financial Instruments Business Operators (Article 29 of the FIEA). What has traditionally been known as the securities business corresponds to Securities Services (Article 28, Paragraph 8) within Type I Financial Instruments. Other Type I Financial Instruments Business include OTC financial futures business (mainly OTC foreign exchange margin business).

The securities business registration system that had been in place since 1948, when the Securities and Exchange Act was first enacted, was replaced by a licensing system in April 1968. The licensing system was designed to help stabilize the management of securities companies by curbing excessive competition and obligating them to specialize (ban, in principle, on concurrently operating non-securities business), thus strengthening the investor protection. As a result, the regulatory regime increasingly took on a defensive bias, and virtually no companies entered the securities business anew.

However, as the securities market developed, the types of financial products handled by securities companies became increasingly diverse. Furthermore, as the years rolled on into the 1990s, customer needs for securities services started to change and vary, from private equity and asset securitization to M&A advisory, asset management, and online brokerage, against the background of the nation's shifting industrial structure, aging population, dying traditional long-term employment practices, and ongoing information technology revolution (such as the proliferation of the Internet).

The licensing system did play a role in stabilizing the management of securities companies. On the other hand, there turned out to be a number of

Table XII-1.   The Scope of Business of Securities Companies (Type I Financial Instruments Businesses), and Requirements

1. Type I Financial Instruments Businesses (Article 28 Paragraph 1, Items (i)–(v) of the Financial Instruments and Exchange Act (FIEA))	Securities-related business (FIEA Article 28, Paragraph 8)
(1) Proprietary securities trading, intermediary, brokerage, or agency service of securities, market transactions of derivatives or foreign market derivatives transactions; intermediary, brokerage, or agency service for the entrustment of the transactions listed above; brokerage for the clearing of securities, etc.; secondary distribution of securities; or the handling of public, primary offering or secondary distribution of securities or the handling of the private placement of securities (2) Intermediary, brokerage, or agency service of commodity-related market derivatives trading; intermediary, brokerage, or agency service for the entrustment of the transactions listed above; or brokerage for clearing (3) Intermediary, brokerage, or agency service of OTC derivatives trading and brokerage for clearing of such transactions (4) "Underwriting" of securities (5) Sale or purchase of securities or intermediary, brokerage, or agency service therefor, which is conducted through an electronic data processing system and in which a large number of persons participate simultaneously as a party or parties of the transaction (business of operating a proprietary trading system (PTS business) (6) Acceptance of deposit of securities, etc., in relation to the transactions, etc., listed above or book-entry transfer of stocks or corporate bonds (securities management business) *Note:* (5) requires approval (Article 30, Paragraph 1). PTS stands for Proprietary Trading System.	Of the Type I Financial Instruments Businesses listed, the business related to securities (in principle, the scope of business which financial institutions are prohibited from conducting). Refusal of Registration (i.e., registration requirements) (Article 29-4, Paragraph 1 of the FIEA, Article 15 of the FIEA Enforcement Order) (1) An applicant who had his/her registration rescinded and for whom five years have not passed since the rescission; an applicant who has been punished by a fine for violating the provision of any applicable law or regulation and for whom five years have not passed since the imposition of the fine (2) An applicant with an officer, etc., who is bankrupt or has received certain criminal punishment and for whom five years have not passed since the completion of the sentence (3) An applicant without appropriate personnel resources to properly conduct the financial instruments business (4) An applicant with stated capital or net worth of less than ¥50 million (5) An applicant that is not a corporation (6) An applicant whose additional business other than incidental or registered/approved concurrent business is found to be against the public interest or to pose difficulty in risk management (7) An applicant whose major shareholder (with 20% or more of voting rights) is disqualified for registration (8) An applicant with a capital-to-risk ratio less than 120% (9) An applicant with a trade name that is the same as or similar to that of an already existing Financial Instruments Business Operator Minimum Capital Requirement (Article 15, Paragraphs 7 and 11 of the FIEA Enforcement Order) (1) When conducting wholesale underwriting as a lead managing underwriter: ¥3 billion (2) All other underwriting: ¥500 million or more (3) Business of operating PTS: ¥300 million (4) All other Type I Financial Instruments Businesses: ¥50 million
2. Incidental businesses (Article 35, Paragraph 1, Items (i)–(xv))	
(1) Lending or borrowing of securities, or intermediary or agency service thereof (2) Making a loan of money incidental to a margin trading (3) Making a loan of money secured by securities held in safekeeping for customers (4) Agency service for customers concerning securities (5) Agency service of the business pertaining to the payment of profit distribution or proceeds from redemption at maturity or at the request of an investment trust (6) Agency service of the business pertaining to the payment of dividends or refunds or distribution of residual assets with regard to investment certificates of an investment corporation (corporate type investment trust) (7) Conclusion of a cumulative investment contract (8) Provision of information or advice in relation to securities (9) Agency service of the business of any other Financial Instruments Business Operator, etc.	(The following items are newly included as incidental businesses under the FIEA.) (10) Custody of assets of a registered investment corporation (11) Provision of consultation to any other business with regard to assignment of a business, merger, spin-off, share exchange or share transfer or intermediation thereof (12) Provision of management consultation to any other business (13) Sale or purchase of currencies and other assets related to derivatives trading or intermediary, brokerage, or agency service thereof (14) Sale or purchase of negotiable deposits or other monetary claims or intermediary, brokerage, or agency service thereof (15) Management of assets under its management as investment in specified assets defined in the Investment Trust Act
3. Other businesses requiring notification (Article 35, Paragraph 2 of the FIEA; Article 68 of the Cabinet Office Order on Financial Instruments Business, etc.)	
(1) Conducting a transaction on a commodity exchange (2) Conducting a transaction in a derivative contract on a commodity price or other benchmark (3) Money-lending business or intermediary service for lending and borrowing of money (4) Business pertaining to building lots and buildings transaction business and lease of building lots or buildings (5) Real estate specified joint enterprise (6) Commodity investment management business (7) Business of investing property entrusted under an investment management contract in assets other than securities or rights pertaining to derivatives trading Among the businesses designated by a Cabinet Office Order, the main businesses include: (1) business pertaining to purchase and sale of gold bullion, or an intermediary, brokerage or agency service therefor; (2) business pertaining to conclusion of a Partnership Contract; (3) business pertaining to conclusion of a Silent Partnership Contract; (4) business pertaining to conclusion of a Loan Participation Contract or an intermediary, brokerage or agency service therefor; (5) business pertaining to insurance solicitation;	(6) business pertaining to lease of real properties owned by a FinancialInstruments Business Operator itself; (7) goods leasing business; (8) business pertaining to creation and sale of computer programs for the business of any other business operator, and a business to accept the entrustment of computing service; (9) business of management of the defined contribution pension; (10) Trust Agreement Agency Business; (11) intermediary service for forming a trust by will or concluding a contract for the disposition of an estate of a deceased party; (12) Financial Institution Agency Service; (13) real property management business; (14) advisory business related to real property investment; (15) business of trading emission rights and emission derivatives or acting as an intermediary, broker or agent therefor; (16) business of undertaking administrative operation entrusted by an investment corporation or a special-purpose company; (17) business of investing money or other properties for other person, as an investment in assets other than securities or rights pertaining to a derivative transaction ; (18) business of concluding a contract for a guarantee or assumption of an obligation, or an intermediary, brokerage or agency service therefor; (19) business of making an arrangement with or introducing another business operator, to customers of its business; (20) business of creating any advertisement or promotion in regard to the business of any other business operator; and (21) funds transfer business.

Notes: 1. A Financial Instruments Business Operator may, in addition to the above, engage in a business for which approval has been obtained from the prime minister (approved business, Article 35, Paragraph 4 of the FIEA).

2. A discretionary investment contract is now included as "investment management business", which is one of the independent investment management businesses that can be conducted without special approval from the prime minister.

drawbacks, including a detriment to creativity in business approaches, such as branch network management and the development of new products and services and a lower sense of self-reliance on the side of securities companies. Increasingly concerned about such negative fallout, the government amended the Securities and Exchange Act as part of the Act on Revision, etc. of Related Acts for the Financial System Reform, and a new registration system replaced the licensing system for the securities business in December 1998.

With the objective of providing an equal and uniform investor safeguard across various financial products and services with considerable risk, the FIEA was subsequently enacted to cover a wider range of objects, including collective investment schemes and derivatives trading. The FIEA is comprehensive legislation that combines the Securities and Exchange Act, the Mortgage Securities Business Regulation Law, the Financial Futures Trading Act, and the Investment Advisory Services Act, and aims at achieving effective regulation of a unified financial instruments business across a securities-related industry once vertically segmented into the securities business, financial futures trading business, and investment advisory business. Also as a result of amendments to the Financial Instruments and Exchange Act in 2012, commodity derivatives trading was added to the Type I Financial Instruments Business.

2. Overview of Financial Instruments Business Operators (Securities Companies) (2)

The former securities intermediary service is redefined as "Financial Instruments Intermediary Service" under the FIEA. The term "Financial Instruments Intermediary Service" means services comprising the following acts conducted under entrustment from a Type I Financial Instruments Businesses, an investment management business, or a registered financial institution (see section 12): (1) intermediation for the sale or purchase of securities (excluding PTS transactions); (2) intermediation for the sale or purchase of securities conducted in an exchange market or market transactions of derivatives; (3) handling of a public, primary offering or secondary distribution of securities or handling of a private placement of securities; and (4) intermediary service for the conclusion of an investment advisory contract or a discretionary investment contract (Article 2, Paragraph 11 of the FIEA). As is common with the items listed above, the provider of the service does not have customer accounts but solicits customers and redirects their orders for transactions to brokers/dealers, etc., from which it receives a commission.

Compared with the former definition for securities intermediary service,

Chart XII-1.   An Outline of Financial Instruments Intermediary Service Providers

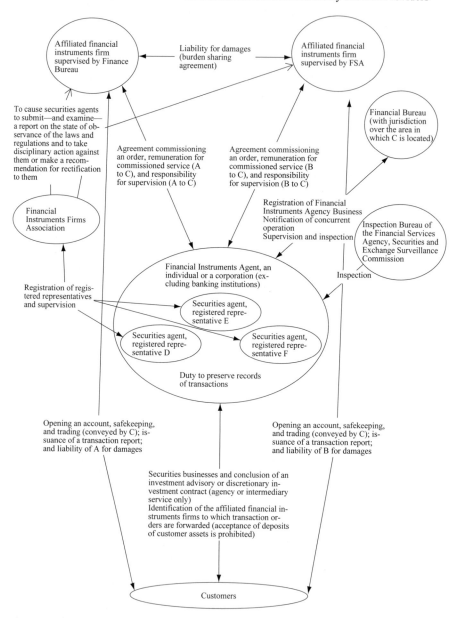

Note: More than one agreement commissioning an order is allowed.

Source: Compiled on the basis of the data drawn from materials published by the Financial Services Agency.

Table XII-2.   Financial Services Intermediary Business

Financial Services Provider Act		Remarks
Article 11.	Definition: To engage in deposit, etc. inter-mediary business, insurance intermediary business, securities intermediary business, or money lending intermediary business in the course of business.	With one registration, multiple mediation (agency) operations can be performed (one-stop service)
Article 18.	Exemption from registration as an agent for electronic settlement, etc.	On condition that an appropriate and reliable execution system and financial foundation are realized in the firm.
Article 22.	Obligation of depositing security deposit (to secure indemnity resources)	Unlike the financial instruments intermediary business, it does not adopt an affiliation system, so it bears its own liability for compensation.

Notes: 1. Items that require highly specialized explanations (structured deposits, unlisted stocks, deriva-tives, etc.) are excluded.
2. The minimum deposit is 10 million yen and 5% of the previous year's compensation (Article 26 of the Enforcement Order of the Financial Services Provision Law).

an intermediary service for derivatives trading and intermediary service for the conclusion of an investment advisory contract or a discretionary invest-ment contract are newly included in the new financial instruments intermedi-ary service. In spite of the expanded coverage, however, the underlying regu-latory principles remain intact. The provisions of the FIEA are designed to ensure the protection of investors by instituting a number of preventive mea-sures. More specifically, they require all financial instruments intermediary service agents to be registered and prevent any disqualified person from be-coming an agent. The FIEA makes all agents subject to the same set of pro-hibited and regulated acts that are applicable to Financial Instruments Busi-ness Operators (the prohibition of loss compensation, the duty to observe the suitability rule, etc.); explicitly defines agents under the control and authority of securities companies employing them; and holds these securities compa-nies legally responsible for supervision and damage compensation. The FIEA also gives the regulatory authority power to inspect and supervise financial instruments agents.

Registration requirements for financial instruments agents under the FIEA are essentially identical to those for the securities intermediary service under the former law. The requirements are less stringent than those for Type I Fi-nancial Instruments Business Operators to facilitate their market entry. More specifically, (1) either an individual or a legal entity can register as an agent and a legal entity does not need to be a corporation and (2) there are no mini-mum requirements for capital, net worth, or capital-to-risk ratio. However, they can only solicit investors for orders and redirect such orders to their bro-ker/dealer. They are not allowed to take a deposit of cash or securities from their customers. (For this reason, they are exempt from joining an investor protection fund.) As is the case with registered representatives of Financial Instruments Business Operators, salespersons of financial instruments agents shall be qualified as registered representatives and register with the Japan Se-curities Dealers Association (JSDA) (as an Authorized Financial Instruments Firms Association).

Financial instruments agents may be affiliated with one or more securities companies. As of the end of May 2021, for example, there were 874 actual financial instruments agents (626 companies and 248 individuals), according to the Financial Services Agency's "List of Financial Instruments Intermediary Service Providers. Many of these are mid-tier securities firms and online securities firms that are looking to expand their sales network as intermediaries.

In June 2020, a Financial Services Intermediary Business system was established (the Financial Instruments Sales Act was changed to the Financial Services Provision Act and came into effect in November 2021). This system has enabled one-stop intermediary businesses that provide all banking, securities, and insurance services (registration required), with several important differences compared to the past financial instruments intermediary businesses (see table on the right).

3. Overview of Financial Instruments Business Operators (Securities Companies) (3)

For quite some time after the war, securities companies in Japan had one characteristic in common: heavy reliance on the stock brokerage business both in terms of revenues and business volume. In the process, (1) there de-veloped a bipolarization of securities companies—integrated securities com-panies that hired a large number of employees and ran multifaceted securities business on a large scale, on the one hand, and small and midsized securities companies that relied on the brokerage business generated by commission-registered representatives, on the other—and (2) the large integrated securi-ties companies—Nomura, Daiwa, Nikko, and Yamaichi, collectively referred to as the "Big Four"—captured a large share of the market in all segments of the securities business. And they had gained an oligopolistic control of the market as a group by creating a network of affiliated small securities compa-nies. This was a major characteristic of the postwar securities market of Ja-pan, unknown before the war or in other countries. And this structure was maintained until the latter half of the 1990s with only minor changes.

Chart XII-2. Net Assets and Number of Firms

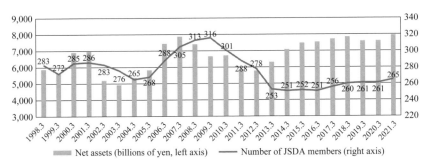

■■ Net assets (billions of yen, left axis) —— Number of JSDA members (right axis)

Note: Excluding firms inactive in business. As of March 31 of each year.
Source: Compiled from "Number of Members and Capitalization", Japan Securities Dealers Association.

Table XII-3. JSDA Member Categories

(July 31, 2021)

	Securities business operator	Non-securities business operator	Breakdown		
			Investment Management Business	FX (FOREX Margin Transactions)	Others
Domestic brokers: 190 firms	149	41	20	16	5
Foreign brokers: 75 firms	46	29	26	3	

Note: Non-securities business operator refers to a business operator whose primary business is not the securities business. "Asset Management Service" refers to investment management and sale of structured funds and securitized products. Foreign brokers are foreign-owned firms whose controlling shareholder (author's estimate).

However, in the 1990s, after the speculative bubble finally burst, the securities slump worsened and Yamaichi Securities and a number of smaller securities companies went bankrupt in the process in 1997 and afterward. In addition, large securities companies abandoned the strategy of forming a network of affiliated small and midsize securities companies, making the management of securities companies increasingly fluid. Around the same time, large banks, etc. acquired the right to manage securities companies while a number of firms that were armed with a unique business style and focused on selected segments of the securities business have entered the market.

In addition, a number of foreign securities companies have opened branches in Japan. Since 1990, some have increased their shares in the equity and derivatives trading markets in their existing securities business, largely

Table XII-4. Breakdown of 150 Japanese Brokers (securities-related) by Controlling Shareholder, Size, Region and Business Characteristics

Independent major securities companies (2 Nomura-affiliated, Daiwa): 3		Bank-affiliated 33 companies		Second-tier small & midsize (face-to-face) 73 companies		Online brokers (including securities which used smartphone) 15 companies
Listed securities companies: 14	Breakdown	Megabank-affiliated: 3	Breakdown	Tokyo: 22		PTS specialists 5 companies
		Regional bank-affiliated: 27		Osaka: 7		
		Other bank-affiliated: 3		Regional: 44		Others 5 companies

Notes: 1. Independent major securities companies include Nomura Financial Products & Services, Inc.
2. "Listed securities companies" are securities companies whose shares are listed. If a holding company is listed, its controlling subsidiary is included in "listed securities companies". However, independent major securities companies and online brokers are excluded. Second-tier small & midsize securities do not include "listed securities".
3. Online brokers include seven "smartphone securities" companies.

thanks to increases in orders received from their overseas customers. They are playing a major role in new types of business, such as the securitization of assets, packaging structured bonds, and M&A.

Following the introduction of new registration system and the abolition of single-business scheme (in 1998) and the relaxation of the member eligibility requirements of the JSDA (in 2007; see Section 9), entities that do not engage in the securities-related business as their primary business have started to register under the Type I Financial Instruments Business, becoming members of the JSDA. Over the twelve years between April 2007 and March 2021, 161 companies left (as a result of mergers, business transfers, voluntary business closures or deregistration), while 120 companies entered the business (including newly registered companies), reflecting the fluidity of the industry. While there are 10 foreign securities companies with operating sites in Japan (as of July 31, 2021), many more foreign entities are actually in operation through the establishment of a local subsidiary, conversion to a Japanese corporation, or acquisition of a domestic securities company (see Table XII-3).

As such, the Japanese securities industry, where the "Big Four" (Nomura, Daiwa, Nikko, and Yamaichi Securities) used to have an oligopolistic control of the market and where brokering was the core and standard operation, changed drastically, resulting in having diverse players, such as foreign entities and banks, hold stakes in securities businesses. And as the securities business itself became increasingly diverse to cover operations other than brokerage, a growing number of firms whose primary business is not a securities-related business have entered the market.

4. Securities Businesses (1)—The Principal Businesses (1)

"Securities Companies" has come to be redefined as "Financial Instruments Business Operators" under the FIFA, and the scope of the businesses are expanded. Securities business are largely divided into those related to stocks, bonds, investment trusts, and derivatives. By type of services, they are largely divided into those relating to (1) dealing—proprietary trading, (2) brokerage—agency trading, (3) investment banking—underwriting, and (4) public offering and private placement—distribution of securities.

The bulk of the securities-related business of brokers/dealers in the secondary market is the brokerage business of executing customer orders on stock exchanges, and the rest is the proprietary trading conducted for their own account. As not many customer orders for bonds—except for convertible bonds, whose prices are linked to underlying stock prices—are executed on stock exchanges, most bond orders are executed by matching them against the positions of securities companies' proprietary accounts (bond dealing). Along with stock exchanges, securities companies play an important role in forming fair prices and maintaining the liquidity of securities through their broker/dealer functions.

In addition to underwriting publicly offered new issues of public bonds (government securities, etc.), nonconvertible bonds of private business corporations, and equity securities (stocks and bonds with subscription rights/ warrants) of public companies, securities companies also underwrite the shares of companies to be listed on exchanges, etc., in the process of initial public offerings. The term "underwriting" means an act of acquiring a security by a securities company with the aim of ensuring successful issuance of a new security or secondary distribution of shares by reselling them to others and, if so agreed, purchasing the unsold portion of the security, if any. More specifically, the act of acquiring new security from the issuer is called "wholesale underwriting" (and the securities company that negotiates a wholesale underwriting agreement with the issuer is called "the managing underwriter"), and acquiring the security from a wholesale underwriter is called "sub-underwriting." Beneficiary certificates of investment trusts are also sold in public offerings, in addition to the new-issue securities mentioned above. Secondary distribution means the placing of already issued securities and includes block sales of major shareholders, etc.

In 1998, over-the-counter derivative trading and PTS services were newly authorized. The former refers to an act of effecting or entrusting to effect

Table XII-5.   Business Volume Handled by TSE and OSE Member Companies

	Cash Stock Transaction Value (Trillions of yen)			Listed Derivatives Trading (Trillions of yen)
	Proprietary	Agency	Traded on margin (%)	Notional principal (stocks, bonds, etc.)
2017/3	280	1,212	14	2,223
2018/3	336	1,429	14	2,870
2019/3	317	1,349	13	3,140
2020/3	288	1,218	13	3,212
2021/3	280	1,514	16	2,769

Notes: 1. The accounting year runs from April 1 to March 31 of the following year.
2. Figures are double the actual volume because both sales and purchases are included.
3. Cash stock transaction volumes are those handled by 88 general members (including foreign securities companies, as of March 31, 2021).
4. Of these members, 75 members also participate in derivatives trading on the OSE.
5. In addition, 21 financial institutions participate in JGB futures trading on the OSE.
6. Derivatives trading include commodity-related (Howerer, thansactions on the Tokyo Commodity Exchange are not included.)
Source: Compiled from statistical data issued by Japan Exchange Group

Table XII-6.   PTS Transactions

(Billions of yen)

	Trading on Exchange (A)	Trading off Exchange (B)	Total (A)+(B)	PTS transactions (C)	Proportion of PTS Trading off Exchange (C/B)	Proportion of PTS Trading to Total (C/(A+B))
2017/3	671,447	83,932	755,379	30,967	36.9%	4.1%
2018/3	787,401	121,446	908,846	35,235	29.0%	3.9%
2019/3	745,182	114,155	859,336	37,339	32.7%	4.3%
2020/3	671,051	88,315	595,011	44,140	50.0%	7.4%
2021/3	766,839	106,954	749,490	70,276	65.7%	9.4%

Notes: 1. The accounting year runs from April 1 to March 31 of the following year.
2. Figures are actual volume because only one side of the transaction is included.
3. Major PTSs include SBI Japannext and Chi-X.
4. ToSNeT (off-auction trading) enters into Trading on Exchange.
Source: Compiled based on statistical data from the PTS Information Network.

Table XII-7. Electronic record transfer rights and handling services (Securities Token Offering, STO)

What is STO (according to the Japan STO Association website)
STO is a system using technology to provide a service for the needs of new financing methods to replace traditional equity and debtfinancing and of new financial instruments to replace stocks and bonds in compliance with laws and regulations is a mechanism called STO. This is called "electronic record transfer right" in Japan.

Financial Instruments and Exchange Law (amended in 2019, effective May 2020)

Electronic record transfer rights	"Deemed securities" as defined in Article 2, Paragraph 2, refers to rights that can be transferred using an electronic data processing system, and is positioned as "securities" as defined in Article 2, Paragraph 1. (Article 2, Paragraph 3, etc.).
Electronic record transfer rights	Since the electronic record transfer right falls under Article 2(1), its purchase and sale, brokerage, handling of offering and sale, and deposit, etc., require "registration of change" when a Type 1 firm handles such business (Article 31(4)).

Note: Electronically recorded rights that are not tradable are considered "deemed securities" under Article 2, Paragraph 2, and the business of handling them is positioned as Type 2 Business.

with a customer a forward or options trading of a stock or a stock index or a swap contract involving, for example, a stock index and an interest rate off the exchange. The PTS service matches orders from investors by utilizing an electronic information processing system. It is a licensed system since it requires specialized technical expertise and advanced risk management skills (see Section 1). As information technology has developed, fund-raising via the internet ("crowdfunding," see Chapter 11, Sections 4 and 5) as well as transactions of digital securities ("electronically recorded transferable rights"), have become more commonplace (see diagram in lower right).

5. Securities Businesses (2)—The Principal Businesses (2)

Because the Financial Instruments and Exchange Act (FIEA) combined the Securities and Exchange Act and the Financial Futures Trading Act, the Type 1 Financial Instruments Businesses includes financial futures, etc., as well as securities derivative trading. Moreover, the OTC derivatives business no longer requires authorization from the authorities (for an overview of the OTC derivatives business, see section 9 of Chapter 8).

The underlying assets of derivatives can comprise financial instruments, such as (1) securities, deposits, and currencies (Article 2, Paragraph 24 of the FIEA) and (2) financial indexes, such as price and interest rate of a financial

Chart XII-3.   OTC FOREX Margin Transactions

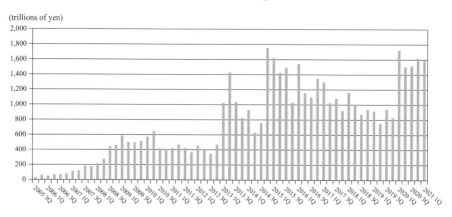

Notes: 1. Figures compiled based on reports from association members and special members.
  2. Trading volume includes both buy and sell sides, including agency transactions.
  3. Foreign currency amounts have been converted into Japanese yen using the spot rate at the end of each period.
Source: The Financial Futures Association of Japan.

instrument, and weather indexes (Article 2, Paragraph 25). In 2012 the definition of financial instrument was expanded to include commodities (excluding rice), and in 2019, crypto-assets were added, making them subject to the Financial Instruments and Exchange Act. The main customers for derivatives are financial institutions or institutional investors. In addition to acting as swap arrangers, securities companies typically use OTC stock options as sweeteners for structured bond issues or conclude interest rate or currency swap agreements with companies issuing foreign currency denominated bonds when underwriting the issue.

Nikkei 225 mini-futures (Osaka Exchange), and foreign exchange (FX) transactions are among the products that individual investors use relatively often. Investors use OTC FX transactions to purchase or sell currencies by depositing a margin with the broker and settle the transaction usually on a net basis. These OTC transactions got their start in Japan when some commodity traders became the first to use them following the deregulation of foreign exchange transactions through the 1998 amendment of the Foreign Currency and Exchange Law (currently Foreign Exchange and Foreign Trade Act.) These FX transactions enable high leverage factors of 20 times on average and up to 100 times on small margins.

Without any laws or regulations initially, problems did occur in the FX market, resulting in the 2005 revision of the Financial Futures Trading Act,

Table XII-8.   OTC CFD Transactions on Securities

	March-end 2013	March-end 2015	March-end 2017	March-end 2019	March-end 2021
Number of Accounts	101,196	105,790	148,692	248,497	409,729
Margin Deposit Balance (100 million yen)	63	107	161	309	678

(Transactions)

	Individual stock related	Stock index related	Bond related	Other securities related	Total
From April 2019 to March 2020					
Transaction amount (100 million yen)	1,526	290,652	1,850	3,193	297,221
Number of transactions	340,010	16,837,419	14,826	2,249,015	19,441,270
Open interest (100 million yen, end of March 2018)	18	440	7	30	495
From April 2020 to March 2021					
Transaction amount (100 million yen)	6,011	484,990	1,477	1,559	494,037
Number of transactions	1,042,447	27,873,722	14,783	1,982,107	30,913,059
Open interest (100 million yen, end of March 2019)	140	805	26	28	999

Note: Transaction amounts and open interest are on a notional principal basis. Open interest is as of the end of the fiscal year. Figures represent the sum of transaction value, etc. of JSDA regular and special members.

Source: Compiled from materials issued by the Japan Securities Dealers Association.

currently included in the Financial Instruments and Exchange Act. The revised law introduced a registration system for the FX business, which eliminated many of the bad operators. As a result, there was a sharp expansion in the use of FX transactions, as can be seen in Chart XII-2. Moreover, in a bid to make FX transactions more transparent, the Tokyo International Financial Futures Exchange (TIFFE, now TFX) listed an FX product in 2005 called Click 365. The ceiling on leverage in FX transactions was lowered to 50 times in August 2010 and again to 25 times in August 2011.

Today, FX transactions, have been shifted from face-to-face transactions with brokers to online. Internet trading specialist FX firms, such as Gaitame. com and Gaitame Online, are, together with internet securities companies, aggressively developing the market. This type of OTC trading, where investors can place orders with low margins and settle the contracts on a net basis, is called contract for difference (CFD transaction) and is available not only for FX but also for securities, indexes, interest rates, and commodities.

6. Securities Businesses (3)—Incidental Business, Concurrent Business, and Other Businesses

In addition to the principal businesses outlined in the foregoing, securities companies may conduct businesses incidental to their principal businesses and other businesses that require notification to the authorities. Management of assets of investment trusts, those entrusted under discretionary investment contracts, or properties pertaining to collective investment schemes used to require notification only, but, under the FIEA, securities companies are required to make registration in order to conduct this type of "investment management business" (Article 28, Paragraph 4). Income from non-principal businesses tends to be recorded as "other fees" (see table on the right and following section).

The volume of margin trading, or transactions in securities that are lent on margin to customers or financed by margin loans extended to them, began to increase around 1999, and it has been accounting for approximately 14 to 20% of agency transactions in the 2000s (see table in Section 4). The term "securities lending and borrowing" refers to the lending and borrowing of stock or bond certificates and is also known as stock lending or bond repurchase agreements (repo). As a lending broker demands a borrowing investor to pledge cash as collateral, these transactions may also be considered as a means of financing secured by stock or bond certificates, and therefore a bond repo transaction is equivalent to a bond gensaki transaction economically. This practice makes it easier for securities companies to finance stocks, bonds, and cash and hence to accept large orders or basket orders from customers. For this reason, it contributes to the formation of fair prices of securities and improves the liquidity of the market. By "consultation with any other business operator with regard to a business assignment, merger, company split, share exchange or share transfer, or intermediation for these matters" is meant the M&A consulting service that an investment bank provides to its clients with respect to the spinning off of a business division, the computation of an IPO price, or an acquisition offer, etc.

Major securities companies of the top- and second-tier brokers, also registered themselves under the investment management service and have started to market a "wrap account" discretionary investment service and to launch and manage collective investment schemes to invest in nonpublic companies, real estate, and others. As of the end of March 2021, according to a survey by the Japan Investment Advisers Association, there were a total of 1,178,396 wrap accounts in the industry, holding approximately ¥11,208.5 billion, reflecting a stable increase. Major brokers, foreign affiliates, and securities subsidiaries of mega-banks focus on M&A; structuring of private

Table XII-9.   Composition and Share of "Other Fees" by Type (FY 2019)

Other Fees	11,323billion yen	Number of companies	Composition	Share
Total		261	(35.3%)	100.0%
Major General and Wholesale		47	37.4%	76.9%
Independent		2	31.2%	21.8%
Megabank Affiliates		4	25.1%	18.1%
Other bank affiliates		3	34.2%	0.5%
Foreign-affiliated		38	72.7%	36.5%
Mainly Retail		131	11.8%	6.3%
Listed securities		14	15.2%	2.8%
Regional bank affiliated		27	11.1%	0.7%
Small and medium-sized securities		73	9.2%	0.7%
Online securities (including foreign-affiliated)		17	10.1%	2.1%
New business entities		83	66.3%	16.7%
Investment management, fund sales, etc. (Japanese-affiliated)		21	83.7%	1.7%
Investment management, fund sales, etc. (foreign-affiliated)		24	95.1%	12.7%
FX (including foreign-affiliated)		19	5.4%	0.3%
PTS (including foreign-affiliated companies)		8	29.5%	0.3%
Others		11	11.9%	1.7%

Notes: 1. Classification criteria are based on "shareholder composition" (independent and listed securities, bank-affiliated, foreign-affiliated, etc.) and "business characteristics". Listed securities are
included if its holding company is listed and it is a controlling subsidiary. Foreign-affiliated securities firms by shareholder composition are 71 (FY2019).
   2. "Online securities" includes foreign-affiliated and smartphone securities.
   3. "Others" includes OTC derivatives, private equity, etc.
   4. "Composition" is the ratio of "other commissions" to net operating revenues.
Source: Prepared based on figures published by each company.

equity funds; and securitization (defined as business to trade monetary claims
and requires notification), collectively known as investment banking services,
along with securities underwriting, which is often conducted in association
with these services.

   In addition, following the full deregulation of brokerage commissions (in
October 1999), low-commission online stock brokers offering service over
the Internet have emerged, and their share of the market has been increasing
rapidly. The number of online brokers stood at 89, with the number of
accounts rising to 33.47 million at the end of March 2021. The value of cash
stock and margin transactions of these online brokers during the period
between October 2020 and March 2021 amounted to ¥218,826.7 billion,
accounting for 24.6% of the total value of agency transactions, and the online
brokers sold ¥1,990.7 billion worth of investment trust units according to the

Table XII-10.   Number of Wrap Accounts and Assets Under Management

(¥100 million)

	Discretionary investment		Investment advisory		Grand Total	
	No.	Amount	No.	Amount	No.	Amount
March-end 2013	51,758	7,689	0	0	51,758	7,689
March-end 2014	105,706	13,760	0	0	105,706	13,760
March-end 2015	307,346	38,973	0	0	307,346	38,973
March-end 2016	482,217	57,776	4	0	482,221	57,776
March-end 2017	564,620	65,700	0	0	564,622	65,702
March-end 2018	716,612	79,841	4	10	716,618	79,853
March-end 2019	868,091	88,271	5	15	868,097	88,287
March-end 2020	1,027,344	87,773	3	7	1,027,347	87,780
March-end 2021	1,178,394	112,079	2	6	1,178,396	112,085

Note: A wrap account is an account that is managed for a flat fee covering fees for investment advisory, trading commission expenses, account management fees, etc. in proportion to the balance of managed assets.
Source: Compiled from statistics produced by the Japan Investment Advisers Association.

JSDA Monthly Report for June 2021. Growth in the business of Internet brokers was particularly notable.

7.   Income and Expenditure of Financial Instruments Business Operators (Securities Companies)

Sources of revenue for securities companies include (1) brokerage commission; (2) management and underwriting fees; (3) selling concessions from public offerings and secondary distributions; (4) trading income (net of trading losses); (5) financial income in the form of interest on loans made in conjunction with margin trading and lending fees on shares lent to customers, lending fees on shares and bonds lent in conjunction with transactions other than margin trading (such as repos), collateral for shares or bonds borrowed, interest, and dividends and other distributions on securities held in inventory; and (6) other fees and commissions, including those received in connection with incidental or concurrent businesses, chiefly among them agency fees received from investment trust management companies for handling the payment of dividends and other distributions and fees from investment banking customers for the provision of information and advice, etc., on best capital policies and M&A opportunities.

Table XII-11. Financial Overview of Regular Member Firms, JSDA

(Millions of yen)	Fiscal year ending March 1991		FY2020	
No. of menbers	260	Percentage of net operating income	262	Percentage of net operating income
Operating income	4,428,700	100.0%	4,114,801	100.0%
(Commissions received)	2,877,500	65.0%	2,319,328	56.4%
(Brokerage commissions)	2,023,000	45.7%	661,064	16.1%
(Underwriting fees)	172,100	3.9%	165,318	4.0%
(Selling concession)	314,300	7.1%	269,919	6.6%
(Other fees and commissions)	368,100	8.3%	1,222,843	29.7%
Trading profit/loss	217,400	4.9%	1,071,523	26.0%
Financial income	1,333,800	30.1%	692,376	16.8%
(Profit from margin trading)	784,300	17.7%	94,309	2.3%
Financial expenses	677,800	15.3%	387,159	9.4%
(Margin trading expenses)	184,400	4.2%	16,192	0.4%
(Interest expense)	467,000	10.5%	50,639	1.2%
Net operating income	3,750,900	84.7%	3,727,561	90.6%
Selling, general and administrative expenses	3,036,100		2,961,825	
(Transaction-related expenses)	562,700		809,188	
(Personnel expenses)	1,264,300		1,077,571	
Operating profit/loss	714,800		765,681	

On the other hand, expenditures of securities companies consist of (1) selling, general and administrative expenses (personnel expenses, rent and other real estate expenses, administrative costs, trade-related expenses, etc., and (2) financial expenses (interest and fees on brokers' loan and stock certificates borrowed from securities finance companies, etc. in connection with margin trading, interest and fees on brokers' loans and bonds borrowed in connection with repos, interest on bank loans and outstanding bonds, etc.). Revenues generated from the securities business are called "operating income." Deducting financial expenses from that amount yields "net operating income," and net operating income less selling, general and administrative expenses is called "operating profit." Nonoperating profit or loss is added to operating profit to reach "current profit." Profit or loss, if any, from the sale of investment securities or real estate holdings and losses due to capital contribution to affiliates, subsidiaries, etc. (such as nonbank lenders) are further added or deducted as extraordinary profit.

Table XII-12.   Breakdown of other fees received (FY2020)

(Breakdown)		Ratio (%)
Equities	106,362	2.6%
Bonds	143,668	3.5%
Beneficiary securities	239,995	5.8%
Others	732,655	17.8%
Profit distribution to Japanese corporations, etc. related to international transactions, etc.	291,587	7.1%
M&A related income	92,666	2.3%
Mutual fund trustee fees	81,083	2.0%
Wrap-related revenues	80,749	2.0%
Discretionary investment management fees	46,134	1.1%
Advisory/Consulting Fees	29,170	0.7%
Administration fees	20,604	0.5%
Insurance-related revenues	15,741	0.4%
Fees for system use/development, etc.	14,533	0.4%

Notes: 1. JSDA members are no longer required to close their books in March after April 2014; FY2020 corresponds to the fiscal year ending March 31, 2021 under the previous notation.
2. Composition ratio is the percentage of operating revenue.
Note: "Other fees" that cannot be classified by product are further subdivided into "Other."
Source: Compiled from Financial Overview of Regular Member Firms, JSDA

Commission income has been on a declining trend over the past thirty years, both in absolute terms and as a proportion of net operating income, while "other fees" have increased. Underwriting fees account for around 7% of net operating income, a large proportion of which is due to investment trust sales. "Other fees" now form the largest revenue stream, including 1) allocation of income from parent companies of foreign securities companies, etc., 2) advisory fees for M&A, 3) agency commission for investment trusts, 4) management fees for investment trusts, discretionary investment advisory fees.

In recent years, the securities business has become increasingly globalized and cooperation with overseas affiliate companies has risen. Investment in foreign bonds by domestic investors has increased, with these transactions typically executed through overseas affiliate-company intermediaries. The increase in M&A involving Japanese companies and the large-scale entry of investment management businesses and fund distributors, both domestic and foreign (Section 13), with most of their income recorded as "other fees" reflects this trend.

8. Financial Condition of Financial Instruments Business Operators (Securities Companies)

Reflecting—and because of—the uniqueness of their business, the balance sheets of securities companies appear to be larger than they actually are. The biggest items on their balance sheets are "loans against the collateral of securities" and "borrowings against the collateral of securities." These are deposits made in connection with the lending and borrowing of securities (see section 6). Funds received from the borrower of a bond or other security to secure them are treated as borrowings, while funds deposited with the lender of a bond or other security to secure them are treated as loans. The trading instrument is one that arises from the dealing of securities, and a net long position in cash securities (securities held for trading purposes) is entered on the debit side, and a net short position is entered on the credit side of the balance sheet. Derivatives (futures, options, and swaps) are marked to market, and unrealized gains are entered under the item of derivatives transactions on the debit side and under unrealized losses on the credit side. In case a transaction was not settled after execution, an amount equivalent to the value of securities sold is entered under the item of collateral account on the debit side, and an amount equivalent to the value of securities purchased is entered on the credit side. Securities companies hold both long and short positions in a security for the purpose of speedy execution of customer orders involving cash security, derivatives, or bond repos, as well as the pursuit of arbitrage gains, and, instead of netting them out, they are required to adhere to the trade-date accounting process with stringent risk management on a contract basis.

Incidentally, a loan to facilitate margin trading is made in an amount equivalent to the amount required to make the margin purchase of a security by a customer, and cash collateral is deposited with a securities finance company as a borrowed securities deposit. On the other hand, the cash for conducting margin trading is borrowed from a securities finance company, and it is equivalent to the amount that needs to be paid to a customer for the securities sold on margin.

Securities companies are required to keep customer assets segregated from their own assets and to hold them in an outside trust (see section 11); this system is called "segregated customer asset trust."

Ceilings on the ratio of individual products to the total net worth were used to control risks. However, as new products have since increased and the lesson was learned from Black Monday of 1987 (the market crash on Wall Street), the industry and the authorities became painfully aware of the need to control risk on a total basis. At the same time, the International Organiza-

Table XII-13.   Major Accounts of Securities Companies in Japan (265 firms) as of March 31, 2021

Assets	In ¥ millions	Liabilities and capital	In ¥ millions
Cash and deposits	10,427,012	Trading products	32,681,698
Deposit	9,960,574	(Trading securities, etc.)	19,851,035
(Segregated customer asset trust)	8,823,080	(Derivatives trading)	12,830,646
Trading products	48,538,363	Collateral-for-contract account	1,153,032
(Trading securities, etc.)	34,363,797	Debt on margin trading	1,519,740
(Derivatives trading)	14,174,553	(Debt for margin trading)	397,750
Collateral-for-contract account	942,649	(Money received for securities lent for margin trading)	1,121,927
Assets for margin trading	3,849,523	Borrowings against the collateral of securities	89,103,702
(Money lent for margin trading)	3,275,358	Deposit received	7,567,248
(Cash collateral deposited to secure the securities lent for margin trading)	574,109	Guarantee money received	6,436,122
Loans against the collateral of securities	89,729,520	Short-term debt	19,300,044
Short-term guarantee money submitted	6,451,620	Total of current liabilities	160,625,976
Short-term loans	1,575,085	Long-term liabilities	6,040,657
Total of current assets	172,801,237	Total liabilities	166,828,232
Tangible fixed assets	235,842	Total Capital	1,815,739
Intangible fixed assets	397,312	Capital surplus	3,124,453
Investment, etc.	1,337,884	Retained earnings	2,843,385
(Investment securities)	946,493		
Total of fixed assets	1,971,240	Total capital	7,944,515
Total of assets	174,772,884	Total of liabilities and capital	174,772,884

Source: Compiled from materials prepared by the Japan Securities Dealers Association. These figures exclude those of companies that have suspended their operations. Totals may not match sums.

tion of Securities Commissions (IOSCO) called for the international harmonization of securities regulations. Against this backdrop, securities companies have been subjected to requirements for their capital-to-risk ratio. (The requirements were put into effect in 1990, and a law institutionalizing them was enacted in 1992.)

As securities companies handle products whose prices fluctuate in the market, their revenues are vulnerable to sudden changes in market prices. Therefore, a framework of capital-to-risk ratio regulations was put into place so that they can maintain their solvency and protect the interests of their customers even when the prices of their assets fall by providing for a sufficient amount of liquid assets against various risk contingencies.

Table XII-14.   Capital-to-Risk Ratio of General Trading Participant Members of the TSE (86 companies) as of March 31, 2021

The minimum ratio	215.1%
The maximum ratio	1835.0%
The median ratio	422.7%
The average ratio	484.2%
Distribution	
Those in the range of 100% to 199%	0 company
200% to 299%	20 companies
300% to 399%	19 companies
400% to 499%	17 companies
500% to 599%	8 companies
600% to 699%	12 companies
700% to 799%	2 companies
800% or higher	8 companies

Source: Compiled from materials produced by the Tokyo Stock Exchange.

Table XII-15.   An Outline of the Capital-to-risk Ratio Requirements for Type I Financial Instruments Business Operators (Securities companies)

(Article 46-6, Paragraph 1 of the FIEA and Article 178 of the Cabinet Office Order on Financial Instruments Business, etc.)

Capital-to-risk ratio = (non-fixed primary capital ÷ the equivalents of various risks) × 100%	
Non-fixed primary capital = Tier I item (equity capital) + complementary item (subordinated debt, allowance) − deducted assets (fixed assets, etc.)	Equivalents of various risks = market risk + customer risk + fundamental risks
Market risk = risk of loss that may arise from a fall in the prices of securities held by securities companies Customer risk = risk of a loss arising from the default by the other party to a transaction effected by securities companies Fundamental risks = risks that may arise in the ordinary course of business by mistakes made by members of the administrative department of securities companies	

Note: Large companies having assets totaling more than ¥1 trillion are designated as "Special Financial Instruments Business Operators" and are subject to primary capital regulations on a consolidated basis (Article 57-2, Paragraph 1 of the FIEA; as of June 30, 2020, 21 companies) Among such companies, since the shareholding companies of two groups—Nomura and Daiwa—correspond to the Designated Parent Companies prescribed in Article 57-12, Paragraph 1 of the FIEA (capital ratio against the entire group including the parent company and fellow subsidiaries), they are eligible for selecting the consolidated capital-to-risk ratio under the Basel III Accord.

Table XII-16.   Orders Issued on the Basis of the Capital-to-Risk Ratio to Take a Prompt
Corrective Action

Capital-to-Risk Ratio		
140% or less	Required to notify the regulatory agency	Art. 179 of the Cabinet Office Order on Financial Instruments Business, etc.
120% or more	Obligated to maintain ratio at such a level	Art. 46-6, Para. 2 of the FIEA
Less than 120%	- Denial to accept a registration application - Orders to change the method of business and deposit its property	Art. 29-4, Para. 1, Item (vi) of the FIEA Art. 53, Para. 1 of the FIEA
Less than 100%	Orders to suspend business for a period of three months or less	Art. 53, Para. 2 of the FIEA
Less than 100% and has no prospects for recovery	Cancellation of registration	Art. 53, Para. 3 of the FIEA

9. Financial Instruments Firms Associations (1)

The former Japan Securities Dealers Association is now regarded as the Authorized Financial Instruments Firms Association under the Financial Instruments and Exchange Act (FIEA). Under the FIEA, the association shall be composed of Type I Financial Instruments Business Operators (excluding OTC financial futures business operators) and must be authorized by the prime minister (Article 67-2, Paragraph 2 of the FIEA). The association aims to ensure the fair and smooth sale and purchase of securities, etc., and to contribute to the protection of investors and is enabled to establish a market where over-the-counter securities are traded (Article 67, Paragraph 1 and 2). The principal functions of the association are (1) self-regulatory operations, (2) businesses that contribute to the development of the financial instruments business and the financial instruments market, and (3) international businesses and promotion international exchange (see Table XII-15). At present, the Japan Securities Dealers Association (JSDA) is the country's only organization established as the Authorized Financial Instruments Firms Association under the FIEA.

In 1940, the government ordered securities companies to form one securities dealers association in every prefecture for the purpose of facilitating the wartime control of the securities market. After the war, the Japan Securities Dealers Joint Association was established in 1949 as a national federation. In 1968, 33 associations were consolidated into 10, and a single national body,

Table XII-17.   Principal Functions of the Japan Securities Dealers Association (JSDA)

1. Self-Regulatory Operations	(1) Drawing up and enforcing self-regulatory rules	With a view to facilitating the efficient operation of the financial instruments market, the JSDA establishes various forms of self-regulatory rules applicable to Financial Instruments Business Operators, etc. and endeavors to ensure the fairness and efficiency of trading of financial instruments. The principal rules regulate: OTC trading in stocks and bonds, underwriting of securities, off-exchange trading in listed stocks, safe custody of securities, code of conduct of directors and officers, internal control system of member companies, qualifications and registration of registered representatives, advertising of member companies, solicitation and management of customers of member companies, financial instruments intermediary service, segregation and management of customers' assets, settlement of disputes with customers, and standardized accounting methods of securities-related businesses.
	(2) Auditing, monitoring, and self-regulating	The JSDA audits member companies to see whether they comply with the laws and regulations, the rules of self-regulation in carrying out business activities and other relevant rules and whether they have an adequate internal control system; monitors the operation of member companies and checks to see whether they segregate customers' assets; and takes actions to discipline member companies and their directors and employees who have violated the laws and the rules of self-regulation.
	(3) Qualification tests, qualification renewal training and registration of registered representative	The JSDA conducts qualification tests on registered representatives and on the personnel in charge of management and control, and carries out training for the renewal of qualifications. (The administrative work relating to the registration of registered representatives is commissioned by the prime minister.)
	(4) General improvement of the securities market and performing the market administration functions.	(i) The JSDA establishes and reviews the rules concerning transactions and practices in the over-the-counter market of bonds. JSDA publishes Reference Statistical Prices (Yields) for OTC Bond Transactions. JSDA collects materials and compiles statistics concerning the bond market. (ii) The JSDA implements upgrades and expansion of securitization-related products and Derivatives market. (iii) The JSDA takes steps to ensure the fairness and efficiency of off-exchange trading in listed stocks and the protection of investors. JSDA collects and publishes data on the volume of listed stocks traded off exchange and publicly announces in real time price quotations, contract, and other information on listed shares traded on PTSs (Proprietary Trading Systems). (iv) The JSDA establishes system regarding unlisted stocks (Equity Crowdfunding Scheme, Shareholders Community System, etc.).
	(5) Settlement of securities-related disputes through the mediation of the JSDA and the handling of trade-related complaints of investors	Consultation regarding complaints concerning the business carried out by a member firm or by Financial Instruments Intermediary Service Providers; and mediation of a dispute between a member firm and a customer pertaining to securities transactions (complaint handling and dispute mediation have been commissioned to the Financial Instruments Mediation Assistance Center (FINMAC), a non-profit organization).
	(6) Services provided by the authorized personal information protection organization	The organization provides services for the proper handling of personal information of members of the JSDA as an authorized personal information protection organization under the Act on the Protection of Personal Information.
2. Services to promote the sound development of financial instruments business and financial instruments market		(i) The JSDA investigates and studies the financial instruments market and considers institutional problems and tax issues and then publishes opinions. (ii) The JSDA makes public statistical material, etc., on the stock and bond markets. (iii) The JSDA disseminates knowledge about financial instruments, indexes, and markets and educates investors. (iv) The JSDA communicates and exchanges views with market-related organizations. (v) The JSDA supports actions to eliminate antisocial forces. (vi) The JSDA supports regarding as business continuity of the entire financial instruments market.
3. International business and international exchange		Participates in international conferences, such as those of the International Council of Securities Association (ICSA), Asia Securities Forum (ASF), and International Organization of Securities Commissions (IOSCO), exchanges information with securities-related organizations of foreign countries, and promotes international exchange.
4. Promotion of public awareness on finance and securities Dissemination and knowledge and learning about financial products		The JSDA facilitates activities to promote public awareness on finance and securities for schools as well as for adults from a fair neutral standpoint so that people would be able to correctly understand knowledge and information about financial products and make proactive judgments on their own.

Note: The Self-Regulatory Organization is responsible for self-regulatory operations and market administration while the Securities Strategy Board is responsible for operations that promote the sound development of the securities market and the securities business.

Table XII-18.   Permissible Forms of Business by Registered Representatives (JSDA Rules: Article 2, Regulations Concerning Qualification and Registration, Etc., of Sales Representatives of Association Members)

Class 1 Sales Representative	Sales representative who is authorized to engage in all acts of a sales representative with the exception of designated over-the-counter transactions of derivatives
Class 2 Sales Representative	Sales representative who is authorized to engage in all Acts of a Sales Representative related to any securities with the exception of stock subscription rights/warrants or covered warrants (excluding Acts of a Sales Representative related to securities derivative transactions or transactions in bonds with options, and limited to the cases prescribed by the detailed rules regarding margin transactions)
Special Member Class 1 Sales Representative	Sales representative who is authorized to engage in all Acts of a Sales Representative related to the business of a registered financial institution (with the exception of designated over-the-counter transactions of derivatives, financial instruments intermediary service of registered financial institution, or brokerage with written orders)
Special Member Class 2 Sales Representative	Sales representative who is authorized to engage in all Acts of a Sales Representative related to transactions of public and corporate bonds, commercial papers, investment trust certificates, etc. (excluding Acts of a Sales Representative related to securities derivatives trading or transactions in bonds with options)
Special Member Class 4 Sales Representative	Sales representative who is authorized to engage in all Acts of a Sales Representative related to "Specified Financial Instruments Business" (marketing of investment trusts and other specified acts of an insurance company or other financial institution)
Margin Trading Sales Representative	Sales representative who is authorized to engage in all Acts of a Sales Representative by a Class 2 Sales Representative and acts of a sales representative relating to margin trading (including "when-issued" trading)

Note: Qualification tests for Special Member Class IV Sales Representative and Margin Trading Sales Representative are not performed (as of July 2021).

the JSDA, with the 10 associations as regional units, was formed. At present, there are 9 regional associations: Hokkaido, Tohoku, Tokyo, Nagoya, Hokuriku, Osaka, Chugoku, Shikoku, and Kyushu. (The regional associations of Kyushu and South Kyushu were consolidated into one in 1995.)

Since securities company scandals came to light, pressure to strengthen the self-regulatory function of the JSDA has mounted, and the status of the JSDA was changed from a public-service corporation under the Civil Code to a legal entity under the Securities and Exchange Act in 1992, and the Ministry of Finance (currently, the prime minister) commissioned the JSDA to handle the registration of registered representatives. This helped define the status of the JSDA as a self-regulatory organization of the securities industry. In July 1998, the Bond Underwriters Association of Japan was consolidated into the

JSDA, and in July 2004 the JSDA was reorganized into a structure consisting of the Self-Regulation Division, the Securities Strategy Division, and the General and Administration Division. As the JASDAQ Securities Exchange was established (see Chapter 10) in December 2004, the OTC securities market was closed, and the JSDA consolidated the Securities Information Center under its wing in April 2005.

In September 2007, the JSDA became the association authorized under the FIEA, and the scope of membership eligibility was expanded from securities companies to Type I Financial Instruments Business Operators. The association established the Code of Conduct Committee in July 2011 to deliberate the code of conduct of member firms and make proposals. Handling of consultation matters and complaints from users of securities transactions and mediation of disputes between users and members have been commissioned to the Financial Instruments Mediation Assistance Center (FINMAC), a non-profit organization, since February 2010.

Registered financial institutions under the provision of Article 2, Paragraph 11 of the FIEA (see section 12) joined the JSDA as special members in 1994. As of June 2021, the JSDA had 270 regular members, 16 specified business members, and 199 special members (including 118 banks, 13 foreign banks, 38 shinkin banks (credit unions), 9 life insurance companies, 4 property and casualty insurance companies, and 17 others).

10. Financial Instruments Firms Associations (2)

Unlike the Securities and Exchange Act, the Financial Instruments and Exchange Act (FIEA) provides for the comprehensive regulation of a diverse range of collective investment schemes (funds) and investment trust beneficiary certificate sales businesses. Self-offerings by funds, investment trust beneficiary certificates sales businesses, and some other businesses are defined under the FIEA as Type II Financial Instruments Businesses ("Type II Businesses"). Because financial instruments, such as funds, etc., are not highly circulated, the registration requirements for Type II Businesses are lenient, such that even individuals may register as businesses. The underlying assets of funds, investment trust beneficiary certificates, and similar products cover a wide range of real estate, specified instruments, and other assets. Registered Type II Businesses, therefore, are not solely securities companies; many real estate companies also have entered the market.

As a result, the number of registered Type II Businesses had risen to 1,167 as of the end of September 2017, exceeding by roughly four times the number of Type I Financial Instruments Businesses (securities business, financial futures trading business, etc., hereinafter referred to as "Type I Businesses").

Table XII-19.   Numbers of Registered Financial Instruments Business Operators and Related Financial Instruments Firms Associations

Business Category	Number of Registered Firms (as of May 31, 2021)	Related Financial Instruments Firms Associations	
Type I	308	(Authorized) Japan Securities Dealers Association	270 Regular members (as of June 2021)
		(Certified) Financial Futures Association of Japan	141 Regular members (as of June 30, 2021)
		(Certified) Japan Security Token Offering Association	13 Reqular members (as of July 31, 2021)
Type II	1,209	(Certified) Type II Financial Instruments Firms Association	532 Regular members (as of August 2019)
Investment advisory and agency business	974	(Certified) Japan Investment Advisers Association	480 Investment advisory and agency members (March 2019)
Investment management business	401		297 Investment management members (March 2019)
		(Certified) The Investment Trusts Association, Japan	104 Investment trust members (August 2019)
			78 REIT members (August 2019)
			6 Infrastructure fund members (August 2019)
Total	2,875 (total number of registrants)		
	1,947 (actual number of firms)		

Notes: 1. Of the 308 Type I businesses, 38 (FX specialists) are not members of JSDA, but have joined the Financial Futures Association of Japan. Because some firms are registered under multiple business categories and with multiple associations, the totals do not match the sum of the individual numbers.

2. In addition to regular members, Japan Securities Dealers Association has "Specified Business Member". These are Type 1 firms that are engaged only in specific businesses. As of July 2021, there are 15 members in total, including those engaged in the specified OTC derivatives business, the Class 1 Small Amount Electronic Offering Business, and the commodity-related market derivatives brokerage business.

Source: Produced using the Financial Services Agency's "List of Certified Financial Instruments Firms Associations" and "List of Registered Financial Instruments Business Operators" and data from associations' websites.

• In addition to the above, there are firms deemed to be Business Operators Engaging in Specially Permitted Business for Qualified Institutional Investors, etc. (the so-called firms handling funds for professional investors) that are not required to register, most of which are not members of any of the above Financial Instruments Firms Associations. (See the Financial Services Agency's "List of Qualified Institutional Investors and other Registered Special Business Operators."

When one or more investor is a Qualified Institutional Investor and other investors (general investors) number 49 or less among investors in a collective investment scheme (fund), under the Special Provisions Concerning Specially Permitted Businesses for Qualified Institutional Investors, the financial instruments firm is exempt from registration and may conduct management and self-offering of the fund by submitting notification of such to authorities. (Art. 63, Para. 1 and 2)

Reference: Essentially, firms or individuals with special investment skills have been allowed to participate in the market without registering and only a duty to submit notification of their businesses in order to enable them to offer their superlative investment instruments to professional investors at low cost. Of course, there are firms or individuals within this group that achieve excellent results and become members of one of the above associations, thereby being covered by self-regulatory rules. However, there are also firms or individuals that clearly have gathered together one (1) Qualified Institutional Investor and 49 individual investors with the intention of using the provisions as a legal loophole to avoid registration of a Type II business or investment management business. Hence the amendments to the FIEA for limiting subscriptions to affluent groups that satisfy certain conditions were promulgated in May 2015 and then enforced in March 2016.

The lax registration requirements, however, have resulted in lawsuits regarding the solicitation for self-offerings, etc., of funds and other incidents requiring administrative discipline because of legal violations.

To address such issues, the Type II Financial Instruments Firms Association was established in November 2010 and designated as a Certified Financial Instruments Firms Association (FIEA, Article 78, Paragraph 1). The association aims to contribute to the fair and smooth operation of Type II Businesses as well as to their sound development and to investor protection. It was set up taking into account the self-regulatory systems of the self-regulatory organizations (SROs) already in place for Type II Businesses, investment management business, investment advisory and agency business, etc.

Establishing an "authorized" association in Japan requires the authorization of the prime minister of Japan. But "certified" associations are granted certification by the prime minister following their establishment. The Japan Securities Dealers Association is the only "authorized" association in Japan's securities market. The country's "certified" associations, however, include the Financial Futures Association of Japan; the Japan Investment Advisers Association; The Investment Trusts Association, Japan; and, of course, the Type II Financial Instruments Firms Association. The major difference between the two types of associations is that "authorized" associations are able to establish and operate OTC securities markets (refer to section 9).

Other than that single difference, "authorized" and "certified" associations carry out the same self-regulatory operations. The associations are responsible for (1) forming rules and regulations, (2) inspecting members to determine their state of compliance with laws and ordinances and self-regulation rules, (3) disciplining members that have violated laws and ordinances and self-regulation rules, (4) resolving complaints and disputes involving members' businesses, (5) mediating conflicts about members' businesses, and (6) carrying out sales representative registration operations when so commissioned by the government authorities.

There are 1,947 firms registered under financial instruments businesses in Japan, with some firms being registered under multiple business categories and some being members of multiple SROs. In addition, there are 2,850 organizations classified as Business Operators Engaging in Specially Permitted Business for Qualified Institutional Investors, etc. that are not registered despite carrying out self-offerings of funds just like Type II Businesses (as of end of April 2021). Since almost all of these Business Operators Engaging in Specially Permitted Business for Qualified Institutional Investors, etc. were not covered by self-regulatory rules, causing troubles to arise, rules were strengthened under the amendment to the FIEA in 2015.

11. Investor Protection Fund

The purpose of an investor protection fund is to protect the credit of general customers from insolvency of the securities companies. As we saw in section 1, the 1998 amendment to the Securities and Exchange Act changed the licensing system of securities companies to a less-demanding registration system for securities business, encouraging non-securities companies to enter the securities market, and relaxed restrictions against conducting side business, liberalizing the lines of business that securities companies can undertake. And this created the need to take measures to protect investors from any unforeseen loss that they may suffer from insolvency of the securities companies they deal with. The government instituted provisions in the 1998 amendment to the Securities and Exchange Act (the present FIEA) with a view (1) to preventing bankruptcy of securities companies, empowering the Financial Services Agency to take a prompt corrective action on the basis of the capital-to-risk ratio (Article 53 of the FIEA) (see section 8) and as a framework to protect investors in case the securities companies they deal with went bankrupt; (2) to requiring securities companies to segregate the customer assets from their own assetts (Articles 43-2 and 3); and (3) to establishing an investor protection fund (Articles 79-20 through 80). In line with this, the law concerning the bankruptcy proceedings of financial institutions (Act on Special Measures for the Reorganization Proceedings of Financial Institutions) was amended, and this amended law has become applicable to securities companies.

The system of the segregated custody of securities is designed to recover the assets of customers in preference to other creditors of a security company if it goes bankrupt by holding the cash and securities of its customers separately from its proper assets. It is done in two ways: (1) securities of its customers are managed separately and (2), with respect to a customer's cash and substitute securities deposited with the securities company as collateral for margin trading, etc., that are impossible to physically identify when they are rehypothecated, the securities company trusts in an outside account an amount equal to its customers' claim, net of their liability, to the securities company (this is called the "customer segregated fund"). If this system of separate management were strictly enforced, customers would not suffer any unforeseen loss even if their securities company went bankrupt. However, the rub is that the customer segregated fund is computed only once a week, and the possibility of misappropriation of its customers' fund by a securities company cannot be ruled out.

Therefore, with a view to strengthening the protection of investors, investor protection funds were established as legal entities under the Securities and

Table XII-20. Investors Eligible for Compensation, Compensation Procedures, and Sources of Funds of the Investor Protection Fund

Those eligible for compensation	(1) Eligible persons (Art. 79-20, Para. 1 of the FIEA)	"General Customer" who conducts a Subject Securities-related Transaction or a Subject Commodity-related Derivatives Trading with a Financial Instruments Business Operator that conducts the securities-related business or commodity-related exchange derivatives trading agency service, etc. (excluding a Qualified Institutional Investor, central or local government, or any other person specified by a Cabinet Order)
	(2) Scope of customer assets eligible for compensation (Art. 79-20, Para. 3)	(i) Money or securities deposited as a margin for exchange transactions of derivatives, etc., or money or securities deposited as guarantee money for margin trading, etc.; (ii) money belonging to the account of or deposited by a customer with regard to a transaction pertaining to the Financial Instruments Business (such as advance payment for purchase, proceeds from a sale that have not been withdrawn, etc.); (iii) securities (securities deposited for sale or held in safekeeping); and (iv) other customer assets specified by a Cabinet Order
Compensation procedures	Notice and recognition (Art. 79-53 and 79-54)	When the Fund receives a notice from a Financial Instruments Business Operator or the Prime Minister, it shall recognize whether or not there is any difficulty for the firm to perform the obligation to return or refund customer assets pertaining to such notice.
	Public notice of recognition (Art. 79-55)	When a Fund has granted recognition to the effect that it is difficult for a notifying Financial Instruments Business Operator to perform the obligation to return or refund customer assets (such a Financial Instruments Business Operator referred to as the "Recognized Financial Instruments Business Operator"), it shall give a public notice that prompts the relevant customers to file a claim for the return or refund of their assets.
	Payment of claims eligible for compensation (Art. 79-57, Para. 4)	A Fund shall, when having made a payment to General Customers, acquire claims eligible for such compensation of the amount commensurate with its payment. The Fund shall collect the claims from the bankrupt Financial Instruments Business Operator through bankruptcy proceedings.
	Loans to a "Notifying Financial Instruments Business Operator" (Art. 79-59)	When the financial position of a "Notifying Financial Instruments Business Operator" has deteriorated to such a point that, while it does not yet face difficulties in returning and refunding customer assets, loans from the Fund could facilitate expedited return or refund, the Fund may make loans to such "Notifying Financial Instruments Business Operator."
Source of funds	Investor Protection Fund (Art. 79-64 and 79-65)	Burden charges collected from member Financial Instruments Business Operators shall be the source of funds.
	Borrowing (Art. 79-72)	Borrowings from financial institutions may be made with the approval of the Prime Minister of Japan and the Minister of Finance.

Table XII-21.   Comparison Between New and Former Systems

	Former System	New System
Name, Year of Establishment	Entrusted Securities Indemnity Fund (August 1969)	Japan Investor Protection Fund (December 1998)
Underlying Entity	Incorporate foundation with no legal basis	Corporation defined under the Securities and Exchange Act (current Financial Instruments and Exchange Act) (must be approved by the Prime Minister and the Minister of Finance)
Membership obligation	Voluntarily by each securities company	Compulsory membership
Contribution	Donation (subject to taxation)	Burden charges (tax deductible as expenses)
Limit of the amount as indemnity (Note)	¥2 billion per bankrupt securities company	¥10 million per customer
Past records	7 cases in and after May 1997 (succeeded by the new fund in December 1998)	· Minami Securities (went bankrupt in March 2000); indemnity amount of approximately ¥5.9 billion (including ¥2.4 billion returned from bankruptcy trustee) · Marudai Securities (went bankrupt in March 2012); indemnity amount of approximately ¥170 million

Note: Up till March 2001, however, a special provision on full indemnity was available (Article 4 of Revision Provisions of the Securities and Exchange Act).

Table XII-22.   An Outline of the Investor Protection Fund

	Japan Investor Protection Fund	Securities Investors Protection Fund
No. of members (at the time the fund was established)	235 companies (224 domestic and 11 foreign-affiliated companies)	46 companies (1 domestic and 45 foreign-affiliated companies)
Scale of the fund	¥30 billion at the time of establishment; ¥50 billion at the end of March 2001	¥10 billion at the time of establishment (¥3 billion in cash and ¥7 billion guaranteed) and ¥5 billion in cash and ¥5 billion guaranteed after April 2001
Burden charge on members	A fixed amount and a fixed rate of burden charge (computed on the basis of the operating income and the number of registered representatives). The total of annual burden charge is ¥4 billion.	1% of the customer assets, and a bank guarantee of an amount equivalent to 50% of margin trading requirement. When the fund falls ¥1 billion or more short of ¥10 billion, members are asked to contribute an additional burden charge.
Remarks	The fund has taken over the compensation service provided by the Entrusted Securities Indemnity Fund and its entire assets and liabilities.	Members are required to have their books audited by outside auditors.

The two organizations were consolidated in July 2002 into the Japan Investor Protection Fund. As of June 30, 2021, there were 267 member firms and the size of the fund was approximately ¥58.4 billion (end of March 2021).

Exchange Act (currently under the FIEA). To accomplish the above purpose, the investor protection fund (hereinafter referred to as the "fund") will (1) pay a specified amount of money (up to ¥10 million per customer to insure the repayment of his/her assets in the case of bankruptcy of a securities company and (2) make loans to securities companies to facilitate the prompt return of customer assets.

To enable the fund to provide such services, it is empowered by law to (1) perform any and all acts that are necessary to preserve customer assets held by securities companies, (2) become a trust manager of securities companies, and (3) create an "Investor Protection Fund" to secure the necessary funds and collect burden charges from its member companies. Members of the fund must be Financial Instruments Business Operators. More than one investor protection fund may be created, and securities companies must participate in one of them.

12. Securities Operations of Financial Institutions

In 1948, banking institutions were prohibited, in principle, from conducting the securities business under Article 65, Paragraph 1 of the Securities and Exchange Act. As the Banking Act did not explicitly authorize banking institutions to conduct certain business related to public bonds or brokerage with written orders, which were provided for as exceptions to the above prohibition (Article 65, Paragraph 2 of the Securities and Exchange Act), banking institutions (except for trust banks, which could pass their customer orders on to a securities company) did not conduct the securities business. Following the issuance of massive amounts of JGBs since 1975, the government enacted a new Banking Act in 1981, explicitly authorizing banking institutions to trade in public bonds, and it also correspondingly amended the Securities and Exchange Act. Accordingly, banking institutions started selling public bonds over the counter in 1983 and dealing in public bonds in 1984.

Subsequently, the following services have been added to types of securities businesses that banking institutions are allowed to provide: (1) brokerage for transactions in bond futures trading (1988); (2) trading, etc., and involvement in private placement of commercial papers (CPs), foreign certificates of deposit (CDs), beneficiary certificates of mortgage bond trusts, etc. (1992); (3) handling of OTC derivatives of securities and public offerings of beneficiary certificates of investment trusts (1998); and (4) securities agent business (2004; currently the financial instruments intermediary service). The registration system of securities companies and the system of authorizing certain securities businesses instituted in 1998 are also applied to banking institutions. And banking institutions that have registered under this system are called

Table XII-23.   Balance of Investment Trusts, by Seller (as of September 30, 2021)

(¥100 million)

	Securities companies		Banks (registered financial institutions)		Direct sales (investment trust management companies)		Total
Stock investment trusts	1,116,589	76.6%	330,729	22.7%	11,243	0.9%	1,458,561
Bond investment trusts	144,498	99.3%	1,028	0.7%	3	0.0%	145,529
Total	1,261,087	78.6%	331,759	20.7%	11,246	0.7%	1,604,090

Note: These figures are only for publicly offered investment trusts. Given the introduction of a negative interest policy by the Bank of Japan, early repayment of MMFs continued, and the balance has been zero since May 2017.
Source: Compiled from the statistics produced by The Investment Trusts Association, Japan.

Table XII-24.   Intermediary service's effect on retail sales performance of Mitsubishi UFJMS Securities (Fiscal year ending March 2021)

(¥100 million)	Balance of assets under custody	Number of outstanding accounts (in thousands)	New accounts opened (in thousands)	Sale of stock investment trusts	Individual investor government bonds	Sale of retail foreign bonds
Amount via intermediary	24,803	278	4	965	188	3,686
	25,674	299	7	492	151	4,091
% of total	6.6%	22.9%	5.3%	8.5%	66.2%	27.1%
	8.9%	24.0%	17.1%	5.5%	68.0%	39.5%

Note: Balance of assets under custody and number of outstanding accounts figures are as of the end of March 2021. Percentages are of total amounts. Assets under custody pertain to domestic sales divisions (including financial institutions). Figures below are for the fiscal term ended March 2020.
Source: Compiled from the Databook provided for the FY2020 investor information meeting of the Mitsubishi UFJ Financial Group.

"registered financial institutions." The revised FIEA of 2007 redefined the scope of the securities business prohibited in principle as securities-related businesses (section 1), no material changes to the provisions of law were made (with the only change being the number of the article: Article 65, Paragraph 1 and 2 became Article 33, Paragraph 1 and 2 of the FIEA).

On the other hand, the 1992 Institutional Reform Law authorized banks, securities companies, and trust banks to enter markets of one another through subsidiaries. Securities subsidiaries of banks were defined as "Specialized Securities Companies" (Article 16-2, Article 52-23 of the Banking Act) and

Table XII-25.   Major Regional Bank-Affiliated Securities Companies

Name of company	Parent bank (investment ratio)	Year established (or the year of making it a subsidiary)	Name of company	Parent bank (investment ratio)	Year established (or the year of making it a subsidiary)
Shizugin TM Securities Co., Ltd.	The Shizuoka Bank Group (100%)	Dec. 2000	Toho Securities Co., Ltd.	The Toho Bank, Ltd. (100%)	January 2016
Daishi Securities Co., Ltd. (former Niigata Securities Co., Ltd.)	The Daishi Bank, Ltd. (100%)	March 2006	Gungin Securities Co., Ltd.	The Gunma Bank, Ltd. (100%)	July 2016
Hachijuni Securities Co., Ltd.	The Hachijuni Bank, Ltd. (100%)	April 2006	Hokuhoku Tokai Tokyo Securities Co., Ltd.	Hokuhoku Financial Group, Inc. (60%)	October 2016
YM Securities Co., Ltd.	Yamaguchi Financial Group, Inc. (60%)	July 2007	77 Securities Co., Ltd.	The 77 Bank, Ltd. (100%)	January 2017
Mebuki Securities Co., Ltd. (former The Joyo Securities Co., Ltd.)	Mebuki Financial Group, Inc. (100%)	November 2007	Kyogin Securities Co., Ltd.	Bank of Kyoto, Ltd. (100%)	March 2017
Hamagin Tokai Tokyo Securities Co., Ltd.	The Bank of Yokohama, Ltd. (60%)	July 2008	Okigin Securities Limited	The Bank of Okinawa, Ltd. (100%)	March 2017
Chugin Securities Co., Ltd.	The Chugoku Bank, Ltd. (100%)	June 2009	Tochigin Tokai Tokyo Securities Co., Ltd. (former Utsunomiya Securities Co., Ltd.)	The Tochigi Bank, LTD. (60%)	April 2017
Hyakugo Securities Co., Ltd.	The Hyakugo Bank, Ltd. (100%)	August 2009	Hirogin Securities Co., Ltd. (former Hirogin Utsumiya Securities Co., Ltd.)	The Hiroshima Bank, Ltd. (100%)	June 2017
Nishi-Nippon City Tokai Tokyo Securities Co., Ltd.	Nishi-Nippon Financial Holdings, Inc. (60%)	May 2010	Kyushu FG Securities, Inc.	Kyushu Financial Group, Inc.	December 2017
Chibagin Securities Co., Ltd.	The Chiba Bank, Ltd. (100%)	January 2011	Juroku Tokai Tokyo Securities Co., Ltd.	The Juroku Bank, Ltd. (60%)	April 2018
Shikoku Alliance Securities Co., Ltd. (former Iyogin Securities Co., Ltd.)	The Iyo Bank, Ltd. (100%)	February 2012	North Pacific Securities Co., Ltd. (former Joko Securities Co., Ltd.)	North Pacific Bank, Ltd. (100%)	October 2018
FFG Securities Co., Ltd. (former Fukuoka Securities Co., Ltd.)	The Bank of Fukuoka (100%)	April 2012	Nanto Mahoroba Securities Co., Ltd. (former Nara Securities Co., Ltd.)	The Nanto Bank, Ltd. (100%)	October 2018
Senshu Ikeda Tokai Tokyo Securities Co., Ltd.	The Senshu Ikeda Bank, Ltd. (60%)	January 2013	OKB Securities Co., Ltd.	The Ogaki Kyoritsu Bank, Ltd. (100%)	March 2019
Gogin Securities Co., Ltd.	The San-In Godo Bank, Ltd. (100%)	August 2015 (Closed October 2020)	Kiraboshi Life Design Securities Co., Ltd.	Tokyo Kiraboshi Financial Group, Lnc.	December 2019

Source: Compiled based on websites of corporations and newspaper coverage.

the scope of their businesses was provided to include the "Securities-Related Business" (Article 28, Paragraph 8 of the FIEA), incidental businesses (items (i) through (viii) in Article 35, Paragraph 1 of the FIEA) and businesses required to be notified to the prime Minister (Article 35, Paragraph 2). At first, with a view to preventing potential adverse effects, the regulatory agency (1) restricted the scope of business that the securities subsidiaries of banks may conduct (i.e., the prohibition of stock brokerage, etc.) and (2) required the installation of a firewall between securities subsidiaries and their parents.

The restrictions on the scope of business were lifted in October 1999. Restrictions of the firewall were also eased in phases. In September 2002, the ban on opening banking and securities joint branch offices was lifted. And in March 2005, banks were allowed to introduce customers to securities companies as initial public offering (IPO) candidates (business-led service). In June 2009, the joint position regulations prohibiting officers and employees of securities companies and banks from working on both sides of the firewall were lifted, and the sharing of confidential information relating to corporate customers was permitted. Simplification of procedures for non-public information sharing is being discussed in 2021. Recently, not only megabank groups but also regional banks have been entering into financial instruments intermediary service agreements with securities companies in developing joint banking and securities businesses through introducing customers, opening accounts and handling orders.

13. Competition Structure of the Securities Industry

The competitive structure of the Japanese securities industry had been called the "Big Four oligopoly" with four major securities companies commanding the largest share of the market and controlling affiliate networks that consisted of a number of small and medium-sized securities companies. However, the Big Four oligopoly broke down in the 1990s as (1) Yamaichi Securities went bankrupt in 1997; (2) Daiwa and Nikko split up their companies into two divisions in 1998—the wholesale division (providing underwriting, M&A advisory, proprietary trading and other services to corporate customers) and the retail division (providing individual investors with a brokerage service and offering the sale of investment trusts) (Daiwa later reintegrated the divisions); and (3) Nomura, Nikko (later changed name to Nikko Cordial), and Daiwa liquidated their holdings of shares in their affiliates. Following an accounting scandal, Nikko Cordial was acquired by Citigroup in 2007 and then was acquired by Sumitomo Mitsui Banking Corporation in October 2009 and became SMBC Nikko Securities.

The conventional business strategy of the former Big Four was to increase

Table XII-26.   Changes in the share of net operating income profits by business type

		Term ending March 1991		Term ending March 1997	
Net operating income (¥100 million)		37,509		24,317	
		No of companies	Share of total	No of companies	Share of total
Domestic securities companies		210	92.4%	225	85.3%
(Exchang Members)	The "Big Four"	4	44.6%	4	47.6%
	Integrated securities companies	42	37.2%	44	28.4%
	Small and Medium Securities companies	83	8.5%	81	5.7%
Exchange Non-members	Small and Medium Securities companies	81	2.1%	77	1.4%
	Bank-offiliated securities subsidiary			19	2.2%
Foreign securities companies		50	7.6%	56	14.7%
	Members	25	6.3%	21	12.4%
	Non-Members	25	1.3%	35	2.3%

Source: Compiled from the Securities Bureau of the Ministry of Finance, Nenpo (Annual Report) (Vol.4 Financial Statements) and the JSDA's Financial Overview of Regular Member Firms, Shoken gyoho (Securities Industry Report))

	Term ending March 2008		FY2019	
Net operating income (¥100 million)	37,038		32,047	
	No of companies	Share of total	No of companies	Share of total
Major General and Wholesale	54	78.7%	47	68.4%
Independent	4	31.4%	2	24.7%
Megabank Affiliates	7	14.1%	4	25.5%
Other bank affiliated	3	0.2%	3	0.5%
Foreign-affiliated	40	33.0%	38	17.7%
Retail Main	173	17.5%	131	18.8%
Listed securities	16	7.3%	14	6.4%
Regional bank affiliated	6	0.4%	27	2.2%
Small and medium-sized securities	137	4.9%	73	2.7%
Online securities (including foreign-affiliated)	14	4.9%	17	7.5%
New business entities	81	3.8%	83	13.0%
Investment management, fund sales, etc. (Japanese-affiliated)	17	0.3%	21	0.7%
Investment management, fund sales, etc. (foreign-affiliated)	22	1.5%	24	4.7%
FX (including foreign-affiliated)	19	0.7%	19	2.2%
PTS (including foreign-affiliated companies)	8	0.3%	8	0.4%
Others	15	1.0%	11	5.0%

Notes: 1. Classification criteria are based on "shareholder composition" (independent and listed securities, bank-affiliated, foreign-affiliated, etc.) and "business characteristics". Listed securities are included if they are listed by a holding company and it is a controlling subsidiary. Foreign-affiliated securities firms by shareholder composition are 71 (FY2019).
2. "Online securities" includes foreign-affiliated and smartphone securities.
3. "Others" includes OTC derivatives, private equity, etc.
Source: "Time-Series Analysis of Securities Companies' Management" (commissioned by JSDA, 2018) written and partly revised by myself. 2019 data calculated from disclosure magazines.

their shares in the brokerage market and win the mandate as the lead manager of equity financing by taking advantage of their share in brokerage. To achieve such goals, they sought to build a nationwide network of branches, hire a large number of employees loyal to their company, and lure many member companies of the stock exchanges under their umbrella. However, as such strategy entailed huge costs and risks, only a small number of securities companies could afford to pursue the strategy by providing full-line services (and by diversifying the sources of income thereby). In consequence, there came into existence only a few big and integrated securities companies that adopted the Japanese-style employment system with many affiliated brokers.

The business strategies and management systems proved effective during the period of high growth as a mechanism to supply large amounts of capital into the industry in a timely manner. However, excess capital tends to lead to over-financing, which became evident during the bubble period in the late 1980s. In the 1990s, after the burst of the bubble economy, the fundamentals of the Japanese economy changed (excess capital) and the traditional management strategies and systems had to be reformed. After the collapse of Yamaichi, major securities companies abandoned the strategy of maintaining affiliate networks of small and medium-sized securities companies. The large banks, which had been keen to enter the securities industry, brought the small-, medium-, and second-tier securities companies that had been the Big Four affiliates under their umbrella.

The stock market experienced dissolution of cross-shareholdings and decline of share prices throughout the 1990s. The financial behavior of corporate managers gradually shifted to focus more on "cost of capital," leading to the reduction of overabundant capital (purchase of treasury stock) and the reallocation of existing capital (disposals of business divisions and M&A). In addition, the overabundant capital, released from companies and absorbed as idle money by the institutional investors, boosted their assets, flowing into foreign bonds and structured bonds which offered higher returns. Foreign securities companies entered the market to provide M&A advisory services or to trade overseas securities. "Trading volume" became less important as a competitive yardstick. The table on the right shows the competitive structure of the industry through changes in the share of net operating income.

CHAPTER XIII

Asset Management Service

1. Management of Individual Financial Assets

According to a survey by the Bank of Japan, "Comparison of the Flow of Funds between Japan, the United States, and Europe," at the end of March 2021 individuals in Japan had ¥1,946 trillion worth of financial assets. Of this amount, 54.3% was invested in cash and deposits and 15.2% in securities (debt securities, investment trusts, stocks, etc.) investments. Compared with the United States and Europe, Japanese individuals' financial assets are heavily skewed toward cash and deposits more so than not only the U.S. but also the Euro area, and thinly invested in securities. In the 2020 survey by The Central Council for Financial Services Information, 37.2% of respondents said that they focused on "safety" as their reason for selecting financial instruments, while 24.5% said "liquidity." Only 22.0% of respondents said that they focused on "profitability. (Nonetheless the percentage of respondents highlighting profitability has increased over the years.)" Individuals' financial assets in Japan thus are mainly invested in low-risk bank deposits, with little preference for more profitable securities. Certainly during the era of deflation, the heavy investment in bank deposits probably turned out to have been the right call. However, it is possible that the focus on safety carries with it the risk that the real value of cash will erode during of inflation.

Under these circumstances, the government introduced a preferential tax treatment investment system (NISA Nippon Individual Saving Account, a small-amount investment tax exemption scheme) (General NISA) in 2014 to promote the "Shift from Savings to Investment." Additionally in 2018, the installment-type (tsumitate) NISA was launched. In 2024, the General NISA is scheduled to be replaced by a new two-tiered system (New NISA) which consists of a general portion and an installment portion. In 2022, the age for participation in iDeCo (individual-type defined contribution pension plan) is due to be raised from under 60 to under 65.

Asset management companies include trust banks, life insurance companies, and discretionary asset management companies that manage the pension and insurance reserves of individuals, i.e. people's security for the future. In-

Chart XIII-1.   Composition of Household Assets (at March 31, 2021)

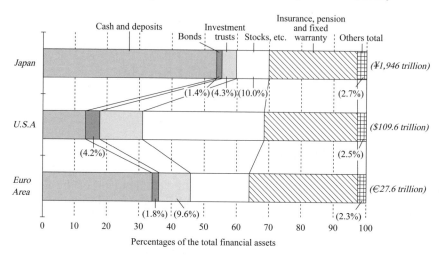

Percentages of the total financial assets

Note: Others total is the remains after deducting "Cash and deposits", "Bonds", "Investment trusts", "Stocks, etc.", and "Insurance, pension and fixed warranty" from total financial assets.
Source: Bank of Japan.

Table XIII-1.   Points of Focus When Selecting Financial Products

<Households Holding Financial Assets>   (%)

	2011	2012	2013	2014	2015	2016	2017	2018	2019	2020
Profitability	18.7	16.9	14.7	16.7	17.6	17.5	18.7	17.6	19.0	22.0
High return	13.8	12.1	9.8	11.7	11.9	12.1	12.9	11.3	11.5	12.4
Anticipated price increase in the future	4.9	4.9	4.9	4.9	5.6	5.4	5.9	6.2	7.5	9.5
Safety	48.0	46.7	47.0	45.7	46.1	45.7	46.6	41.8	41.9	37.2
Principal is guaranteed	30.3	28.7	29.6	29.5	29.3	29.9	30.1	27.8	28.2	26.5
Financial institution handling the product is reliable and secure	17.6	18.0	17.4	16.3	16.8	15.8	16.5	14.0	13.6	10.6
Liquidity	23.7	24.7	25.0	25.0	23.1	24.7	21.0	25.8	22.9	24.5
Easy to convert to cash	4.6	5.3	5.9	6.0	6.0	6.7	5.5	5.7	6.1	7.3
Free to deposit/withdraw even in small amounts	19.0	19.4	19.1	19.1	17.2	18.0	15.5	20.1	16.8	17.2
Product content is easy to understand	2.2	2.5	2.5	3.1	3.2	2.4	3.2	2.2	2.6	4.1
Others	5.4	6.7	8.5	7.9	8.4	7.9	9.1	9.9	10.8	9.6
No response	2.0	2.4	2.2	1.5	1.7	1.9	1.5	2.7	2.8	2.7

Source: The Central Council for Financial Services Information.

vestment trust management companies are also asset management companies, handling investment trusts for individual financial assets. Either indirectly or directly, asset management companies play an important role in financial asset formation by individuals in a society with low birth and mortality rates. These asset management companies also contribute to growth in corporate performances and to the sound development of the economy—and therefore society—through the following two functions. To begin with, they fulfill a role in achieving the efficient allocation of capital by supplying growth companies with capital through the market. Furthermore, they engage in stewardship activities to increase investment returns for customers and beneficiaries on a medium- to long-term basis, thereby contributing to enhancing corporate value and promoting sustainable growth of investee companies.

2. Pension Fund Management

Japan's pension plan system is a three-tier system consisting of (1) a foundational national pension (basic pension benefits) common to all citizens supplemented by (2) employee pension plans for employees of private companies and government employees, and (3) Private pensions (corporate pension plans and private pension plans) for civil servants and private-sector salaried employees. Of these plans, the national pension and employee pension plans utilize a modified pay-as-you-go system which provides support shared among generations in the form of public pensions, while private pension plans use a funding system.

Private pensions can be broadly divided into (1) defined benefit and (2) defined contribution types. For (1) defined benefit pensions, the benefits are determined based on the duration of membership of the scheme or the contributions made. For (2) defined contribution pensions, the contributed premium of each individual is clearly segregated, with pension benefits being determined based on the total of premiums and investment income. (1) Defined benefit pensions include defined benefit corporate pensions (scheme- or fund-type), the national pension fund and the employee fund. (2) Defined contribution types include corporate defined contribution pensions and individual-type defined contribution pensions (iDeCo).

The management of pension plans must be safe and efficient from the perspective of protecting entitlement to pension benefits. With the exception, therefore, of a few large-scale pension funds that manage investments in-house, asset management of the pension fund is commissioned to outside investment companies. According to the Corporate Pensions Survey (fiscal year 2017) by the Pension Fund Association, the allocation of corporate pen-

Chart XIII-2.   Structure of Pension System

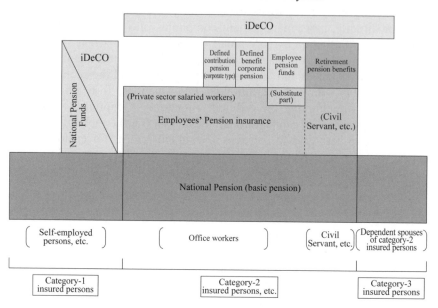

Source: Ministry of Health, Labor and Welfare.

Chart XIII-3.   GPIF's asset/composition ratio (total pension fund)

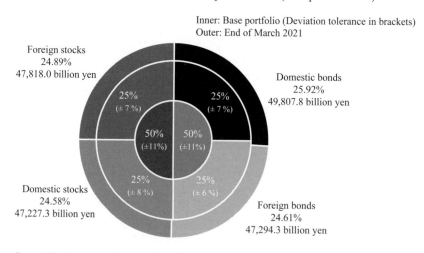

Source: The Government Pension Investment Fund (GPIF).

sion funds (employees' pension funds and defined-benefit corporate pension plans) to asset managers was trust banks, 45.6%; discretionary asset management companies, 27.2%; and life insurance companies, 27.3%. By composition of fund assets, domestic bonds accounted for 22.5%, domestic stocks for 9.1%, foreign bonds for 17.1%, foreign stocks for 12.1%, the general account of life insurance companies for 18.7%, hedge funds for 4.7%, short-term assets for 6.0% and others for 9.7%.

The cumulative reserves of the national pension and employee pension plans, which are public pensions, are administered and managed by the Government Pension Investment Fund (GPIF). By composition of fund assets of GPIF (as of the end of March 2021), domestic bonds accounted for 25.30%, foreign bonds for 24.61%, domestic stocks for 24.58%, foreign stocks for 24.89%. Previously, pension funds invested primarily in domestic bonds. However, the allocation is now more diversified with investments in stocks and foreign currency-denominated assets, (1) because domestic bond yields are negative or very low with little prospect of income gain and (2) in order to hedge against capital losses on bonds in case interest rates surge (and bond prices plummet) once the Japanese economy overcomes deflation. In addition, compared to the corporate pension, which uses a funding system, the public pension system, which utilizes a modified pay-as-you-go system, has a higher risk tolerance in respect of stocks and foreign currency-denominated assets and can be actively managed.

3. Asset Management of Trust Banks

Entrustment occurs when (1) an entity (trustor) transfers its rights to property to an entity that can be depended on (trustee) based on a trust or some other legal agreement and when (2) the trustee is enabled to legally manage and dispose of the entrusted property on behalf of the trustor or a third party (beneficiary). In the case of the entrustment of a fund-based company pension plan trust, for example, the company's pension fund is the trustor and beneficiary, while the trust bank is the trustee. Because the system is premised on the dependability of the trustee, trust banks have a duty of due care of a prudent manager, duty of loyalty, and duty of segregated asset management.

Trust banks can service pension funds in three different ways. They can manage the funds at their own discretion (designated asset management-type trust) or not become involved in management without administering the assets (specified asset management-type trust), or be an intermediary trustee (general manager) representing the trustees. Moreover, when a pension fund commissions asset management to multiple investment institutions, trust

Chart XIII-4.   Trust Scheme

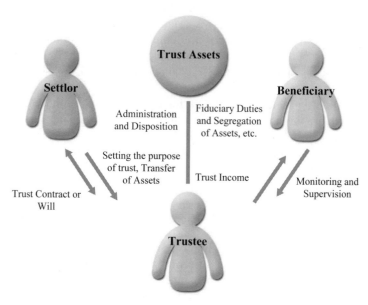

Source: Trust Companies Association of Japan.

banks act as the general manager overseeing multiple investment institutions. One of the characteristics of trust bank operations is their higher proportion of passive investment in comparison with discretionary asset management companies.

Passive management is an investment method that aims to achieve a return in line with movement in a specified benchmark (index). In comparison with active management, where a manager makes trading decisions based on the investment value of individual securities with the aim of outperforming a benchmark, passive management has the advantage of keeping trading turn-over costs low as well as curtailing management fees because detailed re-search and analysis is not required for individual securities. Unlike general commercial banks, trust banks also engage in trust business and brokerage business, in addition to their regular banking business. In terms of business with companies, trust banks can arrange corporate loans as part of banking business, manage an entrusted corporate pension as part of trust business, or administer shareholders' register, etc. as part of securities transfer business. This suggests there are business synergies to be leveraged in terms of trust bank transactions with companies. However, acting simultaneously as a lend-er, a shareholder and a securities agent for a company can give rise to numerous conflicts of interest. In addition, business overlaps in areas such as corporate lending and pension management with commercial banking and asset management operations in the same financial group can lead to inefficiencies (or diseconomies) such as intra-group competition. To this end, Mitsubishi UFJ Trust and Banking Corporation consolidated corporate loans with MUGF Bank, Ltd. and Mizuho Trust & Banking Co., Ltd., Sumitomo Mitsui Trust Bank, Limited, and Resona Bank, Ltd. integrated and consolidated their asset management functions with the asset management companies in their respective groups.

4. Asset Management of Life Insurance Companies

Life insurance policyholders pay a premium based on the likelihood of their living or dying. There are generally two types of life insurance: mortality insurance that insures a policyholder against death and annuities that provide for their livelihood in old age. Life insurance companies (insurers) accumulate the insurance premiums received from policyholders into a liability reserve to provide for future claim distributions and invest them. There are two types of accounts used to manage the investment of insurance premiums; (1) the general account in which individual insurance and corporate pension assets, etc. are jointly managed and operated under one account, and the principal and a specified interest rate are guaranteed (guaranteed rate), with the life insurance company bearing the operational risk, and (2) the special account that is separate from the general account, with the customer bearing the operational risk and benefits varying according to asset management performance.

Under a general account life insurance policy, the insurer promises to pay a certain amount of benefits, and the policyholder agrees to pay a premium that is commensurate with the promised benefit. The premium is computed on the premise of an assumed basic rate comprising such factors as assumed mortality rate, assumed ratio of expenses, and assumed rate of return. Since the assumed basic rate is set conservatively, a positive difference can occur between the assumed and actual rate. When this happens, a portion of the profit is returned to policyholders as a dividend.

According to the 2020 issue of Trends in the Life Insurance Business, published by the Life Insurance Association of Japan, of the total assets under management by life insurance companies at the end of fiscal 2019, securities accounted for 81.9% Looking at the breakdown of securities, Japanese government bonds made up the greatest portion (47.0%), followed by foreign securities (30.5%, of which bonds accounted for 29.3% and equities 1.2%); Japanese corporate bonds (8.8%); Japanese equities (5.8%); and Japanese

Table XIII-2.   Asset Composition

(%)

	Cash and deposits	Call loans	Money trusts	Securities	Loans	Tangible fixed assets	Others	Total assets
FY2015	2.0	0.3	1.0	81.8	9.5	1.7	3.5	100.0
2016	2.0	0.3	1.2	82.5	9.1	1.6	3.3	100.0
2017	2.1	0.4	1.5	82.3	8.6	1.6	3.5	100.0
2018	2.3	0.4	1.6	82.6	8.2	1.6	3.3	100.0
2019	2.7	0.5	1.8	81.9	7.7	1.6	3.8	100.0

Source: The Life Insurance Association of Japan.

Table XIII-3.   Composition of Securities under Management

(100 millions of yen, %)

	Government securities		Municipal bonds		Corporate bonds		Stocks		Foreign securities		Other securities		Total
	Amount	%	Amount	%	Amount	%	Amount	%	Amount	%	Amount	%	Amount
FY2015	1,485,684	49.4	135,178	4.5	253,634	8.4	198,130	6.6	786,531	26.2	146,074	4.9	3,005,235
2016	1,485,538	48.0	129,821	4.2	258,242	8.3	215,146	6.9	851,974	27.5	156,421	5.1	3,097,144
2017	1,473,650	47.0	120,817	3.9	261,876	8.3	231,820	7.4	889,987	28.4	159,314	5.1	3,137,466
2018	1,482,230	46.3	109,400	3.4	271,082	8.5	217,827	6.8	965,262	30.1	157,290	4.9	3,203,095
2019	1,512,024	47.0	101,342	3.1	283,830	8.8	187,661	5.8	981,283	30.5	152,239	4.7	3,218,383

Source: The Life Insurance Association of Japan.

municipal bonds (3.1%).

Investment in foreign securities has consistently increased as domestic long- and short-term interest rates have remained low against the backdrop of a negative interest rate policy. Among foreign securities, investment in public and corporate bonds has increased in particular, and credit assets such as un-hedged open foreign bonds and high yield bonds with higher credit risks, have seen an increase in popularity.

Targeting group pension plans, special account insurance offers several options. In a policy with a Class 1 rider, the assets of multiple customers are managed as a pool based on the investment policies of the life insurance company. In a Class 2 rider policy, the assets of each customer in the group are managed separately using investment policies that reflect the wishes of the individual customer. Within a Class 1 rider policy, there also are balanced-type consolidated accounts for which the life insurer determines the allocation among asset classes and separate designed investment accounts that reflect individual customer preferences in asset allocation.

5. Asset Management of Discretionary Asset Management Companies

Discretionary asset management companies manage the assets of customers based on a discretionary investment contract that gives those companies the necessary authority to make investment decisions and investments on behalf of their customers. Among the major customers of these companies are institutional investors (asset owners), such as pensions. Discretionary asset management is one of the most liberalized and internationalized businesses in the financial services industry, with low barriers to entry for non-financial businesses and foreign companies. As a category for investment specialists, the asset management company category includes investment trust management companies and fund managers that sell units in group investment schemes, such as venture capital funds, as well as discretionary management companies.

The Japan Investment Advisers Association is a self-regulatory body for the discretionary asset management industry. It is designed to protect investors by ensuring the fair and smooth operation of members' investment management business. It also contributes to the sound development of the investment management business and related matters. The investment management industry's business and other activities contribute significantly to the capital market. In consideration of this important role, the association also works to improve corporate governance by collecting and announcing information about initiatives taken by members of the association in adopting the Stewardship Code, by forming study groups on the Stewardship Code, and by carrying out discussions and research.

A special feature of discretionary asset management companies in comparison with trust banks is the high proportion of active investment and customized asset management services that closely reflect the wishes of customers. When commissioned to handle the management of assets, they leave the administration side of the business to trust banks and other financial institutions. Reacting to the pension plan fraud scandal in 2012 and other incidents, trust banks are expanding and reinforcing their monitoring systems by strengthening their independent party checking function and other measures.

Allocation of the assets of customers is done based on investment guidelines and other agreements determined through discussions with pension funds and additional customers. Trends in recent years show that along with the diversification of the investment needs of customers, these funds are not

Chart XIII-5.   Investment of Pension Assets by Discretionary Asset Management Company

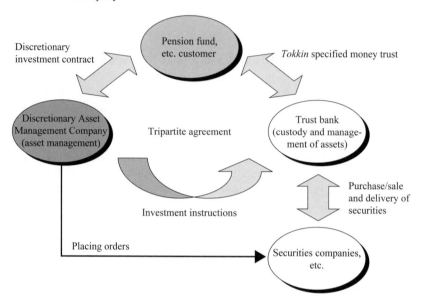

Table XIII-4.   Scheme comparison

	Traditional discretionary investment contract	Real estate private placement fund	Wrap Account
Customer	Institutional investors	Fund	Individual investors
Investment target	Traditional securities	Real estate trust beneficiary rights	Traditional securities
Managing entity	Specialized management company	Specialized management company	Company concurrently engaged in securities business

limited to such traditional investment instruments as stocks and bonds but also involve investments in the stocks and bonds of high-growth emerging countries and alternative investments that target absolute rather than relative returns, such as real-estate-related securities and hedge funds.

In addition to the aforesaid traditional discretionary investment services for institutional investors as customers, schemes for real estate private placement funds as customers as well as the wrap accounts provided by securities companies and trust banks for individual investors have also been attracting attention in the last few years.

6. Asset Management of Investment Trusts

Investment trusts are a type of collective investment scheme based on pooling small investments from many investors and have three significant features. First, they enable the diversification of small investments. Using investment trusts allows individual investors to lower their risk through diversification just the same as institutional investors even with small investments. For example, investment in an investment trust fund that has diversified its investments into no less than one thousand stocks and in 40 or more countries starts from about ¥100. The second feature is that investment trusts are managed by professionals. Building the optimum investment portfolio based on macroeconomic analysis as well as financial trends and stock price analysis requires advanced knowledge, analytic capabilities, and investment technology. Through investment trusts, even individual investors can benefit from the skills of professional fund managers. The third feature of investment trusts is transparency. The mark-to-market net asset value of these investment trust funds is published on a daily basis, and Japanese laws have beefed up disclosure requirements.

An investment trust with instructions from trustors is the representative scheme adopted in Japan. Assets collected from investors (beneficiaries) through subscriptions by distributing companies, such as securities companies and registered financial institutions, are managed by a trustor (investment trust management companies) and held in safekeeping and administered by a trustee (trust banks).

When the investment trust system was first set up, government regulators only approved investments in Japanese stocks. However, the investment regulations have gradually been liberalized, and today it is possible to create a truly wide range of investment instruments based on the products available. For example, by including short-term financial instruments, they can structure investment trusts, such as money reserve funds (MRFs), that mimic bank deposits. Furthermore, since the approval of investment in real estate and commodities, individual investors can take a stake in office buildings, gold, oil, and other investments such as infrastructure or solar power generation facilities through investment trusts. In addition, there are also investment trusts utilizing AI (artificial intelligence).

Entry into the investment trust market has also been liberalized from a limitation to only approved companies associated with major securities companies to a registration system that requires only that companies meet certain conditions. As a result, the industry has grown from only about 10 companies at one time to over 100 investment trust management companies. Moreover, with the lifting of the bans on outsourcing asset management and on invest-

Table XIII-5.   Trends in the Liberalization of Investment Trust Regulations in Japan

1951	Securities companies begin investment trust management business
1959	Investment trust management companies made independent of securities companies
1961	Ban on inclusion of public bonds lifted (Bond investment trusts established)
1970	Ban on inclusion of foreign securities lifted
1978	Ban on use of forward exchange contracts lifted
1986	Ban on inclusion of OTC-registered stocks lifted
1987	Ban on use of derivatives for hedging purposes lifted
1990	Foreign-affiliated investment management companies enter market
1993	Bank-affiliated investment management companies enter market
1995	Ban on use of derivatives for other than hedging purposes lifted (Bull/Bear funds established)
	Exchange traded funds (ETFs) introduced
	Ban on conducting both discretionary asset management and commissioned investment trust management businesses lifted
1998	Financial System Reform Law passed (Japanese Big Bank)
	Deregulation converts investment trust management companies from licensing to approval system
	Ban on outsourcing asset management lifted
	Ban on investment trusts being sold through banks on an agency basis lifted
1999	Ban on fund of funds (FoFs) lifted
2001	Real estate investment trusts (REITs) introduced
2007	Further deregulation converts investment trust management companies from approval system to registration system
2008	Ban on inclusion of commodities lifted
2016	Infrastructure Fund introduced

Chart XIII-6.   The Structure of Investment Trusts with Instructions from Trustors

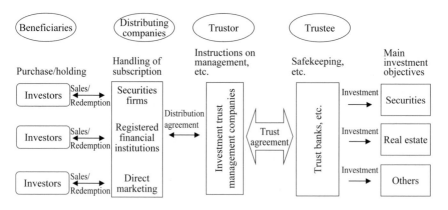

Source: The Investment Trusts Association, Japan.

ing in a fund of funds, investment trusts can also indirectly offer their customers access to the investment services of foreign asset management companies.

7. Stewardship Code (1)

The UK Stewardship Code, on which the Japanese version of the Stewardship Code is based, was established in 2010 to monitor and curb excessive risk-taking by corporate management as the responsibility of shareholders. It was established in response to criticism that shareholders, who have limited liability, were protected even though public funds were used to bail out financial institutions during the crisis that precipitated the Lehman Shock. Given the Cabinet's approval of the Japan Revitalization Strategy in June 2013, the Principles for Responsible Institutional Investors (Japan's Stewardship Code) formulated by the Council of Experts Concerning the Japanese Version of the Stewardship Code (established within the Financial Services Agency (FSA)) were formulated and published in February 2014 as part of a growth strategy, and a revised version was released in May 2017, and then again in March 2020.

The Stewardship Code defines the principles deemed to be helpful for institutional investors in fulfilling their stewardship responsibilities of enhancing the medium-term to long-term investment return for their clients and beneficiaries by increasing the investee companies' corporate value and sustainable growth through conducting "constructive dialog" based on in-depth knowledge of the companies and their business environment, alongside consideration of sustainability issues in accordance with their investment strategies.

The Stewardship Code and the Corporate Governance Code serve as two wheels of a cart so-to-speak, and in expectation that broad penetration and implementation of these two Codes will contribute to realizing effective corporate governance in Japan, over 300 institutional investors have also adopted the Stewardship Code. The Stewardship Code is not a law or a legally binding regulation. Rather than being a set of laws or regulations, it adopts a principles-based approach instead of a rule-based approach. The Code adopts a "comply or explain" approach, according to which an institutional investor either implements the principles or, if not, explains their reasons for non-compliance. In addition, the Guidelines for Dialogue between Investors and Companies, which provide an overview of agenda items on which institutional investors and companies are expected to focus for sustainable growth and medium- to long-term enhancement of corporate value, as required by the Stewardship Code (code of conduct for institutional investors) and the

Table XIII-6.   The Principles of the Stewardship Code

So as to promote sustainable growth of the investee company and enhance the medium- and long-term investment return of clients and beneficiaries,

1. Institutional investors should have a clear policy on how they fulfill their stewardship responsibilities, and publicly disclose it.

2. Institutional investors should have a clear policy on how they manage conflicts of interest in fulfilling their stewardship responsibilities and publicly disclose it.

3. Institutional investors should monitor investee companies so that they can appropriately fulfill their stewardship responsibilities with an orientation towards the sustainable growth of the companies.

4. Institutional investors should seek to arrive at an understanding in common with investee companies and work to solve problems through constructive engagement with investee companies.

5. Institutional investors should have a clear policy on voting rights and disclosure of voting activity. The policy on voting rights should not be comprised only of a mechanical checklist; it should be designed to contribute to the sustainable growth of investee companies.

6. Institutional investors in principle should report periodically on how they fulfill their stewardship responsibilities, including their voting responsibilities, to their clients and beneficiaries.

7. To contribute positively to the sustainable growth of investee companies, institutional investors should develop skills and resources needed to appropriately engage with the companies and to make proper judgments in fulfilling their stewardship activities based on in-depth knowledge of the investee companies and their business environment and consideration of sustainability consistent with their investment management strategies.

8. Service providers for institutional investors should endeavor to contribute to the enhancement of the functions of the entire investment chain by appropriately providing services for institutional investors to fulfill their stewardship responsibilities.

Source: Financial Services Agency.

Corporate Governance Code (code of conduct for companies), were formulated and published in June 2018, as a supplemental document to both codes. The revised version was published in June 2021.

8. Stewardship Code (2)

The Stewardship Code calls for the following three key actions to be taken by institutional investors toward investee companies: (1) monitoring (Principle 3); (2) engagement (Principle 4); and (3) exercise of voting rights (Principle 5).

First, according to the Code, (1) institutional investors should monitor investee companies so that institutional investors can fulfill their stewardship

Chart XIII-7.   Relationship between the two codes and dialogue guidelines

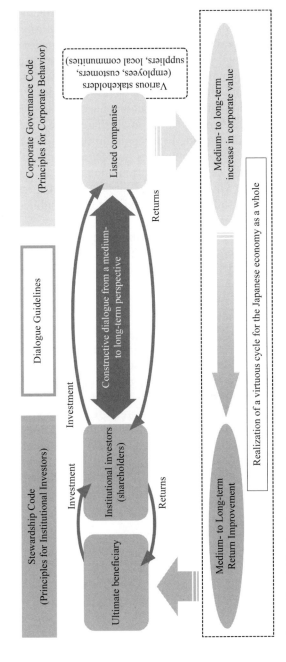

Source: Financial Services Agency.

responsibilities with an orientation towards the sustainable growth of the companies. Monitoring should be performed continuously and effectively.

This includes non-financial matters such as information regarding ESG (environmental, social and corporate governance). Next, (2) engagement refers to having "purposeful dialog" with investee companies in order to arrive at an understanding in common with investee companies and work to solve problems. Institutional investors are expected to have a clear policy in advance on how they design dialog with investee companies. Further, (3) institutional investors should exercise voting rights on all shares held. In exercising their voting rights, they are expected to decide on the vote in light of results of the monitoring of investee companies and the contents of dialog with them. In addition, the Code calls for the formulation and publication of a clear policy on the exercise of voting rights, the publication of the results of the exercise of voting rights for individual proposals, and clear public disclosure of the reasons for approval or non-approval.

Principle 1 requires asset owners such as pension funds to encourage asset managers to engage in effective stewardship activities, and Principle 8 defines the roles of service providers for institutional investors such as proxy advisors and pension management consultants.

Historically, there was a time when the Wall Street Rule was the mainstream approach, whereby institutional investors would sell their holdings in a company if they were dissatisfied with the management of the investee company. However, for passive managers and large public pension funds (universal owners) with widely diversified investments, selling shares is often difficult in practice, and the concept of holding shares and exercising voting rights as a part of fiduciary responsibility has become increasingly widespread. Furthermore, the Stewardship Code now requires engagement from institutional investors with the management of investee companies rather than just the exercise of voting rights. Similarly, with ESG investment, rather than divesting holdings where there is a disagreement on policy, institutional investors are now more open to the notion of holding shares and setting out their opinions to companies through their exercise of voting rights and engagement with management.

CHAPTER XIV

Securities Taxation

1. Transitions in Securities Taxation (1)

Basically, the income tax system of Japan is based on comprehensive taxation (taxation on the total income). It traces its origin to a recommendation made soon after the war by the Shoup Recommendation on Japanese Taxation. Under the Shoup taxation system enforced in 1950, capital gains from sales of securities, as well as interest and dividends, were subject to comprehensive taxation in full (capital losses were fully deductible). After the end of the Allied military occupation, however, the Japanese government authorized separate taxation on interest and exempted from tax, in principle, capital gains from the sale of securities primarily from a policy standpoint to encourage accumulation of capital—with the result that the ideal of comprehensive taxation on income has disintegrated rapidly. And it was a sweeping reform of the taxation system carried out in 1987–1989 that helped the basic framework of the present income tax system take shape. At that time, the structure of income taxation was changed from one consisting of 15 brackets (10.5%–70%) to a flat one consisting of five brackets (10%–50%), and the financial income taxation system was overhauled thoroughly, including the uniform separate withholding taxation on interest income; the abolition of the tax-exempt savings system, in principle; and separate taxation, in principle, on capital gains from the sale of securities. The structure of income tax rates was amended to 4 brackets (10%–37%) in the fiscal 1999 tax reform and to 6 brackets (5%–40%) in the fiscal 2006 tax reform. In the fiscal 2013 tax reform, from the perspective of correcting income disparity and reviving the income redistribution function, starting with income tax for 2015, the rate for taxable income in excess of ¥40 million was set at 45%. Based on the fiscal 2016 tax reform, the basic corporate income tax rate was reduced to 23.4% from 23.9% in FY2016, and was further reduced to 23.2% in FY2018. As a result, the tax rate for national and local combined (the effective corporate tax rate) became 29.74% in FY2018.

Looking at major trends in Japan's securities taxation system during the late 1990s and early 2000s, the government built taxation systems for stock

Table XIV-1.   Securities Taxation Evolution Timeline (1949−2002)

Year	Major amendments	Income tax brackets
1949	Shoup recommendation	
1950	A comprehensive taxation of interest, dividends, and capital gains from the sale of securities is enforced.	8 brackets (20%−55%)
1951	The optional separate withholding tax (50%) on interest is revived.	
1952	The withholding tax on dividends (20%) is revived.	↓
1953	Securities capital gains are exempted from income tax, in principle. The securities transaction tax is instituted (0.15% of the value of stock transaction). A uniform separate withholding tax on interest (10%) is instituted.	11 brackets (15%−65%)
1954	The withholding tax on dividends is reduced (from 20% to 15%).	
1955	Interest is exempted from income tax. The withholding tax on dividends is lowered (from 15% to 10%).	
1957	The separate withholding tax only on interest on short-term savings is revived (10%).	13 brackets (10%−70%)
1959	The separate withholding tax on interest on long-term savings is revived (10%).	
1961	Securities capital gains tax is levied on certain large-lot transactions.	↓
1962		15 brackets (8%−75%)
1963	The withholding tax rate on interest and dividends is lowered (from 10% to 5%).	
1965	The withholding tax rate on interest and dividends is raised (from 5% to 10%). The system of not requiring declaration and the optional separate withholding tax on dividends (15%) are introduced.	
1967	The withholding tax on interest and dividends is raised (from 10% to 15%). The optional withholding tax on dividends is raised (from 15% to 20%).	↓
1969		16 brackets (10%−75%)
1970		19 brackets (10%−75%)
1971	The optional separate withholding tax on interest (20%) is revived.	↓
1973	The optional withholding tax on interest and dividends is raised (from 20% to 25%). The securities transaction tax is raised (from 0.15% to 0.3%).	(The taxable income applicable to tax rate brackets is raised in
1976	The optional withholding tax on interest and dividends is raised (from 25% to 30%).	1971 and again in 1974.)
1978	The withholding tax rate on interest and dividends is raised (from 15% to 20%). The optional withholding tax rate on interest and dividends is raised (from 30% to 35%). The securities transaction tax is raised (from 0.3% to 0.45% for stocks, etc.).	↓
1981	The securities transaction tax is raised (from 0.45% to 0.55%).	
1984		15 brackets (10.5%−70%)
1987	A sweeping tax reform	12 brackets (10.5%−60%)
1988	- The *maruyu* system is abolished, in principle.	↓
1989	- Uniform separate withholding tax on interest (20%) (products similar to financial instruments are also subject to the uniform separate withholding tax). - Securities capital gains are taxed, in principle (introduction of a separate withholding tax of 1% of the stock transaction value). - The securities transaction tax is lowered (from 0.55% to 0.3%).	5 brackets (10%−50%)
1995		(In 1995, the taxable income applicable to tax rate brackets is raised.)
1996	Securities capital gains tax is normalized (from 5% of deemed capital gains to 5.25%). The securities transaction tax is lowered (from 0.3% to 0.12%).	↓
1998	The securities transaction tax is lowered (from 0.12% to 0.06%).	
1999	The securities transaction tax is abolished.	4 brackets (10%−37%)
2001	A tax exemption system is launched for small-amount capital gains from the sale of stocks held long term (abolished after the 2003 tax system reform). An emergency investment tax break is established.	↓
2002	The special account system is established (implemented January 2003).	↓

options, specific-purpose companies, and corporation type investment trusts in 1998. Effective April 1999, it abolished the securities transaction tax and the exchange tax (imposed on futures and options trading), which had long been issues of concern. Further measures followed with the enhancement of the Angels Taxation System in 2000 and the introduction of the tax-exemption system for profits on small sales amounts of stocks being held for the long term (a ¥1 million special tax exemption on stocks, etc., held for more than one year) and an emergency investment tax break (a tax exemption on up to ¥10 million of principal) in 2001. The establishment of the special account system was included in the tax revisions for fiscal 2002 and launched on January 1, 2003. During the same period, the government reorganized its small-amount tax-exemption system for small-sum savings of the elderly, etc. (*Maruyu* savings system for the elderly, etc.), converting it into a small-amount, tax-exemption system for persons with disabilities, etc.

2. Transitions in Securities Taxation (2)

Since 2003, the reforms in the securities taxation system have focused mainly on revisions in the preferential tax system for dividends and capital gains on listed stocks, etc., expanding the scope of offsetting losses against gains, and revisions concerning the systems of non-taxables.

Table XIV-2.   Securities Taxation Evolution Timeline (Since 2003)

Year	Major amendments	Income tax brackets
2003	Non-declaration system is introduced for dividends and capital gains of listed stocks, etc. The tax exemption system for small-amount capital gains from the sale of stocks held long term is abolished	
2004	Preferential tax rate on dividends and capital gains from publicly offered stock investment trusts is introduced Tax rate on capital gains is reduced from the sale of unlisted stock (from 26% to 20%).	
2007	The expiration date of application for a preferential tax rate is extended for a year for dividends and capital gains of listed stocks, etc.	6 brackets (5%–40%)
2009	Mechanism is introduced enabling netting of dividends and capital gains and losses from listed stocks, etc. Preferential tax rate on dividends and capital gains of listed stocks, etc. is extended for three more years	
2011	Preferential tax rate on dividends and capital gains of listed stocks, etc. is extended for two more years	
2014	Nippon Individual Savings Account (NISA) is introduced	
2015		7 brackets (5%–45%)
2016	Tax system for bonds, etc. is changed and scope of profit and loss netting expanded Junior NISA is introduced	
2018	Introduction of installment-type NISA	
2020	Measures to adjust double taxation on investment trusts (foreign tax amount reduction) introduced.	

Chart XIV-1. Review and extension of NISA system (draft)

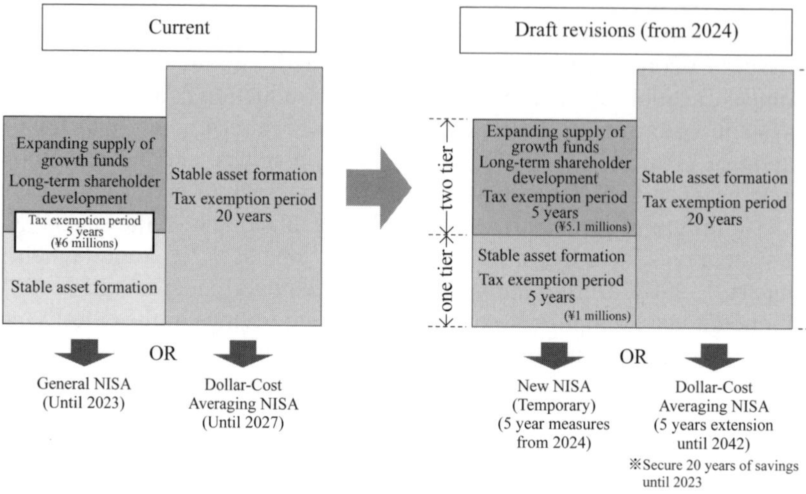

| Current | Draft revisions (from 2024) |

Source: Compiled from the Ministry of Finance pamphlet "Tax Reform for FY 2020".

In terms of the revisions relating to the preferential tax rate, in the fiscal 2003 tax reform, the government introduced a non-declaration requirement system that imposed only a fixed withholding tax of 20% (15% in income tax and 5% in local inhabitant tax) on dividends and capital gains from listed stocks, etc., and distributions of gains from publicly offered stock investment trusts. At the same time, the government introduced a preferential tax rate of 10% on a limited-time basis. In the fiscal 2004 tax reform, the government extended this preferential tax rate to cover taxable gains from publicly offered stock investment trusts. Then in the fiscal 2007 tax reform, the government carried over the preferential tax treatment for dividends and capital gains from listed stocks etc., for another year. In addition, the fiscal 2009 tax reform extended the preferential tax rate for three years, and the 2011 tax reform extended it for two more years, so that the preferential tax rate was in effect until the end of 2013. To help fund the restoration of the areas stricken by the Great East Japan Earthquake, a special income tax for reconstruction is being levied from 2013 to 2037.

Looking at the trend in the scope of allowing netting of losses against gains, the fiscal 2003 tax reform made it possible for investors to offset losses on redemptions (termination of agreement) of publicly offered stock investment trusts on equities, etc., for the year. The fiscal 2004 tax reform added a tax deduction carryforward system (three years) for capital losses on publicly offered stock investment trusts. To reduce the risk of investing in equities for individual investors, the fiscal 2008 tax reform also added a mechanism allowing investors to offset capital losses on listed stocks, etc., against dividends beginning in 2009. Although the application of this mechanism was limited to investors who chose to separately declare their dividend income from listed stocks, etc. in 2009, it became possible to also do so using an income tax withholding account from 2010. Furthermore, the fiscal 2013 tax reform enforced changes to the taxation method for bonds, etc., making it possible to offset income against losses for interest and capital gains on specified bonds, etc., and income from listed stocks starting in 2016.

With regard to the tax exemption system, NISA was introduced in 2014, followed by Junior NISA in 2016 and Installment-type NISA in 2018. In the fiscal 2020 amendment to the taxation system, the review and extension of NISA and the extension of Installment-type NISA are scheduled (Junior NISA will not be extended and will no longer be available after 2023).

In addition, various special tax measures have been implemented in response to the COVID-19 pandemic, including an extension of the allowable period for filing income tax returns.

3. Taxation of Interest

Under the fiscal 2013 tax reform, changes were made to the taxation system regarding interest income to go into effect in 2016. The outline of the current system is as follows. The method of separate taxation on the basis of self-assessment or non-declaration is applied for interest on specified bonds and profits distributed by publicly offered bond investment trusts and investment trusts managing publicly offered bonds, etc. after paying a 20% withholding tax (20.315% including the special income tax for reconstruction). Specified bonds are certain bonds, such as government bonds, local government bonds, foreign government bonds, publicly offered bonds, and listed bonds. Interest on deposits and savings, and bonds other than specified bonds and profits distributed by jointly invested trust accounts and privately placed bond investment trusts are treated, in principle, as interest income, and is subject to a withholding tax at a rate of 20% (20.315% including the special income tax for reconstruction) separately from other income. Interest on deposits for tax payment savings associations, tax reserve deposits and so-called children's bank savings is tax exempt.

Income from similar financial products (including benefits from fixed-term deposits, benefits based on agreements covered by Article 2, Paragraph 4 of the Banking Act, interest on mortgage securities paid under specific contracts, profit on gold investment accounts, foreign exchange gains on foreign currency investment accounts, gains on policies such as single premium en-

Table XIV-3. Interest Taxation System

Classification	Outline
· Interest on specified bonds · Profits distributed by publicly offered bond investment trusts and investment trusts managing publicly offered bonds, etc.	Separate taxation on the basis of self-assessment or no declaration necessary (20% withholding tax including 5% inhabitant tax)
· Interest on deposits and savings · Interest on bonds other than specified bonds (Note 1) · Profits distributed by jointly managed investment trusts and privately placed bond investment trusts	Separate withholding tax (20% including 5% inhabitant tax)
Tax-exempt savings system	· Tax-exempt interest income earned from a small-amount deposit by persons with disabilities, etc. (on principal of up to ¥3.5 million) · Tax-exempt interest income earned from a small-amount investment in public bonds by persons with disabilities, etc. (on principal of up to ¥3.5 million) · Tax-exempt system for the workers' property accumulation savings for house construction plan and the workers' property accumulation savings plan (on principal of up to ¥5.5 million)

Notes: 1. Excluding interest on corporate bonds issued by a family company the payment of which is received by a corporate executive, etc. of the family company either directly or through a related company.
2. Special income tax for reconstruction is levied from 2013 to 2037.
Source: Compiled from materials made by National Tax Administration Agency.

dowment or non-life insurance accounts that meet certain requirements) is uniformly subject to withholding tax at a rate of 20% (20.315% including the special income tax for reconstruction).

Tax-exempt systems of interest income include the tax-exempt small-amount savings system for persons with disabilities, etc. and the tax-exempt system of interest income for workers' property accumulation savings plan (tax-exempt system for property accumulation).

The tax-exempt small-amount savings system for persons with disabilities includes a tax-exempt system for interest income on small-sum savings for persons with disabilities (commonly known as *Maruyu* savings for persons with disabilities, etc.) and one for interest income on small-amount public bonds for persons with disabilities (commonly known as special *Maruyu* for persons with disabilities, etc.). Both of these systems have an upper limit of ¥3.5 million for tax-exempt principal, making earnings on a total of up to ¥7 million in principal tax free when both types of systems are used. The gov-

Table XIV-4.   The Status of Taxation on Interest Income, Etc. (2020)

(millions of yen)

Classification	Amount paid	Taxable amount	Withholding tax amount
Public bonds	3,130,335	37,555	5,936
Corporate bonds	1,339,015	233,345	33,618
Deposits (Banks)	553,220	477,995	72,832
Deposits (Others)	386,013	220,665	33,460
Jointly invested trusts	15,080	9,249	1,402
Bond investment trusts	58,706	53,906	6,467
Interest on specified bonds, etc. (Withholding income tax special amount)	535,012	132,644	20,377
Redemption gains from discount bonds	1,552	1,552	276
Others	767,323	641,691	122,980
Total	6,786,256	1,808,602	297,348

Notes: 1. Taxable amount includes not only that paid to individuals but also that to corporations.
   2. Interest on specified bonds, etc. (Withholding income tax special amount) applies to special cases whereby the payment processor pays the special amount of withholding income tax to the government on behalf of the income payer.
   3. The "amount paid" and "amount of withholding tax" for "gain on redemption of discount bonds" include receipts by individuals as well as corporations.
   4. As fractions were rounded to the nearest whole number, the figures may not add up to the actual total amounts.
Source: Compiled based on the data available on the website of the National Tax Agency of Japan.

ernment abolished the previously available tax-exempt system for interest income on postal savings for persons with disabilities, etc., after the privatization of postal services. Qualified persons with disabilities include persons with a physical disability certificate, persons who receive a disability pension, wives who receive survivors' basic pension benefits or a widow's pension.

The tax-system for property accumulation includes the workers' property accumulation savings for house construction plan and the workers' property accumulation savings plan. These savings are designed to encourage workers below 55 years of age to buy houses and stabilize their retirement lives, and the interest on combined principals of ¥5,500,000 or less would be nontaxable. However, the workers' property accumulation savings plan investing in life insurance and property insurance, etc., have a nontaxable upper limit of ¥3,850,000.

4. Taxation of Dividends

In principle, not taking into consideration the special income tax for reconstruction, the balance of dividends, distributions of gains from publicly offered stock investment trusts, and other applicable income earned by stockholders or investors after the payment of a 20% withholding tax is subject to comprehensive taxation. When comprehensive taxation is levied on dividend income, the Income Tax Act allows the deduction of a certain percentage of dividend income (tax credits for dividends) to avoid double taxation.

For distributions, etc., of gains on publicly offered stock investment trusts and for dividends paid on listed stocks other than those paid on large shareholdings (those paid to a shareholder who holds 3% or more of the outstanding shares of a corporation), the payee of dividends has the option of adopting comprehensive taxation, separate taxation on the basis of self-assessment, or non-declaration of dividend income (withholding tax only on their dividend income). For a limited period, stockholders and investors enjoyed a preferential tax rate of 10% (10.147% in 2013) on this income. However, from 2014 to 2037, the rate is 20.315%, after which a tax rate of 20% will be

Table XIV-5.   An Outline of Dividend Income Taxation

Classification			Outline
Distributions from publicly offered stock investment trusts, etc.			· Comprehensive taxation
Dividend of surplus, dividend of profits, distribution of surplus, etc.	Dividend on listed stocks, etc. (excluding large shareholdings) (Note 1)		Dividend on listed stocks, etc. (5% to 45% income tax; 10% inhabitant tax) (Dividend deduction applicable) · Select either separate taxation on the basis of self-assessment Dividend on listed stocks, etc. (15% income tax; 5% inhabitant tax) (non-declaration is also possible)
	Other than above		Comprehensive taxation (tax credits for dividends) (5% to 45% income tax, 10% inhabitant tax) (20% withholding) (20% income tax)
		Dividend paid at one time is no more than: ¥100,000 × $\dfrac{\text{Dividend computational period}}{12}$ Items below	No declaration necessary (20% withholding) (20% income tax)

Notes: 1. "Dividends on listed stocks, etc. (other than those paid to large shareholders)" means those paid to shareholders holding less than 3% of the outstanding shares of the listed company.
    2. In addition, from January 2013 to December 2037, a 2.1% special income tax for reconstruction is levied against the amount of income tax as a time-limited measure.
Source: Based on the web site of the Ministry of Finance.

Table XIV-6. Taxation of Dividend Income (withheld at source) (2020)

(millions of yen)

Classification	Amount paid	Taxable amount	Tax-exempt amount	Withholding tax amount
Dividends on profit or interest income, distribution of retained earnings, dividends, etc., / on interest on fund corporations, and Dividends, etc. of specified investment corporation investments	33,908,059	22,776,436	11,131,622	4,255,978
Distributions of profits of investment trusts and investment trusts with specific investment purposes	2,281,427	1,577,793	703,634	310,611
Remittance to optional withholding tax account	1,555,142	1,555,142	–	234,126
Total	37,744,627	25,909,371	11,835,256	4,800,715

Notes: 1. Bond investment trusts and investment trusts managing publicly offered bonds, etc., are not included in "investment trusts."
2. "Taxable amount" includes not only that paid to individuals but also that to corporations.
3. As fractions were rounded to the nearest whole number, the figures may not add up to the actual total amounts.
Source: Compiled based on the data available on the website of the National Tax Agency of Japan.

applied. For a limited period, stockholders and investors have enjoyed a preferential tax rate of 10% (10.147% in 2013) even for separate taxation on the basis of self-assessment. However, from 2014 to 2037, the rate will be 20.315%, after which a tax rate of 20% will be applied. It was from 2009 that choosing the separate taxation on the basis of self-assessment became an option. Moreover, from 2010, investors have been able to combine dividends, etc., from listed stock, etc., in their withholding tax accounts. The term "listed stock, etc.," refers to shares that are listed on domestic and foreign stock exchanges and includes ETFs (exchange traded funds).

Meanwhile, dividends on stocks other than listed stocks (unlisted stocks) and those received by large individual shareholders are subject to comprehensive taxation after paying a 20% withholding tax (20.42% from 2013 to 2037). In this case, shareholders have the right to select the non-declaration of dividends paid at one time of no more than the amount derived by proportionally dividing ¥100,000 over the dividend-computation period. However, local inhabitant tax is subject to comprehensive taxation.

Distributions of profit from publicly offered stock investment trusts are treated as dividend income when investors opt for the comprehensive taxation method, entitling the investors to tax credits. However, the rate of deduction varies depending on the ratio of foreign currency denominated assets and non-stock assets of the stock investment trust concerned. If the percentage of either foreign currency denominated assets or non-stock assets is over 75%, the deduction of dividends is not allowed. For profits distributed by privately placed stock investment trusts of the contractual type (see section 10 below), such dividends less withholding tax are subject to comprehensive taxation (dividends are deductible).

For the purpose of computing the amount of dividend income, interest paid on a debt incurred to acquire stocks, etc., may be deducted from the taxable income. However, this is allowed only when the investor files a tax return.

5. Adjustment of Double Taxation Relating to Dividends

Profits generated by a business corporation through its business activities should, basically, be returned to the owners of that corporation. However, corporate income is usually taxed twice: corporate income tax and individual income tax (dividend tax and capital gains tax). Considering that, ultimately, it is the individuals who have the duty of paying taxes, some adjustments have to be made to avoid double taxation. This is the question of consolidating corporate tax and an individual's income tax. Ideally, all forms of double taxation of corporate income—be it retained earnings or dividends—should be rectified. However, adjustments are chiefly made to the dividend portion.

In Japan, in the case of individual shareholders, a dividend tax credit system is applied that makes 10% of their dividend income from sources such as distribution from surplus ("dividend income") (and 2.8% for inhabitant tax) deductible from their tax liability. In the case of individual shareholders, a dividend tax credit system is applied that makes 10% of their dividend income (and 2.8% for inhabitant tax) deductible from their tax liability. However, in the case of those whose taxable income exceeds ¥10 million, 5% of such part of their dividend income that pushes their taxable income over and above ¥10 million (and 1.4% for inhabitant tax) is deductible. For instance, when individual shareholders have a total taxable income of ¥13 million (¥9 million in general income and ¥4 million in dividend income), they are entitled to a tax deduction of 5% of such part of their dividend income that pushes their taxable income over and above ¥10 million, which is ¥3 million (=¥13 million − ¥10 million), and 10% of other part of their income, which is ¥1 million. Therefore, they are entitled to a tax deduction of ¥250,000 (¥150,000 (=(¥13 million − ¥10 million) × 0.05) + (¥100,000 (=(¥10 million − ¥9 million) × 0.1). In the US and Germany, no adjustment measures are used. In the UK and France, the partial dividend income deduction method is used.

Table XIV-7.   Dividend Taxation and Double Taxation Adjustments in Major Countries

(As of January 2021)

	Japan (Note 1)	United States (Note 2)	U.K.	Germany	France
taxation system	Choice between Separate Declaration and Comprehensive Taxation (Separate declaration) 20% (income tax: 15% + individual inhabitant tax: 5%) or (comprehensive taxation) 10% to 55%. Note: It is also possible to choose not to have to file a tax return with only withholding tax (20% (15% income tax + 5% individual inhabitant tax)).	Tiered taxation (separate taxation) (Federal tax) 3 levels 0, 15% and 20%. (Note 3) + Comprehensive taxation (state and local government tax) In New York City state tax: 4.00~8.82% city tax: 2.7~3.4% + 14% additional tax on the tax amount	Tiered taxation (separate taxation) 3 levels 7.5%, 32.5% and 38.1%. (Note 4)	No need to file a tax return (Separate taxation) ※ Comprehensive taxation is also possible (Note 5) 26.375% (income tax: 25% + Additional tax: 5.5% of the tax amount	Choice between separate taxation and comprehensive taxation (Note 6) (Separate taxation) 30% income tax: 12.8% + taxes related to social security: 17.2% or (comprehensive taxation) 17.2% to 62.2% income tax: 0 to 45% + taxes related to social security: 17.2%
Reconciliation with income taxes	Dividend income tax credit method (In the case of electing comprehensive taxation)	No preparation measures	A control and removal method (Deduct £2,000 of dividend income)	No preparation measures	A control and removal method (60% of dividends received are included in the shareholder's taxable income) (In the case of electing comprehensive taxation)

Notes: 1. This is for dividends from listed shares, etc. (other than those paid to large shareholders).
2. This is for qualified dividends (dividends received from a domestic corporation or qualified foreign corporation with respect to shares held for more than 60 days during a total of 121 days before and after the ex-dividend date).
3. Income is accumulated in the order of employment income, dividend income, and long-term capital gains, and a tax rate of 0% is applied to the portion of dividend income and long-term capital gains corresponding to the bracket of $40,400 or less, 15% to the portion corresponding to the bracket of over $40,400, and 20% to the portion corresponding to the bracket of over $445,850. The corresponding portion is subject to a tax rate of 20% (for single taxpayers). The tax rates for state and local government taxes vary from state to state.
4. 7.5% for the portion of dividend income corresponding to the bracket of 37,500 pounds or less, 32.5% for the portion corresponding to the bracket of 150,000 pounds or less, and 38.1% for the portion corresponding to the bracket of over 150,000 pounds, by accumulating income in the following order: employment income, interest income, and dividend income.
5. If the tax rate applicable when capital income is combined with other income is 25% or less, comprehensive taxation can be applied by filing a tax return. However, if the taxpayer is disadvantaged by the choice of comprehensive taxation after filing a tax return, the tax authorities will treat the capital income as if it were not declared and only withholding tax at the rate of 26.375% will be imposed.
6. In principle, interest and dividends are subject to withholding at source, but those whose reference taxable income (taxable income plus certain income deductions (e.g., deductions from dividend income) added back) for the previous year is below a certain level may elect to be taxed separately on a tax return without being subject to withholding.

Source: Compiled from the Ministry of Finance website.

In foreign countries, the imputation method was broadly adopted as a method to adjust for double taxation. In this method, dividends including corporate income tax are included in taxable income for the purposes of calculating income tax, and then the amount equivalent to corporate income tax is deducted from the calculated tax amount. The dividend tax credit (dividend-received deduction) employed in Japan and the partial imputation method employed in the UK are both types of imputation methods. Other methods used to adjust for double taxation include the dividend paid deduction method (which authorizes deduction of dividends paid on the corporate level from corporate taxable income) and the comprehensive business income tax method (CBIT). Interest and dividends are not deductible from taxable income on the corporate level, and such interest and dividends received by individuals are not subject to income tax.

6.　Capital Gains Taxation

In 2003, the system of opting for a separate withholding tax or for separate taxation on the basis of self-assessment for gains on the sale of listed stocks, etc., was abolished, and these taxes were unified into the latter system of separately filing an income tax return. In other words, not taking into account the special income tax for reconstruction, a 20% tax rate (a 15% income tax and a 5% inhabitant tax) is applied to an amount of income arrived at by deducting the cost of acquiring or selling the security and interest paid on the fund used for the purchase of such security from the proceeds of such security. The capital gains from the sale of listed stocks, etc. may be treated so as to deal with issues related to taxable income based on withholding tax only using a specified account which will be discussed later. Previous to 2003, capital losses from the sale of stocks, etc., were deductible only from capital gains from the sale of other stocks, etc., if any, made during the same year, and it was not permissible to carry forward any unused losses. However, since 2003, investors have been able to carry forward capital losses from the sales of listed stocks, etc., for three years starting with the year following their occurrence. Also, since 2009, investors have been able to deduct capital losses on listed stocks, etc., from dividends, etc., received from listed stocks, etc. Furthermore, starting in 2016, based on the change in the taxation method for bonds, etc., it became possible to offset income against losses for interest and capital gains from specified bonds, etc., and income from listed stocks, etc. Separate self-assessment taxation shall apply to general shares and similar.

Along with the abolition of the separate withholding tax system, the authorities sought to lessen the reporting burden on investors by establishing a

Table XIV-8.   Outline of the Capital Gains Taxation System for Stocks, Etc.

	Outline
Listed stocks, etc. · Listed stocks · ETF · Publicly offered investment trusts · Specified bonds, etc.	Separate taxation on the basis of self-assessment
	Capital gains on listed stocks, etc. ×20% (15% income tax: 5% inhabitant tax)
	*Special exception on no declaration necessary for withholding tax account
	For income maintained in a withholding account (specified account selected for tax withholding purpose) from the sale of listed stocks, etc. taxable-income-related issues may be completed based on withholding tax only.
	*Gain/loss offset and carrying-forward of unused deductible losses relating to listed stocks, etc.
	Losses from the sale of listed stocks, etc. may be deducted from the amount of dividend income, etc. on listed stocks, etc. for the same year. For unused deductible losses relating to unlisted stocks, etc., the investor may carry it forward for a three-year period starting from the following year as deduction from the amount of capital gains from listed stocks, etc. (Note 3) and the amount of dividend income, etc. from listed stocks, etc.
General stocks, etc. (Stocks, etc. other than listed stocks)	Separate taxation on the basis of self-assessment
	Capital gains on general stocks × 20% (15% income tax, 5% inhabitant tax)

Notes: From January 2013 to December 2037, a 2.1% special income tax for reconstruction is separately levied against the amount of base income tax as a time-limited measure.
Source: Compiled based on information available on the website of the Ministry of Finance.

special account system. Under this type of account, a securities company computes capital gains or losses, as the case may be, for its customer from the sale of shares of a listed stock, etc., made through a special brokerage account. The account is divided into two categories: the income tax withholding account and the simplified income tax return account (no tax is withheld). When an investor sells his shareholdings through the income tax withholding account, his securities company withholds the income tax, obviating the need for the investor to file an income tax return. Furthermore, from 2010, it became possible for the securities company to deposit dividends from listed stocks, etc. of customers that are subject to withholding tax in the income tax withholding account set up for the customers. However, if an investor using such an account also files a final return, the investor is also allowed to include capital gains or to offset capital losses from the sale of such shares through another account. Further, in conjunction with the change in the taxa-

Chart XIV-2.   Withholding Taxes on Capital Gains on the Sale of Listed Stock, Etc., Managed in Special Brokerage Accounts

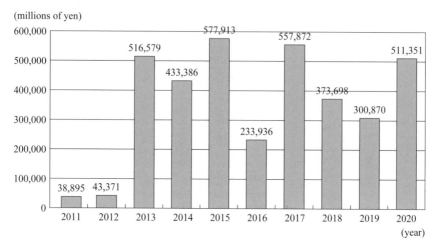

(millions of yen)

Year	Value
2011	38,895
2012	43,371
2013	516,579
2014	433,386
2015	577,913
2016	233,936
2017	557,872
2018	373,698
2019	300,870
2020	511,351

Source: Based on the website of the National Tax Agency of Japan.

tion method for bonds, etc. effective 2016, the scope of application of the special account has also been widened. When an investor opts for the income tax withholding account and does not file a final return, the spousal deduction is not affected. By contrast, if an investor opts for the simplified income tax return account, such an investor may file a simplified version of the income tax return by attaching to it an annual statement of stock trading made under a special brokerage account received from his securities company (Not required after April 1, 2019). Currently, securities companies must send an annual statement of stock trading to the customer and the tax office no matter what type of special brokerage account is selected by the customer.

7.   The Angel Taxation System

The Angel Taxation System is a special taxation measure designed to encourage individual investors (angels) to invest in venture-stage firms (specified small-to-midsize companies and specified new small-to-midsize companies) that meet certain requirements. Specified small-to-midsize companies are joint stock companies as defined in Article 37 of the Act on Special Measures Concerning Taxation, which fall under the category of specified new small-to-midsize companies as defined in Article 6 of the Small and Medium-sized

Table XIV-9.   Specified small and medium-sized companies and specified new small and medium-sized companies

Specified small and medium-sized companies	Specified new small and medium-sized companies
· Joint stock companies that fall under the category of specified new small and medium-sized business operators as stipulated in Article 6 of the Small and Medium-sized Enterprises Business Enhancement Act. · A domestic corporation of which 10 years have not passed since its incorporation (limited to a corporation that falls under the category of small and medium-sized business operator listed in each item of Article 2, paragraph 1 of the Small and Medium-sized Enterprise Act and meets other certain requirements). · Domestic corporations designated under Article 57-2, Paragraph 1 of the Okinawa Promotion Special Measures Law that have been designated under the same provisions during the period from April 1, 2014 to March 31, 2022.	· Joint stock companies that fall under the category of specified new small and medium-sized business operators as stipulated in Article 6 of the Small and Medium-sized Enterprises Business Enhancement Act. (limited to the companies incorporated within one year and satisfying certain other requirements). · A domestic joint stock company that was incorporated within five years (limited to a corporation that falls under the category of small and medium-sized business operator listed in each item of Article 2, paragraph 1 of the Small and Medium-sized Enterprise Act and meets other certain requirements). · Domestic corporations designated under Article 57-2, Paragraph 1 of the Okinawa Promotion Special Measures Law during the period from April 1, 2014 to March 31, 2022. · Joint stock companies stipulated in Article 27-5 of the National Strategic Special Zone Act. · Domestic joint stock companies stipulated in Article 16 of the Regional Revitalization Act that conduct business stipulated in the same Article.

Source: Compiled from the IRS website.

Enterprises Business Enhancement Act. Etc., and domestic corporations which were established less than 10 years ago (limited to those that meet prescribed requirements). On the other hand, specified new small-to-midsize companies are joint stock companies as defined in Article 41 of the Act on Special Measures Concerning Taxation, which fall under the category of specified new small-to-midsize companies as defined in Article 6 of the Small and Medium-sized Enterprises Business Enhancement Act. etc., (limited to those that meet prescribed requirements) and domestic corporations which were established within five years (limited to those that meet the prescribed requirements). This system was established by the amendment to the taxation system in 1997, and has been amended several times since then. The 2005 tax reform extended for another two years the special tax treatment reducing the rate on capital gains for shares of specified small-to-midsize companies (specified shares) to 50%.

The fiscal 2007 tax reform added another two years and liberalized the eli-

Table XIV-10. Structure of the Angel Taxation System
(for investments made on or after April 1, 2020)

The preferential tax treatment available for the year of investment in a venture company
(either (1) or (2) below can be selected).

(1) Deduction of (the amount invested in the target company $-$ ¥2,000) from gross income for the year. ※For companies established less than 5 years before. ※The maximum amount of investment eligible for the deduction is the lower of gross income × 40% or ¥10 million (¥8 million after January 1, 2021).
(2) The entire amount invested in the target company is deducted from the gain on transfer of shares for the year. ※For companies established less than 10 years before. ※No cap on deductible investment.

Preferential treatment available in the year in which unlisted venture company shares are sold
(in the event of a loss on sale).

(3) Not only can losses incurred from the sale of unlisted venture company shares be aggregated (offset) with other gains from the transfer of shares in the same year, but any losses not aggregated (offset) in a given year can be aggregated (offset) with gains from the transfer of shares successively over the following three years. ※Similarly, losses can be carried forward over the following three years if the venture company loses value due to bankruptcy, dissolution, etc., without being listed. ※If the investor received preferential treatment (1) or (2) in the year of investment in the venture company, the loss on sale is calculated by deducting the amount eligible for the deduction from the acquisition price.

Source: Compiled from the website of the Small and Medium Enterprise Agency.

gibility requirements for the special tax treatment and rationalized the approval process. This special tax treatment was abolished under the fiscal 2008 tax reform. However, at the same time, the government set up a contributions tax deduction system for investors that invest in specified start-up small-to-midsize firms. Furthermore, under the fiscal 2020 amendment to the taxation system, the scope of start-up companies eligible is expanded and the procedures are streamlined to encourage a wider range of investors to use the Angels Taxation System.

The outline of the Angels Taxation System as of 2021 is as follows. Investors that have acquired shares issued by a specified new small-to-midsize company (specified new shares) by direct investment may apply the donation deduction for up to ¥8 million of the amount invested in the said company (¥10 million prior to 2020) (investors may choose to apply either (1) or (2)) (2) investors that have acquired shares issued by a specified small and medium-sized company (specified shares) by direct investment may deduct the acquisition costs of shares of the specified small-to-midsize company from their capital gains in the same year; and (3) when investors suffer losses from the sale of the specified stocks up to a day before the listing date, or when they suffer losses from the dissolution and liquidation of issuers, these losses are deductible from gains on the sale of stocks in the same year. Unused deductible losses may be carried forward for three years starting with the following year. The special exception of (3) applies to specified shares acquired through direct investment on or after June 5, 1997.

8. NISA

Based on the fiscal 2013 tax reform, NISA was introduced in Japan in 2014. NISA is another word for a small amount investment tax-exemption scheme, the tax exemption measure on dividends and capital gains on small investments in listed stocks, etc., in tax-free accounts. NISA is modeled on the Individual Savings Account (ISA)—a preferential tax system for investments and savings introduced in the U.K. in 1999—and it was initially referred to

Table XIV-11. Comparison of General NISA and Dollar-Cost Averaging NISA (as of 2021)

	General NISA	Dollar-Cost Averaging NISA
Persons eligible to apply	Persons aged 20 or above	
Account opening	One account per person; select either General NISA or Dollar-Cost Averaging NISA	
Tax benefits	Investment profit is tax-free	
Tax-exempt period	Up to 5 years from the initial year of investment	Up to 20 years from the initial year of investment
Limit of usage (Tax-exempt line)	Up to ¥1.2 million a year	Up to ¥0.4 million a year
Tax-exempt products	Listed stocks, stock investment trusts, etc.	Investment trusts with a certain level of marketability suitable for long-term installment and diversified investment
Investment period	Until December 31, 2023	Until December 31, 2037
Netting of profit and loss	No netting of profit and loss with a specified account and general account	
Withdrawal restrictions	None	
Change of financial institution	Possible to change by year	
Others	Must provide My Number at the time of account opening	
	–	Method of purchase is limited to periodical purchase (e.g. once a month) of a certain amount (installment investment)

Source: Compiled based on the data available on the website of the Japan Securities Dealers Association (JSDA).

Table XIV-12. Outline of Junior NISA (as of 2021)

Tax-Exempt	Small amounts of dividends and capital gains on listed stocks in tax-free Junior NISA account
Eligible account openers (investors)	Residents under the age of 20 on January 1 of the year of account opening or born in the year
Maximum annual investment	¥800,000
Tax-exempt investment amounts	Maximum of ¥4 million
Account opening period	8 years from 2016 to 2023
Tax-exempt period	Maximum of 5 years
Investment management	Investments are made by agency or upon concurrence of a person with parental authority and, in principle, no withdrawal can be made until the account holder reaches the age of 18.

Source: Compiled based on various data issued by the National Tax Agency and the Ministry of Finance

as the Japanese-version ISA. The "N" in NISA stands for NIPPON (Japan). This system may also be referred to as the General NISA.

An outline of NISA as of 2019 is provided below. Dividends, coupons, and capital gains from listed stocks, etc. in the NISA account are tax-exempt. A NISA account may be opened by residents of Japan aged 20 years or older on January 1 of the year of the account opening. The amount of annual investment was initially set at a maximum of ¥1 million making the total tax-exemption investment amount ¥5 million (¥1 million × 5 years). However, starting in 2016, the annual investment amount was increased to a maximum of ¥1.2 million with the total tax-exemption investment amount coming in at ¥6 million. The NISA account may be maintained for 10 years from 2014 to 2023, with a maximum tax-exempt period of five years. Stocks, etc. may be freely sold during the period but the tax-exempt coverage of the sold portion cannot be reused. Although effective January 1, 2015, the rule was changed to allow switching of the financial institution on a yearly basis.

Furthermore, based on the fiscal 2015 tax reform, Junior NISA (a small amount investment tax-exemption scheme on dividends and capital gains on small investments in listed stocks, etc., in tax-free accounts of underaged persons) was introduced from 2016. Under the Junior NISA scheme as of 2019, the tax exemption treatment applies on dividends and capital gains on small investments in listed stocks, etc., in tax-free accounts opened by persons under the age of 20. The maximum annual investment amount is ¥800,000, making the maximum tax-exempt investment amount ¥4 million (¥800,000

×5 years). The account may be opened for eight years from 2016 to 2023 and the maximum tax-exempt period is set at five years. In principle, no withdrawal can be made until the account holder reaches the age of 18.

Furthermore, based on the fiscal 2017 tax reform, the Dollar-Cost Averaging NISA was launched in 2018. The primary characteristics of the product are: (1) investors can start by making contributions in small amounts to tax-exempt investment trusts; (2) investors can contribute up to ¥400,000 a year, with capital gains tax exempt for up to 20 years; (3) investors hold only one NISA account, either the general NISA or the Dollar-Cost Averaging NISA; and (4) the applicable investment trusts are expected to be appropriate for long-term installment and diversified investment aimed at stable asset formation as provided for under relevant laws and regulations.

The NISA system was revised and extended as part of the tax reforms in 2020, and a new system is due to start in 2024 (see Section 2).

9. Taxation of Nonresidents

The Income Tax Act of Japan divides individuals into residents and nonresidents. Residents are individuals who have a domicile in Japan or a temporary residence at which they have been living for one year or more. All individuals other than residents are deemed nonresidents. Of the residents, individuals who do not have Japanese citizenship and who have or have had a domicile in Japan or a temporary residence at which they lived for a total of no more than five years in the past 10 years are referred to as non-permanent residents. The entire income (worldwide income) of residents other than non-permanent residents is subject to income tax. For non-permanent residents, income other than foreign source income and foreign source income (limited to income earned in Japan or income remitted to Japan) is taxable. And for nonresidents, tax is imposed on their domestic source income only. The method of imposition of income tax for nonresidents, i.e. whether the comprehensive taxation applies or the separate withholding tax applies, varies depending on the type of domestic source income, whether the nonresident has a permanent establishment (PE) in Japan or not, and whether the domestic source income is traced to the PE. A permanent establishment (PE) refers to: (1) a branch PE (a place in Japan where a non-resident, etc. manages a business, a branch, office, factory, workshop, or other fixed location for business); (2) a construction PE (a long-term construction site, etc. in Japan for non-residents, etc.); (3) an agent PE (agents, etc. based in Japan on behalf of non-residents, etc. who meet certain requirements).

For example, looking at the taxation system for interest and dividends, of the domestic source income of a nonresident, etc., income attributable to a

Table XIV-13.   Outline of Matters Related to Taxation of Nonresidents, Etc.

Type of income \ Nonresident category	Nonresidents with a permanent establishment in Japan — Income attributable to permanent establishment	Other income sourced in Japan	Nonresidents without a permanent establishment in Japan	Withholding tax
(Business income)		[Tax-Exempt Income]		None
(1) Income arising from investment/holding of assets *Excluding those corresponding to (7) through (15) below	[Comprehensive taxation]	[Comprehensive taxation (partial)]		None
(2) Income arising from transfer of assets				None
(3) Distribution of business profit of partnership		[Tax-Exempt Income]		20.42%
(4) Proceeds from sales of land, etc.		[Separate withholding tax followed by comprehensive taxation]		10.21%
(5) Compensation for personal services	[Separate withholding tax followed by comprehensive taxation]			20.42%
(6) Rental income, etc., from real estate				20.42%
(7) Interest, etc.		[Separate withholding tax]		15.315%
(8) Dividends, etc.				20.42%
(9) Loan interest				20.42%
(10) Usage fees, etc.				20.42%
(11) Salary or other remuneration for personal services, public pension income, severance pay, etc.				20.42%
(12) Prize money from business advertising and promotion				20.42%
(13) Annuity income, etc., from life insurance contract				20.42%
(14) Interest payment from investment savings plan				15.315%
(15) Distribution of profit from anonymous partnership, etc.				20.42%
(16) Other income sourced in Japan	[Comprehensive taxation]	[Comprehensive taxation]		None

Notes: 1. Income attributable to permanent establishment may overlap with income sourced in Japan provided in (1) through (16) above.

2. Regarding income generated from by the transfer of assets in Table 2 above, apart from income corresponding to permanent facility-related income, only income listed under Article 281 Paragraph 1, Items 1 to 8 of the Enforcement Ordinance of the Income Tax Act is subject to tax.

3. Based on the provisions of the Act on Special Measures Concerning Taxation, certain income included in the income subject to comprehensive taxation in the above table may be applicable for separate taxation on the basis of self-assessment or separate withholding tax.

4. Based on the provisions of the Act on Special Measures Concerning Taxation, withholding tax rates relating to certain income among the withholding tax rates in the above table may be reduced or exempted in some cases.

Source: Complied from "Withholding Tax Basics," FY2021 edition, National Tax Agency of Japan.

permanent establishment of the nonresident, etc. (income attributable to PE) is subject to comprehensive taxation after withholding at the source, while income other than that corresponding to income attributable to PE is subject to a separate withholding tax. The withholding tax rate is 15.315% and 20.42%, respectively. The withholding tax rates applied to nonresidents and foreign corporations are finally determined in accordance with the tax treaties Japan has signed with the countries where nonresidents, etc. receiving the payments reside.

Japanese government bonds owned by nonresidents are tax exempt. In other words, interest on government bonds held by a nonresident without a permanent establishment in Japan in an account with a specified central custody and transfer agent or a qualified foreign intermediary is exempt from income tax if it meets certain conditions. In addition, while interest on book-entry government bonds may not be tax-exempt, the withholding tax rates applied to nonresidents and foreign corporations are relaxed in accordance with the tax treaties Japan has signed with the countries where nonresidents, etc. reside.

10. Tax Treatment of New Products

(1) New types of investment trusts

Profits received from a privately placed stock investment trust of the contractual type are, in principle, subject to a withholding tax and then are taxed comprehensively together with other incomes of the recipients of such profits. The tax credit for dividends is also applied, and when the recipient meets certain requirements, he is exempted from the requirement of filing an income tax return. Capital gains from selling beneficiary certificates of such investment trusts are subject to separate taxation on the basis of self-assessment. Profits received from an investment trust managing privately placed bonds are subject to a separate withholding tax, and capital gains, are currently subject to separate taxation on the basis of self-assessment. Tax rates related to open-ended investment trusts and closed-end (listed) investment trusts are the same as those applied to listed stocks. In other words, on dividends received from open-end investment trusts, a withholding tax of 20.315% is imposed before comprehensive taxation, separate taxation on the basis of self-assessment, or non-declaration. A credit for dividends is not applied when the comprehensive taxation is selected on dividends. Capital gains associated with open-ended corporation type investment trusts are subject to the separate taxation on the basis of self-assessment. On the other hand, dividends received from closed-end (unlisted) or privately placed investment trusts are subject to a withholding tax of 20.42% and then to com-

Table XIV-14.   Outline of Taxation Framework for New Investment Trusts

Classification			Profit distribution, etc.	Cancellation (redemption) gains		Capital gains
				Dividend (interest) Income portion	Deemed capital gains/losses portion	
Contractual type	Privately placed stock investment trusts		Comprehensive taxation (dividend income for general stocks, etc.)[1]		Separate taxation on the basis of self-assessment (capital gains on general stocks, etc., 20.315%)	
	Investment trusts managing privately placed asset-management trust bonds, etc.		Separate withholding tax (20.315%)		Separate taxation on the basis of self-assessment (capital gains on general stocks, etc., 20.315%)	
Corporation type	Publicly offered	Open-end type	Comprehensive taxation · Separate taxation on the basis of self · assessment (dividend income for general stocks, etc.)[2]		Separate taxation on the basis of self-assessment (capital gains on general stocks, etc., 20.315%)	
		Closed-end type (Listed)				
		(Unlisted)	Comprehensive taxation (dividend income for general stocks, etc.)[1]		Separate taxation on the basis of self-assessment (capital gains on general stocks, etc., 20.315%)	
	Privately placed					

Notes: 1. Withholding tax at 20.42% at time of receipt. Final income tax return is required except for small dividends.

      2. Withholding tax at 20.315% at time of receipt. Taxpayer may choose not to take any further action; neither comprehensive taxation, separate taxation on the basis of self-assessment nor final income tax return.

Source: Compiled based on the information available in "FY2019 Zeikin no Chishiki (knowledge on taxes)" by SMBC Nikko Securities Solution Planning Division; CHUOKEIZAI-SHA, INC.; pp125 and 132.

Table XIV-15.   Taxation on Stock Options

	At grant of stock options	At exercise of stock options	At the sale of stocks
Qualified stock options	–	–	Separate taxation on the basis of self-assessment on (selling price - exercise price) [Note]
Non-qualified stock options	–	Comprehensive taxation on (market value of stocks at exercise-exercise price)	Separate taxation on the basis of self-assessment on (selling price - market value of stocks at exercise) [Note]

Note: Taxed as income on the sale of stocks.

prehensive taxation. A taxation system is selected that does not require the declaration of such income when certain requirements are satisfied. A credit for dividends is not applied when the comprehensive taxation is selected on dividends. Capital gains associated with open-ended corporation type investment trusts are subject to the separate taxation on the basis of self-assessment. For REITs (real estate investment trusts), if listed would be closed-end, but dividends and capital gains from the sale of listed REITs are subject to the similar taxation as listed stocks. However, a credit for dividends is not applied when comprehensive taxation is selected on dividends.

(2) Stock options
The stock option system is a system under which a company grants its officers and employees the right to purchase its stocks at a certain price (exercise price) for a certain period (exercise period). The company then pays its officers and employees remunerations linked to any increase in its stock price. Stock option is classified into a qualified stock option and a non-qualified stock option, depending on whether it satisfies the requirements stipulated in the Act on Special Measures Concerning Taxation or not. The former is tax deductible on economic benefits gained from its exercise (the difference between the market price and the exercise price). When selling stocks acquired through rights exercise, separate taxation on the basis of self-assessment is applied on the difference between the selling price and the exercise price. For the latter non-qualified stock option, comprehensive taxation is imposed on economic benefits gained from its exercise. Separate taxation on the basis of self-assessment is imposed on the selling price of stocks issued on the exercise, deducting the market price of the stocks at the time of exercise, when the stocks are sold.

11. Tax Treatment of Pension-Type Products

A defined contribution pension plan (the Japanese version of the 401(k) plan) was introduced in October 2001. The defined contribution pension plan is a private pension plan whereby an employee participating in the plan gives instructions about investing his or her contributions, with the understanding that pension benefits may vary depending on the results of such investment. It is divided into the individual type (iDeCo), in which the individual himself makes contributions, and the corporate type, in which the company in principle makes contributions on behalf of its employees. In order to encourage the spread of pension products based on such a system and to enhance the efficiency of the management of such plans, it is essential to give a fixed tax incentive. And in devising such a taxation system, due care must be exercised

Chart XIV-3.   Defined contribution plan eligibility and contribution limits (through September 2022)

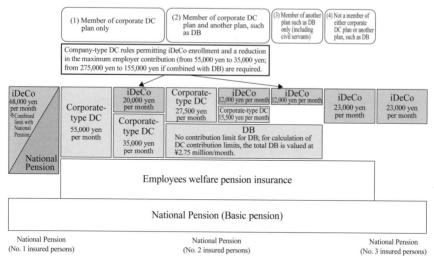

※1   If the corporate DC plan does not allow for matching contributions, the employee can make iDe-Co contributions up to a monthly amount of ¥20,000 (¥12,000 in combination with DB), provided that the plan rules (1) allow employees to join iDeCo and (2) set a maximum monthly employer contribution to the corporate DC of ¥35,000 (¥15,500 in combination with DB).

※2   Matching contributions are permitted for participants in a corporate DC plan if the plan allows for this, provided that the total amount of matching contributions does not exceed the employer contribution to the corporate DC plan and is within the contribution limit (¥55,000 yen per month (¥27,500 yen in the case of a combined DB and DC)).

※3   DB includes the Welfare Pension Fund; the Promotion and Mutual Aid Corporation for Private Schools of Japan System; and the Coal Miner Pension Fund.

Source: Ministry of Health, Labor and Welfare website.

in striking a suitable balance between the taxation system for such pension plans and that for other pension plans as well as in the transferability of pension assets when changing jobs. On May 29, 2020, a revised Defined Contribution Pension Plan Law will be enacted, relaxing the requirements for iDeCo membership for participants in company pension plans.

Tax measures for defined contribution plans are as follows.

(1) The employer's contribution is treated as an expense for the company. On the other hand, the employee's contribution is eligible for income deduction (small enterprise mutual relief deduction). In January 2012, so-called "matching contributions", allowing employees to make additional contributions in corporate pension plans, was introduced. In addition, the "iDeCo plus" payment system was introduced in May 2018 for iDeCo scheme mem-

Table XIV-16. Tax Treatment of Defined Contribution Pension Plans

Division		Outline
Contribution stage:		Counted as a loss of the employer
Portion borne by the employer		
Premiums paid by employee		Premiums to small-scale company mutual aid association are deducted as a loss (Note)
Management stage:		Special corporate income tax is applied (frozen until the end of Fiscal 2016)
Benefits payment stage:		
Old-age benefits	Pension	Miscellaneous income (deduction for public pensions is applied)
	Lump sum	Retirement income (deduction for retirement income is applied)
Disability benefits	Pension	Income and inhabitants' taxes are deductible
	Lump sum	
Lump-sum payment at the time of death		Taxed as an inheritance income
Lump-sum payment at the time of withdrawal		Occasional income

bers who work for small and medium-sized businesses.

(2) At the management stage: The balance of reserves for a pension plan of the individual type and that of the corporate type are subject to a special corporate tax of 1.173% (1% in national tax and 0.173% in local tax). However, this provision has been frozen until March 31, 2020.

(3) At the stage of benefit payment: (i) Old-age pension benefits: The beneficiary can receive pension benefits from the reserve in five or more annual installments or in a lump sum. When the beneficiary opts for benefits in installments, such benefits are deductible from taxable income. It has been noted that income deductibility for benefits such as public pensions is overly generous for high-income pensioners. The system came under review in the fiscal 2018 amendment to the taxation system. (ii) Benefits for persons with disabilities: When a beneficiary has disabilities of a certain level, the beneficiary can receive the payment of benefits from the month in which he or she is disabled, and the benefits are exempted from income tax and inhabitant tax. (iii) Death benefits: Death benefits paid in a lump sum to the survivors when the subscriber died are deemed as inherited property, and up to ¥5 million for each legal heir is exempted from inheritance tax. (iv) Withdrawal benefits: Benefits can be paid in a lump sum upon withdrawal from a pension plan if certain criteria are fulfilled and they are subject to income tax and inhabitant tax.

CHAPTER XV

Prohibited and Regulated Acts of Securities Trading

1. Outline

With a view to establishing a fair securities market and enhancing the market's credibility, the Financial Instruments and Exchange Act (FIEA) provides for various prohibited and regulated acts with respect to securities trading. In addition to prohibiting market manipulation (see Section 2) and regulating insider trading by persons associated with the companies concerned (see Section 3), it also imposes obligations on financial instruments business operators (securities companies) to maintain a trading surveillance system and a corporate information management system to prevent such unfair trading (see Section 4). In addition, the Financial Instruments and Exchange Act requires trade participants to disclose certain transaction-related information, such as the submission of reports of possession of large volume, to ensure the fairness of securities transactions (see section 5).

However, it is practically impossible to list in the Financial Instruments and Exchange Act all unfair trading in connection with securities transactions. In addition, as those securities transactions are complex and their structure changes rapidly, new methods that were unforeseeable at the time of legislation could emerge later. Faced with such issues, Article 157 of the Financial Instruments and Exchange Act bans unfair transactions in broad terms. More specifically, it prohibits the use of wrongful means, schemes, or techniques with regard to the sale, purchase, or other transaction of securities, etc. (Item (i) of the article); the acquisition of money or other property using a document or other indication which contains false indication on important matters or lacks indication about important matters necessary for avoiding misunderstanding with regard to the sale, purchase, or other transaction of securities, etc. (Item (ii)); and the use of false quotations in order to induce the sale, purchase, or other transaction of securities, etc. (Item (iii)) This article is considered to be a general provision that comprehensively prohibits wrongful acts, including new types of unfair trading yet to emerge.

In addition to the above, Article 158 of the FIEA prohibits the spreading of rumor, use of fraudulent means, assault, or intimidation for the purpose of

Table XV-1.   Main Provisions Relating to the Ban on Unfair Trading

	Contents	Article of the Financial Instruments and Exchange Act (FIEA)
General provisions	· Prohibition of wrongful acts	Art. 157
Market manipulation	· Prohibition of fake transactions or prearranged transactions	Art. 159, Para. 1
	· Prohibition of transactions aimed at manipulating securities prices	Art. 159, Para. 2, Item (i)
	· Prohibition of making an indication with the aim of manipulating securities prices	Art. 159, Para. 2, Items (ii) and (iii)
	· Prohibition, in principle, of stabilization transactions	Art. 159, Para. 3, and Arts. 20-26 of the Order for Enforcement of the Act
	· Prohibition of purchase for own account during the stabilization period	Art. 117, Para. 1, Item (xxii) of the Cabinet Office Order on Financial Instruments Business, etc.
	· Prohibition of spreading of rumors or use of fraudulent means, assault, or intimidation	Art. 158
	· Prohibition of securities companies from getting involved in an artificial formation of stock prices	Art. 117, Para. 1, Item (xx) of the Cabinet Office Order on Financial Instruments Business, etc.
	· Prevention of use of corporate share repurchase for manipulating stock prices	Art. 162, Para. 2
Insider trading	· Prohibition of insider trading	Arts. 166 and 167
	· Duty of officers to report securities transactions and the duty to restitute profits made in short-term trading	Arts. 163 and 164
	· Prohibition of short selling by officers	Art. 165
	· Prohibition of disclosure of information and inducement of insider trading	Art. 167-2
	· Prohibition of accepting orders that are suspected to be in violation of insider trading regulations	Art. 117, Para. 1, Item (xiii) of the Cabinet Office Order on Financial Instruments Business, etc.
False indication	· Prohibition of public notice, etc., of false quotations	Art. 168
	· Restriction on the expression of opinion in newspapers, etc., for consideration	Art. 169
	· Prohibition of indication of advantageous purchase, etc.	Art. 170
	· Prohibition of indication of a fixed amount of dividends, etc.	Art. 171
Tender offers	· Regulations on tender offers	Art. 27-2 through 27-22-4
	· Filing of Report of Possession of Large Volume	Art. 27-23 through 27-30
Others	· Prohibition of compensation of loss	Art. 39
	· Restriction on Transactions conducted for their own account and excessive transactions	Art. 161
	· Regulations on short selling	Art. 162
	· Prohibition of massive promotional campaign of particular securities	Art. 117, Para. 1, Item (xvii) of the Cabinet Office Order on Financial Instruments Business, etc.
	· Restriction on front-running	Art. 117, Para. 1, Item (x) of the Cabinet Office Order on Financial Instruments Business, etc.
	· Ban on deliberate market manipulation by means of trading securities for own account	Art. 117, Para. 1, Item (xix) of the Cabinet Office Order on Financial Instruments Business, etc.

carrying out the sale, purchase, or other transaction of securities, etc., or causing a fluctuation of quotations on securities, etc. Article 168 prohibits the publishing of false quotations on market prices of securities, etc. Restrictions on expression of opinions in newspapers, etc., in exchange for consideration are stipulated in Article 169, while Articles 170 and 171 prohibit indication of advantageous purchase, etc., and that of a fixed amount of dividends, etc., respectively.

2. Regulation of Market Manipulation

Market manipulation is an act of artificially influencing securities prices that would otherwise be determined by the securities market through natural supply and demand. With a view, therefore, to ensuring fair price formation in securities markets and protection of investors, the Financial Instruments and Exchange Act prohibits market manipulation and imposes heavy penalties for the violation thereof.

Acts of market manipulation are largely divided into the following five types: (1) fake transactions, (2) prearranged transactions, (3) price manipulation, (4) indication made for the purpose of market manipulation, and (5) stabilization transactions (Article 159).

A fake transaction is a securities transaction in which the same person places purchase and sale orders during the same time frame with no actual change in ownership occurring. With prearranged trades, similar transactions are carried out in collusion with different persons. In both cases, the intention is to mislead other investors into thinking trading in the security is very active; the requisite for being deemed a wash transaction is the existence of someone whose purpose is to mislead other investors regarding trading status. Price manipulation refers to an act of engaging in transactions that could possibly cause a fluctuation in securities prices for the purpose of misleading (inducing) other persons into believing that, despite intentional price manipulation, the prices are determined by natural supply and demand, and thus inducing them to purchase or sell the securities. (Supreme Court ruling on the Kyodo Shiryo case, July 20, 1994)

Stabilization transactions are transactions done for the purpose of pegging, fixing, or stabilizing the prices of specific securities. However, when primary offerings and secondary distributions are made, there is a concern that flooding the market with the securities could result in a large decline in the security price, making it difficult to float the issue. For that reason, stabilization transactions are only permitted with a primary offering or secondary distribution of securities pursuant to the provisions of a cabinet order.

The offense of market manipulation carries a punishment of imprisonment

Table XV-2. Provisions of the Financial Instruments and Exchange Act Relating to
Market Manipulation

Fake transactions	No person shall, for the purpose of misleading other persons about the state of securities transactions, conduct fake sale and purchase of securities without the purpose of transferring a right (Art. 159, Para. 1, Items (i) through (iii)).
Prearranged transactions	No person shall, for the purpose of misleading other persons about the state of securities transactions, conduct sale and purchase of securities at the same time and price, etc., based on collusion with another party (Art. 159, Para. 1, Items (iv) through (viii)).
Price manipulation	No person shall, for the purpose of inducing the sale and purchase of securities in securities markets, conduct sales and purchases of securities that would cause fluctuations in the prices of the securities (Art. 159, Para. 2, latter part of Item (i)).
Market manipulation by indication	No person shall, for the purpose of inducing the sale and purchase of securities in securities markets (1) spread a rumor to the effect that the prices of the securities would fluctuate by his/her own or other party's market manipulation (Art. 159, Para. 2, Item (ii)) or (2) intentionally make a false indication or an indication that would mislead other parties with regard to important matters when making a sale and purchase of securities (Art. 159, Para. 2, Item (iii)).
Stabilization transactions	No person shall conduct sales and purchases of securities in violation of a cabinet order for the purpose of pegging, fixing, or stabilizing the prices of the securities (Art. 159, Para. 3).

with work for not more than 10 years or a fine of not more than ¥10 million. In some cases, both penalties can be inflicted and the property gained through market manipulation confiscated and, if it cannot be confiscated, the value thereof shall be collected from the offender. If market manipulation is conducted by trading securities for the purpose of gaining property benefits (indirect financial benefits), the offense is subject to a punishment of imprisonment with work for not more than 10 years or a fine of not more than ¥30 million. The offense is also subject to an Administrative Surcharge Payment Order. Moreover, there are provisions on liability for compensation for damages claims for investors in violation of market manipulation regulations (Article 160 of the FIEA).

In the Cabinet Office Order on Financial Instruments Business, etc., securities companies are prohibited from accepting the entrustment of orders from customers with the knowledge or expectation that acceptance of the entrustment may lead to artificial market manipulation and are required to have in place trading surveillance systems for the prevention of such violations.

3. Prohibited and Regulated Acts of Corporate Insiders

Regulations concerning the acts of corporate insiders are largely classified into two categories: those prohibiting insider trading per se and those designed for its prevention.

Prohibition of Insider Trading

"Insider trading" refers to acts of effecting the sale, purchase, or other type of transaction of securities pertaining to any unpublished corporate information that may significantly influence the decision-making of investors by an insider of a listed company who has come to know the information through the performance of his/her duties or due to his/her position before such information is publicized (Article 166). If such transactions were to take place, the investing public would be put at a significant disadvantage and the credibility of the securities markets would be seriously undermined.

Japan's insider trading regulations were introduced with the amendment of the law in April 1989 in line with the modernization of the securities market. The framework has since been revised, with legislative changes put in place. In 2013, further amendments (1) expanded the scope of criminal charges and Administrative Surcharge Payment Orders to include disclosure of information and inducement of insider trading by a corporate insider and (2) expanded the scope of regulation to include REIT transactions.

On the other hand, in 2016, the Cabinet Office Ordinance on Restrictions on Securities Transactions, etc. was amended to expand the scope of exemptions from insider trading regulations pertaining to so-called prior knowledge contracts and plans.

Insider trading is punishable by imprisonment with work for not more than five years or a fine of not more than ¥5 million. In some cases, both penalties can be inflicted. For the case of a legal entity, the fine shall be not more than ¥500 million. Any property gained through insider trading shall be confiscated and any deficient amount collected from the offender. In addition, when receiving an Administrative Surcharge Payment Order, the offender must pay an amount equivalent to the profit made (half the profit in the case of disclosure of information and inducement of insider trading by a corporate insider) to the government treasury.

Preventing Insider Trading

Along with the prohibition of insider trading, the officers and principal shareholders of listed companies, etc., are required to officially report any transactions in the shares of the company concerned. They are required to return to the company any short-term trading profit they have made in the shares of

Table XV-3. An Outline of the Targetted People of Regulations, Material Facts, Methods of Announcement Relating to the Regulation of Insider Trading

Item	Outline
1. Targetted People of regulation (1) Persons associated with the company	(i) Directors of the listed company (directors, officers, agents, key employees) → information not announced to the public that came to their knowledge (ii) Persons who have the right to inspect the books and accounting records of the company (for example, those who hold 3% or more of the outstanding shares of the company) → Information not announced to the public that came to their knowledge in the course of the exercise of the right to inspect the books and accounting records of such company (iii) Persons who have the power vested in them by laws and regulations to inspect the books and accounting records of listed companies (for example, officials of the regulatory agencies) → Information not announced to the public that came to their knowledge in the course of the exercise of such power (iv) Persons who have concluded a contract with the listed company (for example, banks, securities companies, certified public accountants, lawyers, etc.) → Information not announced to the public that came to their knowledge in the course of negotiating, signing, and performing a contract. (v) In case any person referred to in (ii) or (iv) above is a corporation or director, etc., of such corporation → Information not announced to the public that came to such person's knowledge in the course of performing his/her official duty
(2) Recipients of information	(i) Persons who have received information concerning a material fact from persons associated with the company (ii) Directors of a corporation to which the person who has received information concerning a material fact from a person associated with the company belongs and who have learned of information not announced to the public in the course of the performance of their duty
2. Material facts (1) Matters decided	A decision made by a decision-making body of the listed company to carry out or not to carry out the matters set forth below: The issuance of new shares, a decrease in capital, the acquisition or disposal of its own shares, a stock split, a change in the amount of dividend, a merger with another company, transfer of business, dissolution of the company, commercial production of a newly developed product or commercial application of a new technology, an assignment or acquisition of fixed assets, etc.
(2) New facts	When any of the facts set forth below has occurred to the listed company: A loss caused by a disaster; a change in major shareholders; a development that could cause a delisting of its shares; lawsuits relating to a claim against the property right of the company; an administrative disciplinary action ordering the suspension of business, etc.; a change in the parent company; a petition for bankruptcy of the company; a failure by the company to honor its notes or bills falling due; suspension of business with its bank; or the discovery of natural resources, etc.
(3) Information on settlement of accounts	When newly announced results, projected or actual, are significantly at variance with those announced earlier: Sales (10% or more up or down); current profit (30% or more up or down, and its ratio to the total net assets is 5% or more up or down); net profit (30% or more up or down, and its ratio to the total net assets is 2.5% or more up or down)
(4) Others	Material facts, other than those listed in (1) − (3) above, relating to the management, business, or property of a listed company that have a profound influence on the investment decisions the investors make
(5) Material facts related to subsidiaries	(1) to (4) above apply
3. Methods of announcing information	When a company notifies the stock exchange on which its stock is listed of material facts and the material facts are placed on the website of the stock exchange that received the information for public inspection. When twelve hours must elapse after the company that has issued the stock in question has disclosed its material facts to two or more news media. When a company has notified the stock exchange on which its stock is listed, and the stock exchange has placed the securities report, etc. containing the information notified on its web site for public inspection.

Note: Any person who had been associated with any listed company and had learned of a material fact of such company as set forth above and who is no longer associated with such listed company is subject to these regulations for one year after that person dissolves association with the company.

the company held for a period of six months or less, and they are prohibited from selling the securities, etc., of the company in excess of the share certificates, etc., of the company that they hold.

Checks by securities companies on orders they receive and internal frameworks of listed companies (to manage and control corporate information and regulate employee trading of company shares) and posting information on J-IRISS play a critical role in preventing insider trading. J-IRSS stands for Japan-Insider Registration & Identification Support System, a searchable database where securities companies regularly register information on their customers and listed companies post information on their directors.

4. Regulations on the Conduct of Financial Instruments Business Operators (Securities Companies)

There are various regulations in place for securities companies (see figure on the right). This section focuses on regulations for ensuring the fairness of transactions.

Trading surveillance system

Securities companies are prohibited from accepting orders if they know there is a risk that such orders could cause a false market formation that will not reflect the actual market conditions or could be an insider trading. Securities companies are required to appropriately check transactions to prevent this. Specifically, they are required monitor all transactions including customers' and proprietary in a timely and accurate manner to identify any possible unfair transactions and examine those. In the event that any unfair transactions are found, securities companies must take appropriate measures (inquiries, alerts, suspension of transactions, etc.) regarding such transaction.

Corporate information management system

Through their underwriting and M&A-related advisory and other businesses, securities companies have access to undisclosed information that could influence the stock price, etc. of issuers (sensitive corporate information). To prevent unfair trading based on such information, securities companies are required to establish appropriate systems. Specifically, securities companies can set up an information barrier between the investment banking and similar divisions and the rest of their operating divisions. In addition, personnel are forbidden to use sensitive corporate information to solicit customers or to engage in trading.

Chart XV-1.   Major Prohibited and Regulated Acts of Securities Companies (Duties and Prohibited Acts)

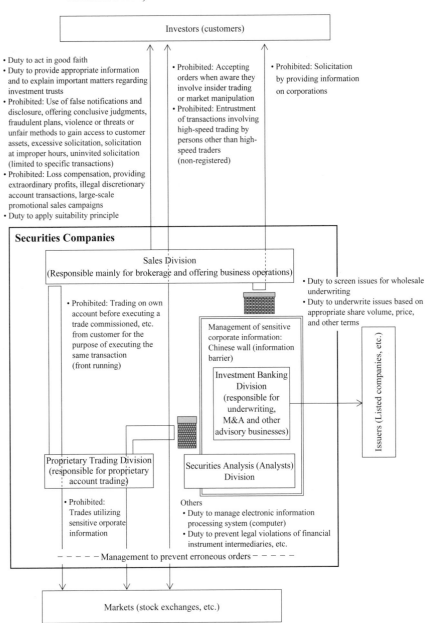

Management system to prevent erroneous orders

Securities companies are required to establish appropriate order management systems to prevent erroneous orders (name of issue, number of shares, share prices, etc.).

Management system for high frequency trading

In April 2018, the Financial Instruments and Exchange Act was amended to introduce a registration system for those who engage in high frequency trading of stocks, etc. Securities companies are prohibited from accepting orders for transactions related to high frequency trading from those who are not registered with the Prime Minister. In addition, as well as securities companies, all those who engage in high frequency trading activities are subject to regulations requrding proper management of computer systems.

Besides the previously mentioned areas, Article 117, Paragraph 1 and Article 123, Paragraph 1 of the Cabinet Office Order on Financial Instruments Business, etc. and the self-regulation rules of the Japan Securities Dealers Association and each Financial Instruments Exchange, etc., set out various strongly advised or required management systems for securities companies.

5. Other Regulated Acts—Information Disclosure to Ensure Fairness of Transactions

A tender offer or takeover bid (TOB) is a type of corporate action in which an acquiring company publicly announces its offer to buy a certain number of share certificates, etc. of a target company at a certain price in a certain period of time in an aim primarily to gain control of the target company. Since such an offer involves purchasing share certificates, etc. from an unspecified number of investors off the exchange, the bidder is expected to disclose information by which investors can judge whether or not to sell the respective shares and deal with shareholders in a fair and rightful manner. Additionally, as it is likely that control over the target company may be transferred as a result of the takeover bid, disclosure of information on the buyer is also required. Given such factors, takeover bidders are required to: (1) publish the purpose of TOB, purchase price, number of shares to be purchased, purchase period, etc.; (2) submit the Tender Offer Notification; (3) issue the Tender Offer Statement, a document explaining the TOB, to applying shareholders; and (4) report the results of the TOB after the completion of the purchase period. In order to prevent the use of TOB for market manipulation or abuse, cancellation of TOB is prohibited as a general rule, and certain restrictions apply for making changes to the terms of purchase. Meanwhile, information on the views of the target company regarding the TOB is

Table XV-4.   Flow of Tender Offer

(1) Begin offer
 · Publicly announce the start of tender offer (TOB) (publish the purpose of TOB, purchase price, number of shares to be purchased, purchase period, etc. in a daily newspaper).
 · On the date of the public notification, file the Tender Offer Notification addressed to the Prime Minister and send copies thereof to the target company of TOB, stock exchanges, and parties that have submitted the Tender Offer Notification regarding the company.
(2) Purchase period (as a general rule, a period of 20 days or more and up to 60 days)
 · Issue the Tender Offer Statement to parties intending to sell or offer stock certificates, etc.
 · Terms of TOB purchase price are consistent; decrease of purchase price and reduction of purchase period are not allowed as a general rule.
 · Withdrawal of application for purchase and cancellation of contract are not allowed as a general rule. Obligation to purchase all shares if the allotment ratio of stock certificates, etc. after the TOB exceeds two-thirds
 · The party intending to sell or offer may cancel the contract at any time
 · The target company submits its Position Statement addressed to the Prime Minister and sends copies thereof to the takeover bidder and the stock exchange.
 · The party intending to execute a TOB is prohibited, as a general rule, from purchasing the respective shares, etc. through a method other than TOB
(3) Completion of purchase
 · Issue a public notice or disclosure regarding the number of stock certificates, etc. associated with the TOB and submit the Tender Offer Report to the Prime Minister.
 · Send the notice containing the number of stock certificates, etc. for TOB to applying shareholders.
 · Settle purchases without delay.

Table XV-5.   Flow of Disclosure of Possession of Large Volume of Shares

(1) Obligation to submit the Report of Possession of Large Volume arises
 · A shareholder or joint shareholder submits, if its holding ratio of share certificates, etc. exceeds 5% of the total number of issued shares, the Report of Possession of Large Volume (containing shareholder or joint shareholder's name and address, business description, matters concerning the holding ratio of share certificates, purpose of holding, matters concerning purchase funds, etc.) to the Prime Minister within five business days from the occurrence of the obligation, and sends copies of the Report to the stock exchange and the issuing company.
 · In the case of an institutional investor, etc., if its holding ratio of share certificates does not exceed 10% of the total number of issued shares, the Report of Possession of Large Volume may be submitted within five business days from the record date on which the obligation arises (twice or more a month) (Special Reporting System).
(2) Subsequent reporting obligation
 · After a Large Volume Holder submits the Report of Possession of Large Volume, if its holding ratio of share certificates, etc. increases or decreases by 1% or more, it submits the Change Report addressed to the Prime Minister within five days, as a general rule, from the date of the aforesaid increase or decrease, and sends copies of the Change Report to the stock exchange and the issuing company.
 · The party that has submitted the Report of Possession of Large Volume or the Change Report of Possession of Large Volume submits the Correction Report to the Prime Minister if any deficiency was found with the content of the report initially submitted.
(3) Public inspection of reports
 · The Prime Minister and stock exchanges disclose the reports for public inspection for a period of five years.

Note: Effective from April 2007, the reports are required to be submitted via EDINET.

extremely important for shareholders in judging whether or not to accept the tender offer. For this reason, the target company of a TOB must immediately submit its Position Statement addressed to the Prime Minister.

While the act of purchasing a large amount of share certificates, etc. in itself does not immediately cause a problem, it can, in many cases, cause fluctuations in stock prices or influence the controlling interests of the company concerned and may lead to inflicting damage on general investors. In consideration of such possibilities, any person or entity, if it becomes a holder of more than 5% of the shares or other equity securities of a listed company, etc., is required to file a Report of Possession of Large Volume to the Prime Minister. In addition, such a person or entity, after having become a Substantial Shareholder, is required to file a Change Report Pertaining to Report of Possession of Large Volume addressed to the Prime Minister if its shareholding ratio in the entity covered by the aforesaid Report increases or decreases by 1% or more or there is a material change to any other entry in the Report. The Reports of Possession of Large Volume and Change Reports are publicly disclosed. This system was put in place with the aim of further protecting investors by encouraging timely and accurate disclosure of information on large-scale purchases and on holding and secondary offering of shares, etc. to investors and promoting high fairness and transparency in the securities market.

CHAPTER XVI

The Information Disclosure System and Investor Protection

1. The Information Disclosure System in the Securities Market

When a company lists its security on the financial instrument market opened on a stock exchange, the issuer of such security is required by the Financial Instruments and Exchange Act and by the rules of the stock exchanges to disclose information concerning certain matters of its business. Such rules are called disclosure requirements, and they consist of statutory disclosure rules under the Financial Instruments and Exchange Act and the timely disclosure required by the securities exchanges.

There are four types of statutory disclosures that the issuers of securities are required to make: (1) issuance disclosure, which requires companies to disclose information concerning certain matters when they publicly offer securities on the primary market; (2) periodic disclosure, which requires companies whose securities are listed and traded on the securities market to disclose information concerning certain matters on a continuing and regular basis; (3) tender offer disclosure; and (4) large volume holding disclosure (shareholdings of 5% or more). Timely disclosure, which is required by the stock exchanges, obliges companies to continuously disclose their information after listing their securities on the exchanges, and the type of information required is classified by the target of disclosure into (1) information on listed companies; (2) information on subsidiaries, etc.; and (3) other information, such as supplemental information on majority shareholders, etc. Information is categorized by the nature as (1) facts decided, (2) facts occurred, and (3) information on financial results. At present, both statutory and timely disclosures are made via an electronic disclosure system using the Internet. Statutory disclosure is made via the EDINET (Electronic Disclosure of Investors' NETwork) while timely disclosure is made using the TDnet (Timely Disclosure network).

Companies that are required to make issuance disclosure and periodic disclosure are also required by the Companies Act to disclose certain information. The disclosure of accounting documents required to be made by the

Chart XVI-1.   The Scheme of the Disclosure System on the Securities Market

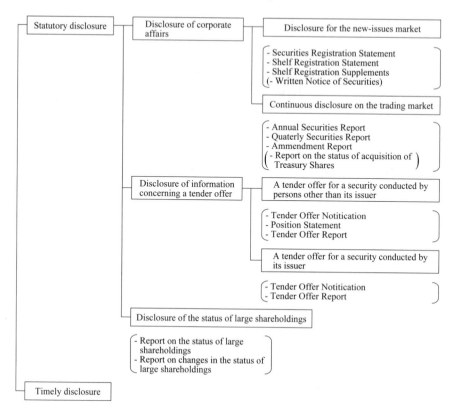

Table XVI-1. Disclosure Systems under the Companies Act and under the Financial Instruments and Exchange Act

Disclosure System under the Financial Instruments and Exchange Act		Disclosure System under the Companies Act
Furnishing information necessary for investors to make an investment judgment	Purpose of disclosure	Report on profits available for dividends and the company's capacity for offering security for loans (solvency)
Investors (including those who are not shareholders of the company at a given time)	Targets for which the disclosure is intended	Shareholders and creditors
Providing disclosure through EDINET and stock exchanges, replying to investor requests for disclosure	Method of disclosure	making of financial documents, keeping of such documents at the head office, and publication of a summary of annual settlement of accounts

Companies Act is aimed at protecting the interest of creditors and at regulating the amount that can be paid in dividends. In contrast, the disclosure required to be made under the Financial Instruments and Exchange Act and under exchanges' regulations is designed to disclose information concerning the state of business of listed companies to help the investors to make informed and reasonable investment decisions.

2. Disclosure of Corporate Affairs under the Financial Instruments and Exchange Act

Issuance Disclosure

When a company publicly offers, or makes a secondary distribution of, securities whose aggregate value is ¥100 million or more, the issuer of such securities must, in principle, file a securities registration statement with the Prime Minister. Information at issuance is disclosed through the securities registration statement. This shall describe (1) matters pertaining to said offering or secondary distribution, and (2) information relating to the issuing company (equivalent information as described in the Securities Report below). In addition, when a securities company solicits investors for the purchase of newly issued securities, it is required to provide investors with a prospectus that furnishes them with information concerning the issue that is deemed necessary for them to assess its value and to make an informed investment decision.

Periodic Disclosure

Issuers of securities listed on stock exchanges must file with the Prime Minister an annual securities report for each business year within three months after the expiration of such business year. The annual securities report constitutes the main document of statutory disclosure for the secondary market. More specifically, it must provide (1) key information on the issuer (such as trends in key management indicators and history), (2) situation of issuer's business (including management policy, business environment, issues to be addressed, business risks, etc., (3) information on the operational status of the issuer (details of shares issued, corporate governance, etc.), and (4) the financial position of the issuer. In addition, companies that are subject to continuous disclosure requirements must file quarterly reports within 45 days of the end of each quarter, and, if necessary, extraordinary reports and reports on their share repurchases.

Issuers in the financial instruments market are expected to make full disclosure of all information necessary for investment decisions to ensure that fair prices are formed for their securities. If they do not disclose information that is to their disadvantage, the prices of their securities will be formed on

Table XVI-2.   Statutory Disclosure Documents Required to be Filed

Classification	Documents filed	Cases requiring the filing of documents (a summary)
Disclosure of corporate affairs, etc. — Issuance Disclosure	Securities Registration Statement	If a company issuing new shares or making a secondary distribution of shares through an offering whose total issuing or secondary distribution price is ¥100 million or more plans to solicit 50 or more investors for the purchase of its new shares or plans to sell to or solicit 50 or more investors for the secondary distribution on uniform terms and conditions, it must file a registration statement. * Small amount offering: In the case of a company issuing new shares or making secondary distribution of shares through an offering whose total issuing or secondary distribution price is less than ¥500 million the contents of the securities registration statement required to be filed by such company are simplified. * Incorporating system: A company that has been filing Annual Securities Reports continuously for one year may substitute the information therein and in the quarterly securities reports other than matters relating to the offering or secondary distribution of securities for securities registration statement securities report and quarterly securities reports filed in its place. * Reference system: When transactions of issued securities fulfill certain requirements of the securities market with which the issuer has been filing Annual Securities Reports for a year and the issuer's corporate information has broadly been disclosed, the description that one should refer to the last Annual Securities Reports, etc., may be substituted for a securities registration statement concerning matters other than the offering or secondary distribution of securities.
	Shelf Registration Statement	When any issuer who is authorized to file a securities registration statement under the reference system plans to issue new shares or make a secondary distribution of shares through an offering whose total issuing or secondary distribution prices are ¥100 million or more, such issuer may in advance file a shelf-registration statement of its shares.
	Shelf Registration Supplement	When a shelf-registration statement of a security is in effect, and when the issuer of such security plans to issue new shares or make a secondary distribution of shares whose total issuing or secondary distribution prices are ¥100 million or more, such issuer is required to file supplementary documents relating thereto.
Periodic disclosure	Annual Securities Report	Any of (1) the issuer of securities listed on a stock exchange; (2) the issuer of securities stipulated by cabinet order as that similar to distribution conditions in (1); (3) the issuer of securities who is required to file a securities registration statement when it issues new shares or makes a secondary distribution of shares through an offering; or (4) the issuer of securities the number of whose owners was 1,000 or more at the end of any of the latest five years (excluding certain cases), is required to file a securities report.
	Quarterly Securities Report	Of the companies required to submit Annual Securities Reports, the issuers of securities listed on stock exchanges or stipulated by cabinet order as being similar in terms of distribution conditions must file quarterly securities reports.
	Extraordinary Report	If any material fact has occurred in a company submitting Annual Securities Reports.
	Share Buyback Report	Any issuer of a security listed on a stock exchange or stipulated by cabinet order as being similar in terms of distribution conditions and that has passed a resolution at a general meeting of its shareholders or at a board of directors' meeting to acquire its own shares must file this report.

the basis of an erroneous assessment of their value that does not reflect such withheld information. This is why the law requires the issuers of securities to periodically disclose all pertinent information, good or bad, in their annual securities reports, and why it contains penal provisions to discipline issuers who file an annual securities report containing false statements.

3. Other Disclosures to Be Made under the Financial Instruments and Exchange Act

Disclosure Relating to a Tender Offer

The act of soliciting an unspecified large number of persons through a public notice for an offer to purchase or to sell shares and of purchasing such shares off the exchange is called a "tender offer." If any person other than the issuer who is required to file an annual securities report proposes the purchase of such shares outside the market of a stock exchange, and in cases that fall within the purview of certain requirements, such as the purchase will result in the ownership of more than 5% of the securities, etc., the person must purchase such shares through a tender offer. The tender offeror is obligated to serve a public notice of (1) the purpose of the tender offer; (2) the purchase prices, etc.; (3) the number of shares to be purchased; (4) the period during which shares will be purchased; and (5) other items stipulated in other cabinet ordinances ("public notice for commencing tender offer") and must also file the tender offer notification with the Prime Minister. In addition, the tender offeror must, on the day immediately following the day on which the tender offer period has expired, serve a public notice or make an announcement indicating the number of shares offered to sell, the number of shares it has actually purchased, and the method of settlement and file with the Prime Minister a tender offer report furnishing information about such matters.

The regulation on tender offers is designed to disclose information for investors in advance and give shareholders equal opportunities to sell their stocks from the standpoint of ensuring the transparency and fairness of off-exchange trading when the transactions would have effects on the control of the target corporation.

Disclosure of Status of Large Volume Holding of Share Certificates, etc.

When the number of shares of a listed company held by a person exceeds 5% of its outstanding shares (large-volume holders), such person is required to file a Report of Possession of Large Volume with the Prime Minister within five days (excluding Sundays and other holidays as may be stipulated in cabinet orders) from the date when such person's holding rate is above 5% (called the "5% rule"). The Report of Possession of Large Volume must fur-

Table XVI-3.   Transitions in Tender Offer Bid (TOB) System

	Major Developments
1971	• Public tender offer system introduced
1990	• Principles set down for forcing tender offers • Percentage share offer that triggers obligation to make tender offer decreased (from 10% to 5%) • Prior notification system abolished • Duration of offer extended • Shareholders' withdrawal rights expanded
2001	• Along with the deregulation, in principle, of purchasing treasury shares, system for making tender offers for a company's own shares introduced
2003	• Scope of acquisitions exempt from the TOB system enlarged
2004	• TOBs restricted to companies with equity securities • Electronic notification system introduced
2005	• ToSTNeT transactions made independent of market transactions
2006	• Disclosure for TOBs upgraded (purpose of acquisition, basis of price calculation, disclosure for MBOs) • Regulations implemented concerning the combined acquisition of shares on and offmarket • Obligating a third party posessing a large stake in a company to make a TOB, if the party increases its posession during the TOB period • Acceptance for lowering TOB price when share split occurs • Reasons for withdrawing TOB expanded • Obligating targeted company to submit a Position Statement • Obligating the offeror to answer targeted company's questions (reply to submitted questions) for the purpose of submitting a Position Statement • Calculation of duration of TOB set using business days • Targeted company allowed to demand extension of TOB period • Obligating the offeror to acquire all tendered shares
2008	• Specified listed securities added to securities eligible for TOBs • Monetary surcharge system introduced regarding TOB rules

nish information concerning (1) matters relating to the ratio of shares held by such person, (2) matters relating to the funds acquired by such person for the purpose of purchasing such shares; and (3) the purpose for which such person has acquired such shares. And when the percentage of shareholdings of such person who must submit the report increases or decreases by 1% or more, such person must file a Change Report indicating the change that occurred in the percentage of such person's holdings of such shares. This disclosure is required because the actions of a single person holding a large volume of shares can have large effects on the formation of stock prices at the market.

4. Timely Disclosure System of Financial Instruments Exchanges (Stock Exchanges)

As described at the start of this chapter, stock exchanges require listed companies to disclose corporate information by their rules. For example, the Tokyo Stock Exchange stipulates in its Listing Rules that listed companies shall, in a timely manner, disclose information having effects on investors' decisions and defines concrete matters to be disclosed and procedures for disclosing such matters (see Table XVI-4). Listed companies need to disclose both the resolutions and decisions adopted by their executive body promptly after such resolutions or decisions were adopted and any incidents caused by external factors at the time the companies had learned of such incidents.

Promptness is a feature of timely disclosure. For example, stock exchanges require listed companies to disclose their financial results immediately after their determination. In response, the listed companies disclose earnings reports (*kessan tanshin*) according to the given format. The earnings report carries more importance in terms of helping investors to learn about financial results because it is released earlier than the annual securities report.

In addition, listed companies are obliged to provide stock exchanges with concise information on inquiries from the stock exchanges immediately if required and to disclose the details of information immediately when the stock exchanges deem it necessary and proper. For example, in the case where there is a broadcast or rumor regarding corporate information but the accuracy of such information is unconfirmed, the stock exchange concerned may make a query to the company about the accuracy of information and require the company to disclose the response to such query.

The Tokyo Stock Exchange has put in place a system for issuing alerts where if the TSE identifies any unclear piece of information among the information about a listed company that can have a material impact on investment decisions of investors and the listed company requires time before offering proper information disclosure regarding the aforesaid unclear piece of information or can disclose only certain information immediately, the TSE issues an alert to investors.

5. Ensuring the Appropriateness of Information Disclosure

In order to ensure the effectiveness of the Listing Rules, including the rules on timely disclosure, stock exchanges may implement prescribed measures against violations found, such as when the disclosed information contains false statements or when there is a violation of matters to be observed under

Table XVI-4.   Main Points of Corporate Information Required by Timely Disclosure (in the case of the Tokyo Stock Exchange)

1. Decisions by Listed Companies	1. Offering of new shares to be issued, treasury shares to be disposed of, issued subscription Rights/warrants, or offering to entities who will subscribe to treasury subscription rights/warrants to be disposed of, or a secondary distribution of shares or subscription rights/warrants 2. Shelf-registration and the commencement of a demand survey 3. Decrease in amount of capital 4. Decrease in amount of capital reserve or profit reserve 5. Acquisition of one's own stock 6. Gratis allotment of shares or gratis allotment of subscription warrants 7. Shelf-registration concerning gratis allotment of subscription rights/warrants or commencement of a demand survey or a survey on intention to exercise the warrants 8. Share split or reverse share split 9. Dividend from surplus 10. Organizational restructuring such as mergers, etc. 11. Takeover bid or take over bid for own shares 12. Announcement of opinions about a takeover bid, etc. 13. Transfer or acquisition of all or part of a business 14. Dissolution (excluding dissolution by means of merger) 15. Commercialization of a new product or new technology 16. Business alliance or dissolution of business alliance 17. Transfer or acquisition of shares or equity interest accompanied by a change in a subsidiary or other matters accompanied by a change in a subsidiary 18. Transfer or acquisition of fixed assets, lease of fixed assets 19. Suspension or abolishment of all or part of a business 20. Application for delisting 21. Petition for commencement of bankruptcy, commencement of rehabilitation proceedings, or commencement of reorganization proceedings 22. Commencement of a new business 23. Change in representative directors or representative executive officers 24. Rationalization such as personnel reduction 25. Change in a trade name or a corporate name 26. Change in the number of shares for a share unit of a stock, or abolition/introduction of provisions for the number of shares for a share unit 27. Change in accounting period (change in the end date of the business year) 28. Petition to the Prime Minister stating an excess of liabilities or possibility of the halt of repayment of deposit, etc. (petition under the provisions of Article 74, Paragraph 5 of the Deposit Insurance Act) 29. Petition for mediation in accordance with specified mediation procedures pursuant to the Act on Specified Mediation for Promoting Adjustment of Specified Liabilities, etc. 30. Early redemption of listed bonds, etc., the convocation of bondholders' meetings, or other important matters relating to rights relating to listed bonds, etc. 31. Change in certified public accountants, etc. 32. Putting notes on matters related to the going concern assumption 33. Submission of application for approval of deadline extension for submission of annual securities report or quarterly securities report 34. Cancellation of entrustment of shareholding services to a shareholding service proxy institution 35. Submission of internal control reports containing content to the effect that there is a material deficiency or that the evaluation result cannot be stated 36. Amendment to the articles of incorporation 37. Acquisition of all classified stocks subject to whole acquisition clause 38. Approval or rejection of a special controlling shareholder's request for sale of shares, etc. 39. Other important matters related to listed company operations, business, assets, or listed company stock certificates, etc.
2. Facts which Occurred for a Listed Company	1. Damage arising from a disaster or in the performance of its operations 2. Change in major shareholders or the largest shareholder 3. Fact which causes delisting 4. Filing of a lawsuit or a court decision 5. Petition for a provisional disposition or decision on such petition, etc. 6. Cancellation of a license, suspension of a business or any other disciplinary action corresponding to these on the basis of laws and regulations by an administrative agency or accusation of violation of laws and regulations by an administrative agency 7. Change in a parent company, change in controlling shareholders (excluding a parent company) or change in other related company 8. Petition or notification for commencement of bankruptcy proceedings, commencement of rehabilitation proceedings, commencement of reorganization proceedings, or execution of enterprise mortgage 9. Dishonor of a bill or check or suspension of trading by a clearing house 10. Petition for commencement of bankruptcy proceedings, commencement of rehabilitation proceedings, commencement of reorganization proceedings, or execution of enterprise mortgage pertaining to a parent company, etc. 11. Default on obligations or delay in collection 12. Suspension of trade with a business partner 13. Financial support, such as exemption of obligations 14. Discovery of natural resources 15. Special controlling shareholder's request for sale of shares, etc. 16. Claim for suspension of issue of stock or subscription rights/warrants 17. Demand for convocation of a general shareholders meeting 18. Unrealized loss of securities held 19. Acceleration of obligations pertaining to a corporate bond 20. Convocation of a bondholders' meeting for a listed bond, etc. and other important facts pertaining to rights of a listed bond, etc. 21. Change in certified public accountants, etc. 22. Delay in submission of annual securities report or the quarterly securities report 23. Approval, etc. of deadline extension for submission of the annual securities report or quarterly securities report 24. The fact that an audit report attached to financial statements, etc. contains an "adverse opinion", "opinions are not expressed", or a "qualified opinion" with making issues concerning a going concern assumption as exceptions 25. An internal control audit report contains an "adverse opinion" or the fact that "opinions are not expressed" 26. Receipt, etc. of a notice of canceling a shareholder services agent agreement 27. Other important matters related to operation, business or assets of such listed company or related to a listed stock certificates, etc.
3. Listed Company Earnings Information	1. Earnings reports (kessan tanshin), quarterly earnings reports (shihanki kessan tanshin) 2. Amendments to performance estimates, differences in estimates and earnings values 3. Amendments to dividend estimates, etc.

Note: In addition to the above, listed companies are required to disclose important decisions and new developments related to subsidiaries and other matters relating to controlling shareholders, etc.

Source: Tokyo Stock Exchange, *Securities Listing Requirements, Guidebook for the Timely Disclosure of Corporate Information.*

Table XVI-5. Measures to ensure effectiveness

○ Penalty measures • Public Announcement Measure • Penalty on breach of the listing agreement	○ Improvement measures • Improvement Report, Improvement Status Report • Designation as Security on Alert

Chart XVI-2. Flow from Designation as Security on Alert to Removal of Designation

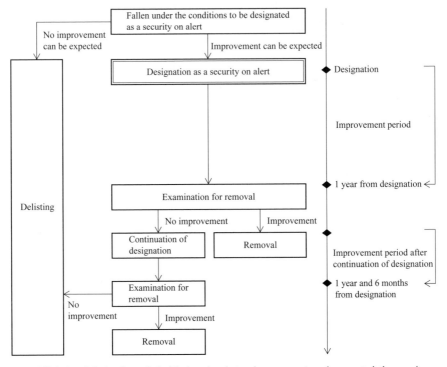

Note: If it is found during the period of designation that no improvement can be expected, the security shall be delisted.

the Code of Corporate Conduct. These measures to ensure the effectiveness are classified into two categories: improvement measures and penalties. The former requires the listed company concerned to make improvements while the latter imposes a penalty on the listed company.

Improvement measures are categorized into the designation as a security on alert and the submission of Improvement Report/Improvement Status Report. For example, if a listed company has made a false statement in its securities report, etc. and a stock exchange recognizes that there is a strong need for the listed company to make improvements to the company's internal management system, etc., the listed company is designated as a "security on alert." The designation as a security on alert is removed if the listed company makes improvements to its internal management system, etc. within the prescribed period for improvement. If, however, no improvement is made within the prescribed period or there is no likelihood of improvement, the company will be delisted. The securities on alert system is a mechanism for having the listed companies concerned make proper improvements while removing the possibility of delisting in the future, and has been introduced as a measure equivalent to delisting. If it is found that there is difficulty in maintaining order on the market unless a stock is immediately delisted, such stock is delisted without receiving the designation as a security on alert.

Meanwhile, if a stock exchange finds that there is a strong need for a listed company to make improvements even when the status of the listed company does not correspond to giving designation as a security on alert, which is a measure leading to possible delisting, the stock exchange may require the listed company to submit an Improvement Report containing the circumstances behind the misconduct and improvement measures. The listed company that has submitted the Improvement Report must submit an Improvement Status Report containing the status of implementation and operation of improvement measures in a timely way after six months have passed since the submission of the initial Improvement Report. The Improvement Report and the Improvement Status Report submitted by the listed company concerned are made available for public inspection on the website of the stock exchange.

Meanwhile, penalties are categorized into a penalty (a fine) against a breach of listing contract and a disclosure measure. Depending on the degree of damage given to the trust that shareholders and investors place in the market, a judgment will be made on whether to apply the penalty (a fine) against a breach of contract, which is the more serious treatment.

6. Recent Moves of Information Disclosure

Movement toward Introduction of International Financial Reporting Standards (IFRS)

International Financial Reporting Standards (IFRS) are accounting standards developed by the International Accounting Standards Board (IASB). In recent years, the adoption of IFRS has been on the increase around the world. In Japan, listing companies have been allowed to voluntarily adopt IFRS since 2010. In addition, given the recommendations proposed by the govern-

Chart XVI-3. Number of Companies Adopting IFRS on the TSE

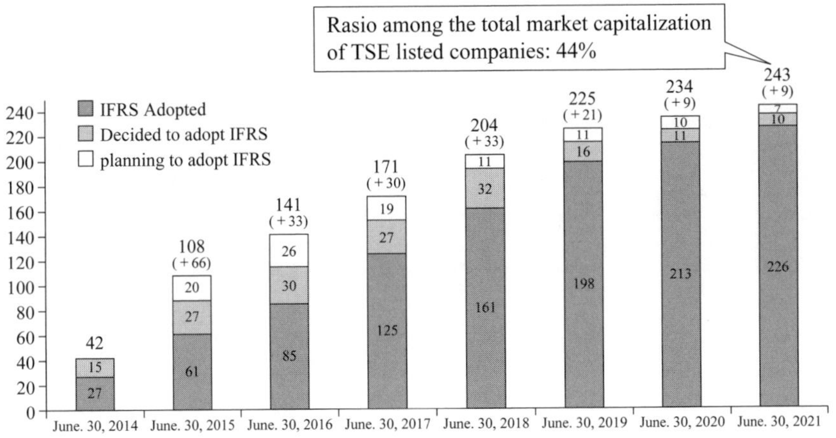

Rasio among the total market capitalization of TSE listed companies: 44%

Source: Tokyo Stock Exchange, Analysis of Disclosure of Basic Approach to Adoption of Accounting Standards (September 2021).

Table XVI-5. English disclosure implementation status by market (by number of companies)

Market segment	Market capitalization (trillion yen)	Number of companies	Timely Disclosure Materials			Notice of Convocation of General Meeting of Shareholders	IR Presentation Materials	CG Reports	Annual Securities Report
			Financial Statements	Other					
First Section	666.7	2,186	28.0%	55.5%	29.1%	50.3%	46.0%	16.7%	8.6%
Second Section	6.8	475	1.3%	7.2%	1.5%	4.4%	2.9%	0.8%	0.6%
Mothers	9.5	346	7.2%	16.8%	8.1%	6.4%	16.5%	2.9%	1.4%
JASDAQ Standard	10.1	667	1.6%	8.5%	1.6%	1.3%	4.0%	0.1%	0.1%
JASDAQ Growth	0.3	37	8.1%	16.2%	8.1%	2.7%	5.4%	0.0%	2.7%
All Markets	693.5	3,711	17.7%	36.9%	18.5%	31.1%	29.8%	10.2%	5.3%

Source: Tokyo Stock Exchange, Summary Report of the English Disclosure Implementation Status Survey (December 31, 2020).

Chart XVI-4.   Questionnaire Survey on English Disclosure to Foreign Investors

(1) Assessment of English disclosure   (2) Investment materials
   of listed companies

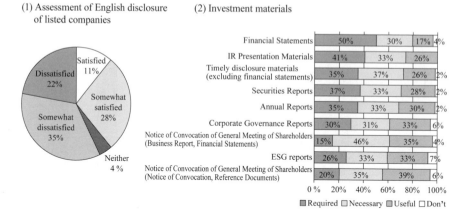

Source: Tokyo Stock Exchange, Report of the Survey to Overseas Investors on English Disclosure by Japanese Companies (August 2021).

ment in its growth strategy, initiatives were taken toward expanding the scope of application, including the release of a report by the FSA in 2014 that summarized the objectives of companies pursuing voluntary adoption of the IFRS at the time of shifting to the IFRS and the advantages of adopting the IFRS. Currently, there are 243 companies (44% of the overall market in terms of market capitalization.) listed on the TSE that have either already adopted the IFRS or are scheduled to adopt the standards.

Movement toward enhanced disclosure of descriptive information

In order to promote a constructive dialogue between investors and companies and to boost corporate value over the medium to long term, it is considered important to enhance descriptive disclosure of financial information and ESG information (environment, society, governance).

The report by the Working Group on Corporate Disclosure of the Financial System Council released in June 2018 stated that measures must be implemented to streamline the disclosure system, such as "enhancing financial and descriptive information", "providing governance information to facilitate a constructive dialogue with investors". Thereafter, efforts have been made to enhance disclosure of descriptive information in the Annual Securities Report, such as the revision in January 2019 of the Cabinet Office Ordinance on Disclosure of Corporate Information etc., and the publication of "Principles Regarding the Disclosure of Descriptive Information" and "Case Studies of Disclosure of Descriptive Information" by the Financial Services Agency in

March 2019. In addition, the revised Corporate Governance Code published in June 2021 states that companies should provide appropriate disclosure of their approach to sustainability, including ESG factors, on a medium- to long-term view.

Moreover, as the percentage of shares traded and held by overseas investors increases, companies are more and more expected to improve their English-language disclosure. According to a questionnaire survey conducted by the TSE as of the end of December 2020, the percentage of companies listed on the First Section that indicated that they publish timely disclosure materials in English was 28.0% (increase of 5.3% over the previous year in the number of companies.), showing a good progress in this area. However, institutional investors are still requesting further improvement.

CHAPTER XVII

The Securities Regulatory System

1. Financial Instruments and Exchange Act

In 2006, the Securities and Exchange Act underwent major revisions and was renamed the Financial Instruments and Exchange Act (FIEA). These revisions were enforced for the purpose of introducing cross-sectional regulations and flexibility into the financial system. Introduction of cross-sectional regulations meant reviewing vertical regulations and applying the same types of rules to financial instruments with similar economic functions and risks. This was achieved by expanding the FIEA's scope of application and by revising various related laws and regulations. More specifically, the scope of application was extended to include not only general investment trust beneficiary rights and mortgage securities, etc. but also collective investment schemes, making it possible to implement regulations comprehensively. In addition, various related laws were revised to establish a regulatory framework where financial instruments not covered by the FIEA but sharing many of the same aspects were subject to similar rules. Another move to cross-sectional application was the standardization of the registration of sales and solicitation, investment advisory, asset management, and asset administration, etc., businesses under the umbrella of Financial Instruments Business Operators with the aim of applying as common a code of conduct as possible.

The authorities introduced flexibility into the law through (1) disclosure regulations, (2) industry regulations, and (3) separating rules for dealing with different classes of investors. More specifically, (1) they placed strict disclosure obligations on highly liquid securities, strengthening the disclosure system by requiring listed companies. In contrast, illiquid securities, in principle, are exempt from these disclosure regulations. (2) While all Financial Instruments Business Operators are required to register under the comprehensive industry regulations, businesses are classified into the three categories of Type I and Type II Financial Instruments Businesses, Investment Advisory and Agency Business, and Asset Management Business, with separate rules applying for each category. In addition, (3) customers are classified into professional investors and general investors, with various exceptions to the gen-

Chart XVII-1. Transition from Securities and Exchange Act to Financial Instruments and Exchange Act

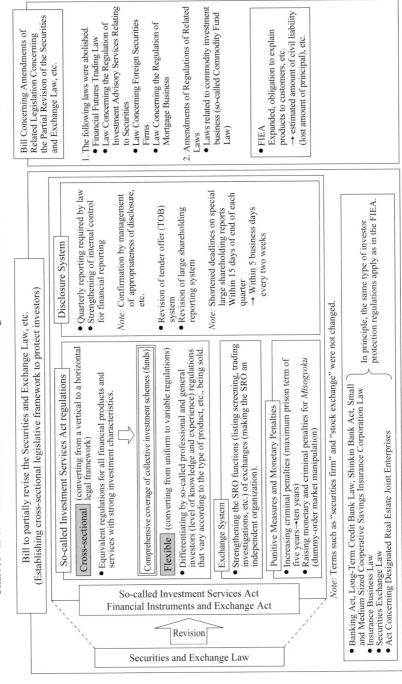

Source: Materials produced by the FSA.

eral industry code of conduct applying to dealing with professional investors.

Major revisions to the FIEA included those relating to firewall regulations between securities companies, banks and insurance companies enforced in 2008, the introduction of public regulations on credit-rating agencies, establishment of the Alternative Dispute Resolution (ADR) System in the financial sector, establishment of a framework for alliances among financial instruments exchanges and commodity exchanges that went into effect based on the revisions in 2009, and the introduction of a disclosure system relating to rights offering that was made based on the revisions enforced in 2011. Subsequently, in the 2015 revision, regulations on funds for professionals (specially permitted businesses for Qualified Institutional Investor, etc.) were amended. And the 2017 amendments included the introduction of rules on high-speed trading (HST) where a registration system for high-speed traders was adopted and the introduction of the Fair Disclosure Rules. The 2019 amendment (1) established regulations on derivative transactions involving crypto-assets and (2) established electronically recorded transferable rights as "paragraph 1 securities", bringing the trading thereof under the regulations pertaining to Type-I Financial Instruments Business Operators. The 2021 amendment established a notification system for the investment management business for overseas investors.

2. Other Laws and Regulations Related to the Securities Market

While the Financial Instruments and Exchange Act (FIEA) serves as the most fundamental law concerning securities, securities business operators, and transactions on the securities markets, there are, in fact, many other related laws and regulations.

As previously stated, in addition to the enforcement of the FIEA, from the point of view of investor protection, other laws were revised so that they shared, to the extent possible, common regulations with the FIEA for financial instruments not covered by the FIEA but having the same economic function. For example, such related laws as the Banking Act (Art. 13-4), Insurance Business Act (Art. 300-2) and the Trust Business Act (Art. 24-2) implemented provisions equivalent to the FIEA's code of conduct. Specifically, these laws have regulation of advertising, etc.; obligation to clarify conditions of transactions in advance; delivery of document prior to conclusion of contract; behavior prohibitions; prohibition of compensations of loss, etc.; and best execution policy.

The Act on Sales, etc. of Financial Instruments (renamed to Act on the Provision of Financial Services (Financial Services Provision Act) in the 2020 amendment) was formulated to provide cross-sectional regulations re-

Table XVII-1.   Banking Act, Insurance Business Act, and Trust Business Act

> 1. Acts that have sales and solicitation rules equivalent to those of the FIEA for deposits, insurance policies, and investment trusts with strong investment characteristics

(Points of view on which regulations have been implemented for each act)

	Banking Act (specified deposits, etc.)	Insurance Business Act (specified insurance policies, etc.)	Trust Business Act (specified trust agreements)
Advertising, regulations, etc.	• In the case of derivative deposits, if the bank has the right to extend the term of the deposit, it must indicate to the customer the risk that the interest rate could fall below the market rate to the disadvantage of the customer.		
Obligation to deliver written documents	• Exceptions to the obligation to deliver written documents - When a document on foreign currency deposit, etc. was delivered within the past year - When a similar document was delivered within the past year *Note:* Establish transitional measures at the time of enforcement (can be issued prior to enforcement; can be issued within three months of enforcement) • In the case of derivative deposits, the document prior to conclusion of contract must contain the same contents as the items shown in the advertisement, etc.	• The document prior to conclusion of contract must contain notes on material items in accordance with provisions in supervisory guidelines regarding the contract outline and cautionary information Eg.: The contract outline is dictated on the statutory level, while cautionary information is dictated on the cabinet office order level. • Items covered in the document delivered upon conclusion of contract can be adjusted in line with the items included in the insurance policy, etc. Eg.: Items regarding the type and content of the contract can be omitted from the document delivered upon conclusion of contract if they are contained in the insurance policy, etc.	• Exceptions to the obligation to deliver the document prior to conclusion of contract (Documents regarding a similar contract has previously been delivered, and the customer has made it clear that issuance of documents is not necessary, etc.)
Prohibited acts	• Generally prohibited acts in the banking business • Concluding a contract without adequate explanation necessary for understanding the document prior to conclusion of contract or the document on foreign currency deposits, etc.	• Generally prohibited acts for concluding or soliciting purchase of insurance policy • Concluding a contract without adequate explanation necessary for understanding the document prior to conclusion of contract	• Generally prohibited acts in underwriting trusts • Concluding a contract without adequate explanation necessary for understanding the document prior to conclusion of contract
Professional investors (*Tokutei Toushika*) (Type of contract)	• One type (contract for specified deposits, etc.)	• One type (contract for specified insurance policies, etc.)	• One type (contract for specified trusts)

> 2. Business scope of banks and insurance companies (Auxilliary businesses)

• Expanded to include agency or intermediary business for concluding investment advisory and discretionary investment contracts (banks only).
• Expanded to include emission rights derivatives trading. (intermediary and consulting services for emission rights trading also permitted as incidental businesses).

> 3. Business scope of banking and insurance company subsidiaries

• Business scope of securities subsidiaries expanded (full coverage of Financial Instruments Businesses).
• Scope of financial-related businesses expanded (private placements, investment advisory and agency business, self-management, emission rights trading, emission rights derivatives trading, etc.).

Source: The FSA.

Chart XVII-2.   Enhancement of the Act on Sales, etc. of Financial Instruments

Principles on actions for damages under
civil act (section 709 of the Civil Law)

Customers (sufferers) shall prove all the
requirements from① to ④ to win actions for
damages against financial firms.

Financial Products Sales Act

The act prescribes special treatment on actions for
damages regarding a wide range of financial products.
including deposits, insurance, securities, etc.

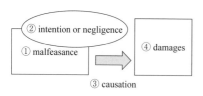

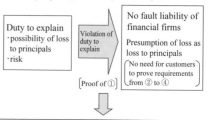

Strengthening Financial Products Sales Act

● Enlarging the scope of duty to explain
  ·Adding a possibility of losses beyond original principals
   and important part of schemes of financial instruments in
   the scope of duty to explain
● Introducing prohibition of provision of conclusive judgment
  ·no-fault liability and presumption of loss in case of the
   violation

Source: The FSA.

garding the sale and solicitation of sales for deposits, investment trusts, insurance, securities, and other financial instruments. The law was revised in
2006 at the same time the FIEA came into force to make it easier for customers to press civil liability suits. For example, the law expanded the scope of
obligation to explain products to customers (Article 3, Paragraph 1, Items
(ii), (iv) and (vi)) and added a suitability rule (Article 3, Paragraph 2). These
revisions defined the responsibility, in the case of a violation of the suitability
rule, to compensate the customer for damages, which are presumed to be any
loss of principal (Article 6). The Commodity Exchange Act (currently the
Commodity Derivatives Transaction Act) was also reformed to include similar regulations for its financial instruments. The revisions implemented advertising regulations and inserted an obligation to explain financial products
in a manner appropriate to the customer. Furthermore, loss compensation was
prohibited and made punishable by penalties. The 2020 amendment created a
new category of financial services intermediary business (Article 11(1)) (see
Chapter 12).

　While most of the business and code of conduct regulations regarding the
investment trust intermediary business and asset management business of investment corporations have been included in the FIEA, the Act on Investment Trusts and Investment Corporations (Investment Trust Act) was left to

focus solely on investment trust regulations and to serve as one of the pillars of investment trust regulations along with the FIEA.

There are several laws pertaining to issuance of securities. Issuing of public bonds is approved based on the provisions of the Public Finance Act and the Local Government Finance Act while deficit-covering bonds are governed by the special law of each fiscal year (The Special Deficit-Financing Bond Law of 2021 set the issuance period for special bonds up to 2025, maintaining the multi-year framework adopted from 2012). There are also laws concerning issuing administration for government bonds. For private securities, the Companies Act provides for the issuance of stocks and corporate bonds by corporations. As for corporate bonds and other bonds, the Secured Bond Trust Act and the Enterprise Mortgage Act are separately enforced in regard to collateral. In addition, the Act on the Securitization of Assets is in place regarding the issuance of asset-backed securities.

3. Organization of the Securities Regulatory System

After the war, the Securities and Exchange Act was in place and the Securities and Exchange Commission was modeled after the U.S. Securities and Exchange Commission (SEC) was established as an external bureau of the Ministry of Finance to oversee the securities regulatory system. However, after the end of the U.S. occupation in 1952, the securities regulatory system was once again placed under the control of the Securities Business Division in the Finance Bureau of the Ministry of Finance. Then in 1964, the Securities Bureau was created within the Ministry of Finance. The Securities Bureau regulated the securities business as a core authority for overseeing the license system of securities business operators over a period of about 30 years under the revised Securities and Exchange Act of 1965. During Japan's bubble economy years, the country's securities market demonstrated significant growth to become one of the major markets on a global level. On the other hand, the market came under severe criticism for lacking openness and being scandal-ridden. This, in particular the major financial and securities scandals in 1991, prompted efforts to strongly promote reforms of the securities regulatory system along with market reforms.

In 1992, the Ministry of Finance bolstered its market surveillance by establishing the Securities and Exchange Surveillance Commission (SESC) and transferring surveillance to this body. Further change came in June 1998 when the government set up the Financial Supervisory Agency as an external bureau (Article 3, "Committees" of the National Government Organization Act) of the Prime Minister's Office, to which the Ministry of Finance transferred the SESC. Subsequently, with the enforcement of the Act on Revision,

Chart XVII-3.   Securities Administration and the Monitoring System for Securities Transactions, etc.

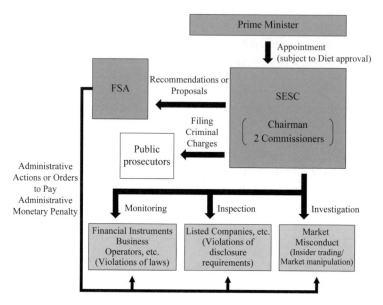

Source: Materials available on the website of the Securities and Exchange Surveillance Commission.

etc. of Related Acts for the Financial System Reform in December 1998, the Financial Supervisory Agency took over the role of overseeing the securities regulatory system. Concurrently, the Financial Reconstruction Commission, which was established around the same time, was given the highest responsibility over the financial and securities regulatory system.

Then in 2000, the Financial Supervisory Agency was reorganized as the Financial Services Agency (FSA) to which the Ministry of Finance transferred the financial system planning and law drafting functions in 2001, the same year as the Financial Reconstruction Commission was transferred to the FSA and the SESC also became part of the FSA. Through this process, the major portion of securities regulation in Japan was consolidated into a system administered by the FSA and the SESC. And the policy on securities regulation shifted from preventative administration to regulatory violation surveillance. Behind this shift was the clarification of the objective of the administration to increase the welfare of people in Japan primarily through promoting sustainable growth of corporations and the economy and stable asset formation, following the winding-down of a bad debt issue among others after the collapse of the bubble economy.

Chart XVII-4.　Securities Administration Organization Chart

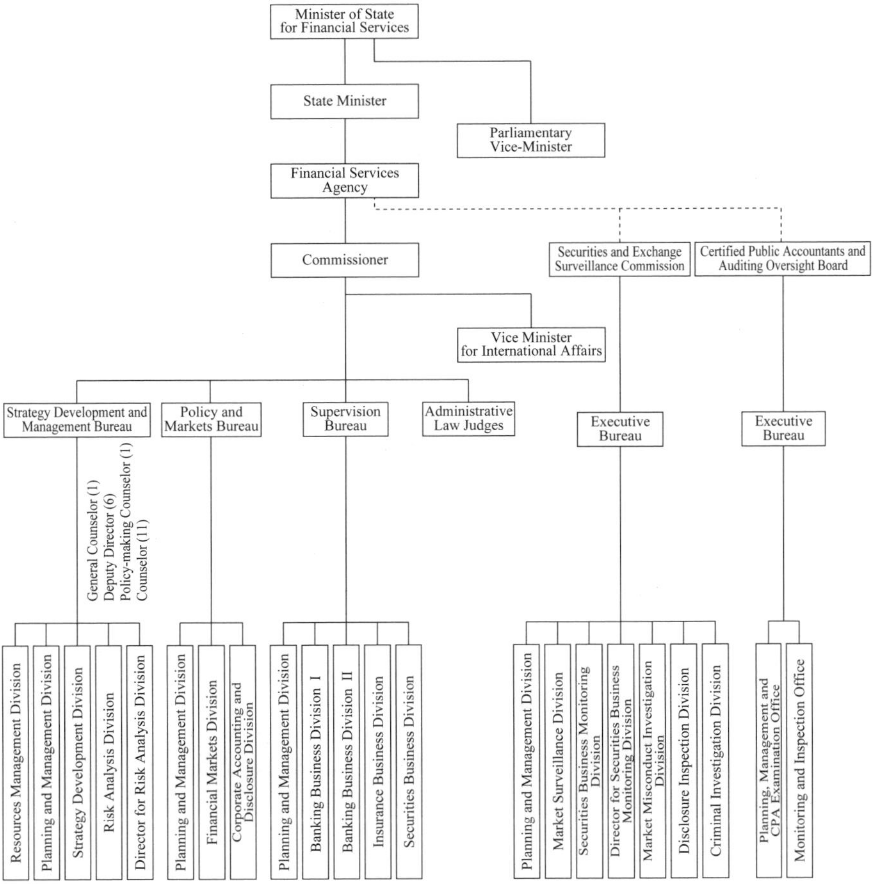

Minister of State for Financial Services

State Minister

Parliamentary Vice-Minister

Financial Services Agency

Commissioner

Securities and Exchange Surveillance Commission

Certified Public Accountants and Auditing Oversight Board

Vice Minister for International Affairs

Strategy Development and Management Bureau

Policy and Markets Bureau

Supervision Bureau

Administrative Law Judges

Executive Bureau

Executive Bureau

General Counselor (1)
Deputy Director (6)
Policy-making Counselor (1)
Counselor (11)

Strategy Development and Management Bureau divisions:
- Resources Management Division
- Planning and Management Division
- Strategy Development Division
- Risk Analysis Division
- Director for Risk Analysis Division

Policy and Markets Bureau divisions:
- Planning and Management Division
- Financial Markets Division
- Corporate Accounting and Disclosure Division

Supervision Bureau divisions:
- Planning and Management Division
- Banking Business Division I
- Banking Business Division II
- Insurance Business Division
- Securities Business Division

Executive Bureau divisions:
- Planning and Management Division
- Market Surveillance Division
- Securities Business Monitoring Division
- Director for Securities Business Monitoring Division
- Market Misconduct Investigation Division
- Disclosure Inspection Division
- Criminal Investigation Division

Executive Bureau offices:
- Planning, Management and CPA Examination Office
- Monitoring and Inspection Office

Source: FSA materials.

The FSA was reorganized in July 2018 into three bureaus-Strategy Development and Management Bureau; Policy and Markets Bureau and Supervision Bureau-with an eye toward enhancing strategy planning function and expertise of the FSA as an administrative body, and strengthening its ability to deal with the advancement of Fintech, etc. Under this system, the following measures are being implemented: (1) promotion of digital innovation; (2) development of an international financial center; (3) promotion of sustainable finance; (4) revitalization of capital markets and smooth supply of growth capital; (5) spread of user-oriented financial services, and preparation for dealing with various risks, including money laundering measures (as of August 2021).

4. Law Enforcement by the Financial Services Agency

The executive authority for the Financial Instruments and Exchange Act lies with the prime minister of Japan, the top cabinet minister, who in turn oversees the Financial Services Agency (FSA). In actual practice, the prime minister delegates this authority (with some exceptions such as the authority on approval and other treatment) to the commissioner of the FSA as stipulated in Article 194-7 "Delegation of Authority to the Commissioner of the FSA." Major types of authority delegated to the commissioner include the authority to issue a Business Improvement Order to Financial Instrument Business Operators and Registered Financial Institutions (Article 51, Article 51-2) or an order to suspend operations or rescind their registration or approval (Article 52, Article 52-2). The FSA commissioner is also required to issue an Administrative Surcharge Payment Order if certain conditions are met. Primary examples subject to the issuance of the Administrative Surcharge Payment Order include non-submission of securities registration statements, etc. and false statement (Articles 172, 172-2, 172-3, and 172-4) and non-submission, misrepresentation and false statement of the public announcement of the start of an offering or the Tender Offer Notification (Articles 172-5 and 172-6). When any case of unfair trading practice is noted based on facts of spreading rumors, use of fraudulent means, market manipulation, or insider trading (Articles 173, 174, 174-2, 174-3, and 175), an Administrative Surcharge Payment Order is normally decided through a trial procedure and based on a draft produced by examiners (Articles 178, 185-6, and 185-7).

In addition, the following inspection authority for issuing disciplinary action by order or measures by the FSA is delegated by the commissioner to the SESC. Certain other matters and some of the matters delegated to the commission may be delegated to the Director-General of the Finance Bureau or to the Director-General of the local finance bureau. The Director-General of the Finance Bureau collaborates with the Director of Securities and Exchange Surveillance Department of each location.

(1) The authority to require Financial Instruments Business Operators and parties executing transactions with Financial Instruments Business Operators to produce or submit for inspection reports related to the business and assets of such operators

(2) Similar authority over Authorized On-Exchange Transaction Service Operators (Foreign Securities Companies), etc.

(3) Similar authority over licensing and accrediting associations or those

Chart XVII-5. Flow Leading to the Payment of Administrative Surcharge

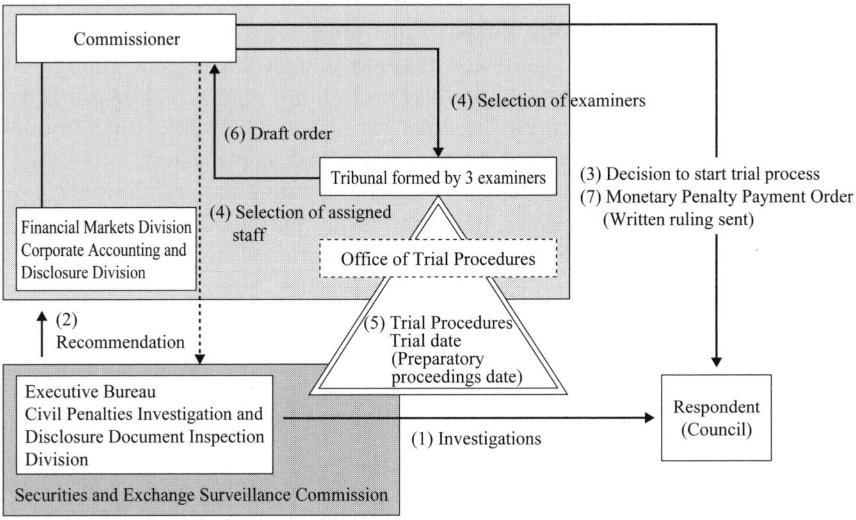

Note: Designated staff members are selected among the employees by the FSA Commissioner to assert and verify the violations, etc., in the trial proceedings. They submit preparatory documents and give evidence, etc.

Source: Materials available on the website of the Securities and Exchange Surveillance Commission.

Table XVII-2. Major Legal Basis of Inspection and Supervision by the FSA

Financial Instruments and Exchange Act		
	Article 56-2	Financial Instruments Business Operators, Etc.
	Article 60-11	Authorized On-Exchange Transaction Service Operators, Etc.
	Article 63-6	Specially Permitted Business Notifying Persons, Etc.
	Article 66-22	Financial Instruments Intermediary Service Providers, Etc.
	Article 75	Authorized Financial Instruments Firms Association, Etc.
	Article 79-77	Investor Protection Fund, Etc.
	Article 106-6, Article 106-20	Major Shareholders, Etc. of Financial Instruments Exchanges and Their Holding Companies
	Article 151	Financial Instruments Exchange, Etc.
	Article 153-4	Self-Regulatory Organizations
	Article 155-9	Foreign Financial Instruments Exchange, Etc.
	Article 156-5-8	Major Shareholders, Etc. of Clearing Organization
Act on Investment Trusts and Investment Corporations		
	Article 22	Investment Trust Management Companies and Trustee Companies, Etc.
	Article 213	Investment Corporations, Etc.

entrusted by such associations

(4) Similar authority over issuers of OTC or tradable securities

(5) The authority to require financial instruments exchanges and their subsidiaries, issuers of securities listed on respective exchanges and foreign financial instruments exchanges to produce and submit reports and be inspected

(6) The authority to require related parties of incidents subject to administrative surcharge to produce and submit reports and be inspected

The commission carry out their investigations within the permissible scope and when considered necessary, the commission may recommend the prime minister or the FSA commissioner to take an administrative disciplinary action (Act for Establishment of the Financial Services Agency, Article 20) and other measures.

5. The Securities and Exchange Surveillance Commission

The Securities and Exchange Surveillance Commission (SESC) comprises a chairman and two members appointed by the prime minister with the approval of the house of representatives and the house of councilors (Act for Establishment of the Financial Services Agency, Arts. 10 to 12). As described in the preceding section, the commission has the authority delegated by the FSA commissioner to require a wide range of people related to Financial Instruments Business Operators and registered financial institutions to produce or submit for inspection reports and materials (FIEA Art. 56-2, Art. 60-11, Art. 63, Art. 66-22, Art. 75, Art. 79-4, Art. 79-77, Art. 151, Art. 156-15, Art. 156-34, etc.). The commission also has the authority to demand the production or

Table XVII-3.   Number of criminal accusations by Business Year (as of March 31, 2021)

Business Year	92 − 15	2016	2017	2018	2019	2020
Fake statement of Disclosure documents	41	0	0	3	1	0
Disseminating Unfounder Rumors · Fraudulent Means	26	2	0	0	0	0
Market manipulation	26	3	2	0	0	1
Insider trading	77	2	2	5	1	1
Others	11	0	0	0	1	0
Total	181	7	4	8	3	2

Source: The website of the Securities and Exchange Surveillance Commission's Initiatives (August 2021).

Chart XVII-6.   Activities of the SESC

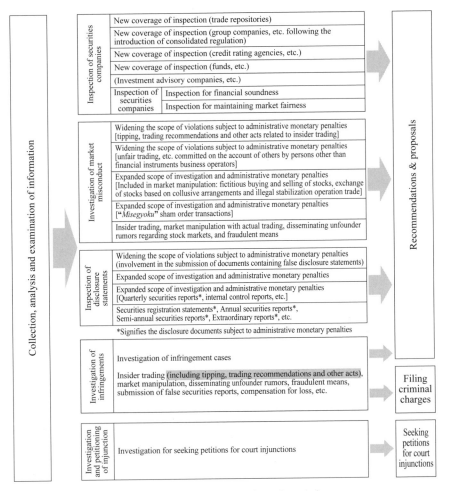

Source: Data disclosed by Securities and Exchange Surveillance Commission.

submission for inspection of reports and materials from the submitters of securities registration statements or Statements of Large Volume Holders and tender offers (FIEA Art. 26, Art. 27-22, Art. 27-30, etc.).

Based on this process, the commission mainly carries out the following tasks: (1) market analysis screening (daily market surveillance) involving a review of the securities trading activity of Financial Instruments Business Operators; (2) securities inspections involving wide-ranging and detailed branch inspections of Financial Instruments Business Operators and registered financial institutions; (3) disclosure inspections to ensure the appropriateness of disclosure by submitters of securities registration statements and annual securities reports; and (4) administrative surcharge investigations undertaken to determine whether certain behavior requiring an Administrative Surcharge Payment Order, such as unfair trading practices or disclosure violations, has occurred. Furthermore, in the case of a criminal investigation, such as the misrepresentation of material facts in a securities registration statement or annual securities report submitted or market manipulation, officials of the commission are authorized to arbitrarily investigate by questioning, examination, retention, etc. and keeping documents in custody (FIEA Article 210). In such criminal investigations, the officials also have inspection, search, and seizure authority within the scope of the warrant issued by a judge (FIEA Article 211, etc.).

As described in the preceding section, after the commission has made its recommendations based on its securities investigations, the FSA commissioner issues orders to improve business operations, rescinds registration, or suspends operations. When the commission recommends action as a result of its administrative surcharge investigations, the commissioner issues an Administrative Surcharge Payment Order when he/she is convinced that regulations have been violated. Furthermore, when the commission is convinced that irregularities have been committed following the investigation in a criminal case, it must report the case to the Public Prosecutors Office pursuant to the provision of Article 226, Paragraph 1 of the FIEA.

In the 2008 revision of the FIEA, the authority to petition for Prohibition and Stay Orders (Article 192, Paragraph 1) was delegated from the court to the Securities and Exchange Surveillance Commission. It first used this power to crack down on a business operator not registered as a Financial Instruments Business Operator in 2010. More recently, petitions for the issuance of Prohibition and Stay Orders were submitted to the court for misconducts by D.U. corporation and IFP Tokyo in 2019, and SKY PREMIUM INTERNATIONAL PTE.LTD. in 2021.

6. Self-Regulatory Organizations

A self-regulatory organization is an organization established voluntarily by intermediaries, etc. under the respective legal framework with the purpose of ensuring fair and smooth trading of securities and other transactions and of contributing to the protection of investors. It takes on the role of securing the public nature of the securities market through formulating its own rules and ensuring adherence to those rules along with the laws, regulations and other rules set out by the government.

Table XVII-4.   List of Self-Regulatory Organizations Governed by the FIEA (September 2021)

Rules, etc.		Organization
Financial Instruments Exchange	Licensed	Japan Exchange Regulation (see main text)
	Same as above	Nagoya Stock Exchange
	Same as above	Fukuoka Stock Exchange
	Same as above	Sapporo Securities Exchange
Financial Instruments Firms Associations	Authorized	JSDA
	Certified	The Investment Trusts Association, Japan
	Same as above	Japan Investment Advisers Association
	Same as above	Financial Futures Association of Japan
	Same as above	Type II Financial Instruments Firms Association
	Same as above	Japan Virtual and Crypto assets Exchange Association
	Same as above	Japan Security Token Offering Association
Investor Protection Organization	Certified	Financial Instruments Mediation Assistance Center (FINMAC)

Source: Compiled based on data available on the website of the FSA, etc.

Table XVII-5.   Principal Rules of the Japan Securities Dealers Association (as of September 2021)

Self-Regulatory Rules
Rules Concerning Solicitation for Investments and Management of Customers, Etc. by Association Members
Rules Concerning Establishment of Confidential Corporate Information Management System by Association Members
Rules Concerning Establishment of Order Management System by Association Members
Rules Concerning Application for Confirmation, Examination, Confirmation, Etc. of Incidents
Rules Concerning Financial Instruments Intermediary Services Providers
Rules Concerning Elimination of Relationships with Antisocial Forces
Rules Concerning Qualification and Registration, Etc., of Sales Representatives of Association Members
Guideline for Protection of Personal Information
Rules Concerning Maintenance of and Compliance With Ethical Code by Association Members
Uniform Practice Rules
Rules Concerning Handling of OTC Incident-Related Securities
Rules Concerning Processing of Rights in Case of Forgetting Entry of a Name Change on Stocks
Rules Concerning Exchanges of Bonds Drawn for Redemption by Lottery in OTC Trading
Rules Concerning Elimination of Fails in Bonds, Etc.
Dispute Handling Rules
Rules Concerning Outsourcing, etc. for Resolution of Disputes, Etc. Between Customers and Association Members
Rules Concerning Mediation of Disputes Between Association Members

The Financial Services Agency (FSA) acknowledges the money lending associations, certified payment service associations and designated dispute resolution organizations as self-regulatory organizations in addition to the Financial Instruments Firms Associations. Financial Instruments Firms Associations are categorized into authorized financial instruments firms associations approved by the prime minister under the FIEA (Article 67-2) and certified financial instruments firms associations designated by the prime minister under the FIEA (Article 78). The JSDA is currently the only Authorized Financial Instruments Firms Association and its members comprise Financial Instruments Business Operators and registered financial institutions. The JSDA has in place Articles of Association; fair, conventional regulations; board resolutions; and dispute handling rules; and its members are required to carry out securities transactions in compliance with these regulations and rules. The JSDA is also empowered to take disciplinary action when its members violate these association rules. The scope of its disciplinary action may include reprimand, imposition of monetary penalties, suspension or limitation of membership or expulsion, or the issuing of a formal warning (JSDA Articles of Association, Article 28, Article 29).

Certified Financial Instruments Firms Associations include The Investment Trusts Association, Japan that has investment trust management companies, trust companies, etc. that serve as trustees in investment trusts without instruction by trustor, and securities companies and registered financial institutions that purchase and sell beneficiary certificates of investment trusts as members, and The Japan Investment Advisers Association having investment advisory companies as members.

The Financial Instruments and Exchange Act (FIEA) distinguishes between a "stock company that operates financial instruments exchange markets" and a "self-regulatory organization" and recognizes a "financial instruments exchange" or "its self-regulatory organization" as a self-regulatory organization relating to the exchange market. With the authorization of the prime minister, the self-regulation-related service of Japan Exchange has been commissioned to Japan Exchange Regulation pursuant to Article 85 of the FIEA. Those services include the listing and delisting of financial instruments, inspections of compliance of members with laws and regulations, etc., and other measures specified by cabinet office order for the purpose of ensuring fair trading practices (Article 84, Paragraph 2). Japan Exchange Regulation's organizational structure contains a listing examination department that screens listing applicants for suitability; a listing compliance department that maintains and improves the quality of the financial instruments listed on the exchange; a market surveillance and compliance department that investigates and seeks to prevent unfair trading practices; and a participant examination and inspection department that monitors compliance and implements disciplinary action. Under rule 34 of the Trading Participant Rules, violations of laws or rules and regulations by participants are punishable by revocation of trading qualifications, suspension or restriction of trading, and monetary penalties or official warnings, etc.

7. International Organization for Securities Regulation

The International Organization of Securities Commissions (IOSCO) is an international organ that sets forth global standards for the securities sector in various countries. It takes on the role of promoting, in particular, the development and implementation of, and compliance with, internationally recognized securities regulations. In the process of implementing reforms to the international rules after the financial crisis, IOSCO worked in cooperation with the G20 and the Financial Stability Board (FSB) below. The IOSCO framework was established in 1974 as the Inter-American Association of Securities Commissions. In 1983, the code of the organ was revised to expand membership beyond the Americas, and the organization was renamed as IOSCO at the Paris Annual Conference in 1986. As of September 2021, there were a total of 230 member organizations, representing the regulators of over 95% of the world's securities markets. The Securities Bureau of Japan's Ministry of Finance became an ordinary member in 1988. The FSA has succeeded the position and is an ordinary member at present. Besides the FSA, the Securities and Exchange Surveillance Commission is an associate member, along with the Ministry of Economy, Trade and Industry and the Ministry of Agriculture, Forestry and Fisheries, both of which oversee commodity futures. Meanwhile, Japan Exchange Group, Inc. and the JSDA are affiliate members. IOSCO has published a wide range of principles, policies, standards, guidance, codes, recommendations, and practices regarding securities trading that have been implemented in many countries. IOSCO's documents are important also for Japan's securities regulators, which have taken steps to implement policies through defining laws and self-regulatory systems. The Financial Services Agency closely follows IOSCO trends and publishes them on its website.

The Financial Services Board (FSB) was established as an international body in April 2009, as the successor to the Financial Stability Forum (FSF) founded in 1999, with a broadened mandate to promote financial stability, the function of the FSF. Members of the FSB include financial supervising organs and central banks of 25 major countries and regions, including Japan. In addition, international organizations such as IOSCO, IMF, the World Bank, the Bank for International Settlements (BIS), and the Basel Committee on Banking Supervision are also members of the FSB. From Japan, the Bank of

Chart XVII-7.   IOSCO Organization Chart

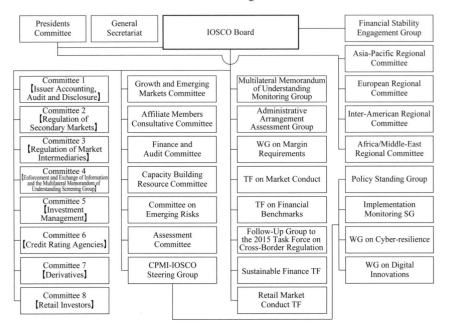

Table XVII-6.   Major IOSCO Committees

Presidents Committee	The Presidents Committee is composed of all the Presidents (Chairs) of ordinary and associate members and meets once a year during the Annual Conference. It has the right to make decisions on all matters necessary for the IOSCO to achieve its objectives.
The IOSCO Board	The IOSCO Board is comprised of securities regulators of 34 countries, including the FSA. It is the governing and international standard-setting body for the securities industry. Under the Board are (1) policy committees that discuss policy issues and conduct policy work; among other committees is (2) the Growth and Emerging Markets Committee, comprised of regulators of emerging markets and countries, which seeks to promote the development and greater efficiency of emerging markets by establishing principles and standards and providing training, etc.
Regional Committees	There are four regional committees—Asia-Pacific Regional Committee, Inter-American Regional Committee, European Regional Committee, and African/Middle-East Regional Committee—and they discuss specific issues pertinent to their own regions. Japan belongs to the Asia-Pacific Regional Committee.

Source: Websites of IOSCO and the FSA.

Japan, the FSA and the Ministry of Finance are participating members. According to the FSB Charter, the organization is responsible for the monitoring and assessment of vulnerabilities affecting the global financial system and for identifying and reviewing regulations, supervisory and related actions needed to address these vulnerabilities and their outcomes. Particularly important tasks of the FSB include the authorization of global systemically important financial institutions (G-SIFI) crucial for systems that are in place across borders and the formulation of guidelines for establishing the supervisory college. The organization also examines international standards and principles relating to the shadow banking system and other activities that have not been subject to regulations thus far, and serves as an intermediary function to coordinate matters among related entities. The outcomes of activities of the FSB are reported and addressed as recommendations when appropriate at the G20 summit.

APPENDIX

Chronology of Events Related to Securities

(1870−2021)

Year Date	Changes implemented
Apr. 23, 1870	The Japanese government publicly offers 9% coupon bonds on the London market (the first public bond ever to be so offered).
Oct. 13, 1874	The stock trading ordinance is enacted (the nation's first securities law), but it is not enforced.
May 4, 1878	The stock exchange ordinance is promulgated.
May 15, 1878	The Tokyo Stock Exchange is established.
June 17, 1878	The Osaka Securities Exchange is established.
Mar. 4, 1893	The Securities Exchange Law is promulgated.
Aug. 1, 1894	The Sino-Japanese War breaks out.
Mar. 9, 1899	The Commercial Code is promulgated (the basic law of to-day's Companies Act).
Feb.10, 1904	The Russo-Japanese War breaks out.
Mar. 13, 1905	The Secured Bonds Trust Act is promulgated.
Feb. 1910	Securities brokers engage in sub-underwriting in the issuance of the No. 1 issue of public bond with 4-percent interest.
July 28. 1914	World War I breaks out.
Apr. 1, 1918	The Securities Installment Sales Act is promulgated.
Mar. 15, 1920	Stock prices crash, touching off a reactionary depression.
Apr. 20, 1922	The Securities Exchange Law is amended: development of membership-based exchange, two transaction categories - spot transactions and net-balance settlement transactions
Sept. 1, 1922	Osaka Securities Exchange starts short-term futures transactions (time bargains).

Sept. 1, 1923	Great Kanto Earthquake, September 7 Moratorium.
June 2, 1924	The Tokyo Stock Exchange starts short-term futures transactions (time bargains).
Mar. 15, 1927	Financial crisis occurs.
Mar. 30, 1927	The Banking Act is promulgated.
Apr. 22, 1927	Financial crisis continues, 3-week moratorium is implemented.
1928	The Tokyo Stock Exchange and the Osaka Securities Exchange mark their 50th anniversaries. The Tokyo Stock Exchange computes a stock price index for the first time (Fisher's ideal index, monthly average) and starts publishing it.
Oct. 24, 1929	The New York Stock Exchange crashes (Black Thursday), setting off a world-wide depression.
Jan. 11, 1930	Gold embargo is lifted, causing an outflow of massive amount of specie and an outbreak of industrial depression (Showa Depression).
Sept. 18, 1931	The Manchurian Incident breaks out.
Sept. 21, 1931	U.K. decides to terminate the gold standard, setting off a worldwide financial crisis.
Dec. 13, 1931	Reimposition of gold embargo is executed.
May 15, 1932	The Bank of Japan begins underwriting issuance of deficit-covering government bonds.
May 5, 1933	Banks and trust banks as trustees of corporate bonds initiate a clean-up movement of corporate bonds, disallowing issuance of unsecured corporate bonds.
May 27, 1933	The U.S. enacts the Securities Law.
June 6, 1934	The U.S. enacts the Securities and Exchange Law.
July 7, 1937 あ	Marco Polo Bridge Incident occurs, setting off the Second Sino-Japanese War.
July 17, 1937	Fujimoto Bill Broker Securities forms a securities investment partnership–the first investment trust.
Mar. 29, 1938	The Securities Business Control Act is promulgated.
Mar. 31, 1938	The Securities Underwriting Business Act is promulgated.

Sept. 3, 1939	World War II breaks out.
Aug. 30, 1941	The Stock Price Control Ordinance is promulgated.
Dec. 8, 1941	The Pacific War breaks out.
Feb. 18, 1942	The Act for Registration of Corporate Bonds, etc. is promulgated.
Mar. 11, 1943	The Japan Securities and Exchange Act is promulgated. On June 30, the Japan Securities Exchange is established, and the 11 stock exchanges (as corporations) are abolished to become branch exchanges of the Japan Securities Exchange.
Oct. 19, 1943	Exchange Member Administration Guidelines are issued; Securities Business Administration Guidelines are issued (December 17)
Mar. 10, 1945	After the Great Tokyo Air Raid, the Wartime Finance Bank decides to provide unlimited support by buying at the March 9 price.
Aug. 10, 1945	Japanese stock exchanges nationwide temporarily suspend operations.
Aug. 15, 1945	Japan loses the war.
Sept. 26, 1945	The GHQ releases a memorandum (dated Sept. 25) banning the resumption of business by the securities exchange.
Dec. 1945	Investors start group trading in stocks in Tokyo and Osaka.
Apr. 17, 1946	Shinnihon-Kogyo Corporation's stock is publicly offered as the first public stock offering after the war.
Aug. 8, 1946	The Holding Company Liquidation Commission is established and begins designation of holding companies.
Jan. 18, 1947	The Act Concerning Adjustment, etc. of Disposal of Securities is promulgated.
Mar. 28, 1947	The Act Concerning Dissolution of Japan Securities Exchange is promulgated, and the securities exchange is dissolved on April 16.
Mar. 28, 1947	The Securities and Exchange Law (of 1947) is promulgated.
Apr. 14, 1947	The Antimonopoly Act is promulgated.
July 23, 1947	The Securities and Exchange Commission is established.

Apr. 13, 1948	The revised Securities and Exchange Act (of 1948) is promulgated, and it makes securities companies subject to registration.
Nov. 7, 1948	Article 65 of the Securities and Exchange Act is enforced.
Jan. 31, 1949	The GHQ announces a policy authorizing the resumption of securities trading.
Feb. 12, 1949	Securities companies hold inauguration meetings of stock exchanges in Tokyo (Feb. 12), Osaka (Feb. 15), and Nagoya (Mar. 7).
Apr. 20, 1949	Adams GHQ Officer in charge of securities instructs the three principles of securities exchange.
May 9, 1949	The Japan Securities Dealers Association is founded (as a federation of securities dealers associations).
May 16, 1949	The stock exchanges of Tokyo, Osaka, and Nagoya start floor trading.
July 4, 1949	Stock exchanges in Fukuoka, Hiroshima, Kobe, Kyoto, and Niigata start floor trading.
Apr. 1, 1950	The Sapporo Stock Exchange starts floor trading.
June 25, 1950	Disturbance outbreaks in Korea.
June 1, 1951	Margin trading is started.
June 1, 1951	The Securities Investment Trust Act is promulgated and enforced, and stock investment trusts start operating on June 15.
Jan. 4, 1952	Based on the Dow Jones stock pricing method, average stock prices (TSE average stock price) are adopted on exchanges and announced.
Apr. 28, 1952	Treaty of Peace with Japan and the U.S.-Japan Security Treaty come into effect.
Aug. 1, 1952	The Securities and Exchange Commission is abolished, and its function is transferred to the Securities Section of the Finance Bureau of the Ministry of Finance.
Sept. 10, 1952	The Securities and Exchange Council is created.
Mar. 5, 1953	Nationwide stock markets crash at the news of Russian leader Stalin is in a critical condition.

Oct. 26, 1954	The Tokyo Stock Exchange's labor union goes on strike, demanding improvements in labor conditions.
June 1955	Movements to revive term (time bargain) transactions reach a peak.
Apr. 2, 1956	The stock exchanges in Tokyo and Osaka open a bond trading market.
Oct. 7, 1958	Trading on the Tokyo Stock Exchange tops 100 million stocks for the first time.
Feb. 18, 1959	Foreign currency-denominated bonds (USD public bonds) are issued for the first time after the war.
Jan. 11, 1961	Bond investment trusts are launched.
July 18, 1961	The Dow Jones average stock price hits the peak at 1,829.74.
Oct. 2, 1961	The stock exchanges of Tokyo, Osaka, and Nagoya open Second Sections.
July 18, 1963	President Kennedy of the United States proposes the creation of an interest equalization tax, and stock prices on the Tokyo Stock Exchange crash on July 19.
Jan. 20, 1964	Japan Joint Securities is founded and continues to buy stocks from the fall season to the end of the year.
Sept. 25, 1964	Capitalization Coordinating Committee agrees to restrain capital increases after February 1965.
Jan.12, 1965	Japan Securities Holding Association is founded, takes on stock holdings of investment trusts.
May 21, 1965	Talks about the rehabilitation of the near-bankrupt Yamaichi Securities are reported, plunging the market into a semi-crash.
May 28, 1965	The Bank of Japan decides to provide special loans to 19 management companies including Yamaichi Securities.
July 27, 1965	Economic reconstruction measures, including the policy for issuing deficit-covering government bonds, are decided.
Oct. 1, 1965	The amended Securities and Exchange Act is enforced; among other things, it requires securities companies to obtain a license from the government.
July 1, 1967	Liberalization of capital transactions (first round) is implemented.

Apr. 1, 1968	Securities companies are fully transfered to a license system.
June 4, 1968	The Tokyo Stock Exchange's market capitalization on its 1st section reaches ¥10 trillion.
Jan. 31, 1969	Nihon Gakki pursues capital increase by issuing shares on market with preferential terms for shareholders. Issuing of shares on market becomes active.
July 1, 1969	TOPIX is introduced.
Mar. 3, 1971	The Law Concerning Foreign Securities Firms is promulgated.
Jan. 24, 1973	The Dow Jones average stock price hits a peak of 5,359.74.
Feb. 13, 1973	The government shifts the exchange rate system to a floating exchange rate system.
June 2, 1973	Agreement reached with OPEC on major oil companies and raising of oil prices; the first oil crisis begins.
1975	The Ministry of Finance starts issuing a massive amount of government bonds, and the turnover of bonds on the OTC market increases sharply.
May 15, 1978	The Tokyo Stock Exchange celebrates its 100 year anniversary and enters its second century.
Mar. 30, 1979	Unsecured corporate bonds (Sears, Roebuck and Company) are issued for the first time since the end of the war.
Dec. 1, 1980	A new Foreign Exchange and Foreign Trade Act is enforced, and in- and out-bound securities investments are liberalized, in principle.
Oct. 1, 1982	Revised Commercial Code is enforced, unit share system is introduced, and the face value of newly founded company's stock is set at ¥50,000.
Apr. 9, 1983	City banks and other financial institutions start OTC sale of government bonds.
Apr. 20, 1984	The Law Concerning the Custody and Transfer of Stock Certificates is promulgated.
Oct.19, 1985	The Tokyo Stock Exchange starts bond futures trading, the first securities futures trading since the end of the war.
Dec. 24, 1985	Merrill Lynch and five other foreign securities firms are admitted to the Tokyo Stock Exchange for the first time.

Oct.11, 1986	NTT begins offering its shares to the general public.
Nov. 25, 1986	The Law Concerning the Regulation of Investment Advisers Relating to Securities is enforced.
June 9, 1987	The Osaka Securities Exchange starts Futures 50 trading as the first stock futures trading market.
Oct. 20, 1987	The Tokyo Stock Exchange records the largest fall (14.9%) following the crash of the New York market, Black Monday; stock price crash ripples throughout the world.
Dec. 15, 1987	The Law Concerning the Regulation of Mortgage-Backed Securities Business is enforced.
Sep. 3, 1988	The Tokyo Stock Exchange (TOPIX) and the Osaka Securities Exchange (the Nikkei 225) start stock index futures trading on full scale.
June 12, 1989	The stock exchanges in Osaka (Nikkei 225); Nagoya (Option 25, on Oct. 17); and Tokyo (TOPIX) start trading stock index options.
Dec. 29, 1989	The Dow Jones average (the Nikkei average) shoots up to an all-time high of 38,915.87.
Mar. 20, 1990	With the rapid plunge in stock prices, public offering of stocks on the market has come to a halt.
Oct. 1, 1990	Given the plunge in stock prices, the Finance Minister quickly announces measures to bolster stock prices.
June 24, 1991	Following the involvement of the big four securities companies in the loss compensation issue with corporate clients and in transactions with antisocial forces, the President of Nomura Securities and the President of Nikko Securities take responsibility and resign, which leads unfolding securities scandals over the subsequent several months.
Oct. 3, 1991	The revised Securities and Exchange Act is approved. Revisions include the prohibition of discretionary account transactions and prohibition of loss compensation dealings.
June 26, 1992	The Law Concerning Realignment of Related Laws for a Reform of the Financial System and the Securities Trading System is promulgated, and the Securities and Exchange Surveillance Commission is launched on July 20.

Aug. 18, 1992	The Nikkei stock average plunge to 14,309.41 and emergency measures are quickly announced. Comprehensive economic measures, including the injection of public funds, are revealed (August 28).
July 2, 1993	Kogin Securities and other securities companies affiliated with financial institutions were established for the first time.
Apr. 1, 1994	Brokerage commissions securities companies charge on block trading are liberalized.
Oct. 1, 1994	Amendment to the Commercial Code for deregulating treasury stock purchases is enforced.
Feb. 26, 1995	Barings Securities of U.K. goes bankrupt.
Aug. 30, 1995	Hyogo Bank goes bankrupt under the Banking Act for the first time after the war and the BOJ provides a special loan.
Sept. 8, 1995	The Bank of Japan cuts the discount rate to an all-time low of 0.5%.
Jan. 1, 1996	The regulation of the issuance of corporate bonds is abolished.
June 21, 1996	Six laws relating to housing-loan and financial matters are promulgated.
Nov. 11, 1996	Prime Minister Ryutaro Hashimoto instructs his cabinet to come up with ideas for a sweeping financial system reform to revive the Tokyo market in preparation for the 21st century (a Japanese version of the "financial Big Bang").
Apr. 25, 1997	Nissan Life Insurance becomes the first bankrupt life insurer after the war.
June 13, 1997	The Securities and Exchange Council, the Financial System Research Committee, and the Insurance Council submit reports on measures to be taken to achieve the goals of the Japanese Big Bang.
June 20, 1997	The Act for Establishing Financial Supervisory Agency is promulgated.
Nov. 3, 1997	San'yo Securities, Hokkaido Takushoku Bank (Nov. 17), and Yamaichi Securities (Nov. 22) go virtually bankrupt.
Apr. 1, 1998	The government starts carrying out Big Bang reforms, the amended Foreign Exchange and Foreign Trade Act is enforced, and the brokerage commission on trades worth ¥50 million or more and less than ¥1 billion are liberalized.

June 22, 1998	The Financial Supervisory Agency is launched.
Sept. 1, 1998	The SPC Act is enforced.
Oct. 16, 1998	Eight laws related to financial reconstruction are promulgated.
Oct. 23, 1998	The Long-Term Credit Bank of Japan and Nippon Credit Bank, Ltd. (December 13) are placed under temporary government control.
Dec. 1, 1998	The Act on Revision, etc. of Related Acts for the Financial System Reform is enforced.
Dec. 15, 1998	The Financial Reconstruction Commission is launched.
Apr. 1, 1999	Securities companies start managing their customers' assets separately from their own.
Oct. 1, 1999	Brokerage commissions on stock transactions are liberalized.
Nov. 11, 1999	The Tokyo Stock Exchange launches Mothers market, a market for high-growth and start-up stocks.
Mar. 1, 2000	The Niigata Stock Exchange and the Hiroshima Stock Exchange are consolidated into the Tokyo Stock Exchange.
Mar. 17, 2000	The regulatory agency cancels the securities registration of Minami Securities, the first such cancellation ever in Japan.
May 8, 2000	The Osaka Securities Exchange opens the NASDAQ Japan market, later converted to the Hercules market for start-up companies on Dec. 16, 2002.
May 31, 2000	The Securities and Exchange Act as amended in 2000 is promulgated, and the portion of the Securities and Exchange Act that provides for reorganizing stock exchanges into corporations is enforced on Dec. 1.
May 31, 2000	The Act on Sales, etc. of Financial Instruments is promulgated.
July 1, 2000	The Financial Services Agency goes into operation.
Mar. 1, 2001	The Kyoto Stock Exchange is consolidated into the Osaka Securities Exchange.
Apr. 1, 2001	The special measure for the protection of the entire deposit of investors at the time of bankruptcy of a securities company is abolished.

Apr. 1, 2001	The Osaka Securities Exchange reorganizes itself into a coorporation.
June 1, 2001	The system of electronically disclosing the contents of securities reports, etc. (Electronic Disclosure for Investors' NETwork "EDINET") goes into operation.
Oct. 1, 2001	The amended Commercial Code—lifting the ban on treasury stocks and instituting the system of trading units of shares—is enforced.
Nov. 30, 2001	The amended securities taxation system (which reduces the tax rate applicable to capital gains made by individuals from the sale of shares) is enforced.
Dec. 17, 2001	Nomura Holdings is listed on the NYSE.
Jan. 30, 2002	Banks' Shareholdings Purchase Corporation is established.
Apr. 1, 2002	The special measure for the protection of the entire deposit of investors expires, and the blanket government guarantee of deposits is partially lifted.
June 5, 2002	The Act on Securities Settlement System Reform Law is enacted.
Nov. 29, 2002	The Bank of Japan starts buying up cross-held shares released by banks.
Apr. 28, 2003	The Nikkei average drops to a 21-year low of ¥7,607.88.
Dec. 1, 2004	The ban on banking institutions against engaging in the securities intermediary service business is lifted.
Dec. 13, 2004	The JASDAQ Stock Exchange opens for business.
Apr. 1, 2005	The blanket government deposit guarantee is scrapped (excluding deposits used for settlement purposes).
Jan. 16, 2006	The Livedoor scandal occurs, leading to the Murakami fund problem in June.
June 14, 2006	The Financial Instruments and Exchange Act is published and goes into effect Sept. 30, 2007.
Sept. 15, 2008	Lehman Brothers Holdings Inc. files for protection under Chapter 11 of the U.S. Bankruptcy Code, creating the Lehman Shock that spins the world into financial crisis.
Jan. 5, 2009	Japan implements a fully dematerialized registration system for stocks.

Jan. 19, 2010	Japan Airlines Co., Ltd., files with the Tokyo District Court for protection under the Corporate Reorganization Law becoming the largest business failure in Japan's post-war history.
Feb. 4, 2010	European markets plunge due to the sovereign debt crisis in Greece.
Sept. 10, 2010	The Incubator Bank of Japan, Limited declares its bankruptcy to the FSA, which announces the first ever triggering of the government's deposit insurance cap system.
Mar. 11, 2011	Great East Japan Earthquake occurs, followed by a hydrogen explosion at Tokyo Electric Power Company's Fukushima nuclear power facility on March 13.
Aug. 5, 2011	S&P lowers the long-term credit rating for U.S. government bonds from AAA to AA+.
Jan. 1, 2013	The Tokyo Stock Exchange Group, Inc. and Osaka Securities Exchange Co., Ltd., merged their operations, giving birth to the Japan Exchange Group, Inc. (JPX)
April 4, 2013	The Bank of Japan introduced a quantitative and qualitative monetary easing program aimed at achieving 2% inflation in the Japanese economy within two years.
Jan. 1, 2014	NISA, a tax saving scheme for small-amount investments, is launched.
Mar. 5, 2015	FSA and TSE decide on the Corporate Governance Code.
Nov. 27, 2015	MOF records negative yield for the first time in the 2-year JGB auction.
Jan. 29, 2016	BOJ decides on additional monetary easing policy of applying negative interest rates in part on excess reserves at its Monetary Policy Meeting.
Aug. 31, 2016	Nomura Asset Management ends the management of MMFs.
May. 29, 2017	FSA recommends individual disclosure of the results of voting rights exercise for institutional investors.
Apr. 1, 2018	GPIF allowed to invest in domestic high yield bonds.
Apr. 1, 2018	FSA opens registration system for High Frequency Trading (HFT) operators.
Jun. 12, 2018	US-North Korea summit held in Singapore.

Nov. 15, 2018	London Stock Exchange Group ETF is listed on TSE.
Jun. 25, 2019	Cross-listing of ETFs on JPX and Shanghai Stock Exchange initiated.
Jul. 30, 2019	JPX announces a definitive agreement to acquire Tokyo Commodity Exchange to create a single consolidated exchange.
Oct. 1, 2019	Charles Schwab cuts trading fees for stocks, ETFs and options to zero.
Oct. 25, 2019	Toyota Finance Corporation issues 0% yïeld bond.
Feb. 25, 2020	Nomura Securities announces investment trust with 0% trust fee.
Mar. 30, 2020	Nomura Securities and Nomura Research Institute issue bonds using blockchain technology.
Dec. 25, 2020	The Tokyo Stock Exchange announces the abolition of the four existing markets and reorganization into three markets: Prime, Standard, and Growth from April 2022.
Mar. 24, 2021	CBOE Global Markets announces the acquisition of Chi-X Japan.
Apr. 20, 2021	SBI Securities issues corporate bond-type digital securities, the first security token offering for general investors in Japan.

The "Chronology of Events Related to Securities" that covers more details of events from 1945 is available on the Japanese-language website of the Japan Securities Research Institute (JSRI) (https://www.jsri.or.jp/). Events may be searched by name.

The "Chronology of Events Related to Securities" is also contained in the following publication issued by the JSRI:

"Chronology of Events Related to Securities (Meiji, Taisho, Showa)" (1595 to January 7, 1989)

Published September 1989; B5 size; 1,026 pages; ¥11,650

From 1989 up to 2011, the "Chronology of Events Related to Securities" in *Shoken Shiryo* is published each year for the events of the previous year.